Convent Life

Show me, O Lord, Your way,
and grant me the faith
and courage and love
to follow wherever
it may lead. Amen.

CONVENT LIFE

Roman Catholic Religious Orders
for Women in North America

Edited and with an introduction by
Joan M. Lexau

Forward by
Sister Maria del Rey
of Maryknoll

Dial Press 1964 New York

NIHIL OBSTAT

Rt. Rev. Msgr. James T. Clarke
Censor Librorum
March 19, 1964

IMPRIMATUR

Most Reverend Jerome D. Hannan, D.D.
Bishop of the Diocese of Scranton, Pennsylvania
March 24, 1964

Library of Congress Catalog Card Number: 64-15224
DESIGNED BY VINCENT TORRE
Manufactured in the United States of America

Acknowledgments

I would like to thank the sisters and editors who gave assistance and advice, especially Sister I. H., and those who offered prayers on behalf of this work. To Fordham University my gratitude for allowing me the use of their library for research. And a special thanks to Miss Lila Mitchell for her help in compiling and checking the list of congregations.

"Show me, O Lord, Your way" from the booklet "If You Really Love . . ." published by Geo. A. Pflaum, Publisher, Inc., Dayton, Ohio.

"The Bride in the Castle" by Marie Dishongh condensed from an article entitled "Why Be a Nun?" in the September, 1959 issue of *The Magnificat*, published by the Sisters of Mercy, 131 Laurel St., Box 154, Manchester, New Hampshire. Used by permission of the magazine.

"I Would Never Know Another Happy Day" as told to Joe Breig condensed from an article entitled "Dearest Freshness Deep Down Things" in the October 7, 1961 issue of *Ave Maria*, © 1961 by Ave Maria Press, Notre Dame, Indiana. Used by permission of the magazine.

"From Convert to Convent" by Sister X, R.S.M., condensed from the book *Why I Entered the Convent*, edited by Rev. George L. Kane, © 1953 by the Newman Press, Westminster, Maryland. Used by permission of the publisher.

"How Cathy Became a Nun" by her Mother condensed from the December 1955 issue of *The Catholic Digest*, © 1955 by The Catholic Digest, Inc., 2959 N. Hamline Ave., St. Paul 13, Minnesota. Used by permission of the publisher.

"The Ad Said Generous Souls" by Sister Mary Augustine, S.M.S.M., condensed from the book *Why I Became a Missionary*, edited by Rev. George L. Kane, © 1958 by the Newman Press, Westminster, Maryland. Used by permission of the publisher.

"Some Call It Madness, Some Call It Love" condensed from the book *Shepherd's Tartan* by Sister Mary Jean Dorcy, O.P., Copyright 1953 by Sheed & Ward, Inc., New York. Used by permission of the publisher.

"The Arrival" by Sister M. Deborah, S.L., condensed from the January 10, 1959 issue of *Ave Maria*, © 1959 by Ave Maria Press, Notre Dame, Indiana. Used by permission of the author.

"From Decision to Final Vows" by Sister Mary Josette, s.n.d., condensed from an article which appeared originally in the January, 1953 issue of *Extension* under the title "Inside Story," © 1953 by the Catholic Church Extension Society of the United States of America, 1307 S. Wabash Ave., Chicago 5, Illinois; published in pamphlet form in 1963 under the title "All Hers to Give" by Our Sunday Visitor, Inc., Huntington, Indiana. Used by permission.

"Obedient Virgins" and "What Do They Do All Day?" condensed from the book *A Right To Be Merry* by Sister Mary Francis, p.c., Copyright 1956 by Sheed & Ward, Inc., New York. Used by permission of the publisher.

"The Relaxed Grasp" reprinted with permission of The Macmillan Company from *My First Seventy Years* by Sister M. Madeleva, c.s.c. Copyright 1959 by Sister M. Madeleva, c.s.c.

"By Rule, By Custom, By Unwritten Law" by Sister Mary Gilbert, s.n.j.m., appeared in the February 6, 1954 issue of *America* under the title "Differences of Communities of Religious Women." Reprinted with permission from *America, the National Catholic Weekly Review*, 920 Broadway, New York 10, New York.

"Here Cut and Here Burn" condensed from *Inside Out* by Sister M. Ann Edward, o.p., published by the Academy Library Guild of Fresno, California. Used by permission of publisher and author.

"Specialists in Prayer" condensed and reprinted with permission of McGraw-Hill Book Co., Inc., from *My Beloved: The Story of a Carmelite Nun* by Mother Catherine Thomas, d.c. Copyright © 1955 by Mother Catherine Thomas.

"Death of an Obscure Nun" by Rev. Joseph E. Manton, c.ss.r., condensed from an article in the November 17, 1962 issue of *Ave Maria* entitled "Jewel in a Casket." © 1962 by Ave Maria Press, Notre Dame, Indiana. Used by permission of the author.

"The Teaching Sister" by Robert T. Reilly condensed from an article in the January and February, 1960, issues of *U.S. Catholic* (formerly *St. Jude*), 221 West Madison St., Chicago 6, Illinois, entitled "The Teaching Nun: Saint and Woman." Used by permission of the author.

"Sisters of the Bayous" by M. F. Everett condensed from an article in the August 17, 1957, issue of *Ave Maria* entitled "Nuns of the Bayous," © 1957 by Ave Maria Press, Notre Dame, Indiana. Used by permission of the author.

"Shepherdess of the Strayed" by Rev. Brendan Mitchell, o.f.m., condensed from the March, 1955 issue of *The Way of Saint Francis*, 109 Golden Gate Ave., San Francisco 2, California. Copyright 1955 by the Franciscan Fathers of California, Inc. Used by permission of the magazine.

"New Life for Modern Magdalenes" by Antoinette Bosco, Woman's Editor of *The Long Island Catholic*, condensed from the September 9, 1961 issue of *Ave Maria*, © 1961 by Ave Maria Press, Notre Dame, Indiana. Used by permission of the author.

"Sisters of the Forgotten" by Vincent J. Giese appeared in the January 28, 1956 issue of *America* under the title "The Little Sisters of Jesus Come to Chicago." Reprinted with permission from *America, the National Catholic Weekly Review*, 920 Broadway, New York 10, New York.

"Charity is a Heavy Burden" condensed and reprinted with the permission of Charles Scribner's Sons from *In and Out the Andes*, pp. 136-139, by Sister Maria del Rey. Copyright 1954 by the Foreign Mission Sisters of St. Dominic, Inc.

"Glorifying God with a Camera" by Sister M. Noemi Weygant, o.s.b., appeared in the June, 1962 issue of *The American Benedictine Review*, Collegeville, Minnesota, under the title "Glorifying God with a Camera Lens." Used by permission of the magazine.

"The Nuns Who Catch Fishermen" by Robert M. Debevec from the June, 1961 issue of *The Catholic Digest*, © 1961 by The Catholic Digest, Inc., 2959 N. Hamline Ave., St. Paul 13, Minnesota. Used by permission of the publisher.

"The Secular Institute" by William B. Faherty condensed from an article in the April, 1961 issue of *Direction* entitled "Meet the Secular Institute," Copyright 1961 by The Queen's Work. Reprinted from *Direction*, national magazine for Sodality readers, published by The Queen's Work, St. Louis. Used by permission of the magazine.

"Sister Formation" by Robert A. Broenen appeared in *Ave Maria* under the title "Outline for Excellence," © 1960 by Ave Maria Press. Used by permission of the author.

"West Point for Nuns" by Edward Wakin from the March, 1963 issue of *The Sign*, Copyright © 1963 by the Passionist Missions, Inc. Used by permission of the author. A more detailed account of Marillac College appears in *The Catholic Campus* (Macmillan Co.) by Edward Wakin.

"Doffing the Bonnets" by Sister M. Roberta, o.s.u., appeared in the May, 1958 issue of *The Catholic Digest* under the title "The 'New Look' at Our Convent," © 1958 by The Catholic Digest, Inc., 2959 N. Hamline Ave., St. Paul 13, Minnesota. Used by permission of the publisher.

for my mother

Table of Contents

Foreword

AN ELEPHANT whom I knew very well told me this story. He had a friend, a flea, who lived in his ear as a sort of permanent house guest. The flea was a cocky fellow; the elephant was lumbering, slow, good-natured and easily imposed upon.

One day the elephant went over a bridge in the jungle. The twisted vines trembled and barely held up under the elephant's bulk. As he stepped onto solid ground, the flea came out from hiding, threw out his chest, and remarked to his host, "Say! We surely did make that bridge tremble, didn't we!"

This is somewhat the case of a sister. She is awfully small herself, capable of making no bridges tremble. But the grace of God carries her through jungles and over chasms. And, after all, she contributes her whole self, whatever little weight she has, to the elephant's triumphs. Maybe not bridges, but devils tremble when she is around.

Perhaps that is the secret joy that shines in the faces of 175,000 American women now wearing the odd habits of religious orders. Joining their puny strength with the grace of vocation, they fully expect to move mountains. Sometimes they do.

I used to think that I would have to write books and take pictures, and then storm my way into editors' offices to let them know the type of life we live and the type of women we are. But before I could get around to it, the editors woke up. Magazines, newspapers, radio, and TV decided to capitalize on the aura of mystery which surrounds the very matter-of-fact person who wears a religious habit.

Of recent years books galore have tried to give the inside story of convent life. They have ranged from the disillusioned to the false-illusioned. Some have been straightforward accounts of the things sisters do. Magazine stories by and about sisters pop up every month.

In this book Joan Lexau has taken pains to show the vast variety of sisters. Rich girls and poor ones, artistic temperaments and stolid types, young and fairly old, those from old Catholic families and some who are converts of just a few years—the backgrounds are like a patchwork quilt. Some even have prison records. A few have been invalids from childhood. Most are just normal girls from Catholic families.

Their work, too, runs the gamut of possibility. In this book the reader finds convents supported by cancer research—or by making fishing lures. One Benedictine is a full-time photographer, another an abstract painter, a third sets to work to dig foundations and erect a convent.

It would be foolish to try to type sisters. There is no type. God made each of us with her own personality, just as He gave us the shape of our noses and the color of our eyes. There's nothing to be done but to develop that personality into the highest potential for good.

Most lay writers are wont to stress the sacrifice in a dedicated life. This is true enough, but we sisters don't feel so heroic about it. Indeed, it seems to us that our married brothers and sisters often make greater sacrifices for God than are asked of us. Religious life is a disciplined life and, in a sense, unnatural. Faithfulness to the daily schedule, constant striving for perfection, in fact, just living in a large house, require stamina of body and soul.

But with it all, there is joy. Most sisters are merry, many are jovial, and all who live the life fully are happy. This dedication satisfies the deepest part of woman. I have a private theory that no woman is happy unless she is sacrificed on some altar. It may be her family and home; it may be the welfare of others: education, perhaps, or medicine or reclaiming alcoholics. Whatever it is, the woman who spends herself down to the last penny is the woman most satisfiied with life.

SISTER MARIA DEL REY
Maryknoll

Introduction

IN SPITE of all we hear about the sister shortage, Catholic convents are not exactly empty. In 1963, there were 177,154 sisters in the United States and over 47,000 in Canada. But the increase in the number of sisters is not keeping pace with the growth of the Catholic population.

The lack is especially felt in schools. Since 1950 the Catholic school population has grown by 102 per cent, but the number of teaching sisters has increased only about 24 per cent. A parish makes great financial sacrifices to build a school for the children and then discovers there are no sisters to staff it. The pastor pleads, the bishop begs, to no avail. One mother superior after another says a heartfelt, "I'm sorry—we just don't have the sisters to send." Mother superiors do not like to say No, especially to bishops, and not too long ago such pleas would have been answered by sending out half-trained sisters from the novitiate. But now the superiors have gotten together to talk over their problems and they have decided that it isn't fair or wise to send out sisters until they are fully trained, both spiritually and professionally, and the training programs are being improved to suit the needs of the times. It is expected that in the long run this will ease the shortage, as the better trained sisters inspire more girls to follow their example, but in the meantime it is increasing the problem. Dedicated lay teachers are helping to fill the gap, but there are not nearly enough of them to go around. Often parents object when they find that their children, sent to a parochial school to be taught by "the good nuns," are actually being instructed by a Miss Smith.

The schools are only part of the problem. The United States contributes 75 per cent of all the money going to the Catholic foreign missions but less than 5 per cent of the Catholic mission personnel—priests, brothers, sisters, and lay people. In 1962 U.S. Catholics had approximately 7,100 missionaries abroad, while the figure for U.S. Protestants was 25,000.

The need in Latin America is so great that in August, 1961, Monsignor Augustina Casseroli, speaking for the Vatican Pontifical Commission for Latin America, asked that a tithe of the U.S. religious be sent there in the next ten years. Yet there is a mission need in the United States. The priestless areas in the United States together make up an area greater than France, Germany, and Great Britain combined. The scattered Catholic population in these sections (mostly in the South) need more sisters to help them keep the faith, to teach Catholic doctrine to the children, to spread the faith, and by their example to help overcome anti-Catholic prejudice. Lay missionaries are at work there, as in the foreign missions, but their number so far is negligible and for many it is a temporary apostolate. Large parts of northern Canada are also still considered mission territory.

More sisters are needed in hospitals, mental institutions, orphanages, and homes for the aged. Sisters are needed to help Negroes, Indians, and the hard-to-reach migrant workers, Catholic and non-Catholic. In 1962 there were more than 664,000 Catholic Negroes in the United States and over 150,000 Catholic Indians. Many Indians are still living on reservations in conditions of extreme hardship.

There are approximately one million Puerto Ricans in this country, over 90 per cent Catholic by baptism but only about 10 per cent are estimated to be practicing Catholics. They come here as unskilled workers, unable to speak English, facing vastly changed living conditions. Many are ignorant of their religion, have their own informal marriage customs, and some still practice voodoo. More Spanish-speaking sisters are needed for this work. In Puerto Rico itself there are only 950 sisters for the 2,100,000 Catholic population.

Pope Pius XII one said, "The Church's apostolate is scarcely conceivable without the co-operation of religious women in works of charity, in the school, in assistance to the priestly ministry, in the mission."

A vocation is a call by God to a particular state in life in which the individual works for his own perfection. States of life are usually classified as the diocesan priesthood, membership in a religious institute, marriage, and the single state. St. Paul told the Corinthians, "Everyone has his own vocation, in which he has been called; let him keep to it." Bishop John J. Wright said at a retreat for young people in Pittsburgh, "Once people get the idea that they have an individual vocation in life, then we'll have more priests, more sisters and men and women with a sense that they are working for eternal life, not just drifting about making a living."

It is believed that enough young women are being called to the religious life but too few are answering. God invites but does not force. No one knows for sure why so few girls enter religion. Some believe it is because we pamper our young people, shielding them from problems and not giving them a chance to become mature adults willing to make sacrifices. Others think it is because we place an undue emphasis on material security. Years ago a girl gave up less materially when she entered the convent. The sisters were poor but many of our homes were even poorer. Today most homes have luxuries which are taken for granted. Some blame it on the worldly atmosphere in which we live.

The idea is growing that many young people are searching for a challenge and purpose but don't know enough about the religious life or have wrong ideas about it. If a girl believes that only saints become sisters, she isn't likely to be able to picture herself in the convent. Then if she meets a sister who is obviously not a saint, she is disillusioned.

Some concepts about sisters come from movies, books, and cartoons. Thus we learn that a sister is an incredibly naive woman who grovels before a tyrannical superior and spends most of her time playing baseball or riding around in a jeep, smiling sweetly all the while and performing a few miracles every day on the side. Books by former nuns who, however sincere they may be, never quite caught on to the purpose of the life, show us that it is an endless round of seemingly ridiculous and petty practices, performed for no earthly reason. (That last at least is right.) Ask a sister about these books and she may reply, "Do you learn about marriage from a divorcee, about military life from a deserter?"

The similarity in their dress makes us view sisters as stereotypes. But each sister has her own personality, and they don't really look alike. Some are short, some tall, fat, thin, pretty and not-so-very. Nor are they all dressed alike. There are brown habits, white habits, blue, and violet—as well as black. The Redemptoristines, whom we don't see because they are cloistered, have red-white-and-blue habits. The Daughters of Charity of St. Vincent de Paul wear winglike headdresses. Most sisters wear veils, some wear hats or bonnets or caps. While many habits are patterned after the peasant dress of centuries ago, some sisters are dressed in the style of the 1930's or even more recent times. The sisters in the Congregation of the Divine Spirit, founded in 1955, wear a gray skirt and jacket, white blouse, navy hat for outdoors, nylons, and navy pumps with a medium heel. There are congregations in which all or some of the sisters wear ordinary street dress. Each order or congregation differs in its work, in details of its training, rules, and so on.

We think of sisters as all leading restricted and old-fashioned lives. Still we are not as surprised to hear of a sister flying a plane, getting a law degree, or making a scientific discovery as we are to learn of a group of sisters having a hilarious time swimming.

Sometimes even those who are often with sisters find them awesome, mysterious creatures. We manage to say but little in a torrent of words; sisters, used to silence, are able to communicate a good deal to each other by a nod of the head, a raised eyebrow, a glance, and a rattle of the rosary beads. Questioned about her life, a sister may tell you about vows, prayer, novitiates, and so on, forgetting that even the details of her hour-to-hour existence are unknown to us. Sister M. Alician, B.V.M., a high school English teacher, in an article in the *Catholic Educator* wrote of answering the repeated question of her students, "What do the sisters *do*?"

She told them about eating, house-cleaning, grocery shopping, visits to the dentist, preparing school lessons, recreation—and they found it all terribly prosaic and not at all mysterious. "But you pray so much," they protested. "Strange, isn't it," she wrote, "that though the early arrivals are with us in school at seven-thirty in the morning and the late departing sometimes say good-bye close to five in the evening, many of our girls believe we spend countless hours each day at community prayers? To wonder how we could fit all those imagined prayers into our crowded teaching day has never occurred to them. So beginning with morning prayers and meditation, we total the minutes of devotions till the end of night prayers. The sum is surprisingly less than they expect, and scattered through the day as the exercises are, none seems excessively long even for their restless bones."

In an article in *America* Father Walter E. Stokes, S.J., quotes two surveys of high school girls on the religious life.

One survey of six hundred high school girls disclosed that 94 per cent at one time or another had thought of entering the convent, and 65 per cent of the seniors still thought about it now and then. But a great many were unable to answer correctly questions about the purpose of religious life.

In the other survey of 15,000 girls throughout the country, the answers showed that the girls were not against the idea of sacrifice. A girl wrote, "One must sacrifice oneself no matter what vocation one follows." Another said, "Religious life is not hard, because if you love God enough you will be willing to make sacrifices." But ignorance of the life was felt to be a handicap. "The sisters are too mysterious themselves." "No one wants to take such a big step blindfolded." "This is my last year in high school, and I have found out for the first time that my teachers really have a happy life together. Most girls think it is all work and no play, and it certainly appeared that way up to now." One girl replied, "The religious life should be presented as something appealing, as an interesting life in which wonderful things can be accomplished both for God and others, and in which there is some scope for individual development."

This book is an attempt to clear up some of the mystery of the convent. It is meant for girls who might be interested in the religious life; for parents, who often try to dissuade their daughters from becoming sisters, some for selfish reasons and others in honest horror; and for anyone who would like to know more about this life.

The articles selected are deliberately varied. Some are deeply thoughtful; others reveal sadness or laughter, just as the sisters' daily life is variously composed of soul searching, compassion, and joy.

I

Why Is a Nun?

Why Is a Nun?

THE WORDS "sister" and "nun" are, in everyday speech, used interchangeably and are so used in this book, although there are actually technical differences between the two. To simplify matters, it can be said that nuns are contemplatives and are cloistered in a major or minor degree; the active religious, those who teach, nurse, etc., are sisters. The word "religious" refers to both sisters and nuns (also to brothers and to priests who are members of religious institutes). The same can be said for "order" and "congregation"—they have different meanings but no one, unless he is trying to interpret Canon Law, worries too much about it. Both are also referred to as "institutes" and "communities."

Basically a woman becomes a nun because she is convinced that that is what God wants her to do even though for some the idea of entering the convent is at first repellent. Her object is the closest possible union with God and she is often referred to as the "bride of Christ." Pope Pius XII said her primary purpose is "to aim only at the divine, to turn thereto the whole mind and soul; to want to please God in everything, to think of Him continually, to consecrate body and soul completely to Him."

3

In some ways a sister tries to fulfill what all Christians are required to do: "Thou shalt love the Lord thy God with thy whole heart, with thy whole soul, and with thy whole mind," and, "Thou shalt love thy neighbor as thyself."

To do this in the most perfect way, a sister gives up everything that could come between herself and union with God. Christ said, "If any man will come after me, let him deny himself, and take up his cross, and follow me. For he that will save his life, shall lose it: and he that shall lose his life for my sake, shall find it."

She takes vows of poverty, chastity, and obedience. These are also known as the evangelical counsels. Christ didn't say we have to follow these counsels in order to be saved. They lead to a greater perfection. The religious life is a higher, a more perfect, life. (It isn't the taking of the vows but the keeping of them that leads to perfection.) A sister gives up material things, marriage, and her own desires because these things could stand in the way of her union with God. Some women first think of entering the convent because they want to be missionaries, to teach, to nurse, and so on. But there are lay teachers, lay missionaries, lay nurses. These careers are secondary to the religious state of life.

All this may sound quite dismal to some. Actually it isn't. Novices are famous for their giggling, and the gift of laughter is highly prized in the convent. Sisters speak again and again of their happiness, peace, and joy. There is a great feeling of contentment in knowing one is doing what one was meant to do. Christ promised, "And everyone who has left house, or brothers, or sisters, or father, or mother, or children, or lands, for my name's sake and for the gospel's sake, shall receive now in the present time a hundredfold as much, houses, and brothers, and sisters, and mothers, and children, and lands—along with persecutions—and in the age to come life everlasting."

The following "fairy tale" was written by a fourteen-year-old girl and is part of her prize-winning entry in an essay contest on religious vocations sponsored by the Serra Club of Houston, Texas. (The Serra Club is a group of laymen who promote vocations.)

The Bride in the Castle

Marie Dishongh

Christ the King looks down from His castle wall. Every convent that ever was built for love of Him is His castle.

He looks down from the castle window into the courtyard where stands the beggar maid. (What woman, young or old, but knows herself a beggar in God's sight?) And Christ loves this needy beggar maid.

So He goes down and takes the hand of the beggar maid in His. "You shall be My bride," He says, "and I will make you queen."

She follows Him reluctantly. She looks back upon the world that lies outside His convent-castle and sees how fair it is. The wind blows, flowers bloom, and she hears strong men laughing.

Can she give up all this lovely world with its brightness and freedom for the cold solitude behind those high castle walls? Has she the courage to face a life of companionship (she feels ashamed that she should dread it) with Christ alone?

Liberty becomes suddenly so dear to her, and a little house somewhere in a little garden or even a tiny pigeonhole in a tenement— anything but this stately castle-convent with its beautiful austerity. Yet she follows Christ.

Then comes the moment when she is dressed in her bridal white.

She feels God's hand close over her own and sees Him smiling. Slowly she pronounces her bridal vows. To her astonishment she sees that into the cold castle have come all the things she had dreaded to lose.

II

Who Me, God?— the Vocation

Who Me, God?—the Vocation

THE AWARENESS of a vocation begins with an insistent feeling that God is calling one to a particular state in life. For a woman this can mean the religious life, marriage, or the voluntary single state. The convent is not a hiding place for women who haven't been able to snag a husband any more than marriage is a make-do for those who can't bring themselves to become nuns.

A vocation to the religious life should not be confused with a desire for this state. Not every girl who is called is ecstatically happy about the idea at first. On the other hand, if a girl wants to be a nun but doesn't qualify, she doesn't have a vocation to the religious state, although there is nothing to stop her from leading a more perfect life in the secular state.

There is no "type" for the religious life. As soon as a girl announces her intention to be a nun the first thing she is likely to be told by family and friends is that she is not the type. Convents are full of sisters who were not "the type."

You might say that God goes so far to make sure a girl has a free choice in accepting that He hardly lets her know she's being invited. Very few girls are completely sure they have a vocation. It is sometimes said that the invitation is given to all who are qualified.

Actually all that is needed is the willingness to enter, the qualifications for the life, and acceptance by a community. During the postulancy and novitiate the candidate will learn about the religious life and test her vocation. If she doesn't seem to have one, her superiors will be the first to let her know and she is free to leave at any time before taking vows.

According to Canon Law (the body of Catholic Church law) any girl can be admitted to religion who is (1) Catholic, (2) not debarred by any legitimate impediment, (3) inspired by a right intention, (4) fit to bear the burdens of religious life.

Converts are included in the first requirement. However, they are usually asked to get used to practicing their new faith before taking such a big additional step.

A girl has an impediment to admission if: she has left the Catholic Church and joined another sect; she has not reached her fifteenth birthday; she was forced to enter religion because of violence or grave fear—and whoever does the forcing is excommunicated; she entered religion through fraud, either fraud on the part of others to make her enter or fraud on her part; she is married, unless her marriage was annulled or she is a widow (Sister Maryanna, O.P., author of the book *With Love and Laughter*, received a letter from one of her readers saying, "Sister, I'm married to a wonderful guy and we have three darling children. But, Sister, every now and then I get this overpowering urge to become a nun. Should I study Latin? . . ." The Church considers it a little late to change one's mind at that point.); she has left a religious institute after taking vows, temporary or perpetual; she is in danger of being punished for a *grave* crime for which she has been or could be accused; she has debts which she cannot pay; she is involved in the administration of affairs which could go into litigation (she has to uninvolve herself before she can enter—religious institutes don't like to take a chance on getting involved in lawsuits); she has parents or grandparents who cannot support themselves without her help, or children of her own who need her support; she is a member of an Oriental Catholic rite, in which case she cannot enter an institute of a Latin rite without written permission of the Sacred Congregation for the Oriental Church.

Anyone who wishes to be a nun but seems to have one of these impediments should see her confessor or parish priest for more precise information. It is *sometimes* possible to be dispensed from an impediment by the Pope or a bishop. For instance, a wife who is permanently separated from her husband might, under certain circumstances, be able to enter a convent. Or a sister who left after taking vows to care for a sick parent might be permitted to return when she is no longer needed at home (that is, if she had been permanently dispensed from her vows for such a reason; if she just left temporarily, with permission, there would be no question about her return). It is sometimes possible to obtain a dispensation to switch from one community to another, but this is difficult and not to be done lightly.

If a girl is of age, the consent of her parents is not necessary. Obedience to parents is important, but obedience to God is more important.

The right intention has already been discussed. Without the right intention, one wouldn't be likely to want to stay in any case.

Fitness to bear the burdens of religious life concerns mental and physical health, intelligence, and character. Some institutes require more physical stamina than others, for instance, a strict cloistered order in which the nuns fast much of the time. Intelligence requirements vary according to the type of work. The religious life has a certain appeal for the emotionally or mentally unstable, and congregations are taking greater precautions in this respect.

In addition to the above impediments, individual congregations have further requirements or restrictions. The usual age limits given for entrance are sixteen to thirty. After the age of thirty the candidate may be considered too set in her ways to adjust to religious life. Some place the limit at thirty-five, and there are exceptions even to this. Some institutes admit girls as young as thirteen or fourteen to a preparatory period called the aspirancy. Educational requirements vary greatly from grade school to completion of college. The requirement of a dowry is often waived and is seldom a real problem. A dowry is a sum of money, varying in amount according to the order, provided by the candidate. At her death the community acquires the dowry, but if she leaves the order, the dowry is returned to her. Some communities do not even ask for a dowry and others ask a girl to pay for her clothing and other expenses during the training period. The dowry is especially important in cloistered communities which necessarily depend more on them. A sister who has not provided a dowry and leaves the con-

vent after taking vows may be given financial assistance if necessary until she is able to support herself, but this can be a hardship
to a community which is low on funds. Individuals or parish societies promoting vocations can help in this regard by setting up
dowry funds with a community of their choice or for the benefit of
young people in their parish.

The lack of a good Catholic upbringing, a broken-home background, or illegitimacy can also be barriers. The candidate must
provide baptismal and confirmation certificates and the superior of
her institute is required by Canon Law to make inquiries about her
character and conduct. The religious life demands such things as
a solid faith, self-control, humility, perseverance, unselfishness, and
an ability to take correction and to get along with others. Community life is very close and a happy family background is considered a good preparation for it. If a girl couldn't get along at all
with one sister at home, what is she going to do with ten, fifty, or
a hundred sisters all around her every day? A sense of humor is a
great asset and some communities list it as a requirement. Of course
a candidate is hardly expected to be perfect (that is what she will
be aiming at all her life) and she will receive careful training, but
she is expected to have something to begin with. It is a good idea
to practice cheerful obedience in the home before entrance.

Once a girl feels she may have a vocation, she should do a lot of
praying and see her confessor, parish priest, or a sister she knows for
advice. They can help her decide if, how, and where she should
apply for entrance. She should keep in mind that the final choice
about entering and the community she chooses is strictly up to her,
but she will probably need all the guidance she can get in these
decisions. She shouldn't pack her bags and go rushing off to a
convent the moment the idea occurs to her. She would only be told
to go home and think it over some more. On the other hand, she
shouldn't wait too long to come to a decision. A vocation is a grace
and the longer nothing is done about it, the more danger there is
of losing it. This is why many sisters and vocation directors are
against the idea of finishing college, nursing school, or whatever
before entrance, unless the community chosen happens to require
it. No community requires a last "wild fling," which doesn't mean,
of course, that a girl planning to enter the convent has to be a
hermit. Sisters see nothing intrinsically wrong in dating, but dating
leads to marriage, not to the convent, and it is not advised for
those who have already made the decision to be a nun.

There are two main types of religious institutes—contemplative (with the emphasis on prayer), and active (with the emphasis on work), but there are all sorts of stages in between.

Active sisters do a great many types of work, and cloistered nuns cannot be considered really inactive. Besides praying, they accomplish a great many other things within the cloister. Over and over like a theme song, sisters of all types repeat, "Prayer is work and work is prayer." They all serve God by seeking their own sanctification and through helping others by their prayers and labor.

A prospective nun should choose a community which does the type of work she wants or feels best suited for. But her actual assignment to a job will depend on her own qualifications *and* the needs of the community. Her superiors may even find unexpected talents in her that she never dreamed of. Another aspect to consider is the matter of home visits. Some communities allow a sister to go home for visits and some do not.

Several communities offer girls a chance to see a little of the religious life before deciding. The Recluse Missionaries of Jesus and Mary have an "observation period," a few days' private retreat which they offer free of charge to girls interested in the religious life. Groups are also welcome to visit. (For further information, write to: Vocation Directress, Recluse Missionaries of Jesus and Mary, Route 1, Box 170, Lafayette, Louisiana.) The Benedictines have two vocational workshops each summer during the week following the fourth Sunday in June and the fourth Sunday in July. Girls attending take part in the activities of the community with a schedule of prayer, work, study, and recreation. There is, of course, no obligation to enter the order. Girls must be at least fifteen and must have a recommendation from their parish pastor. (For information or reservations, write to: St. Joseph's Convent, Benedictine Sisters, 303 Church Street, St. Mary's, Pennsylvania.) The Franciscan Sisters of the Poor, Warwick, New York, and Cincinnati, Ohio, invite interested girls to visit for a weekend or retreat. Those who live near a convent of the Little Sisters of the Poor can become acquainted with their work by spending some spare time helping them. Girls may also volunteer to help the Dominican Sisters of the Sick Poor as nurses' aides and secretaries or may visit for a weekend. Volunteer helpers and visitors are also welcomed by the Society Devoted to the Sacred Heart.

But suppose a woman feels she may have a vocation and her confessor agrees with her, but she cannot find a community which will accept her. Perhaps she is too old for most communities, or any one of a number of other reasons. Her confessor may not have enough detailed information on the various congregations to advise her. There is a priest who has made assisting "difficult vocations" in the United States and Canada his special work. Anyone having difficulty finding the right community for herself should write to: Rev. Jean-Marie J. Bauchet, Ph.D., Secrétariat St. Gertrude, 3202 McKinley Street N.W., Washington 15, D.C., giving her name, age, health, education, why she wants to be a sister and the history of her vocation, and what sort of congregation she is seeking. Father Bauchet will do his best to help.

Many roads lead to the convent; the story for each sister is different. The following articles tell the story of four vocations, both hesitant and eager.

"I Would Never Know
Another Happy Day"

as told to Joe Breig

For a couple of years a nagging restlessness and discontent had been growing which I couldn't explain or dispel. I couldn't understand why all the things I had once enjoyed so much—my job, my friends, my social life—had grown stale.

This unhappiness finally culminated in a talk with my confessor, who, I found to my amazement, had been convinced for some time that I had a religious vocation.

Finally, after some weeks of anguished indecision, I made an appointment with the mother superior of the community where I had gone to school. She was wise with the wisdom of years of holy living and suggested that I forget about the whole idea for at least two months. What a relief!

But I soon discovered that forgetting wasn't so easy as that.

Every book that I opened held only one message. Every evening spent seeking pleasure and forgetfulness ended in frustration. Every day convinced me more strongly that "not here lies happiness."

There fell into my hands a pamphlet by the late great Jesuit, Daniel A. Lord, titled *Shall I Be a Nun?* which I tucked inside the covers of a book and read as I traveled in a streetcar to and from the hospital where I was private secretary to a noted surgeon.

Extra time in lunch hour was spent in a nearby church alternately praying for the idea to go away or for strength to know and do God's will.

Father Lord had written, "Normal, natural young women are asked by God to dedicate their lives to Him and to work for His Kingdom on earth." I was just that—not particularly gifted, not even particularly pious, just an average American girl who enjoyed life.

Following another interview with the mother superior, at which I "petitioned" to be admitted, a calm peace enveloped my soul while I shopped and planned. But with my name signed on the dotted line, my physical examination passed, my acceptance papers received, the date set, my old doubts returned.

Most sisters taught school. I hated the very idea. I was past twenty-five and had no experience outside the business world.

The sight of a neighbor's two-year-old daughter's golden curls and blue eyes as she ran in and out of our house brought tears. How could I give up every hope of ever holding a child of my own in my arms? And yet, somehow or other, I knew I had to see this thing through.

I knew without doubt that I was giving up everything I treasured in life and was sure I would never know another happy day. How wrong I was!

From that day to this—nearly thirty-three years later—I have never known a moment of unhappiness. There were, of course, difficult days in the first years. Only in fairy tales is life made up of "sugar and spice and everything nice."

After having known several years of independence—freedom to go where and when I wanted—it was trying to have to ask permission to obtain a toothbrush or a cake of soap. Having enjoyed the privacy of my own room, it was not easy to become accustomed to living in a dormitory with six or eight other postulants, many of whom were ten years younger than I. It was anything but easy to drop what I was doing and proceed with religious decorum to the chapel for prayers two or three times a day. It was hard for me to have every moment of the day completely mapped out by "the rule."

But these were minor disturbances, because my heart sang all the while. In a convent one finds that "dearest freshness deep down things" which Gerard Manley Hopkins mentions in one of his poems. Someone has compared religious life to a ring—one is conscious of it for a while, then completely forgets it is on the finger.

That is true. At first everything is so new and so different; life seems fenced around with rules and customs. But soon one becomes so accustomed to this that one hardly knows she ever lived differently.

There is such peace, such security, such happiness, in sharing the joys and sorrows of all the members of one's great "family"; living with people of one's own age who have the same education, interests, and ideals; walking into a strange convent to be received as an honored guest by nuns one has never seen before; separating each fall to take one's place on the missions, then returning in the summer to renew old friendships, exchange experiences.

There is much joy in spiritual motherhood. My heart skips a beat when I see one of my students take her place among the "babies" of the community in the novitiate; it beats with pride when another proudly introduces her husband and one, two, three, four, five, or six children; it glows with warmth when I meet a smiling alumna who recalls some forgotten remark dropped in class which was a great influence for good in her life.

But most important of all is the fact that one lives day by day under the same roof with Our Lord in the Blessed Sacrament, and feeling that closeness one experiences a happiness which is so intense as to be at times frightening.

One lives always with the consciousness that of all the millions of girls who walked the same city streets with her, she was chosen to be bride of the King of Kings. The Lord cannot be outdone in generosity, and His "hundredfold" expands to a thousandfold and a millionfold with each passing year.

From Convert to Convent

Sister X, R.S.M.

I was a modern, sophisticated American girl who smoked and liked her fun. I was only one of the countless teen-agers who "knew all the answers" and who, deep down inside, wished desperately that they really did know them.

I went along pretty much with the crowd, except that I had a few ideas that were considered bizarre, running counter to the current philosophy. Don't ask me why, but I clung stubbornly to the ideal that you don't give out your kisses casually to every Tom, Dick, and Jack, but save them for the fellow you intend to marry. That alone was enough to brand me as prudish, but since I was a pretty good sport otherwise, the gang looked on me tolerantly. And I tried to be broad-minded.

It seemed odd when my favorite sister, Sallie, became a Catholic. Well, it was just one of those things. It was a free country, wasn't it? Anyhow, it didn't keep me from going over to Hilton to visit her every chance I could get. I even went to church with her, so broad-minded was I, and so immune to any possible Catholic influence.

The group of young people I met in Hilton intrigued me. They found much of their fun in their homes, just dancing to records, playing cards, making candy, and that sort of thing. Imagine that!

18

True, most of them were Catholics, but I would not let that ruin my fun. Besides, for added interest, there was Tony. All he had to do was turn that slow grin of his toward me, and my heart would turn flip-flops.

It wasn't long before people knew that Tony and I were head-over-heels in love. Religion? It was not mentioned.

So events stood until that never-to-be-forgotten night. Playfully, Tony had confiscated my handkerchief, and I was searching through his pockets, a little exasperated.

"Tony, you goon!" I began, but just then my exploring fingers pulled out—a rosary. I gasped and stared at it in surprise. I had seen rosaries before, and they had left me cold, just as everything else Catholic had. But this time something happened to me.

"Do you carry that all the time?" I asked.

"Sure. What about it?" he wanted to know.

I stared at him a moment, and then said, "Tony, take me home."

"But, honey, the party's just started," he protested.

"Take me home," I repeated. He did.

"Honey, are you feeling well?" Tony asked, searching my face anxiously.

"Of course, darling," I answered. "I just have to do some thinking." But I couldn't say more.

Then he rested his cheek against my hair, saying, "Stay as sweet as you are, Jan, honey, and don't let anything happen to you. We've got a lot of living to do together, you know."

A little breathless, I went to bed early. But it was not to relive those moments so precious to lovers; instead, it was to face a drastic alteration of outlook. There was no weighing of pros and cons. It was just the incredible fact that one moment I was heading in a certain direction, and in the next I had performed an abrupt about-face. I couldn't explain it, and I didn't try.

Next evening found me sitting in Father O'Brien's study. "So you think you want to be a Catholic, eh?" he said, half jokingly.

"I know so," I answered firmly. "I just want to go through the formalities, that's all, beginning right now." I didn't dream that he might put me off for a while or question my resolution. My presumption must have amused him; at any rate, he humored me.

I didn't miss one instruction class. What a revelation truth was! How wonderful to discover a real foundation for my ideals! At last I could very nearly say that truly I "knew all the answers."

Then came the evening, about four months later, when I was baptized and made my first general confession. Next morning I received my God for the first time in Holy Communion. But He was still a strange God, whom I took to myself in cold, blind faith.

Tony was exultant. Our plans were taking more definite shape. We were to have a ranch-style house, with yellow curtains in the kitchen, and fishing poles and picnic baskets and a car in the garage, and babies and toys and dogs underfoot. What more could I ask of life? It must have been at this point that God decided it was time to hint that there *could* be more in life.

Before long I returned to Pineridge to let my parents get acquainted with me all over again. There was no comment on religion. Mom and Dad always said that whatever religion or career we might choose, we could always count on their backing.

Then came that memorable day. I was doing the dishes for Mom while waiting for the morning mail, and a letter from Tony. Not only did Tony fill my fancies; I had also my newly found faith and the glad wonder that thrilled me and the deep gratitude that made me feel sorry that such a large portion of the world did not know how wonderful it was to be a Catholic.

"You poor world," I sighed. "How I would like to help God take care of you!" As if uttered by someone standing next to me, the words echoed within me: "You can be a nun."

I remember how I gasped, and nearly dropped the plate I had been polishing dreamily for ten minutes. I was staring at that same plate when Mom came into the kitchen.

"You must be miles away," she said. "The mailman came and left without being pounced on. Here's your letter."

I received it eagerly, and fled to a far corner to enjoy it. "Jan, my sweetheart . . ." and everything else was relegated to oblivion, for the time being, that is.

During a visit back to Hilton, I received another jolt. I was attending one of the parish ice-cream socials. Father O'Brien was teasing Peggy Quinn, but I wasn't paying much attention until it dawned on me that he had just said, "Now, why don't you become a nun, as Jan here is going to do?"

Again I nearly dropped a dish—with ice cream in it—as I gasped, "Why, Father, how can you say that!" He merely chuckled and went on to the next group. He knew that Tony and I were in love with each other, didn't he? I began to feel uneasy. For didn't

Father O'Brien know my soul as no one else could know it (except God)? Yet, not even to him had I revealed that new something which had been struggling in my soul for recognition. I hadn't even admitted to myself that it was there.

I took to stopping in at the church rather frequently to convince Our Lady of the fact. She was my best pal; besides, I had a sneaking notion that somehow she had something to do with my predicament. As yet I hadn't learned that cajoling her would merely hasten my own defeat.

"I simply can't give up Tony," I informed her firmly. I didn't argue; I merely stated facts. But somehow my firmness began to waver. And I resorted to the use of every woman's weapon—tears. "It's just impossible," I wailed. "God wouldn't ask such a thing." But Our Lady just looked down silently, lovingly, her arms outstretched, until I couldn't resist any longer. I finally looked at her imploringly, and went to kneel as close to the tabernacle as I could to make my whispered surrender, "Okay, Lord, You win." It didn't seem at all strange that He had worked it through His Mother.

Well, my mind was made up, and that was that, as far as I was concerned. But I wonder how many circles I paced on the living room rug, and how many cigarettes I tossed away as I prepared to tell Tony.

I was surprisingly calm as I gently broke the news to him. His jaw was set as he stared at me, his hands gripping my shoulders till they hurt. I heard him say, half to himself, "So that's it! I knew there was something about you, something I could never get at. Well, all I can say is that I'm glad it's God who gets you and not some other man." I bit my lips to keep them from trembling, and through tears I watched him stride down the steps and out of my life.

What did I think awaited me behind the cloistered doors of the convent? Frankly, I wasn't sure. A paradise on earth? No. The anticipation of lifelong self-denial and the loss of my independence repelled me. But that repulsion was outweighed by the attractiveness of doing something special for the God who had been so generous with me, as well as by the prospect of living close to Him and His sweet Mother. Whatever aversion I might feel, I felt that He would give me the grace to "take it."

And so at last I became a postulant in that sisterhood dedicated in a special manner to Our Lady of Mercy. You may wonder, did I ever look back? Well, would it surprise you were I to tell you that some of the bitterest tears of my life were shed the night before I received the religious habit? But there was no wavering in my resolve, and next day I was happily stumbling about in its voluminous skirts.

I did nurse my hurt a wee bit, perhaps. I thought I was making such a huge sacrifice. And, confidentially, I rather had the idea that I was doing God a favor by becoming a nun. And certainly I thought I was putting love out of my life forever.

But that was only because I did not as yet comprehend the meaning of the religious life. How long was it before I realized that my sacrifice wasn't really so much, after all?

I smile as I reflect that perhaps God made it seem difficult just so that He could give me the merit of renunciation. I have realized long since that it was not a matter of my doing God a favor; rather, it was a matter of His bestowing upon me a most precious gift, a very special favor He reserves only for His chosen ones.

How Cathy Became a Nun

by her Mother

Three-year-old Cathy was pretty mad. She wanted more bedtime stories, and I wanted to stop. When I gave her my final No, she announced, in a carefully controlled voice, "If you won't read me another story, I'll leave this house and go to the poor Little Sisters of the Poor!"

She tossed her brown curls defiantly, packed her pajamas in her doll suitcase, struggled into her coat, and thrust her red velvet bonnet onto her rebellious little head. Then, with the air of a princess, she strode out the front door to carry out her threat.

I followed her and told her, as calmly as possible, that I would call a cab for her, because it was too dark and cold for her to walk the three blocks alone. Then I closed the door and watched her through a window.

Presently, the doorbell rang. My little rebel said meekly, "I've changed my mind."

I gathered her close, and the whole family said they were glad she had reconsidered. Cathy unpacked and prepared for bed. I was tempted to read the extra story, after all; but I did not yield.

That was my daughter's first announcement concerning the Little Sisters. The next time, when she was sixteen and a half, it was not so amusing.

Cathy was the first baby in our family in six years, and she held the title of baby for eleven years more. She was born the day before Christmas Eve, and thus identified herself forever with this beautiful season. She was an exquisite child, healthy and happy; the idol of grandmother, uncles, and aunts; the joy of my heart.

I had maintained my own music studies for years before Cathy was born, and it was necessary for me to continue my work in music after she came. But this adorable child was my rarest blessing from God, and I determined that no career, however necessary, should encroach upon time that belonged to her. I gave up music teaching and turned to writing. From Cathy's fourth to twelfth year I worked in the program and advertising departments of a radio network. I could choose my own working hours.

Suddenly my baby was six years old and ready for school. Every mother knows the pain of the first wrenching away, and how big and empty a house can be without childish prattle and gay laughter.

As Cathy grew up she and I went on vacation jaunts, which I could not afford. How often did I remark when we were on a delightful excursion, "Oh, these are good days!" I was all-important to Cathy; she wanted me to share her every experience.

I prayed daily to the Holy Ghost for wisdom and courage to "let go" when the time should be over for "holding." I had seen children maimed in spirit by mothers who, in their selfishness, refused to abdicate at the proper time.

Meanwhile, I had organized neighborhood children into a group called the Back Yard Players, in summer, and the Fireside Players, in winter. Sometimes we would go to the home of the Little Sisters and entertain them and the old folks with songs, readings, and music.

Cathy was even more musical than I; when she was very small she showed extraordinary musical talent. She loved the rhythm of poetry, and began playing the piano when she was four. Soon, she was playing whole songs by ear after hearing them once.

One of my radio accounts was a music store. Cathy made friends there with a German violin maker. He made a violin especially for her, and gave it to her as a Christmas-birthday gift when she was eleven. Before six months of lessons had elapsed, we knew that Cathy was no ordinary music pupil.

Honors were soon coming to her in rapid succession. Two weeks before her thirteenth birthday she appeared as soloist with the Youth Symphony, playing first violin. Applause was deafening and prolonged; she was recalled six times. On the streets, in restaurants, and in stores people would stop her and praise her.

Now she was invited to play full programs at colleges and universities, at home and in other cities. I always played her accompaniments. Those concerts and the daily practice hours are among my richest memories of my precious, fleeting years with Cathy. By this time, she was earning money from television, radio, and civic-club engagements.

While she was in high school three offers of college scholarships came her way. A summer music camp awarded her a five-week scholarship; she could play under the baton of some of the finest conductors in America. Cathy accepted it, but only on condition that she could continue her habit of attending daily Mass.

Cathy loved swimming, dancing, and horseback riding. Her uncle and aunt let her use their membership card in a country club, and she often took her friends there for swimming and lunches. Her aunt and uncle honored her on her sixteenth birthday with a dance. She loved every minute of it, as well as the exquisite blue formal dress they gave her. My cup of joy ran over when, in one school year, Cathy won high dramatic, oratorical, and literary honors.

I now believe that God gave Cathy those triumphs that they might be my consolation later. Cathy herself remained unaffected and talked more and more about her "vocation." I listened with pride, and always my comment was the same: that I would be honored if God should choose her—after college, at twenty-one— but I never prayed that she would have a vocation. I prayed only that she might do God's will in all things and remain always on good terms with Him.

In January, after her sixteenth birthday, Cathy said, "Mother, would you be dreadfully disappointed if I did not go to college? I do so want to enter the convent, soon."

My reply did not come immediately. Then I told her that if she should wish to marry after high school I should have to give my consent; therefore, I would make the same allowance for a religious vocation. "But," I added, "we'll discuss it fully when the time comes." I do not like to recall the agony I knew after Cathy's momentous request to skip college.

Cathy's pleas became more insistent. I began grasping at moral straws; I set myself up as a sort of "devil's advocate."

For two years Cathy had gone every Saturday, after symphony rehearsal, to help the Little Sisters of the Poor for three hours. Rehearsals were strenuous. I told Cathy that she needed relaxation after them. She said that she found helping the Little Sisters just the right kind of relaxation. She had been slipping in some extra weekday visits. I took a stand. I told her she should go less often to the Little Sisters—and that she would enter no convent until her eighteenth birthday.

I told myself that I was acting in Cathy's best interest. When I took time to analyze my reasons carefully, I knew that I was primarily concerned with my own selfish ambitions. "The Little Sisters, of all communities!" The sparkle in my little girl's big brown eyes could now be seen only after her visits to the Little Sisters.

Once I remarked to Cathy that perhaps when she was old enough to enter, she would want to join a teaching order. Her simple reply was, "Mother, I don't have a vocation to teach."

That settled it. No child of mine would be forced into any profession distasteful to her. But I did not give up entirely. "Since nursing appeals to you, there are children's hospitals staffed by nuns. And old people are trying and cantankerous, even revolting at times."

"Mother," Cathy answered, "there will always be girls who want to take care of the children. Few like old people; that is why I want to be a Little Sister of the Poor."

Nevertheless, I argued on. My aunt, a nun, had once said that she was glad she had been a teaching sister because she had prepared so many little ones for First Communion.

Cathy explained that after a child was prepared for First Communion no one knew where he would go from there; "but," she said, "when we prepare the old people for death we know where they are going."

On another occasion I said, "How can you condemn yourself to live with old people?"

"Mother, dear," was the surprising answer, "I'll not live with the old people, I'll work for them, just as you work for your employers. I shall live with my community."

Who could beat such arguments? They seemed inspired.

I reminded her of her music. That would be a dreadful sacrifice, indeed, she agreed, but one that would have to be made, just as it probably would have to be made if she should marry. It dawned on me that her violin, like her dolls and books and skates, must be abandoned in favor of more important things.

"You have been influenced by the sisters," I charged frantically.

Unruffled, Cathy explained that we have all been influenced by someone: the girl who marries, by the man who asks her; the public, by advertisers. "The Little Sisters," she went on, "by their love of God, their devotion to religious duties, and their service to the aged have revealed the kind of life that appeals to me. Yes, indirectly, they *have* influenced me."

"Does a girl have to enter a convent to lead a pious life?"

"Of course not," Cathy said, "but the routine of convent life— daily Mass, meditations, spiritual exercises, and, most of all, the freedom from worldly distractions—all these enable one to draw closer to God."

"But the *begging!*"

"Oh, Mother," said Cathy, "many Little Sisters never go out begging. It takes a special talent for that, and I doubt very much that I have such a talent."

"Just the same," I blazed away, "I'll sign no papers for you to enter at sixteen. It's absurd." But even as I spoke, I knew that I had lost the fight.

Desperately I turned to St. Anne. I had prayed to her before Cathy was born, asking simply that Cathy might be good. I began a novena which was to end on St. Anne's feast day. Next day Cathy asked me if she might enter on the feast of St. Anne!

On July 24, two days before St. Anne's feast, Cathy returned home from a date. I asked her if she had enjoyed it. She replied sadly, "Mother, it's a sin for me to let Joe spend money on me when I know exactly what I want to do with my life." She put her arms around me as she spoke.

"Oh, that again?" I remarked dully.

"Mother, you asked for it when you inquired about my date."

Suddenly I became angry—with myself. How did I know whether she was too young to know what she wanted? What she wanted to do was noble and good. I was refusing my child the right to choose her own way of life. The time had come to "let go."

Hopelessly, I said, "Cathy, darling, if this is your happiness that

I am holding in my hands, I shall give it to you. I'll sign your papers, and you may enter the convent on St. Anne's day."

Cathy threw her arms about me and danced me around the room. My heart died within me. The sisters were stunned. The following Sunday, at 1:45 P.M., Cathy walked out of the home where she had been so tenderly loved for sixteen and a half years.

This time, as I mentioned before, her departure was not amusing. I knew that no doorbell would ring announcing her return. She strode down the steps, and went straight to the home of the Little Sisters, three blocks away.

The conflict within me was frightful. One moment I knew that I had done right; the next, I was convinced that I had made a wretched mistake.

I visited Cathy frequently in the local home, and always found her in high spirits and glowing health. By the grace of God, I shed no tears in her presence, but nothing could stop my weeping at home. The sight of her violin on the top of the piano was unbearable. My sister understood, and packed it away. I asked myself over and over, "How can she be happy?"

On my visits to Cathy I avoided the subject of music. She always walked to the gate with me, bubbling with happiness. But one day she seemed wistful. "Oh, Mother, I miss our practice hours so terribly! And my violin! How I long to play it!"

My heart leaped. Maybe the silent strings would call her home! But I determined that it would be they, not I, that would do it. I told her that she could come at any time, and would be greeted with open arms; on the other hand, if she decided to go on to her profession, I would be behind her every step of the way. In parting, I said, "Anything worth having is costly. If the violin is worth more to you than this life you have chosen, God will let you know. He gave you a great talent. He will make it known to you whether you are to use that talent in His service or offer it as payment for the privilege of a vocation."

I did not mention the matter again, nor did Cathy, until after she had gone to the provincial house in another city. Then, when I visited her for the first time there, she told me that no price was too great to pay for the great blessing of her vocation. "Am I," she said, "to continue looking backward to the lovely life I've left, or shall I look forward to the lovely life I've chosen?"

As I took my leave I again told her that she could come home if she became unhappy.

"Mother," she smiled, "the sorriest thing in the world would be a Little Sister who was not happy. She'd be no good to anybody. Never fear. They'd send me home if I became unhappy!"

That night I wept while others slept in the train that roared toward home, and away from Cathy. I knew that she was already a Little Sister of the Poor.

Upon every visit since Cathy entered, I have been more and more impressed with the gaiety that pervades the homes of the Little Sisters. They make a fourth vow, of hospitality, and they fulfill it faithfully. Every time I visit Cathy I am once more aware of the old-world charm and culture which permeates this order that was founded in France more than a hundred years ago. When I arrive, the sisters seem to say, "At last!" and at leave-taking, "So soon?"

I soon learned that the communities have a cosmopolitan atmosphere. In a single group of twelve or thirteen sisters you may find five nationalities represented. Among them are linguists and teachers, musicians and artists, who take no personal pride in the gifts received from God. They chose to be Little Sisters because they can completely and utterly lose themselves in striving toward the perfection of the rule of the order.

As a parent of a Little Sister, I find myself treated with the deference, courtesy, and consideration that might be accorded royalty. I am honored not only by my own daughter but by every sister in the community.

No, never, by word or deed, do I intend to mar Cathy's happiness. I don't understand the mystery of a vocation. But neither can parents always understand why a son or daughter must marry a certain girl or man. It is the lot of parents to be perplexed; enough for them to realize that each child is a separate entity, cast by God each in a different mold.

Indeed, since Cathy became a nun peace is the undercurrent of all my emotions. I can rest in the knowledge that she is secure and safe and supremely happy. I have the satisfaction of knowing that I gave her this joy; I could have made her wait until she was twenty-one.

My hour of triumph came when Cathy told me that throughout eternity she would thank God for a mother who permitted her to give Him her life while she was still so young. Day by day I am realizing more fully the words of Holy Scripture: "Honor the Lord with thy substance, and with the first of all thy fruits: and the barns shall be filled with abundance, and thy presses shall run over with wine."

The Ad Said "Generous Souls"

Sister Mary Augustine, S.M.S.M.

I rang the doorbell of old Saint Patrick's Rectory in downtown Washington and waited. I wondered impishly though somewhat anxiously what Father Kelly would say to this one. The question of my having a vocation to the religious life had been satisfactorily settled some months before, but the "where" was still pending. So far, the various ideas I had come up with had elicited a quizzical look at best, followed by the smiling suggestion, "Look some more!" The day I had mentioned the Poor Clares, he had really laughed.

"Honestly, Father!" I was piqued. "What's so funny about me being a Poor Clare? I want to get away from all this—really shut the door and say good-bye to the world forever. And the poverty of St. Francis appeals to me. I like the idea of doing something hard, never eating meat again, for instance, sleeping on boards and going barefooted." And then, noting his frankly appraising look, I added vigorously, "Don't think I can't take it. Why, I'd rather go barefooted than wear shoes, any day!"

". . . or mend stockings?" he quipped. And that's when he laughed. "No," he said reflectively. "No, I don't think you're meant for the cloister. There's more to it than just doing something hard. It's the 'why' that makes the contemplative, not the boards. Someday you'll be a contemplative, I hope, but I don't think it will be in the cloister. You're too active. Look around some more, and pray. Then come back."

I smiled ruefully and left. But a trace of rebellion tagged at my mind. Just what was Father driving at! It seemed perfectly clear to me that the "why" meant doing something big—going the whole way, not just settling down with the sisters in the parish to teach school. From the time I was old enough to toddle, I had always strained for the horizon. In the days when baby-sitting was a cherished privilege and happy pastime for the little girls of my neighborhood, I had scornfully closeted myself with a book in my self-designated "studio" in the attic, to dream of the day when I would be, unquestionably, one of the world's greats.

When others, freshmen, elected commercial courses in high school with a view to a quick job after graduation, I acquiesced to a straight academic, secretly nourishing the ambition to study medicine one day. But I was ahead of my time. Women doctors in the 1920's were rare enough to be classed as oddities, so small wonder I wasn't taken seriously.

A few years more and a number of barely tried jobs behind me, I found myself one of the thousands of Uncle Sam's daughters milling about in the 8:30 and 4:30 rush for the Pennsylvania Avenue streetcars. I wouldn't stay with this, I promised—the call to "something big" was still pushing me on.

Fortunately at this point God stepped into the picture. Already I had experienced the truth that success, of itself, carries with it the seeds of a strange unrest. Echoes of a chance phrase, too, recurred to plague me. I was realizing, painfully at times, that one can perhaps conquer worlds, yet lose one's soul. Religion, for the better part of my then twenty-six years, had been just one of these accepted things, to be endured, like death and taxes. Now, in the humbling self-knowledge that even mountain-climbing aspirants can wind up in small gutters, the world of grace opened up to me, bringing new dreams, new visions, and, most important, a new love. To this new, vitalizing factor in my life I responded quite characteristically. Once again I was reaching out for something big—this time for God Himself!

Now I felt I had it. And here I was, cooling my heels at the rectory door, wondering how I would fare when Father heard the re-

sults of my "looking some more." I was prepared to argue on this
one, for I had prayed, as he suggested, most earnestly at the foot of
Our Lady's altar (my very first novena!), and in the middle of the
week, leaving the church, I had chanced to pick up a *Sacred Heart
Messenger*—to find my answer before my eyes on the first page.

It read, "Wanted: Generous Souls." Generous souls for what?
As I read, all my unphrased longings found expression. Everything
seemed to fall into place. But what would Father think?

As it happened, Father himself answered the doorbell. I had
planned, woman-wise, to work around the subject, introducing the
idea bit by bit. Instead, I heard myself blurting out my news before
he had even settled himself in his chair.

"I've got it, Father, where I want to go, I mean." I hated myself
for stammering when I had planned to be so adult and calmly sure.
"Now don't laugh, Father," I pleaded, "and don't hit the ceiling
. . ." I stopped, suddenly shy. Pulling the dog-eared *Messenger*
from my bag, I thrust it into his hands, pointing out the ad.

Slowly he scanned it, his face inscrutable as that of Buddha.
Then he read it aloud, enunciating each word in a measured ca-
dence which seemed drowned out by the loud pounding of my
heart. "Wanted: Generous Souls," he proclaimed, "who wish to
devote their lives to the conversion and education of the natives of
Oceania and to the care of victims of leprosy . . ." His voice trailed
off. In the silence that followed I could only stare fixedly at my
hands and wish miserably he'd say something. Good heavens! I remembered too late that I hadn't looked up Oceania to see where
it was. What if he should ask me that!

"So you feel generous! Heroic, too, I suppose?" But the quiet
desperation in my eye checked his intended raillery. Father sat up
abruptly. "Fine," he said, "just what I've been waiting for!"

The room did a circle, then righted itself, only to lose all di-
mensions in the sudden blur of stinging tears that rushed to my
eyes.

"Good, very good!" He grinned at me as I tried vainly to stem
the salty mess. "Now you're on the right track! What you've been
talking about, your wanting to do something hard for the Lord,
might find fulfillment here, and in line with your temperament.
Something like this will keep you so occupied you won't have time
to be involved in aimless dreams." His eyes moved back to the ad.
"Have you written for details yet?"

Self-control flowed back into me at his matter-of-fact manner. "No," I protested, still blinking, "I wanted your approval first."

"Good girl," he said, "you're catching on to the religious spirit fast. Well, you have my blessing—on the idea, that is," he added hastily. "I don't know anything about this particular group—the ad doesn't give much to go by. What about this leprosy deal?" he queried. "What makes you think you'd like that? There's more to it than heroics, you know. Didn't you tell me once you are very sensitive to bad odors, sickrooms, and the like?"

"That's just the point, Father!" Now that I had his vote of confidence, I found my tongue. "That's what I can give God—those countless things I don't like. Oh, I'm not kidding myself that I'm made of heroic stuff.

"I need something, Father, to keep throwing me back on God," I continued musingly, really seeing myself for the first time. "I'm too self-centered, too self-assured and confident. I need the poverty of the missions—the poverty of real want that I can't do anything about, so that I'll trust in God for my very necessities. Isolation, too, not by shutting a door on the world, but the isolation of being thousands of miles removed from all that is familiar—strange food, stranger customs, an alien tongue. These can be my daily sacrifice to God. And I can offer the tropical heat, the fevers, the lack of gratitude that probably goes with it all, just as the Poor Clare does, for souls."

"Stop, or you'll have me crying," Father bantered. "Besides I have to get ready for an appointment. But go ahead and write for information. Then we can talk about decisions. In the meanwhile keep on praying—you've got a long way to go yet. And keep on thinking it out for yourself, for you'll need more than feelings to carry it through." He spoke brusquely, but I grasped at the encouraging light in his eyes.

I fairly floated out of the rectory and through the week that followed. When the envelope postmarked "Bedford, Massachusetts" turned up in the mailbox, fortunately before the family had returned home, I handled it as if it had come from heaven. One by one I examined its various contents. I could just see myself, all in white, standing under a waving palm, gazing out across the cobalt blue of the Pacific, surrounded with tropical beauty and blissful peace, ten thousand miles away from nowhere, the world well lost!

My next visit to Father brought me up with a jerk. I had floated back in the rectory on a roseate cloud, greeting him with a mystically remote smile as he strode into the room.

"Oh, oh!" he jibed, sizing up the situation. "Any ecstasies lately?" I flushed, then grinned, as the bubble burst and I laughed with him. "But wait 'til you see, Father," I giggled. "They're real missionaries, all right. Wait 'til you see the leprosy booklet! And there's a letter here from Tin Can Island, wherever that is . . ." I fumbled in my bag.

"So?" Father smiled patiently. "But *who* are they? What community is it?" By this time I had fished out the envelope and the precious folders. He stopped at the leaflet with Our Lady's picture. "Queen of the Marist Missions, eh? I didn't know the Society of Mary had sisters too. But I'm glad—that brings Our Lady into the picture and that's what you need most. If she is calling you, it is a mark of predilection."

He turned to the leprosy booklet. "These poor people," I exclaimed. "I have a feeling that this is where God needs me." The pictures didn't impress him as much as I thought they would. At least he showed no reaction other than a terse, "It says here the sisters get up at four-thirty in the Fiji Islands!" And his eyebrows shot up as he looked at me.

"Oh," I replied airily, "I've always been an early riser. Besides, that's all to the good. That's that much more work I can get done . . . and more time to watch the sun go down over the ocean."

He replaced the literature in the envelope thoughtfully, then looked me over as if seeing me for the first time. "If I worry about you at all, it's not so much on the score of illusions as on your activity, your ambitious projects. That's an illusion too, this idea of God needing you, needing your work."

He leaned back again. "Get this straight, and never forget it. God doesn't need you. He doesn't need me—He doesn't need anyone. He doesn't need big brains, talents, or any of the social graces that we think, too often, as being a necessary part of the picture. Out of His love for you, His love for me, He opens to us a share in His love for His creatures. He deigns to use us as instruments, sometimes very weak instruments, to accomplish His purposes.

"You talk about going the 'whole way.' That's just another way of saying 'sanctity.' But the 'whole way' is different for each soul, the circumstances, that is. In every case, however, the whole way means nothing more or less than God's holy will—all the way, in every way—His will."

He opened the envelope again and pulled out the mimeographed letter. "You probably passed over this part," he remarked, and then read it out to me: " 'Here we have schools for both boys and girls.' Schools," he repeated. "So what will you do if you are sent not to nurse but to teach?"

I squirmed. It was true. I had glided over that part of the letter, to dream about the romantic solitude. I faced the issue. "Well," I began, "maybe it's just the idea of teaching here at home that I don't like, where we have everything, and expect so much from the children. Maybe in the missions it would be different." He started to speak, but thought better of it. "Anyway," I said firmly, "if after I've gone ten thousand miles away to get away from teaching, I'm put to doing just that, I'll have to take it as God's will for me, and do it!"

"Yes," and he finished it for me, "do it, and be sure it's done with a smile!" He played with an unlit cigarette for a minute, attempting to balance it across his forefinger. "Okay," he said, "write and see if they will accept you. You may give my name for reference. Now's the time for you to really pray, but don't worry," he assured me, "if Our Lady wants you—and I think she does—nothing can stop you, except you yourself!"

The next letter from Bedford brought an application blank, detailed requirements, and more information about the Marist Missionaries. I learned that the first of their sisters had left for the Islands in 1857, from France, at a time when cannibalism was still rife in the Pacific. In 1922 an American foundation had been made. Already there were forty-three American sisters in the missions (this was in 1936) with others in Bedford preparing to go.

With Father's help and suggestions the application form was filled in and my request for admission mailed in. With the subsequent acceptance came the necessity to announce my plans to my family and intimate circle of friends. The reaction, as I expected, brought a spate of objections and the puzzled query, "But why? Why go so far away? There's plenty of work to be done right here in your own country—even in your own family, for that matter!"

The argument was a good one, but, as I reminded them, it overlooked a point. "Look at it this way," I argued patiently. "There will always be work to be done, even in the most Catholic of countries, as long as there is fallen human nature—and, meanwhile, there are distant lands where people have never even heard of God, nor have had opened to them the avenues of grace they need, too. The big thing is to go where God calls. If God wants me in the missions, I'd be no good in the classrooms. Father Kelly told me," I added, "not to worry about the work in the parish—and I think that goes for the family problems too. He said that what is given to the missions always comes back double."

"But if you have to be a missionary, why choose an order nobody knows? After all, the Holy Cross Sisters who taught you have foreign missions in India!" The argument was a valid one, but I sensed it stemmed from the hope that once in a teaching congregation I might not be sent to the missions. I had thought of this myself, but what would have been a source of hope for the family was, for me, a threat. "No," I replied, "I want to enter where everybody goes to the missions. The Marists are one hundred per cent foreign missionaries, and they go, not for just so many years, but with no thought of return. I want to make my sacrifice complete."

When it came time to hand in my resignation at work, the personnel director refused it, granting me instead a four-month leave of absence. "It won't take you two weeks to know you're making a mistake," he growled, "but you're so stubborn it will be a few months before you'll admit it. No sense losing your seniority for a passing idea. Your place will be waiting for you when you decide to come back."

Come back? The idea rankled. I was sure of myself, but the idea persisted in my subconscious the next few weeks. There was the morning I was dressing quietly in the predawn dark, to slip out to an early Mass. It's thrilling and satisfying now, I found myself thinking, to rise early and hasten to the Lord when everybody else is asleep. But what about the days, the years, the lifetime ahead— getting up because you're expected to, with everybody else doing the same? And one evening, after I had packed my trunk, the thought occurred to me—ten thousand miles away, ten *thousand* miles away! Is it just some romantic nonsense of mine? I squirmed uneasily. After all, once one is there it's not ten thousand miles away any more—it'll be *there*, and palm trees will be just backyard scenery, with nothing left to fan my zeal but a love of God which might be just as abstract as behind the walls of the cloister. But I swallowed my doubts, one by one, and went on. I found a real comfort in the lines of my class song, which came more and more to mind: "Lord, for tomorrow and its needs, I do not pray. Keep me, my God . . . just for today!"

Go to the missions I did, but not to the South Seas. The story of how I became a missioner in the leprosarium at Old Spanish Town, Jamaica, in the British West Indies, is another chapter. I learned, however, among other things, that leprosy work, medical work, orphanages, and the more glamorous works of charity are but preludes to the real missionary work, which is teaching. As for leprosy, I discovered to my amazement that I was so taken up with the individual personality behind the suffering sores that I forgot to notice the odors that I had thought would be part of my immolation. And in the work of conversion I had patients who themselves taught me a lesson in seeing and loving God's holy will.

I even found out there is a "why" behind the missionary, too, and hundreds more of American Marist Missionary Sisters have found it out since those days when there were only forty-three of them and I weighed the pros and cons of the cloister versus the missions.

Truly I found the "big thing" and, with it, the humbling, heroic fact that missionaries face not one big sacrifice but a lifetime of little ones. And sanctity, for the Marist, consists in joyfully making each sacrifice with Mary, for love, and with a smile!

III

Early Days

Early Days

At some time or another the decision must be made. A girl often puts off telling her parents as long as possible and then suddenly drops the bombshell with, "Uh, I'm going to be a nun." However she does it, the news may be greeted with hysterical laughter or tears.

Results of surveys on the number of parents who object to their children's religious vocations vary widely. But there is no doubt that it is a problem and that it does keep some girls out of the convent or prevents them from persevering in the religious life. St. Alphonsus had this to say about it: "Parents who without a just and certain cause prevent their children from entering the religious state cannot be excused from mortal sin; and not only parents, but anyone who prevents another from following a religious vocation, sins mortally."

Parents give various reasons for their objections. "You're too young" is common. Children, especially girls, are always too young in their parents' eyes, and even more so when it comes to the convent.

The fault is not entirely in the parents' unwillingness to let go.

Most sincerely believe their daughter will be unhappy in the convent. The religious life is incomprehensible in the light of the weakened faith of today and the atheism and religious indifference all around us. Instead of total dedication, the attitude is more, "I'll let you know when I need you, God." The large number of communicants here has often been noted, but when Mother Marie des Douleurs came to the United States from France in 1954 to find a suitable spot for a convent for her Congregation of Jesus Crucified, she also noticed the lack of recollection afterward: "People leave church with a disconcerting haste. I realize that your motto is 'Save time,' but even so, one would like to find a piety which is more profound, more lively, and more personal." Rare is the family in which God has first place as a day-in, day-out reality. In most families God comes in a poor second, and the afterlife is a good retirement plan with social security supplemented by a pension. So we have parents crying, "Anything but the convent. The sisters are fine, I respect them, but it isn't for *you*." It is an extremely difficult problem because, like any prejudice, it is emotional rather than intellectual.

Not that it is easy for parents even in a truly Catholic home, especially where the community concerned doesn't allow the sisters to make visits home. Joe Breig had a series of articles in *Ave Maria* about nuns, one of which is in the previous section. Afterward he received a letter from a mother who had always felt that her children belonged to God and were only loaned to her. She said about her feelings after a daughter announced she wanted to be a nun, "We had no objection to our daughter entering religious life. And yet what happened to her father and me in the ensuing weeks was an agony of soul, and such a longing and yearning to say 'No, no, no' that it was almost indescribable. I couldn't eat, sleep, think or work. This, all the while I was trying to be a great, big noble creature in front of our daughter."

Few parents are so noble. That mother eventually found peace, as most parents do, but often they make life miserable for their daughters, who are having a hard enough time in any case in reconciling themselves to leaving home. And yet one mother of a nun told me, "You never lose a daughter in the convent. Married children grow away from you but a girl in the convent grows closer." Love in a convent is not restricted to husband and children but is expected to embrace all mankind, certainly not forgetting parents.

What comes after the decision is made and the application is accepted? For one thing a light-headed joy sets in. But there is a good deal of shopping and planning to keep one busy. These are described in the article by Sister Mary Jean Dorcy.

At some point in the preparations there is usually a traumatic experience which could be called the "last-minute jitters." A girl says to herself, "Am I crazy or something? What am I doing?" It is, after all, a big step she is taking. And as in any big change, she tries to look ahead, to see herself in the new life. If only she could picture those first few hours! But all she gets is a big blank nothing. The first few hours will seem different for each entrant, of course, but Sister Deborah has described her experience in "The Arrival."

After the arrival comes the postulancy and the novitiate, described in Sister Mary Josette's article. The postulants are considered the infants of the community and mistakes are expected. Life in the novitiate is stricter but the novice mistress, all the while she corrects her charges, is probably remembering she did the same zany things herself. The article in Section IV called "Here Cut and Here Burn" was written by a present novice mistress about her own early life in the convent.

To enter the novitiate a girl must be fifteen; to take temporary vows, sixteen; to take perpetual vows, twenty-one. Girls of early high school age often spend the first few years in the aspirancy. The postulancy and novitiate are training periods for the religious life and the aspirancy is sort of a training period for the training period. In a good aspirant school the girls are not expected to buckle down to a full convent regime. They are allowed plenty of time for study and sports as well as prayer, with frequent visits home. Many communities have a short pre-postulancy period which is also called the aspirancy.

The girls in the aspirancy are not sure they want to be sisters. They are finding out. So in a sense are the postulants and novices. They are free to leave at any time, and sisters with temporary vows are free to leave after their vows run out. And, of course, one often hears these days of sisters with perpetual vows getting permission to leave the convent. The saying goes that it is a lot easier to get out than it is to get in. Most sisters never find out if the saying is true—they like the life they've chosen.

Some Call It Madness, Some Call It Love

Sister Mary Jean Dorcy, o.p.

The surprising thing I had to learn, by going through it myself, is that a girl on her way to the convent can be just as balmy as anyone else in love. There is really nothing so strange in this, for the attraction of a girl for God is in a very real sense a love affair. It is one singularly free of the cheap connotations sometimes attached to those words in this age. But human nature is always pretty consistent, and love when it is new can do odd things to people.

The average girl goes into a genuinely dizzy whirl of preparations when the date is finally set for her wedding. However many items she may have in her dower chest, there is still the delightful necessity of shopping early and late for the wilderness of things that she and her mother feel are indispensable.

A bride of Christ, too, has a trousseau to prepare, not only in a spiritual way—which one would expect—but in a material way as well. There is first of all a cash dowry required by most communities, which varies in amount with the type of sisterhood and the work it does. In most of the apostolic groups a useful education—for instance, for teaching, nursing, etc.—will supply in whole or in part the cash dowry. (This of itself shows a difference in the position of women from the days when a daughter of the nobility would come to the convent laden with the family jewels and a land grant or two. Today, nobility or not, she probably has a typewriter, a tennis racquet, an assortment of work aprons, and an education, all of which she knows how to use.) In a cloistered monastery where the dowry is a necessary part of the house revenue, the amount of the dowry is usually greater and can be commuted only by the bishop. However, it is so rare as to be almost an impossibility that a girl with a real vocation would be kept out of the convent for lack of funds.

Each community also has a clothing list which is given out to prospective postulants after their application blank has been satisfactorily filled out and passed on by authority. In this trousseau there is a noticeable lack of the silk, satin, and laces that make other bridal shopping such fun. Prosaic at best, the list abounds in practical items not chosen for their aesthetic qualities. Some of the more traditional articles are utterly foreign to an up-to-date miss who hasn't a great-grandmother handy for reference purposes. Most girls weather this sacrifice without much ado, being very much in love. But if you think it makes no demands on feminine human nature, just go buy yourself a pair of black cotton stockings and consider how you'd like to wear them for a lifetime. A trousseau shower for a prospective postulant usually provides her with enough gloves and handkerchiefs to last a decade or two, for the good and simple reason that nobody ever knows what to buy for a sister, even a prospective one. Very smart girls have avoided this situation by providing an obliging friend—or aunt or big sister—with a selected list of things from the clothing list: necessary prayer books, towels, and other small articles that would make good shower gifts.

You have to go through it once to believe it, the amazing rumors that people tell you (for your own good, of course) when the news gets out that you are entering the convent. Louise, one of the senior boarders, was planning to enter the same summer I did, though a different community. Through the lovely spring days when we should have been studying we dreamed, giggled, planned, and wept together over our futures and life's futilities. One day Louise flung herself into my room and collapsed on the bed. "It's all off," she said. "I can't go through with it. I was just down by the washlines. They wear canvas underwear."

I said I didn't believe it and went on with my painting.

"I saw it with my own eyes," she insisted. "You just come right on down and see for yourself!"

Like most of the rumors we picked up, this one collapsed on inspection. The petticoat she showed me was a pretty sturdy contraption, all right, but it was middy twill, not canvas. We tried unsuccessfully to figure out how the various funny little stringed pieces of linen went together to make that snug headdress. Louise tried on a nightgown for size and said it felt like a circus tent. I told her she had canvas on the brain, and we slipped silently back to the boarders' quarters.

That ghost was barely laid when someone told us we had to have long hair or the sisters wouldn't accept us. Louise brought back a bottle of hair-grower from a weekend at home, and we did what we could to expedite matters, to the utter amazement of the sisters. Eventually we both reached the point where, with an entire package of bobby pins, we could get our reluctant locks into the "do" affected by lady preachers of the time. Mine looked so evangelical that my sister Margie refused to ride on the same bus with me. Our sanity was saved by one of the "old" boarders who remembered that one of the novices, when *she* was a senior boarder, had worn rouge when she went home for weekends. Unconfirmed rumor said she had even smoked on the same occasions. And the sisters hadn't refused to accept her. We breathed again.

My clothing list came first and Louise's arrived some time later. Hastily we compared notes. I had been telling her for months that she had better come to the Dominicans instead, and the list she received convinced me. I looked at Louise, pretty rascal that she was, and tried to think how she would look in a gray flannel bathrobe like the shapeless article pictured on her list. Or the nightgown that looked like the two Mrs. Noah might have had on the Ark. And that wasn't all. Days later, when we went shopping together, we still hadn't mentioned the great weight that sat like a tombstone on both our hearts.

We lurked by the underwear counter for a full twenty minutes before getting up courage enough to hail a clerk. Louise whispered her request timorously, but there was nothing timorous about that clerk. Perhaps she was only startled. She boomed back "LONG UNDERWEAR! !" and everyone within hearing distance turned and stared at us.

Louise wilted and stood speechless. "You know," I said helpfully to the clerk, "the long kind—with *ankles.* . ."

"Do you realize that it is the first of May and that all our winter stock is put away?" bleated the clerk.

I gulped. "Yes, but you see, she's going to. . . ."

"ALASKA!" shouted Louise, giving me a sharp kick in the shin. Everybody in the department stared at us as we bolted with our packages for the nearest exit.

The person who is in love is often isolated from the ordinary current of life; she has her own world for the time being and does not urgently require any other. If it happens that she is in love with another creature, the most ordinary (and, in most cases, the most satisfactory) way of settling the difficulty is to marry him, a solution which most other people will understand. But the person in love with God must very often face heartbreaking opposition from those nearest and best equipped to understand her. Why this should be so is a puzzle to anyone who takes time to think about it, but the fact that it *is* so has been a growing headache to the religious orders in this country for many years.

People of a certain western city famous both for its hills and its Irish police force swear that the following story is true. They caution me not to use any names, so I don't, but here is the story.

A young lady whose twenty-one years had been spent in very high society made up her mind to be a cloistered nun. The idea didn't set well at all with the family. They had always been discreetly public about their Catholicity and they admired nuns—at a distance. They embarked on a round of activities designed to take the girl's mind off such nonsense.

They kept her pretty busy, but being a girl of no mean ability at getting what she wanted, she proceeded quietly to get herself accepted at an eastern cloister, pack her things, and buy her ticket. After several attempts to win her parents over, she finally shipped her trunk, wrote a note of farewell, and slipped out of the house. She was actually on her way to the airport when her parents discovered the plot and, furious, set out in pursuit.

They were speeding down the highway on the outskirts of the aforementioned city when there was the screech of a police whistle, and a motorcycle policeman waved them over to the curb. He was polite but unimpressed. He didn't care *who* Mr. Moneybags was, there was a forty-five-mile limit on this highway. But like any true gentleman he rose to the tears of the mother. "Eloping, eh?" he said. "To the convent, eh? Hmmmm." There was a thoughtful gleam in his eye as he whistled for another policeman. "I'll give ye an escort," he said magnanimously. "The tracks are up on Market Street and ye'll never get through without it."

So, with one motorcycle before and another aft, with sirens howling and curious people staring, the Moneybags party went seventy miles an hour up hills, around curves, over bridges, covering forty miles of Skyline highway that avoided traffic by going a good forty miles out of the way, for the longest and most scenic ride to the airport within the memory of man. The politeness of the two policemen was beautiful to see as they waved a don't-mention-it farewell at the airport an hour or so after the plane was on its way. No one has ever been able to identify the two knights in blue who so gallantly assisted a lady in distress. Indeed, Mr. Moneybags did his best to find and hang them. But somewhere in a peaceful cloister I hope that a Carmelite remembers.

Not everyone must elope to the convent, of course, and neither does every girl find her family solidly behind her. Most of us come from that vast middle ground where there is just enough opposition to make us determined to go ahead with our plans. Sometimes it takes heroic courage; sometimes a heroic amount of tact. A family that has seen you through the pigtail and bicycle stage, and suffered you to survive adolescence, isn't apt to take you seriously when you suddenly announce that this is IT.

It has taken me many years to discover that even this opposition, which can cause real heartache at the time, can be a definite part of God's plan. Indeed, there is an amusing simplicity in the way He chose to point it out to me, as though in addition to making His Will known, God would like also from time to time to have His own little joke.

My family—good, sensible people who had seen me through many an ephemeral enthusiasm, from writing operettas to playing the xylophone—could be easily pardoned for thinking it was just another one of those things. They were most unenthusiastic about the whole idea. As one of them put it, "Good heavens, are they *that* hard up for nuns?" Having stubbornly resisted all their logical arguments, I was on my knees packing a suitcase the day before leaving home when Margie came in to let me know what she thought about it.

"You've never had an ounce of sense," she assured me with sisterly candor, "and you won't develop it there. You won't like religious life one bit, and you won't have sense enough to come home. I thought if you'd just give me a code word, so that if you were unhappy—as I'm sure you will be—you could let me know and I'd come after you. . . ."

I assured her I wouldn't need any code word, but she insisted. "All right," I said, holding up my mother's best dressmaking scissors as I packed them, "if I say 'black-handled scissors,' you come after me."

"That's silly," she said. "How could you ever possibly find anything to say about scissors?" But we agreed.

The imaginative, the unsystematic, and the undisciplined find little to soothe their nerves in the average novitiate. By the end of the first year I was in hot water so much of the time that the available edifying subjects to write home about became progressively fewer. So I was charmed beyond measure to find a neutral subject beginning: "Dear Mama, You'll be interested to know I've cut a silhouette, something like the ones Pussie makes. I used your black-handled—" and there I pulled up short, terrified. Tomorrow Margie would be on the front porch with fire in her eyes, and all my arguments would be in vain.

I could hardly tell it the way it happened. Sister Novice-Mistress had sent for me one day, a usual procedure. I examined my conscience and it was uncomfortably crowded with the sort of things novices find on their consciences. But she merely looked at me reflectively and said, "Why don't I ever see *you* cutting any silhouettes? Your sister does lovely ones."

"I've never made any," I said lamely.

"That's just what I said," she agreed. "Why don't you? You certainly know how to handle scissors."

Now, it is common knowledge that novice-mistresses are not easily shaken off an idea, any more than a barnacle will let go a rock for a novice's notion. A week or so later I got another summons and this time she simply handed me a picture which she had borrowed from an obliging gift-shop manager, an Austrian cutting of the Flight into Egypt. "I presume you have scissors," she said off-handedly. "Go make one—*just like it.*"

"Well, Helen was right," I thought resignedly. "They tell you to do something perfectly silly, just to see if you'll do it or not. If you

do, it's supposed to burst into blossom and confound those who
laughed at you. If you don't, they send you home." I hadn't much
choice. I didn't want to be sent home, so I sat down and made one
just like it.

At least four times that year I had to start my letter home all
over again because of the scissors. The novice-mistress, who had
tried me and found me wanting in practically every useful art, was
relieved to find there was something I could do. She encouraged
and coaxed and suggested and corrected and comforted, and even
today I judge all my pictures as though she were looking over my
shoulder.

The black-handled scissors have been lost years ago. Three thousand silhouettes later I can still remember the queer sensation that
ran along my spine when God's little joke first became evident to
me. And I still wonder why, out of all the miscellany I was putting
into that suitcase (but of course you have never seen me pack), it
had to be *scissors* that I casually picked up and tagged with destiny.

Or do you agree with me, there just aren't any accidents?

The Arrival

Sister M. Deborah, S.L.

We stepped down from the train into the night. Somewhere in the darkness would be two sisters who had come to meet us. For months I had been rehearsing that meeting. Now I stared straight ahead, afraid to turn to either side, afraid I would see them. My companion—a tall, even-featured girl, bound for the same novitiate —peered apprehensively past me and up the track.

"There they are," she muttered.

I turned. A glow of harsh yellow light suffused the tiny country station and its surrounding platform. Silhouetted against the light, two Sisters of Loretto were advancing toward us, the sides of their veils flapping as they walked along the crunchy cinder siding. One of the figures was tall, the other short. Since the light was behind them, I could not see their faces; but I knew that the smaller one would be the mistress of postulants whom I had once met. "Her eyes look right through you"—that's what I'd been told.

Then the sisters were upon us, exclaiming over us, making introductions and inquiring about our trip. The tall sister, it developed, was the assistant mistress of novices, a close friend of one of my favorite teachers. I observed her curiously.

We walked back along the cinder siding the way they had come.

The February night was damply cold. A station wagon waited for us under the glaring yellow light. Suitcases were handed in. We postulants hung back until told where to sit. It wouldn't do to be forward with these sisters; they were our superiors—awesome thought! I wondered, in the midst of this tea-party cordiality, what novitiate discipline under them would be like in the years ahead—such long years.

I sat tensely in the back seat next to the mistress of postulants, answering questions about the musicale then in rehearsal at the college I had so recently left. The fact that she seemed interested in such a topic reassured me, and there was a refined gentleness in her voice that I found attractive. Despite what I'd been told, her eyes did *not* seem to be looking through me.

The car swung off the main road and began to climb a dark hill. I leaned forward, searching through the blackness for the outdoor stations of the cross that I had seen and liked on that one memorable visit to the motherhouse* three years before. Suddenly the headlights swept over them. A hundred yards farther up the gravel drive the car stopped. We got out.

The place was just as I had remembered it: angular buildings, most of them quaintly old, forming three sides of a long quadrangle of dark trees. Here and there an old-fashioned street lamp spotlighted a doorway, a porch, a sidewalk. Dead leaves rustled on the ground. An asphalt walk, hardly visible in the darkness, crossed the quadrangle from where we stood and ended in a lighted area between the dark, lofty novitiate building and the miter-shaped façade of the church. Oblongs of saffron light fell through the church windows and lay in a row on the ground outside. No one was to be seen.

"They're all at prayers," said the mistress of postulants. "Are you hungry?" We assured her that we were not. I, for one, felt almost incapable of swallowing.

"Are you sure? Well, let's go make a visit; then you can go right to bed."

We crept into the rear of the church, genuflected, and slid into an empty pew. Rows and rows of sisters knelt silently with their backs toward us, black veils on the left, white on the right. I looked down the right side, trying to pick out my friends Vron and Ann in

*The central house or headquarters of a congregation. Usually, the novitiate is at the same location.

their white, starched postulant caps. I had friends among the novices, too, but there was no use looking for them among all those blankly anonymous veils. Way up front the altar glimmered faintly in the light of the sanctuary lamp. A feeling of having arrived in the right place stole over me and calmed, somewhat, the fear that still churned my stomach and made electric buzzers in the palms of my hands.

The mistress of postulants was kneeling across the aisle from us. Instinctively I kept the corner of my eye on her; and when she rose to go, I rose. So did my companion. We two began sliding cautiously out of the pew, trying to balance on the balls of our feet so our heels would not click against the floor. Outside, under one of the street lamps that made this quadrangle of buildings seem like a little town, we picked up our suitcases and, following the small black-garbed figure of the mistress, crossed a few feet of sidewalk and climbed the stairs to a high porch. An iron handrail ran up along the staircase, its vertical bars cutting the wan lamplight into strips that crookedly carpeted the stairs. Sister opened the door, and we stepped after her into the novitiate building.

Inside stretched a long, highly polished corridor. Its waxy, amber-colored floor and wainscoting gleamed mellowly in the light of the chandelier. Farther on, the corridor was unlighted—dim and shadowy. The mistress turned to us.

"We don't talk at night," she said in a soft but definite voice. Then she led the way up a solid-looking staircase of dark, polished wood, with a heavy carved newel post at its foot. As I climbed the stairs behind her toward the cloister (oh, my, a real cloister!) my mind kept repeating her words, carefully recording that first command. For the quiet statement had been a command, I knew, though it hadn't sounded like one. "We don't talk at night." The information was not new to me; I had heard sisters refer casually to what they called "sacred silence." Vaguely I thought of those sisters keeping tonight an obedient silence at my college, three hundred miles away. It pleased me to think that now I had something in common with them. But more impressive was the awareness that for me, tonight, the whole of religious obedience was summed up in the observance of that one regulation.

The long hall at the top of the stairs was dusky-dark, though halfway down it a small orange bulb burned on a cord from the ceiling. Shadowy pictures looked down on us from enormous frames as we followed Sister down the hall. Then, to one side, I saw a lighted room. Just inside the door a woman—another postulant, I assumed—sat hunched on a suitcase. She raised her face as we entered, and I was startled to see it red and bloated as if from long weeping. Sister bent toward her.

"Margaret," she said softly, "you go down to my office. I'll be there in a minute." Sister turned to us. "She came in just this morning. She's terribly homesick."

I sensed that Margaret's lugubrious frame of mind was not exactly what Sister might have preferred us to encounter at that point. My own feelings, however, were far too vehement to allow me to worry about other people's. Pangs of fear and unfamiliarity writhed within me; but, at the same time, bubbles of amusement kept rising to the surface. This room, for instance, with its green linoleum floor and its rows of curtained stalls, was, I knew, a type of dressing room.

On my previous visit I had seen its mate in another building on the premises, a building at that time accessible to seculars. My whole high school class had been visiting the motherhouse, and we had had a hilarious time, ducking in and out of just such alcoves as these, finding conventual living arrangements a great joke. Imagine that I should now be moving into one of these "horse stalls" in real earnest!

"Your alcove is over here," the mistress was saying as she led the way down a narrow aisle between rows of stalls. Sure enough, there was a bit of paper with my name on it pasted up next to one of the white curtains. Lifting the curtain, I looked into a white-walled space about four feet square. A washstand, covered with a green and orange plaid dresser scarf and equipped with soap dish, plastic glass, and white enamel basin, was built in against the back wall. On the side walls were clothes hooks, on the floor a wooden box, painted white.

Sister had led my companion farther down the aisle to another alcove. Now she returned and scratched with her fingernail on the canvas curtain opposite mine. "Maxine," she called softly. One side of the curtain was pulled aside from within, and a tall girl with a sweet, thin face stepped out. She looked about sixteen or so. Her dark hair, parted in the middle, fell long and almost straight to the shoulders of her old-fashioned nightgown, with its gathered yoke and long sleeves. Her gray-blue eyes were large and round and timid.

Like some little wild thing, I thought. A deer.

"Maxine," said the mistress, "these two just got off the train. They ought to have a nice, warm bath. You'll show them where everything is, won't you?"

"Yes, S'ter." The voice had a little country quaver in it.

"I'll come back in a few minutes and show you where your beds are." Sister walked down the narrow aisle, then suddenly turned back to us. "Oh, and in the morning, now, don't get up at the first bell. You'll hear the others getting up, but just stay in bed. I'll come and get you when it's time."

"Yes, Sister," we answered.

Maxine with a minimum of comment showed us the bathtub, enclosed in still another wooden stall in the corner of the room. I was amused to see that it was exactly the same kind we had at home—one of those old models, standing up off the floor on ornate feet, claws clasping round balls. "Queen Anne bathtubs," my mother called them.

"You get some water from the hopper," said Maxine, pointing to a deep sink, "and you take it back to your alcove to wash your teeth. You've got a glass and a basin in your alcove."

I registered in my vocabulary the word *hopper*, till then beyond my ken. Hopper? What hopper?

"All right," I said softly, remembering the ban on unnecessary conversation. "Thank you."

I looked inquiringly at the other new postulant. "You go on first," she said.

Judging from the number of alcoves in the room, there would be considerable competition for that bathtub as soon as prayers were over, and speed seemed desirable. Back in my alcove, I undressed as quickly as I could and slid into a voluminous white nightgown, much like Maxine's. In it I felt self-consciously quaint, as if I were in costume for a play. Peculiar thing, though—this play was real.

The bath was warm, relaxing. It was also something I had known all my life, something reassuringly familiar. If baths inside convents were like baths outside convents, perhaps life inside convents was not unreasonably different from life outside convents. I did not stop to reason out the matter; I just felt better about being where I was.

Back in my alcove again, I sat down on the wooden box, set my suitcase on my knees and opened it. Inside the silky top pocket of the suitcase were two letters—one from my mother, the other from a family friend, a good Protestant lady who found this convent business noble, if puzzling. Both letters had been given to me with instructions that they must not be read until I arrived. Both were long and heartbreakingly loving. I dared not read them thoroughly but skimmed them with deliberate coldness. One could cope with only so much emotion.

There was a sound of feet ascending a staircase. Some went past the door of the room; others came in. Cautiously I pulled back a corner of my curtain and peeked down the aisle between the two rows of alcoves. A plump postulant passed by, then another, then one of the girls I'd known at college. Her brown hair was slicked up and back until it looked like a boy's under the starched frill of her cap. There was a nonchalant swing to the short black cape around her shoulders. Right behind her was another friend of mine, her face rounder and ruddier than I had ever seen it. They seemed so much at home. As first one, then the other disappeared behind a row of alcoves, I felt the bar of discipline clang down impressively between myself and them. "We don't talk at night."

The alcoves around me bustled now with quiet activity. I could hear the swish of garments going on or off, the splashing of water, and little muffled clicks and clumps that meant cabinets were opening and shoes being removed. I had heard Sister say she would come back to show us the way to bed, and I dared not venture out of my cubbyhole without a guide. So I sat on the wooden box, my open suitcase on my knees, unpacking the new-feeling, new-smelling black and white clothes I would wear the next day. More costuming for the play. Carefully I stowed little piles of my possessions in the cabinet under the washstand. Even so, the alcove was becoming as cluttered as a closet. My scarlet topcoat, with its fashionable full back, full sleeves, and full length, hung against one wall, rather notably reducing the already minimal space. The suitcase wasn't much help either.

There was a light knock on the wall of my alcove. Lifting the curtain again, I looked out. In the aisle stood a small, slender girl in a black bathrobe, her dark hair slicked back from her shiny-clean face.

"Sister says I'm to show you where your bed is," she whispered.

I stepped out of my nook to join her in the aisle.

"Where's your robe?" she asked.

"I don't have one. I mean, it's coming in my trunk. It wouldn't fit in my suitcase." (It certainly wouldn't! I thought of my second-hand suitcase, one hinge of which had popped open at the crucial moment early that morning. I had knelt on the living-room rug at home—how far away it seemed!—and had rather precariously re-fastened the hinge with a bobby pin.)

"You can't go out without a robe!"

I felt silly, but the horror in her tone did amuse me. After all, in this tentlike gown I was more than fully clothed. Besides, I could not possibly wear a robe that I did not have, no matter how sorely the novitiate's sensibilities were offended by its lack. Just then an-other new postulant, equally lost but at least possessed of a bath-robe, appeared at the end of the aisle, and my guide abandoned me to conduct the other girl to bed. I crept after them, feeling that the best refuge for me at the moment was bed. At the door of the al-cove room I stopped and peered cautiously into the dim hall, look-ing first one way then the other, like a person about to cross a street. There was no one to see my custom-defying lack of robe!

Relieved, I scuttled across the hall and through the ceiling-high doorway of the dormitory. The room was dark and I could see little except what appeared to be long rows of sheets hanging on clothes-lines. Perplexed, I stopped. A fresh, cool breeze, full of the fra-grance of clean linen, swept over me, drawn by the draft from the open door to the hall. Then a light in the center of the room went on, and I could see that the "sheets" were bed curtains, hung from a framework of poles. Legs of white iron beds, set at regular inter-vals down the length of the room, appeared from under the cur-tains. The center light, a bare bulb on a long cord, swung rhythmically, switching irregular swaths and patches of light and shadow over the white walls, the high white ceiling, the white bed curtains. Under the light stood the two postulants.

The experienced one beckoned to me, pulling back a curtain to indicate the location of my bed. I lifted the side of the curtain nearer to me and slid under it, squeezing along the foot of the bed which I encountered just inside. Instantly the postulant's head poked around her side of the curtain, the same look of concern on her face.

"You're supposed to go in over here," she whispered.

"Oh," I said.

Her head disappeared. I stood staring after her, choking back a giggle. Good heavens! Did they even have a rule about which side

of a curtain you could walk around? Then I noticed that the bed
was set over to one side of the curtained enclosure. Had I entered
at the point she indicated, I need not have squeezed along the foot
of the bed; there was an open space through which I might have
walked. Oh!

The center bulb clicked off, but a kind of twilight still poured
into the room through the transom over the high door. Fascinated,
I surveyed my "bedroom." White curtains formed three sides of the
enclosure. Behind the head of the bed rose the dark frame of an
immense window, long, narrow shutters folded back on either side.
Beside the bed stood a straight white chair. I knelt down and said
an excited, distracted prayer or two, then got into bed, sliding carefully between the sheets.

The bed had been turned down for me—a nice gesture. It made
a person feel expected. My feet slithered appreciatively over the
slick sheets. At home our sheets were rough-dried. "Poverty!" my
mother had once scoffed jokingly. "I'll bet you'll have ironed
sheets!" Sure enough, these were ironed sheets. I laughed to myself; but, even so, I lay stiff and straight in that stiff, straight bed.
Everything about it seemed so austere—its white iron frame, its
firm mattress, its narrow width. Stretching and yawning and flop-
ping comfortably about seemed hardly appropriate. I lay still and
looked at the white curtains and listened.

Now and then the big door opened, then shut with a soft clump.
Slippered feet padded across the floor. I wondered how many people slept in this immense room and who on earth they were. I
wondered what the bell would sound like in the early morning. I
thought of the next day, swallowing apprehensively as I pictured
the big church where I would not know where to sit; a big dining
room in which I would not know where I belonged; a big new
strict life in which I would not know what to do when, or why, or
how.

But the warm bed, like the warm bath, began to comfort me.
Ironed sheets—m-m-m. I would survive; others had. My friends
were surviving. I would get used to it. No use worrying . . . too
sleepy . . . too tired. And God was here—and ironed sheets.

From Decision to Final Vows

Sister Mary Josette, S.N.D.

When any girl arrives at the conclusion that the religious life is the life for her, she contacts the superiors of the community in which she is interested. As a rule she presents herself for a personal interview. Often her parents go with her for this interview and at its close, if the young woman is accepted as a candidate, she receives her wardrobe list and a few forms for conventual records. In addition to this, she usually learns the date on which she will be accepted as a postulant. The time between the first interview with the superiors and the date of entrance varies with the community, the candidate, and the wishes of the parents, especially if the candidate is a minor. In general, the Church gives the same advice to prospective candidates for religious life as she does to engaged couples—the period should not be too long.

Time speeds. It is one of the most sensational eras in the life of a girl. Everything around her takes on a new hue—often one of added attractiveness. It's "the last time for this" and "the last time for that" everywhere she turns. She is the guest of honor at several or many going-away parties. As the day draws closer her parents hate to see her go out. The time that they will have her for their own is so short.

On the day of entrance she arrives at the convent with her parents. There is one thing she realizes as she steps across the threshold. She is not the one making the biggest sacrifice. Her mother and father are getting the dregs of it. She is getting what she wants for happiness in time and eternity.

Her life as a religious begins the first day she enters. She is taken to a special part of the house reserved for novices and postulants— the novitiate. There she receives the distinctive garb of her postulate. There, too, she meets the other young women with whom she will live. Some are just a few hours older in religion than she.

Everything is new—the prayers, the work, the study, the food, the recreation, even the conversation. Sometimes the newness keeps her from getting homesick, but often it increases a tendency to get blue. Almost everybody gets homesick at some time and in some degree, and the lovelier the home a girl has left and the finer her sensibilities, the more homesick she is likely to become.

Time brightens the horizon. She learns to know the people with whom she associates. She masters the correct response to the multitudinous convent bells.

Her novitiate life, and of course her entire religious life thereafter, will differ according to her choice of an active or a contemplative order. Here we consider the preparation of a sister for an active religious community—a community that engages in any kind of work which necessitates contact with people outside the religious family itself.

After a week or two the postulant feels at ease in the routine of the day. An early rising, meditation, Holy Mass, and Holy Communion take up the first hours of her day. Breakfast follows. After that her household chores, study, prayer, succeed each other. Experience and special orientation conferences open up to her the way of life she is expected to follow as a postulant.

In each week there is enough variety to keep the postulancy interesting. There are games of all types—ball games, roller skating, shuffleboard, badminton. There are hikes on holidays and evening treats once in a while. There are the special feast days of the community. Topping all are the spiritual advantages of frequent exposition of the Most Blessed Sacrament; in some communities even Nocturnal Adoration on specified days of the month. There are daily conferences on the religious life, explanations of the rule, and study of the vows.

Before long the postulant gets to know that the superiors are nothing like their counterparts on stage and screen. She has nothing to be afraid of. Their encouragement is much more frequent than their admonition. Their patience, justice, and kindness toward everyone is striking. Their sympathy in any distress points up the fact that in the new family of which the young woman is a member she has the best of care, direction, and mothering.

Once a month in most religious communities there is an opportunity for the family to visit with the postulant or for the postulant to write to her family. Often there are additional opportunities for correspondence given to postulants whose families live at such a distance that they can come only once or a few times a year.

The postulancy lasts from six months to a year. Ten days before its close the postulant enters her first long retreat. She is required to make a retreat of eight full days, but many communities count the evening of the opening as the first day and the morning of its conclusion as the tenth. Before the retreat she wonders whether she will be able to keep silence for so long a time. It will probably be easier than it seems. In the first place she will probably have no one to talk to—the other novices and postulants will be making the retreat too; in the second place, over the period of time between her entrance and her retreat she has been trying to cultivate the habit of talking silently to God in her heart as she works. Just as a young woman strives to know her fiancé through frequent contact, so the postulant who wishes to take Christ as her Spouse tries to know Him through intimate contact with Him in prayer. When this same young woman had come as a casual visitor to the convent before her entrance she probably noticed the silent atmosphere that prevailed and remarked on it. Now she understands its significance.

Finally the great day of religious investment arrives. It will be a twofold thrill for the postulant. She will get the habit of the order and her religious name. In some communities she dresses as a bride; in others she receives a part of her religious habit in the cloister and a part in the public ceremony in the chapel. The ceremonies differ from community to community, but the essential portion of blessing and receiving the religious habit remains the same.

After the celebration everyone is eager to meet the new novice and, if she did not receive her name as part of the public ceremony,

to find out what it is. In some communities she is permitted to ask
for her name, in others she suggests two or three names that she
would prefer, in still others she is given a name. In the latter instance all her relatives and the sister herself look forward with great
expectation to the new name, hoping they will be able to pro-
nounce, spell, and get accustomed to it.

After her investment the novice goes into the intensive training
period required by the Church for the validity of religious profession. Because the period is required by Canon Law it is known as
the canonical novitiate, and often the novices training are known
as canonicals. Many religious communities permit no visits during
this year and reduce correspondence to the minimum. Others allow visitors three or four times a year, and some every two months.
The canonical novices do not teach, nurse, or engage in other activities which would necessitate their leaving the novitiate center
or devoting the greater amount of their time to professional duties.
The main duty of the novice during this year is to learn the religious life according to the spirit of the order or congregation in
which she is to take vows. Various household chores, study of
Christian Doctrine, the Bible, the liturgy, prescribed community
prayer, and recreation fill out her waking hours. As in the postulancy there is variety in the daily schedule throughout the week to
avoid monotony.

During the time of the postulancy and canonical year the superiors of the religious community study the new member to discover the type of work for which she is best suited. She may be
questioned about the things she likes to do best and about her
special talents. Natural aptitude and the needs of the community
will finally determine the task or field of work assigned to her.

According to the law of the Church she may take her temporary
vows at the end of her canonical year. However, the rules of many
communities prescribe another year of novitate to allow her time to
test herself in the activities proper to the institute she wishes to
join. She may be sent to teach, to nurse, to help out in orphanages,
to study for her degree, to train for mission work.

Three months before the time of her temporary profession she
goes back to the novitiate center to make final preparation for the
big day. This preparation consists of another intensive study of the
vows, rules, customs, and history of the congregation. During this
time she is given ample opportunity for spiritual preparation for

the day. The many hours that the ardent earthly bride spends in choosing her trousseau, arranging her apartment and negotiating with the florist, the novice spends in making her soul more beautiful for her Heavenly Bridegroom.

Ten days before her profession, she makes another retreat. This time she understands the purpose, seriousness, and value of the retreat a little better than in her postulant days.

The ten days drag by on leaden feet. She can hardly wait.

Before her retreat many of the other sisters of the community have made it a point to see the bride-to-be, asking her one favor— to remember them on her profession day. The Fathers of the Church hold that the religious oblation is so great and pleasing to God that at the making of religious profession, the soul is cleansed of all sin and punishment due to sin so that it stands before God in baptismal innocence. Because of the purity of soul, everyone feels that the person has special influence with God and wishes to be remembered.

Sometimes the religious profession ceremony is open to the public. Again, it may be private. That depends on the community. But whether it be public or private, the novices take temporary vows, i.e., they promise to observe poverty, chastity, and obedience for one year, two years, or another specified term. The period for which they take vows is specified by the Rule. The vows are usually pronounced in the presence of the bishop.

The wedding day is one of great rejoicing. In most communities the bride receives her ring. In some few she waits until the day of her final espousals for that. She also receives the black veil to replace the white one she has worn as a novice. To distinguish her from the rest of the sisters for the day she is crowned with a special wreath, a coronet of flowers or a crown of thorns.

Usually she moves from the novitiate into the part of the house reserved for the professed religious. When assignments are given out for the coming year, she may find that she will continue her studies if she still has to complete them. She may teach, be charged with a group of children at an orphanage, receive a nursing assignment, or be entrusted with the care of the house in one of the missions. The care of the aged or a mission field at home or abroad may be her portion. One thing is certain, she will have some direct part in the labor of the community no matter what her charge.

It is comparatively seldom that religious leave the convent after temporary vows. Their attitude all along is not, "If I like it, I'll stay," but rather, "God make me worthy of the grace of perseverance."

Each year for her annual retreat the young religious returns to the center of the community in the area in which she works. In addition to this week spent at the center, she may spend her entire vacation there and she may be called in at various times in the year for special "helps" in the religious life and in her professional work. These helps are not just a matter of reading and study. Nor are they just for teachers, nurses, or missionaries; they are given for every young religious. Special conferences on the problems they are meeting and frequent private interviews with the superiors give the junior members an opportunity to get any advice they may need. Older religious offer them the value of their experience in the professional fields. Often an older religious is assigned by the superior to help the beginner in her professional difficulties. All in all, complete and careful training of every sister in the religious spirit and in her professional work is the utmost concern of the superiors.

At the close of the period prescribed by Canon Law for temporary vows, the sister makes ready for the day of final espousals. The law of the Church prescribes at least three years of temporary vows, which may be for a year at a time, renewed annually, before the making of perpetual vows. Most communities have a longer time prescribed by the rule. The usual number is five or six. In many communities this final step in the making of a full-fledged religious is preceded by a second novitiate extending from three to six months.

Again during that time the religious reviews her obligations and devotes a large amount of time to prayer. The day of the final vows is preceded by a ten-day retreat.

On the morning of its conclusion, usually at the Communion of Holy Mass, the priest stands before the religious, holding the Sacred Host aloft for her to see. There, with her eyes on God, she promises that for the term of her whole life—for better or for worse, in sickness and in health, in poverty and persecution—she will cast her lot with Him until death will unite them in unending embrace.

IV

The Goal Is Merely Perfection

The Goal Is Merely Perfection

IF YOU would be perfect, go sell all you have, give to the poor and come follow Me." The sisters would be perfect, so they follow Christ in the rules laid down for everyone and the rules He gave for those who would follow Him all the way. They do this by following the evangelical counsels of poverty, chastity, and obedience, and by obeying the rules and constitutions of their particular order, with charity above and around all else.

Unfortunately there is nothing automatic or easy about it. Perfection isn't a bonus that comes with the profession of vows. A sister has to try to practice the vows and follow her rule every day, all her life.

The main rules used are those given by St. Basil, St. Augustine, St. Benedict, St. Francis of Assisi, and St. Ignatius. The rules are lists of statutes defining the objectives of the order and the principal means of reaching them. The rule gives the general principles, and the constitutions give the particular laws for the details of the life in the institute. The constitutions may be changed as the times change. The terms *rule* and *constitutions* are often used synonymously. These laws are meant to give order to the religious life and are aids to perfection. Infractions of the rule are not always sins. St. Dominic said he would rather cut up the rule book than let it be a burden to anyone's conscience.

Poverty varies from community to community. Individually, nuns with solemn vows, contemplatives, can't own property even if it is willed to them; a sister with simple vows may have property in her own name but may not use or dispose of it without permission. In some institutes poverty is dire; in others, a mere lack of luxuries. Not too long ago money was being raised in this country for some of the destitute nuns in Europe in a "race with death." The sisters in the United States and Canada are more fortunate, but they can use help, especially those in the cloistered orders. The gifts the religious most appreciate may be surprising. A sister at Maryknoll was overjoyed one Christmas at receiving a power saw. It should be remembered, too, that the outside of a convent gives no clue to the poverty within. When sisters plan a new building they don't say, "Now let's put up something really ugly and make sure it will tumble down in a few years."

A girl who is used to throwing away a pair of shoes or a lamp when she happens to tire of them may not appreciate at first taking special care of every little thing in the convent because it is not hers but "ours," or asking permission to keep a trinket someone has sent her. With obedience, especially, the letter of the vow is indeed deadly and only the spirit leads to survival. Obedience doesn't mean that every time a superior opens her mouth and Sister doesn't jump to obey that she has committed a mortal sin. If Sister has been gently advised to straighten out the mess on her work table and doesn't get around to it right away, she may be scolded but not threatened with perdition. In the rare cases where drastic measures are needed, the superior may give a formal command in a set phrase provided for in the constitutions, and in this situation Sister is in no doubt that she had better do what she is told. Mother Catherine Thomas, in her book *My Beloved, the Story of a Carmelite Nun*, says the modern girl is not more reluctant to obey but she does like to know the reason for the act, and this attitude is encouraged. Senseless commands, in spite of what most girls hear before they enter, are not likely to be given in today's convent. Possibly there are a few old-fashioned convents where this is still practiced, but most sisters have never experienced it and say that ordinary obedience is hard enough without any silly commands to test it.

Common life is both a blessing and a trial. The sisters *are* sisters in a true sense, with all the joys that come from a close-knit happy family. But, especially in a small convent, they know each other so well that there is no chance for the subterfuges pride is accustomed to. And as Sister M. Ann Edward says in her book *Inside Out,* "If there are twenty-five sisters in a room, there are also twenty-five opinions as to when moving air is a breeze and when it is a draft, when the room is warm and when it is stuffy."

The means used to bring about perfection are often misunderstood. Sisters heartily objected to the book *The Nun's Story* on several counts. First of all, the heroine never left off being Gabrielle Van Der Mal to become a true Sister Luke. A nun is expected to "die to her old self," something more drastic than our "turning over a new leaf" or making a New Year's resolution, and this death to the worldly self is symbolized by her prostration in the ceremony in which she receives her habit. Sister Luke thought more of being a nurse than being a sister. No one should enter the convent merely to be a nurse; she can do that in the world. Furthermore, says Sister Bertrande, D.C., in an article in the *Catholic Library World,* "Gabrielle fought a good fight—but she wanted the 'crown' in the here and now. She wanted to know herself a victor. It isn't like that in the battles of the soul. So she laid down her arms—and therein lies her failure."

Penitential practices are often presented in books by ex-nuns without giving their spiritual reason and traditional background. This is something like trying to explain saluting without any reference to military life and customs. ("Mama, why is the man hitting his head?" "He isn't hitting his head, dear. He's putting his hand up to his forehead because that other man is passing by. Look, now the other man is doing it." "But *why,* Mama?") This can only lead to the ridiculous. The sisters who stick it out know these are means to a goal, not the goal itself.

There are some other pitfalls in the religious life that should be mentioned. Mother Catherine Thomas of Carmel says, "When a nun goes blissfully along for months on end without any trials or problems we suspect that there is something wrong somewhere." Carmel, of course, is a cloistered, strict order, but the road to perfection is bumpy for everyone.

Even after a sister has been in the convent for some time she may sit back one day and wonder, "What am I doing here? Do I really have a vocation?" Or her constant soul-searching and introspection may lead to the disease of scrupulosity, when small faults suddenly appear to her as mortal sins. (This happens also in secular life and it doesn't help to say it's all in the person's mind. It's a real tragedy to the one who suffers from it.) Or she may very well come to a spiritual dryness that St. John of the Cross spoke of in his book *The Dark Night of the Soul*. This is described very well in an article in *Time*, April 11, 1955, on the religious life:

> Without any apparent cause, all the warm joy and pleasure that the religious normally finds in prayer and the monastic routine suddenly disappears. As one contemporary has described it: "The entire spiritual world seems meaningless and unreal; even one's own most vivid spiritual experiences fade out like half-forgotten dreams. One becomes keenly, sometimes agonizingly aware of everything prosaic: heat, cold, stuffy rooms . . . excessive weariness, the irritation of the heavy, uncomfortable garments . . . other people's maddening 'little ways,' the 'sinking feeling' and depression that are inseparable from fasting; the appalling monotony of the rule-imposed routine . . ."

This is said of the cloister, but much of it applies as well to the active sister and also to the layman who practices contemplation.

There is also the shock of adjustments to life after the close confinement and strict training of the novitiate when the new sister mingles with the other professed sisters and discovers they are often not as perfect as she had thought, and suddenly she realizes with horror, neither is she. She has to learn when to tone down some of the practices she has learned—for instance, custody of the eyes, the intentional lack of curiosity about her surroundings, is for the convent, not practical in the classroom. Her long hours of work as teacher, nurse, or whatever may sometimes leave her too exhausted for fervent prayer. Sister is also subject to such ordinary everyday trials as headaches, corns, and getting up on the wrong side of the bed.

But through it all, most of the sisters keep their eyes on the goal, faltering because they are human, refusing to give up because they are reaching out for the Divine.

Obedient Virgins

Sister Mary Francis, P.C.

The ceremonial for profession of vows in the monastery is so pre-occupied with the vow of virginity that you would think it the only vow the novice was making. In ancient times the ritual was known simply as that for the "consecration of virgins," and it is a great mistake to think that the state of virginity solemnly vowed to God is no different from the state of single persons in the world. The unmarried woman is free to change her state of life whenever she wishes. The consecrated virgin has given her entire future into the hands of God, signed with a changeless seal. The motives of a girl in the world for remaining single may be as varied as the sands on the seashore. The motive of the religious is unique: she wishes to give herself, body and soul, to God.

This positive aspect of holy virginity is far too often entirely ignored. Virginity is thought to be a mere abstention. Many, daz-zled by the coruscating if specious logic of psychologists of the Freudian school, think it a blight on the development of the per-sonality. One cannot experience the fullness of happiness in the virginal state, they maintain. It needs only one long look at the faces of nuns, one long listen to their laughter, to blow this propo-sition sky-high—or, better, earth-low.

Religious life without obedience would be a three-ring circus. Complete, continual, unswerving obedience comes naturally to no one. Our first parents planted the seed of disobedience in the soul of each of their children. It is true, though, that the seed bears more luxuriant fruit in some, and only sickly plants, easily uprooted, in others. In other words, obedience comes easier to some characters than to other characters.

A vocation to the cloister does not presuppose an insatiable thirst to be told what to do. Most modern girls are remarkably adept at ordering all details of their own lives. And most girls find obedience the big hurdle in religious life. Self-will is said to die only fifteen minutes before we do—or is it fifteen minutes *after!* At any rate, the feeling of being captain of this ship, mistress of one's own affairs, is the last luxury nature is willing to forego.

To add to nature's objections, the devil has a very fine sand especially prepared for the state of emergency into which each new religious vocation throws all hell. He scatters this light powder into a postulant's eyes during the first weeks of her religious life so that she can no longer see certain details of her past. Being told at every turn what to do and how to do it in approved monastic form, she forgets that she has actually been taking orders all her life. We all move within a tight orbit of obedience even in adulthood, obeying superiors ranging from the dean of the college or the head of office personnel to the traffic policemen who tell us when we may cross the street and when we may not.

An obedient religious simply cannot blunder while she obeys. The superior may be wrong in commanding, but the subject is still right in obeying. Too many persons think of being bound to obey. Actually it is the headiest exercise of our liberty to be free to obey. Adam was the lord of the world when he was free to obey. When he surrendered that glorious freedom in order to disobey . . . well, which human heart does not keep the record of his sorry loss?

The idea of the nobility in being free to surrender our wills even in the smallest matters is never, however, swallowed at one gulp in the first weeks of postulancy. The little fetters by which we freely elect to be bound to our dear Lord seem irksome until we get the taste of the world out of our mouths and forget its talk and its false values. When I was striking out into the deeps of the Divine Office as a postulant, Dear Mistress told me to turn to the Magnificat at Vespers each day. I did not turn. Next day, she inquired into this curious fact, and I informed her brightly that I knew the Magnificat by heart, expecting to be commended for lore so outstanding in one so young. Dear Mistress, however, did not pat me fondly on the shoulder. She did not even smile, proudly or otherwise. She said in a flat, firm voice: "That is entirely beside the point. Turn to the Magnificat and read it. It is the custom." That is the first of my store of recollections about obedience in small matters. And as I turn to the Magnificat at Vespers on my eighty-third birthday, I am sure I shall still find those words, "It is the custom," just as momentous as I did in the novitiate.

The grim tone of so many pious books that urge us to obey our superior, however unlovable she may be by nature, suggests that this is the normal cut of superiors. Such tomes cheer us on with dubiously joyous thoughts about all the warehousefuls of merits we are stacking up for ourselves by taking orders from someone for whom we feel a great aversion. The climax of all this would seem to be that you ought to pray to have an ogre as abbess; she would touch off your latent sanctity like a match set to a firecracker.

Of course, there is a wholesome truth at the bottom of all this, but it has been exaggerated out of all bounds. It is the business of the subject to obey her abbess whether she has any personal love for that dignitary or not. But it is not the business of the abbess to get a good grip on her authority and let love go by the board. St. Clare wants the abbesses of her order to be leaders in virtue and superior to the other nuns in holy behavior. For mere authority as such never takes hold of our hearts, but virtue and holy lovableness do. We are directed in the ways of obedience by a lawful superior. We are led by a lovable one.

The Relaxed Grasp

Sister M. Madeleva, C.S.C.

Before I was in the novitiate four months the only sister who had counseled me in any way regarding the religious life was sent on mission. I never saw her again. Sister Rita, my dream lady, died just a month before I left the novitiate. I never had a day's opportunity of knowing her simply as a sister-friend. By these two tokens, and even then, I understood that God meant me to live without props. He was making my natural independence an asset rather than an obstacle. My friendships rested on mutual interests, enthusiasms, objectives. I had to do my own thinking, make my own decisions, with proper deference to others. This gives one a capacity to be alone. Sometimes it almost imposes aloneness on one. There are compensations.

When I was a very young sister I came upon an essay by Louise Imogene Guiney, entitled "La Sainte Indifférente." I found just what I needed and at the exact moment of my need. Let me quote the paragraphs which have dominated my life, this description of the saint of holy indifference:

> Of all his store, unconsciously increased, he can always part
> with sixteen-seventeenths, by way of concessions to his indi-

viduality, and think the subtraction so much concealing marble chipped from the heroic figure of himself. . . .

He has gone through volition, and come out at the other side of it; everything with him is a specific act; he has no habits.

Nothing is so vulgar as close suction. He will never tighten his fingers on loaned opportunity; he is a gentleman, the hero of the habitually relaxed grasp.

When I left Saint Mary's, my school and convent home for thirteen years, I loosed my hold on friends, pupils, places, things. I went to a world of missionary possibilities, of compensatory rich friendships, of the majesty of mountains, a new world of birds and wild flowers. It was a life one spent on tiptoe, at least for me.

Three years later it was exchanged for California spring in February, a world rose-filled in April, and exotic summers until the winter rains. Then I watched the orange and other citrus fruits hanging heavy on the trees bleach rather than ripen. The Pacific gave itself to me down all the miles of its matchless coast. The trees, from pepper to redwood, were mine, the purple finches, the mockingbirds.

Better, there were the colleges that I knew, some before they were born, some in their robust youth, all in their beautiful promise and fulfillment. I think of Dominican College of San Rafael, which I knew when its enrollment numbered five students, two of whom were sisters. I was studying with the Sisters of Notre Dame de Namur when they pulled themselves up by the roots in San Jose and moved to Belmont. This was a major lesson in the relaxed grasp. I spoke to the first students at Mount Saint Mary's College, Los Angeles, when I had to step on a box to enter the only accessible door of the first building then under construction. I remember watching the fog roll over twin peaks in San Francisco long before the College of San Francisco transfigured that great eminence. Best of all, new worlds of the mind and of the soul opened in California, with new friends to stimulate and to share them. These, too, must teach me the relaxed grasp. These, too, I left to return to the work of building a college on a mountainside.

Living among the mountains involves mountain climbing. This calls for hiking sticks. When I left Saint Mary-of-the-Wasatch I had in my office a collection of hand-picked carved and polished hiking sticks that had journeyed miles with me to the tops of all our surrounding mountains and back. They had shared our quest of wild flowers: fritillary, lupine, lungwort, pentstemon, cliff rose, columbine. They had shared with us the first call of the meadow lark, the iridescence of the lazuli bunting, the splendor of the western oriole. They were friends to leave behind.

On returning to Saint Mary's after fifteen years I did not have enough to fill one small trunk. This is at least an outward sign of the emancipation achieved by the relaxed grasp.

For twenty-five years I have occupied an outer and inner office in Le Mans Hall at Saint Mary's. Either could be mistaken for an old curiosity shop. A half-dozen or more hiking sticks make a curious collection in the corner of the inner office. Some day I may put them as a holocaust on the roaring fire in our Great Hall, a perfect burnt offering. But not yet!

When, before dawn, on August 15 of last year, God came for Bill Cotter, the realization left me bereaved as no other death could have. The relaxed grasp—how could I translate it into comfort for Evarista, his sweetheart-wife, my schoolmate-friend? When a fortnight later Helen Holland Voll died, my grasp relaxed on a second of my lifetime and most dear friends. On Thanksgiving Day the astounding word came that John O'Laughlin, after a day in his office working in apparent good health, had died before all of his family could reach him. I began to understand that God was taking me in earnest. He loves these friends of mine even better than I do. I am learning to let go in deference to Him.

A little Chinese sister came to study with us some time ago. She had seen her family shattered, her young religious community dispersed. Her entire world, materially, consisted of two small suitcases, filled with absolutely essential clothing. She understood little English and spoke less. During our annual retreat, which she was trying to make with us, I thought to help her by talking over with her slowly and simply the matter of each conference. After the instruction on poverty, I asked, "Sister, did you understand Father's talk?" "He talk on poverty," she answered; then added, "Sister, you come to my room." We went upstairs together. She opened her suitcases, put their entire contents out on the bed, everything, I believe, except her toothbrush and soap. "Now, Sister," she said, "you take what I do not need." Here was an Oriental girl of twenty-five, a refugee, alone in every possible way, understanding

and practicing as I had never had to do the absolutes of detach-
ment, of holy poverty. What had my years taught me of the relaxed
grasp?

I am, however, en route. I like to go to Marshall Field's in Chicago just to see how many things there are in the world that I do
not want. There have been, still are, books that I should like at
least to try to write, cuds of song upon which I still hope to chew.
I should like to watch my seedling oaks and beeches grow into
great trees. Thinking of things to be done, hopes to be realized,
persons to be helped, I say laughingly that I go to a multitude of
funerals daily, burying so many deceased projects, so much of what
I have had to let die and must bury without regret. Some day I
shall have only One, Infinite, Absolute want. I shall not even want,
for the time being, my body. I shall not even want the breath I
breathe. When the last nonessentials of encumbering humanity
have been cut away, when the last tenacious grasp has been relaxed, what shall I say? What shall I say when I see God?

By Rule, By Custom, By Unwritten Law

Sister Mary Gilbert, S.N.J.M.

"Why, of course you can have gold frames," the optometrist insisted gently. "I've sold them to lots of the sisters myself." He reached for a file of accounts and began thumbing through it.

"I'll call again and let you know," I replied firmly, and left. I would have to check on that with Mother Superior. I had never seen anyone in our community wearing them.

It's never wise to generalize about what nuns may or may not do. Some may wear gold eyeglass frames and some may not. There are sisters who must write home once a week and others who may write only twice a year. There are sisters who visit their parents regularly and sisters who may not even enter their old home except when someone is dying. There are those who wear wrist watches and those who are allowed nothing more personal than an alarm clock. There are those who must go everywhere in pairs and those who thread their solitary way along the city streets.

Of course a few lay people don't quite see that nuns differ from the rest of the world. One of these was the magazine editor who began his form letter, "Reverend dear Sister," and then went on to invite me and my family to a cocktail party "after you get off the ski lift at the foot of Mt. P—." I declined, of course, just as

78

Sister M does when the alumni office sends her repeated invitations to her university's beer parties. Thus far, no community of religious women that I know of has proved that adaptable.

The same mistaken attitude is responsible for the weird assortment of Christmas gifts we receive—tantalizing perfumes like those that Sister A's superior passed on to her high school students; or fancy stationery like the stuff that Sister B donated to the parish bazaar; or lovely lingerie like that which Sister C gave enthusiastic thanks for and then presented to the convent cook.

Communities of religious women are as various as the Church. Wherever there arises a new need among the members of Christ's Mystical Body, a new community is formed or an existing one modified to serve that need.

Although Canon Law gives certain broad directives governing communities of religious women, the details are regulated by rule and custom and by unwritten observance in each institute. These, in turn, grow out of the particular objectives of the order. Sometimes, it is true, an observance may outlive the situation which gave rise to it, for change comes slowly in religious institutes.

Even within a single community, circumstances may give rise to unusual permissions. Most rules and customs are flexible enough to allow of interpretation by the superior, or, for valid reasons, even temporary dispensation. Without this elasticity our obedience would lose much of its merit, for it is in yielding to the human judgment of the superior that the sisters find many opportunities for the exercise of faith.

Sisters themselves accept these differences cheerfully. Members of distinct "families" within the Church, they have embraced a particular rule with knowledge and forethought. They know that the life of sacrifice common to all precludes envy and discontent at the fancied freedom of others.

Laymen often fail to understand this point. I remember, for example, the time our city celebrated Business-Education Day. Two from our community, a sister of another order, and a Jesuit scholastic were with a group of lay people visiting a radio station. We had just seen the transmitter and were preparing to get back into the cars that would take us to a hotel for lunch. We waited for our host to direct us. He had something to say, and we huddled closer together to catch his words.

"There are some among us," he began, not without a hint of

melodrama, "who are living dedicated lives." We exchanged covert glances and wondered what next.

"We know," our guide continued in his best radio manner, "that their lives demand sacrifice, and we respect and admire them for it. Now, we are going to the hotel for lunch, and you may notice that some among our number will no longer be with us. Their rules require them to have their meal apart from the group. They will rejoin us afterwards."

My companion and I looked over at the other sister and saw her flushed cheeks. "Where did he get that 'they' business?" we wondered. The Jesuit scholastic grinned boyishly, and the groups moved to their respective cars.

Back at the hotel, we learned that "they" meant "she," and while the other sister went elsewhere, we three remaining black-robes entered the dining room with the secular visitors, feeling embarrassingly "undedicated."

Such differences among various communities of nuns prove puzzling to the average layman, especially the convert or the non-Catholic, but they are wholesome signs, indicating a noble ideal. Each religious institute has its peculiar spirit, bequeathed to it by its founder, embodied in its rule, and sanctioned by the Church. It is the duty of religious superiors to inculcate that spirit and of subjects to sanctify themselves in accord with it and no other.

But it may pose a problem when Mrs. X decides to take a "mixed" group of sisters for an afternoon outing. Sister A may go for the ride, but she can't get out of the car or eat an ice-cream cone on the way. Sister B may go for the ride and get out of the car, but refreshments are taboo. Sister C may go for the ride and have her ice cream, but all within the sanctuary of the car. Sister D may go for the ride, get out of the car, and eat the ice-cream cone. She may even name her own flavor if Mrs. X isn't a dictator. Sister E? She may come out to the car and wave good-bye to the others.

If this proves too inconvenient for the layman, he can always play safe by letting them write their own ticket. Or he can go directly to the highest convenient authority, as a certain science professor in a state university did. He wrote to the bishop, urging that a nun in his class adopt a fireproof garb. A few days later he casually informed the sister in question, "Oh, by the way, I wrote to that man Shanahan about you the other day."

Here Cut and Here Burn

Sister M. Ann Edward, O.P.

My famous first thought when entering the novitiate was a maxim from the life of St. Louis Bertrand, patron of novice-masters and novice-mistresses: "Here cut and here burn, but spare me in eternity." It's passing strange how literally God fulfills some unspoken prayers.

The instructions of our chaplain and novice-mistress would have remained fruitless if they had been given to souls distracted by noise and worldly surroundings. Therefore silence and separation from the world were our spiritual food and drink, night and day. I'm sure it was only the grace of God and the intercession of St. Dominic that made me love silence and solitude. By temperament I would much rather tell a joke at ten in the morning than salt it away until the noon recreation hour. I would much rather hum some melody while I'm dusting a room than do so in hushed solemnity. I could do my work more quickly if I could shove furniture around instead of gently picking it up, quietly carrying it half a league, and then noiselessly setting it down. But the Spirit of God is not in the earthquake. So, out of respect to the Divine Spirit, I learned to prevent my body, and especially my tongue, from setting the sound waves in motion.

I didn't acquire this habit in the twinkling of an eye. Certain serious people seriously doubt whether I really have acquired it. I give myself the benefit of the doubt. One sparkling cold day in December I was doing my pre-Christmas cleaning in the music corridor. Our habit skirt, sleeves, and veil were pinned up, under, and back according to regulation Number 17. With my left hand I hung on to the stepladder, with my right I flourished a long-handled mop, poking viciously and thoroughly into the corners. That's where spiders hibernate for the winter, so I had been told. Time was short and Christmas was nigh, so, to save fleeting moments, I shoved the ladder along without even dismounting. That was a real acrobatic feat. I was complimenting myself on this ability to make haste without waste, when lo! Sister Davidica suddenly stood in the doorway of Room 6. King David in all his glory never looked more regal than his namesake. "I could have known it was a novice," she said in a very unregal tone of voice. "Don't you know this is a convent, not a big-top circus?"

With a humble heart and contrite spirit I descended from my trapeze and cleaned in solemn silence to the end of the music corridor.

Custody over the eyes, the windows of the soul, was the hallmark of some saints. Blessed Henry Suso* made a covenant with his eyes and never permitted them to see what was going on more than six feet away. Although I made repeated covenants with my eyes, they refused to stick to the terms. I used to console myself with the reflection that I didn't merit Christ's indictment of the Pharisees, "Eyes have they and see not."

Conscientiousness in the little things, like doing my cleaning charge thoroughly, was another one of my sins of omission. Cat's Alley was such a dark place that I felt it was sufficient to dust the mopboards once a week. Only God can see in the dark, and what's a little dust to Him? He made the dust and therefore loves it as much as the sunbeam. I soon found out that in the convent God's all-seeing eye has many assistants. "This hallway is where the milkman and groceryman deliver their products," I one day overheard the cook informing the all-informed prioress. "What must they think when they see those dusty mopboards? When we were novices, we were given public penance for such negligence."

*A 14th Century Dominican preacher and mystic, born in Switzerland, who reformed women's convents.

Whew! That was a narrow escape. I practically rubbed off the varnish that day, and hoped the complaint would not reach the novitiate. At chapter that week we were told not to "count the boards" when we did our cleaning, whatever that meant. I didn't think it referred to me. I hadn't counted boards. Such a waste of time! So I kept my spirits up and my nose to the mopboards.

One Sunday afternoon I was walking meditatively in the convent yard, close to the laundry on the south side. I noticed that the windows in the laundry offered me a full-length profile of myself. Instead of meditating on heavenly things, I suddenly began admiring the graceful folds in our habit. "Sure is good to be a Dominican," I reflected, and proceeded to rearrange the folds at my left side, then at my right. "Vanity of vanities, and all is vanity!" Somebody's voice jerked me out of my feminine reverie. I twirled around. There stood Sister Frieda, the novitiate sewing instructor. I suddenly felt hot and cold at the same time. I wanted to say something to excuse myself, but no words came. Then I did a really clever, unpremeditated thing. I walked quietly away as if I hadn't heard the remark. Without even reflecting, I had imitated the Little Flower, who also took refuge in flight when beset by a similar temptation.

Before Christmas, Sister Helene and I were sent to get the mail from the niche in the novitiate staircase. I squinted sideways, crossways, and every which way, trying to see if there was a package for me from home. When I set down my load inside the novitiate door, our mistress said, "Did you find out what you wanted to know?"

Here again I edged close to the borderline of sanctity: I made no reply. But for days afterward I walked around with my eyes on my feet, trying to convince our mistress that I was not really curious. This self-nourishment nullified my initial victory.

I found one religious exercise as uncomfortable as a pair of ill-fitting shoes. It was chapter of faults. Spiritual writers describe it with such ambiguous terms as "an admirable means of advancing in holiness," "a school of self-abasement," and "the devil's funeral."

The key word of the phrase chapter of faults is "chapter." In monastic terminology a chapter is a regular meeting or assembly for business or conference of the canons of a cathedral or collegiate church, or of canonesses, monks, or members of a religious order.

In the early days of monasticism these meetings were opened by the reading of a chapter of scripture or of the Rule. Hence the word "chapter."

With the development and expansion of religious orders, founders and superiors noticed the need for a periodical disciplinary meeting of the entire community. At this meeting, originally held once a day, the superior read a chapter from the Rule and made whatever recommendations he judged necessary for the correction of faults against it. This was eventually followed by the custom of having each individual subject accuse himself or herself of exterior faults against the Rule and Constitutions, and accept the penance imposed by the presiding superior.

The purpose of chapter of faults is comparable to that of the sacrament of penance: forgiveness and amendment. The difference lies in the matter of accusation. Penance is concerned with sins; chapter with external faults.

I consider chapter of faults a great help to holiness. But I've never found it pleasant to stand up before my companions and accuse myself of having failed in silence so many times, of neglecting my cleaning charge that many times, of laughing boisterously at recreation this many times, and other peccadilloes of varying degrees of intensity and numerosity an embarrassing number of times. I don't ever expect to enjoy it either. But I want to spend my eternity doing what the saints do in heaven, so I'll keep on doing what they did while on earth.

There have been times when I've had to hold my sides during another sister's accusation. One time a novice murmured with all the gravity of an undertaker, "Three times I crossed my legs and ran up the stairs." I had visions of a cross-legged race horse. Too bad some stately senior sister didn't see those calisthenics!

After chapter was over one day, our mistress called me to her desk. "What on earth did you mean by that accusation, 'I left some pussies in Cat's Alley'?"

"Did I say that?"

"I'm not in the habit of imagining things, Sister."

"Oh. I guess I meant the time you corrected me for not sweeping the hallway outside the refectory for two days. That place reminds me of an alley."

"But the pussies?" Sister scrutinized me.

"That's those dust flurries that gather in the corners."

"Sister John Baptist! Sometimes you worry me."

I have strong suspicions that my companions were more than once in stitches because of my quizzical self-accusations. But I will never know for sure. Recommendation 69 forbids the sisters to discuss among themselves anything that was said at chapter. That recommendation must have been composed by someone who understood the relationship between sanity and sanctity.

V

Walls Around but Sky Above—Contemplatives

Walls Around but Sky Above—
Contemplatives

Ever since Martha complained that Mary wasn't helping her and Our Lord rebuked Martha instead, there has been a controversy about the prayer life and the active life.

On the one hand are those who say what a shame it is when so many sisters are needed in schools, hospitals, orphanages, and everywhere that some nuns are content to be walled up in cloisters and refuse to do any work. Oh, sure, they pray, but they don't get anything *done;* you can't feed a hungry child with a prayer.

The other school says that since the active sisters want to be so holy and all, it's a pity they aren't good enough to go all the way and be contemplatives.

Christ, who led both an active and a prayer life, didn't rebuke Martha for feeding Him, but for being in such a dither about it and for wanting to take something even more important away from her sister. The contemplative life is usually considered a higher, more perfect life because it is reaching out for God in the most direct way, tearing oneself away from anything, however good in itself, that could stand between the soul and God. Contemplation is the contemplative's life's work and aim, an anticipation of life in heaven.

Active sisters, of course, also pray, and their work itself is a prayer, being done for God, just as the prayer of contemplatives is also their work. It's a matter of specialization. A contemplative may sometimes wish she could be out on the missions where she could see the results of her labors, and her active sister must frequently be on her feet working when she would prefer to have more time to spend on her knees in prayer. There are great sacrifices involved for both. There have been great saints from both walks of life. The active sister loves her neighbor by showing him the Christian life by example, and by teaching him, nursing him, etc. The contemplative prays for him and by her sacrifices and mortifications helps to atone for his sins.

All in all, it is an extremely useless argument. St. Thomas Aquinas, who belonged to the Dominican Order, a combination of the active and contemplative, said that the contemplative life is higher than the active, except sometimes, and that the mixed life of contemplation and teaching or preaching is even better because it is a sharing of the fruits of contemplation with others. For a girl making a decision in favor of one or the other, the important thing is to do what she is called to do, according to the talents given by God for this purpose.

All convents are cloistered in some degree. The active sisters have a certain part of the convent reserved for them alone, forbidden to outsiders. The contemplative cloister is of two kinds—major and minor papal enclosure. In a major enclosure practically all of the monastery, including the garden, is cloistered, except for parlors where visitors may talk to the nuns through a grille, the part of the monastery reserved to the extern sisters, any guest apartments, a place for a priest to hear the nuns' confessions, and the chapel except for the part called the choir which is reserved to the nuns. The enclosure is so strict that any professed nun leaving the monastery unlawfully or any visitor entering the cloister unlawfully is excommunicated. Naturally if the monastery is on fire or bombs are falling on it, the nuns leave. Permissions may be granted for plumbers and doctors to enter or for nuns to go to the hospital, eye doctor, to vote in elections, and so on. But the rules for papal enclosure in Canon Law are extremely strict.

Minor papal enclosure is also strict, but it makes it possible for nuns who wish to lead both an active and contemplative life to do such apostolic work as teaching, giving retreats, works of charity, and so forth. Part of the monastery is strictly cloistered and part is reserved for the work. The nuns engaged in the work may leave the monastery if their duties or training for the work require it.

If only a few nuns are engaged in apostolic work and a great deal of space is not needed for it, they may still be allowed to have major papal enclosure. Work such as farming, making altar vestments, and so on, which is performed for the support of the community or to avoid idleness, does not come under the heading of "active" work in the sense used here and the areas for it are in the enclosure.

Some orders with major papal enclosure are the Nuns of the Perpetual Adoration of the Blessed Sacrament; Carmelite Nuns of the Ancient Observance, who pray especially for priests and religious; Discalced (shoeless) Carmelites; Cistercian Nuns of the Strict Observance (Trappistines); Poor Clares and Poor Clare Colettines—their monastery at Chicago is especially dedicated to the Immaculate Heart of Mary for the Russian apostolate and is training sisters for a monastery of the Eastern Byzantine rite; Dominican Nuns of the Second Order of Perpetual Adoration; Franciscan Nuns of the Most Blessed Sacrament; Passionist Nuns; and Sister-Servants of the Holy Ghost of Perpetual Adoration (also called Pink Sisters because of the pink habits), who pray for the propagation of the faith and the sanctification of the priesthood.

Monasteries of minor papal enclosure and examples of their work are: Religious of the Perpetual Adoration of the Blessed Sacrament (retreats, providing vestments and sacred vessels to the missions and directing an association for this purpose); Religious of the Blessed Sacrament and of Our Lady, or Sacramentine Nuns (teaching and retreats); Sisters of Jesus Crucified, most members of which are ill or physically handicapped (retreats for the sick, labs for the detection of cancer); and Good Shepherd Sisters and Sisters of Our Lady of Charity of Refuge (both caring for disturbed and problem girls).

Some of the Visitation Nuns are in major papal enclosure, some minor—teaching and retreats. These nuns have no age limit requirements but there is a limit to the number of older candidates per monastery. This order is less strict than many of the others.

This is not a full list, of course. There are other contemplative orders, such as the Redemptoristine Nuns, which is also less strict; the Recluse Missionaries of Jesus and Mary, who are mostly contemplatives but have a few active sisters; the Benedictine Nuns of the Primitive Observance; and the Dominican Sisters of the Perpetual Rosary who take turns day and night praying the rosary in Latin before the altar.

The life in the Benedictine Order is one of prayer, study, and work; "pray and work" is their motto. Those who are not strictly contemplative lead a mixed life. The Congregation of the Oblates of Bethany and the Institute of Our Lady of Mount Carmel (not to be confused with the Order of Our Lady of Mount Carmel) have contemplation and domestic service for all. The Carmelite Sisters of the Divine Heart of Jesus are semicloistered and their work includes taking care of orphans and the aged, social work, and foreign missions. Many others could be cited as leading a life of both contemplation and active work. Many of the mixed institutes are not cloistered, and the line between them and the active congregations is a hard one to draw.

The Maryknoll Sisters began a contemplative branch in 1932, twenty years after their missionary congregation began, and there are now twenty sisters in it. Several institutes have a few contemplatives among their active sisters—the Sisters of the Order of St. Basil the Great, Ukrainian Byzantine Rite; the Franciscan Sisters of the Poor in Cincinnati; Little Servant Sisters of the Immaculate Conception; and the Sisters of the Precious Blood.

Prayer can be either vocal or mental. The Divine Office is the official public daily prayer of the Church, which follows the liturgical cycle and consists of psalms, antiphons, responsories, prayers, the lives of saints, and readings from Scripture and theological writing. It is divided into "hours" (not an hour in length), although the exact time at which each part is said varies from order to order, and there are various editions of the breviary, or book, which contains the Office. This practice has been going on since the time of the Apostles and grew out of the Jewish custom of going to the temple at certain hours to chant the psalms and other prayers. At first the laity took part in the Office, but today it is mostly confined to priests, monks, and contemplative nuns as representatives of the entire Church and is also said by some active sisters, although they are not required by Canon Law to do so. It is usually chanted or recited in Latin. Some active sisters, and lay people increasingly, are using a shorter office, the Little Office of the Blessed Virgin, and some religious recite only some of the hours of the Divine Office. Chanting the Divine Office in choir, learning what to respond when, when and how to bow or kneel, and so on take a good deal of study and practice. Ordinarily it takes something over an hour to say the Office privately but much longer when it is chanted in choir.

In a way, mental prayer sounds easy, but to keep one's mind concentrated solely on God for a half-hour or an hour at a time is a difficult task. We can remove all possible distractions from our surroundings, but memories and impressions have a way of creeping into the best intentioned meditation. Some sisters who fall asleep easily have a hard time keeping awake during a quiet hour of meditation. The contemplative nun must pray at set hours whether she happens to be in the mood for it or not.

There is a book on mental prayer, written for sisters but also valuable to the laity, called *Greater Perfection* by Sister Miriam Teresa, available in paperback from The Paulist Press, Harristown Road, Glen Rock, New Jersey. The author, a Sister of Charity in New Jersey (an active congregation, incidentally), died in 1927 at the age of twenty-six, two years after entering the convent, and her beatification cause is in the early stages of being considered. The articles on prayer were written while she was a novice at the request of her spiritual director.

The striving after perfection which has been spoken of before is necessary to growth in prayer. If one is striving after union with God in this life, it is necessary not only to shut out worldly affairs but to get rid of self and self-love so there is room only for God in the soul. This is much easier to say than to do and not everyone who seeks this goal reaches it. The important thing is to keep trying, not to give up in discouragement. The contemplative cloister is no place for those who think of it as something glamorous or romantic or as a leisurely life for the lazy. Since mysticism today is often confused with visions and voices and so on, it might be well to add that these, while they do very infrequently happen to a few souls, are not the aim of prayer. Praying while keeping one eye on the floorboards to see if one is levitating leads only to an awareness of the floor, not of God.

The higher the goal, the stricter is the road leading to it. But there are degrees of strictness. The Redemptoristine Nuns, for instance, sleep on straw mattresses, but they may eat meat and they don't get up in the middle of the night to pray, depending on how you look at it—their day begins at 4:30 A.M. The Poor Clares fast every day in the year and never eat meat and they do hop out of bed in the small hours of the morning to pray for a while before going back to sleep. For some reason their life span, according to one study, is 14 per cent longer than the average.

If this sort of life seems too mild, consider the Trappistines. They abstain from meat, fish, and eggs, have their night office at 2 A.M., do a good deal of outdoor work, and observe perpetual silence. This last might not be too difficult considering their seven hours of vocal prayer. The amount of time spent at mental and vocal prayer varies from order to order. The Dominican Nuns of the Second Order of Perpetual Adoration and the Sister Servants of the Holy Ghost of Perpetual Adoration have five hours of vocal prayer and one of mental prayer. For the Poor Clares it's four hours of vocal prayer, one of mental. The Parish Visitors of Mary Immaculate, an active-contemplative institute, spend an hour and a half each at mental and vocal prayer.

The contemplative nuns also have the periods of postulancy, novitiate, and temporary vows. A college education is highly appreciated, although not usually required, in the cloister. Some orders require a knowledge of Latin for entrance. A healthy constitution is necessary for the austere life of most contemplative orders. Since the cloistered family is usually fairly small, from fifteen to thirty or so sisters who are faced with each other's company for a lifetime, a sense of humor is a great asset, or as the Redemptoristine Nuns put it, what is wanted is a "buoyant extrovert with contagious laughter."

Many cloistered orders have separate classes of sisters. The choir nuns recite the Divine Office, and lay or coadjutrix sisters take care of the major share of the housework and handle the material affairs. The lay sisters live within the cloister but do not recite the Divine Office and lead a less strict life, and the requirements for entrance, education, knowledge of Latin, and so forth, are also less strict. They take no part in the government of the order and are usually distinguished by some difference in the habit—it may be black while the choir nuns wear white, for instance, or the veil may be a different color. The details of their life vary from order to order. Extern sisters, on the other hand, have separate living quarters in the monastery outside the cloister. They are sometimes called "outdoor" sisters and take care of business outside the monastery, answering the door, doing the shopping, and so on, and also wear a distinctive habit. They may or may not see much of the inside of the cloister, depending on the order, aside from their training. In the Poor Clare Order, the extern sisters are looked on as an indispensable part of the family. In addition to her many other duties, when a member of a choir nun's family is dying, a Poor Clare extern sister will attend the sickbed in her place if at all possible.

There are far fewer contemplative nuns than active sisters in this country, but they are actually increasing at a faster rate. They are coming to be more and more understood and appreciated, and while at one time they were not particularly welcome here, in this century bishops have often asked for them in their dioceses. When Bishop Alfred Mendez, C.S.C., was named to the See of Arecibo, Puerto Rico, in 1960, he was asked what he intended to do first. His reply was, "I intend to thank the Holy Father and to ask the Poor Clares to make a foundation in my diocese." In somewhat the same spirit a parish priest recently decided to ask for a retired active sister to join the teaching sisters in their convent, not to help them in their work, but simply to pray for the parish.

It is difficult for us in the world to imagine living in a small area where a short walk in any direction will take one to the limits of the territory of a lifetime. We are inclined to pity contemplatives for being walled up, but it is not so much they who are walled in as the world that is walled out. They live in an atmosphere in which everything possible that could be an impediment to their goal has been removed, and they are surrounded by companions who are seeking that same goal.

As for their confinement, in an article in *Cross and Crown*, Sister Mary Jordan, a Dominican, puts it this way:

> People tend to forget that religious imprisonment is a three-sided affair. The inmates of a convent are boxed up, but the box is without a lid. We can never complain of claustrophobia when overhead are the still unvisited stars. And on those clear nights when they shine out all together, they can instill a sense of proportion beyond the powers of other natural things. The walls then shrink to mere fences; we could bestride them like giants. To travel around this tiny earth appears as the occupation of insects. The great exploration, on every level, lies upwards.

Specialists in Prayer

Mother Catherine Thomas, D.C.

A Carmelite nun should be, by the very nature of her vocation, a specialist in prayer. Besides the time we spend in private devotions, each day seven hours are spent in formal, community prayer, the greater part of which is devoted to the recitation of the Divine Office, the official prayer of the Church. Each one of us tries to substitute herself for those who have no love for God, or very little; for those who do not pray, or pray very badly.

Carmel, from the first week of postulancy, impressed me as being a spiritual headquarters far up in the battle area. The nuns seemed almost to "stand at attention" whenever the prioress read an urgent request for prayers. Prayer seemed like a sort of warfare: silence was our fortress; penance and mortification were our strategy.

Everyone's problems, trials, and aspirations are the concern of Carmel; and the explicit confidence placed in the power of our prayer terrifies and humbles us. Perhaps it is the faith others have in our prayers that enables us to pray with greater confidence.

In Carmel each year we divide up the whole world geographically, and each nun is responsible for a portion of it. (The Little Flower, for example, prayed especially for America the year before she died.) So, in a general way, I might offer my prayers and sacri-

fices this year for Africa, next year for Europe, and so on. The
areas are written on slips of paper (called billets) and chosen on
the Feast of the Epiphany.

Besides the large areas of the world, we make everyone and every
plan for good an object of our prayers. We pray for those who
may die each day, that they may die in the state of grace; we pray
for those in mortal sin, that they may have the stain removed; we
pray for those who zealously work for peace, and even for those
who foolishly try to bring about disharmony in the world, we pray
that God may change their hearts.

I dare say there are few places in our country where our heroes—
both living and dead—are held in greater esteem and more loving
memory than in Carmel. The world is so busy about many things—
it is our business to remember.

So we pray for those who are in danger and for those who are
sick. We pray not only that they may get well quickly, but, what is
more important, we pray they may have courage to see in their
illness the hand of God and use their suffering for the purification
of their own souls and the good of mankind.

We pray for the virtuous and devout in offices and factories who
are mocked and ridiculed for no other reason than that they are
trying to follow the delicate dictates of their conscience.

We pray for students, especially for those whose faith is exposed
to the poisonous insinuations of godless professors; we pray that
all searchers for the truth may find it and, finding it, may face it
squarely and accept it completely.

We pray for those suffering behind the Iron Curtain, for the
children who may not know Our Lord's name or that there is a
Christmas still in the rest of the world—those poor children, more
sinned against than sinning, from whose eyes the limpid look of
childhood has long since disappeared.

We pray for all those who have strayed from the path of virtue
and are stumbling blindly along the alleys of sin; we pray that they
may return to their Father's house, where alone they can find peace
and rest. We pray that all those who have habits of sin may not
only know but *do* what is right. How our hearts go out to the man
or woman who has become the victim of alcoholism.

The first point of our holy rule states that we are to "pray without ceasing." This is our most important duty. Penance and
mortification will follow easily; for we shall not be self-indulgent

when we are on our knees pleading for others. The saintly Teresa warned all of those who were to follow her, "If ever we should fail to offer our prayers and sacrifices for souls we would cease to be Carmelites."

To say for whom we pray and try to indicate why we pray are relatively easy chores. But now, in as simple a manner as I am able, let me attempt briefly to tell you how we pray.

"Lord, teach us to pray . . ." That was the pleading request of the disciples who followed Our Blessed Lord and watched Him absorbed in prayer.

Following the instructions and suggestions of Saint Teresa, our first requisite in prayer is to *love* and to *think* when we pray. We must consider who God is, to Whom we are talking, and we must consider who we are. Then we shall be reverent and humble. If we do not keep in mind the dignity of the Person to Whom we speak —nor our own insignificance—no matter how many prayerful words our lips may utter, we cannot call that prayer. We must be reverent when we address God; we must be careful to speak humbly to Him and have our minds on what we are saying. It is not enough to say the words, no matter how distinctly pronounced; we cannot speak to God and listen to the world.

"Lord, teach us to pray. . ." Listen again to the words of the Master as He instructs us: "When thou prayest, go into thy room, and closing thy door, pray to thy Father in secret; and thy Father who sees in secret will reward thee. But in praying, do not multiply words, as the Gentiles do, for they think that by saying a great deal they will be heard. So, do not be like them; for your Father knows what you need before you ask Him. In this manner therefore shall you pray: Our Father Who art in heaven, hallowed be Thy name! . . ."

Picture Our Lord beside you teaching you how to pray. And as He slowly speaks the words to you, you repeat them slowly and deliberately, thinking of their inexhaustible meaning and beauty. Our Lord makes Himself one with us: "Our Father." Then He teaches us how to address the Heavenly Father.

I think all will agree that an indispensable aspect of prayer for everyone is recollection. Recollection is not, of course, the same as contemplation, about which we shall say a few words in a moment.

In its negative aspect recollection is primarily the opposite of distraction. When we find it difficult to concentrate our attention on the matter of our prayer, we say we are distracted—we cannot "collect ourselves"; we are fitfully flying from one image to another or from one thought to another, never giving much attention to any image or any thought.

When we are recollected, we are wide-awake to the essential object of our prayer, we are unhindered by any superficial diversion, we refuse to dwell on any trivial matter.

Our memory and our senses combine to make it difficult to collect ourselves as we should wish. This should not discourage anyone from making the effort. No one finds it easy. Saint Teresa, mistress of prayer, confessed that she found mental prayer so difficult at the beginning of her religious life that there was no penance she would not have preferred to the penance of trying to recollect herself. She would even shake the hourglass to make the time move more quickly! I was comforted when I read about Saint Teresa's difficulties. I would say that it is quite unusual for anyone to go through an hour's meditation and remain completely recollected for the entire hour—at least, I think it safe to say that I have not yet, after twenty-five years in the cloister, been able to do so.

I repeat, even the saints had difficulty in recollecting themselves; but the reason they succeeded in reaching the heights is that they never became discouraged.

This effort to be recollected we try gently to carry over throughout the whole day in all our activities, all our prayers, all our thoughts—we try never to separate ourselves from God, the ultimate center of our being. We give to each scheduled act that place which it can rightfully claim in the eyes of God; we look at everything from God's point of view. The awareness of God's presence continues to resound in our soul; it forms the background for all our external acts and interests.

Closely connected with the idea of deliberate recollection is the state of *contemplation*.

"Mary hath chosen the best part." Our Blessed Lord in these words indicates the primacy of contemplation. He does not mean that we are to spend all our time in contemplation, nor that everyone is called to spend more time in contemplation than in action. He merely wants to point out that contemplation is the higher of the two, the goal at which ultimately all of us who will be numbered among the elect are to arrive.

Supernatural contemplation is not merely *thinking* about an object, nor does it have anything to do with "contemplating" a future action. It is the conscious dwelling on a truth, dwelling in the bliss derived from the light of beauty and goodness. Contemplation is *absorption* and *enjoyment*. Mary Magdalen not only listened to the words of Jesus; with deep love, she immersed herself in the beatific presence of her Master, in Whom she saw her God. As Saint Teresa puts it, "Contemplation is a divine union in which Our Lord takes His delight in a soul, while the soul rejoices in Him." It is the science of love, calm and peaceful. I do not mean by this to imply that contemplation is not activity. It represents the highest form of spiritual activity. It is "a simple gaze at truth," as Saint Thomas Aquinas says, adding "under the influence of love."

The object of a Carmelite's contemplation obviously is the Triune God.

When I am not only truly recollected but also in an attitude of contemplation—as I might be, for example, at the Elevation of the Sacred Host during Mass—time, for a moment, seems to halt. This is a momentous moment, a "now," in which the rest of the world fades away.

Perfect infused contemplation is a pure gift of God. Our part is to prepare for it by making our vocal prayer and our mental prayer as perfect as we can possibly make them.

How essential it is, then, that I first get rid of everything that cannot be held up before the face of my Beloved!

Here again is where our religious vows help to fit us for our role of contemplatives: by our vows of poverty and chastity we rid ourselves of all preoccupation with material things—we "empty" ourselves of everything; by our vow of obedience we renounce our own will and give that, too, to God. Now we are ready to face the Divine Reality; now we belong entirely to God.

To arrive at the goal of contemplation, spiritual writers and the experts in prayer like Saint John of the Cross, Saint Ignatius, and Saint Teresa suggest that, at least in the beginning, we follow carefully a method. Thank God, I was able to overcome my repugnance to using a system; otherwise I might still be beating the air and wasting my time.

We repeat, the first and most important step in our prayer or meditation is to recall to Whom we are speaking; we thereby recall

to mind the presence of God. We think of an attribute or aspect
of God or Our Blessed Lord, and in this way we recollect ourselves.
We then dwell on the subject of our meditation, turn it over in
our minds, and draw from it sentiments or affections of love and
praise. From these affections we may enjoy moments of contemplation, losing ourselves in adoration of the Beloved. We end by
resolving to remain close to Our Blessed Lord, to please Him and
do something special for Him that day.

As we have seen, this ideal condition in which the soul is always
in a state of recollection is not easy to achieve; yet a surprising
number of people—outside as well as within the cloister—do experience it. Contemplatives can be found even in the din of our
factories. However, even in Carmel we do not let this recollected
attitude interfere with the assigned duties of the nuns. Jokingly
we say, "Sister, if you can make the soup and at the same time keep
in the presence of God, that is wonderful; but if in striving for
recollection you let the soup burn, better for you to keep in the
presence of the soup."

Of course, work can be a great help to recollection and prayer.
Saint John of the Cross says, "Work and silence recollect the soul
in God." The phrase *"ora et labora"* ("pray and work") indicates
that even for us in Carmel, whose primary purpose is contemplation, work is not to be wholly foregone.

In the enclosure we have an advantage: we have fewer distractions; our seven hours of scheduled community prayers give us the
practice and the atmosphere that is needed. But I plead with you
who do not have our advantage to make a place in your life for
contemplation. You do not have to be in vows to be a contemplative. Don't, we pray, let the uninterrupted tension of modern living
sap the spiritual life from your soul.

Consecrate even a small part of an hour each day to mental
prayer, to thinking about Our Blessed Lord, Who loves you so
much and has done so much for you, and in Whose company you
are to spend your eternity. Separate yourself for this short interval
of silence from all the "weighty concerns" that seem to demand
your attention. Forget them for this moment, and think rather of
the one thing that really matters, your soul, and its relationship
to its Creator.

Don't, I plead, don't permit your daily obligations to make you
forget your chief purpose in life; don't be "troubled about many

things," like Martha, and be unmindful of the one thing that is necessary.

The world needs the perfume of your prayers as much as it needs the help of cloistered nuns; the unwholesome air of lust and avarice cannot be purified in any other way. One faint spark from your heart burning with love could set the world on fire.

What Do They Do All Day?

Sister Mary Francis, P.C.

Not long after midnight a nun who may happen to be awake, for some strange reason not common among Poor Clares, will hear the warning summons of Sister Sacristan's alarm clock. When that dignitary has gathered her wits sufficiently to shut the thing off, she sets her jaw for what is at once a beautiful and a grim task: to rouse all the other sleeping nuns. It is a beautiful task because the sacristan's bell is summoning the community to a midnight tryst with God. It is a grim business because Poor Clares unfortunately carry their souls about in the same clay casing found on the rest of humanity. Consequently, though the soul is ready and waiting to go to the choir and begin the chants of the night Office, the flesh finds the idea not at all stimulating. That is why the night Office is a cloistered nun's greatest privilege and joy and also her greatest external penance. That is also why the night Office is so precious in the sight of God.

Once you get Brother Ass standing, things begin to take shape in the mists of your mind. You remember what feast it is, and you start gathering all the sinning and suffering world into your heart as you make your sleepy way to the choir. Poor Clares observe the ancient monastic custom of sleeping fully garbed, which not only simplifies night rising but also endows even their sleep with beauty and significance. Our Lord has warned us that we know not the day nor the hour when death will come like a thief in the night. A cloistered daughter of St. Francis is garbed in all her monastic livery whenever this welcome thief chooses to break the locks on her life. And in a very practical sense, sleeping in the full monastic garb is a great advantage when all one's powers of concentration are needed to sweep the cobwebby sleep from one's mind. All a Poor Clare need do, as far as apparel is concerned, when she hears the Matins bell, is to spring up, tighten her cord, and throw her choir veil over her head to replace the short veil worn in bed.

Once you arrive in the choir where Our Lord waits exposed in the Blessed Sacrament, the full beauty of the night Office takes hold of your heart and soul. The chantress intones a hymn proper to the feast and then the great Office of the Church for the new day begins. When I was a postulant, I used to thrill to the sound of the nuns' voices chanting an invitation to all creation: *"Venite, adoremus"*—"Oh, come, let us adore!" I still thrill to the utter rightness of it each dark morning anew.

All the petitions for which we have been asked to pray are gathered into these morning songs of Holy Church. And all the anguish and loneliness and fear of those who have never heard of us and of whom we have never heard are gathered, too. I always feel, at the night Office, that we are walking down all the avenues of the universe, lighting God's lamps on every corner.

The nun who goes back to her cell after Matins and Lauds may be tired, but she is the happiest person in the world. She will work, later in the day, giving her hands and her mind to many tasks; but these first hours of the day which is still as young as night are sacrosanct for the work which will occupy all of us throughout all eternity.

There is another short period of sleep after Lauds until Sister Sacristan again takes bell in hand and peals out the message that it is time for Prime. Now there are full morning ablutions to perform, day habits and Communion guimpes and veils to don; and there soon follows a great scampering of the junior division to the choir to get the stalls dusted before Mother Abbess arrives to begin the morning Office.

When the last veil has fluttered into choir, Mother Abbess begins the short morning prayer which precedes Prime. Again, all the intentions of friends and benefactors and the needs of the whole world are offered up like a chalice of tears to a compassionate God. Prime itself is sheer poetry, from the glorious cadences of its opening hymn through the tremendous plea: "O Christ, Son of the living God, have mercy on us!" to the final petition that God will show quick mercy to the souls in Purgatory and bring them into the rest which He is.

In the midst of Prime, the versicular leaves her stall and goes to the lectern to call the roll of the saints of the next day. It is a kind of liturgical preview of the next showing, but has a thunder and a glory all its own. On the greatest solemnities, two candle-bearer novices stand beside the versicular, and the announcement of the next feast is chanted with all possible solemnity.

There is a half hour of meditation after Prime, followed by Terce, that part of the Office which summons the Holy Spirit upon the new day, and is our immediate preparation for the holy sacrifice of the Mass. Mass has an entirely new significance for the heart which has been prepared for it by the Divine Office. Beginning with the night Office of Matins, you have gradually become saturated with the spiritual joy of the day's feast or the grave beauty of the feria. Now comes the great and climactic sacrifice for which your soul has been well briefed. The conventual Mass is the great event in the monastic day. To it all things lead, and from it all others progress.

The period of private thanksgiving after Holy Mass and Benediction is followed by the community's corporate invocation of the Holy Spirit upon the day's work. Our Blessed Mother is summoned to lend her love and protection to our toil, and the blessing of our holy Mother St. Clare is asked.

Breakfast is a brief affair of bread and coffee. The most important thing about it is that the abbess now subjoins her blessing to that of St. Clare. "Dear Sisters, may God grant you a good day. Begin your work with the blessing of God." This stirring monastic form of "good morning" is repeated in chorus by all the kneeling nuns. "Reverend Mother Abbess and holy community, may God grant you a good day." You have a good feeling in the heart, too. Since the short period of sleep following the night Office, you have again given your full and undivided attention to God from 5:10 until 7:30. You have every reason to believe that this day, as all monastic days, will indeed be a good day.

Now the big monastery stretches its long cloisters like arms, the windows yawn wide with sunlight, and sounds and smells awaken everywhere. Soon the fragrant odor of cooking apples and baking bread comes spiraling out of the kitchen. Typewriters begin their tap dance. Suppressed giggles drift through the windows on the west side where the postulants are dragging yard-long roots of Bermuda grass out of the field so that the harassed peas and squash can get through. The sacristan goes to see about the Lord's accessories for His next public appearance. Mother Abbess says: *"Te cum Prole pia benedicat Virgo Maria"*—"May the Virgin Mary bless you with her holy Child," to an extern sister going out to beg. A sewing machine begins to hum to the tune of someone's new choir mantle. The portress comes from the turn* with a broad grin and a gallon of—ice cream! A benefactor has remembered with ice cream that this day is the anniversary of our coming to Roswell.

The silence that pervades the monastery during the time of work is a quiet full of busy sounds.

The hum of work ceases at eleven o'clock when the Offices of Sext and None are chanted. Again the monastery sinks down contentedly into the bosom of God, its whole life regathered into the chanting voices of the nuns. If it is summer, you come into the cool shadows of the choir with your garden habit damp against your back and your sunburned bare feet grateful for the coldness of the bare wood floor. In winter you take up your breviary into red and roughened hands and let your soul enjoy the warmth of God's Sacramental Presence.

Sext and None were St. Clare's favorite canonical hours, for they are especially commemorative of the crucifixion and death of Our Blessed Lord. She would often chant Sext and None with the tears streaming down her cheeks.

This Office chanted, consciences looked into and burnished, and prayers said for the benefactors whose charity provides for our needs, we go to dinner, chanting in the procession that magnificent psalm *"Miserere mei, Deus!"*—"Have mercy on me, O God!" There is reading during dinner, an ascentical book and then either a hagiographical work or something "light." This amused me no end when I entered, for I knew that what Poor Clares call "light reading" would be considered by most persons outside to be very

* Turn: a revolving cabinet-like device through which articles are passed in and out of the cloister.

solid stuff. Any book which does not stand you up in front of your
own soul in a broad daylight that reveals its every dusty crack and
hidden cranny of fault or compromise is called "light" by the community. However, the books are never dull. I do not know why
anyone should suppose monastic reading would be dull, but I remember that I was most agreeably surprised as a postulant to
discover what really excellent works were read in the refectory.

Sometimes the reading is momentarily interrupted by an important announcement from Mother Abbess to the effect that "the
squash is for potatoes. The salad is the third portion." After years
of listening to these quaint flashes, I still relish them with secret
mirth, and not least because of the judgelike gravity of countenance and tone with which Mother Abbess unfailingly makes
them.

A Poor Clare dinner consists always of soup, a vegetable, potato, fruit, and the famous "third portion." That last is an ancient
monastic term for the main dish of the meal, supposed to be some
sort of substitute for the meat we never eat. You are expected to
take a substantial helping of "third portion," since Brother Ass
must labor on the strength of it until the next day's dinner. Now
an innocent-looking salad may be just that, an unimportant side-
car to your vegetable and potato. However, who knows what
depths of canned salmon its surface may conceal! Such caches
would raise the salad to the rank of a third portion. Consequently,
a solemn announcement from the abbess is in order.

Also, the nuns are very set in their monastic ways. If we have
no potatoes, then some understudy must be summoned from the
culinary wings to play their role. Thus, the pronouncement: "Dear
Sisters, the turnips are for potatoes."

The nuns return in procession to the choir after dinner, and
more prayers are recited for the benefactors of the community.
When the dishes are washed and the Rosary recited, all scatter to
their private work until the house bell rings out that 2 P.M. message of Vespers. This is the great dividing line of the monastic day.
If the next day's Office is a major one, it will commence with today's first Vespers. All hearts now turn to a new day. All things
are now directed to the coming feast, all becomes a preparation
for the next morning's Mass and Holy Communion. Having la-
bored all the morning, we look now toward evening. It is a perfect
hour for Vespers. In winter, the day is giving you the fullness of

its gray light, as if it, too, magnified the Lord at that hour. In summer, the skies in Roswell are intensely blue, and the sunlight laughs and sings at every window and dances in shimmers on the broad choir floor.

You are given ten minutes to prepare for the glory of Vespers, kneeling quietly in your choir stall and gathering the past morning and early afternoon into the folds of that love you wish to offer God at Vespers. Then, at 2:10, the great Maria bell swings in a deep-throated song: Vespers, Vespers, Evensong.

After the Maria bell has swung out the message of Vespers and the nuns have chanted the beautiful evensong of holy Church, there is a period of spiritual reading and another Cross prayer. These Cross prayers, by which are meant certain prayers recited with the arms extended wide, are beams of prayers set crosswise on many different hours of the monastic day. They intrigue some new postulants who conceive the idea of praying privately in that position for an hour, and are hauled out the back door of the choir by their long-suffering mistress and disabused of their fond notions regarding such unorthodox penances.

Once a young priest visited the monastery. He had two potential postulants, he said. Wonderful girls. Saints (preshrunk, apparently). They spent many hours at a time praying with their arms extended. Old Sister Mechtilde squinted through the grate and leaned hard on her cane. "That's the kind that lasts about two weeks here," she volunteered. Father was shaken, but Sister was sound in her pronouncement. Those who indulge in extraordinary penitential feats in the world are almost unfailingly stubbornly attached to them. The normal girl who finds penitential practices penitential, but sweetens them with joy and roofs them under obedience, is the one who will persevere in the cloister with God's grace.

As the brightness of the monastic day begins to dwindle into evening, work again proceeds apace. No one accomplishes so much with her head or her hands as the one who is nourished by much prayer and fortified by silence.

In the two periods of work between breakfast and Sext, and between Vespers and evening meditation, habits are made and books are written, vegetables are raised and flowers are cultivated, psalmody is learned and musicianship is schooled, a big monastery is swept and burnished, a chapel kept lovely for the King, vest-

ments made and altar linens sewn. And through all these and so
many more occupations, contemplative prayer always whispers and
sometimes sings.

Ordinary afternoons are never ordinary. They may bring anything from a bushel of overripe fruit, to whose deck all hands are
hastily summoned for a canning session, to an emergency practice
of the play to be presented for Archbishop Byrne when he comes
to Roswell to officiate on the feast of our holy Mother St. Clare.
Nothing makes a Poor Clare smile as quickly as those good old
pious tomes which urge nuns to bear up under the monotony of
the cloister and to keep a stiff upper lip in the face of the tedious
sameness of monastic living. I have not been able to lay hold on
any monotony so far, though I have sighed after it more than once.

At 4:45 P.M., the nuns bring the fatigues of the day to the refreshment which is the Lord. So the day which began in Him and
flowed in minutes and hours out of His Heart, now returns to give
Him its contented fatigue.

After a hymn and the Rosary, you disappear into the utter solitude of the evening meditation. You kneel in your stall with all
your sisters around and your Lord on His throne before you. And
you are completely alone in the company you love best on earth.
At 5:30 you emerge from the depths of your solitude and affirm
your refreshment with another hymn.

Again the monastic procession forms to the soul-stirring measures of the *"Miserere mei, Deus,"* and comes into the summer sunlight or winter twilight of the refectory for collation. Before that
simple repast is taken, another very beautiful monastic usage finds
its place. All the nuns fall to their knees and prostrate on the floor,
each to beg pardon of all the others for anything she may have
done during the day to give pain or mortification to her sisters.
Each nun begs her companions to pray that she may receive Our
Lord more worthily the next morning in Holy Communion for His
greater honor and her own salvation and perfection. The abbess
then recommends the intentions of our civil and spiritual superiors
and of all those to whom the community's prayers have been asked
that day. It is a cleansing and transforming little ceremony. We
rise up feeling washed and forgiven, ready to begin again.

There is free time after collation for the Stations of the Cross,
for an informal visit to the Lord Jesus, or what you will. And then,
at 6:30, there is recreation. I remember feeling warmly happy when

one retreat master, an aged and experienced friar, declared that the unfailing gauge of a community's fervor is the hilarity of its recreations. All's well, I thought, all's well.

Prospective postulants often inquire about what we do at recreation. Read? Play games? No? Well, what *do* we do? We talk. Reading at recreation is forbidden. Games exist in the form of a standing joke. Silence alone fits us to speak. Conversation, which started out to be an art and a tremendous God-given privilege, is well on the way to becoming a lost art today. Except in cloisters. Only the silent know how to talk, and that is why we cannot imagine anything more delightful to do at recreation.

The wonderful hour over, the community returns to the choir for Compline. "Into thy hands, O Lord, I commend my spirit," chant the postulants in eager young voices. "Into Thy hands," sing out the superiors, who place all the burdens of office in those Divine hands. "I commend my spirit," the old nuns tremulously chant. And each nun rehearses the moment when Sister Death will come to take her own hand: "Now, O Lord, Thou dost dismiss Thy servant . . . for my eyes have seen Thy salvation." Compline is more than the perfect night prayer. It is an immediate preparation for death, which is always the possible splendor of each night.

The lights are lowered. The great silence takes the monastery into its velvet arms. Each nun enters the private castle which is her little cell and kisses the floor of it. "The Heart of Jesus is the place of my rest," she says. The day is ended. Her lamp is trimmed for the midnight summons of the Bridegroom.

Death of an Obscure Nun

Rev. Joseph E. Manton, C.SS.R.

I suppose there were the usual number of funerals that sunny May morning last spring in Boston. But I am sure there was none like hers. Even the undertaker's men leaned forward with staring eyes and parted lips. Even the clergy, most of us anyway, had never seen anything quite like this.

The corpse was a Carmelite nun, and as she had lived for almost fifty years within those dark brick walls of the old Roxbury monastery, she would not leave them even now in death, but would be buried in body where for half a century she had been buried in spirit.

Though in the course of more than twenty years I had given her Holy Communion hundreds of times, her veil draped down to the lips, I found out her name only now, when no one would ever call her again. In religion that name was Sister Teresita, or little Teresa, a name of double glory in Carmelite history. In the world she had been Helen Dwight. Her father had been Dr. Thomas Dwight, Parkman professor of anatomy at Harvard Medical School where the Catholic Club is called the Dwight Society in his honor.

But we didn't know this then. All we knew was that lying here in death was an obscure nun, her fingers like little white sticks that once flashed skillful needle and thimble as she stiched some of the most gorgeous vestments that ever glowed against the marble altars of our majestic basilica.

This morning in the Carmelite private chapel the celebrant of the Solemn Funeral Mass was wearing one such flowing cope of velvety black for the obsequies, as we priests formed a mournful circle round the casket. The casket lay on a kind of simple couch in the center of a tan linoleum floor. Incidentally, when you walked on the thin-worn pattern, every step squeaked poverty; not picturesque, romantic, idealistic poverty, but just plain need.

But yes, the casket—and did I say casket? Think rather of the manger of Bethlehem and you will come closer to the fact. We all knew that the Carmelite nuns, doing penance for a pleasure-loving world, never touched a morsel of meat and slept not on a Beautyform mattress but on hard penitential planks. But we had never dreamed that they carried austerity even into the grave.

But there it was, the casket. It looked as though some carpenter had hastily hammered together a plain narrow box, maybe twice as thick as a soapbox, but made from the same white wood, streaked with the same grain, and spotted with the same rough brown knots. This particular homemade coffin started out a bit wider at the head and tapered in toward the feet.

The Carpenter of Nazareth would have appreciated the workmanlike skill that went into Sister Teresita's box. There also went into it, till it was half filled, clean bristly straw, so that you could not help thinking of a Christmas crib. On either side hung two loops of clean white rope as handles for the pallbearers.

So there she lay on the fresh straw (or was it excelsior?) in the plain narrow box, garbed in the brown and white Carmelite habit of coarse wool, but on her head a frail wreath of tiny white roses and in her lifeless fingers a small wooden cross. Fingers and cross both fascinated, each in its own way. Carmelites forswear cosmetics even in death, so those fingers looked like shriveled white wax. And the cross was strange because it was only a cross and not a crucifix. In the Carmelite's cell there hangs a similar larger cross, with no Christ hanging upon it.

It is the awesome vocation of a Carmelite, by her fasts and vigils and thorny mortifications and endless self-denial, to take the place of the Christ on the cross; to suffer with Him, in penance for a pleasure-mad world.

While the obsequies were being sung, the community of some eighteen or twenty nuns were kneeling on the flat floor (they do not even have kneeling benches), their black veils drooping completely over their faces and weird yellow candles flickering in their hands.

Now the chanting stopped, and one of the Carmelites, I presume Mother Superior, flung back her veil, quietly arose and approached the deceased. Out of the stiffly curved fingers she gently withdrew the cross and placed in its stead a simple and eloquent white flower, as if to say, "Your penance is over, your reward has begun." Then she took a simple white cloth and reverently laid it over the upturned, unseeing face. I thought she lingered then for the fraction of a second, a Carmelite's farewell.

After that the burial procession slowly moved out of the chapel. As the chanting line wound through the convent corridor and past the open windows, I looked out and saw a glimpse of what the world never sees. This was their lovely convent garden, gay with all the beauty of a golden day in spring. Your eye left the gorgeous blossoms for the stone pillars of the cloister walk and the red-tiled Spanish roof that stood out so bravely amid all the greenery. I thought how the nuns had dug and planted and pruned this stained-glass window of growing things.

But I also saw in this bright hidden garden a symbol. When I had met Carmelite nuns as patients in the hospital, they were the merriest people you could meet. Generally another nun, who is also a nurse, goes along as a companion, and their room always seems the happiest in the hospital. At the grille, too, when you could not see them but heard only bell-like voices, they seemed bubbling with joy.

That garden somehow explained how austerity, gilded with the grace of God, not only lights the tapers of happiness in the convent but throws the beams even into a wicked world.

Now we were marching down the stone stairs to the burial crypt. The great cellar felt cool and shadowy. It was whitewashed all around like a tomb in the New Testament. One wall stretched out as a long burial vault where perhaps fifty nuns had been laid away. On each square marble slab you could read the inscription of Sister Somebody, then her name as a young lady in the world, and finally the date of death. Nothing else, except that on one slab it said, "Foundress of the Carmel in Iceland." There were three or four empty oblong shelves, lined with red brick, still available, and our coffin came to a halt before one of them now.

Solemnly this "grave" was blessed, the holy water sprinkled into the long narrow opening, the fragrant incense was swung, the last pleading prayer sung and the echoes hovered mournfully amid the candles. Then the undertaker's men carefully fitted a plain white board over the coffin box, lifted it silently into its waiting niche, and stood aside for a mason to seal the marble slab. It read, "Sister Teresita, alias Helen Dwight, May 31, 1962."

VI

Work Is Prayer

Work Is Prayer

THE WORKS of the active life can be spiritual, directly bearing on the soul (preaching, retreats, etc.) or temporal (teaching, nursing, social work, and the like). St. Gregory the Great said it meant, "to feed the hungry, to teach the ignorant, to correct the erring, to recall our neighbor to the path of humility when he becomes proud, to care for the sick, to dispense to all that which they need, and to provide for those entrusted to our care."

Of course contemplatives work to support themselves by making altar breads, vestments, altar linens, rosaries and other religious articles, by writing, printing, painting, illuminating manuscripts, ceramics, wood carving, stained-glass work, needlework, weaving, farming, laundering, translating, and bookbinding. The Trappistines in Wrentham, Massachusetts make candy to sell to the public.

But "active" is commonly used in regard to religious communities as distinguished from "contemplative." Teaching is the occupation most frequently listed but by no means the only one, and teaching itself is wonderfully varied. Teachers are found in elementary schools, high schools, and colleges, teaching many kinds of courses. Some specialize in teaching the deaf, the blind, the mentally retarded, cerebral palsy victims, aphasics, slow readers and others.

Nursing is done in hospitals, private homes, institutes for the aged, mental institutions, sanitariums, leprosariums, dispensaries, and clinics. Sisters nurse convalescents, the incurable, the chronically ill, aged and infirm priests, and ill sisters in the convent infirmary. Sisters are also trained as doctors, psychologists, psychiatrists, dentists, X-ray and lab technicians, pharmacists, anesthetists, and therapists.

Sisters also care for orphans, foundlings, neglected, disturbed, and delinquent children, and unwed mothers. They run residences for working girls and students, camps for children, day nurseries and playgrounds, take parish censuses, instruct converts, teach religion to public school children, train lay apostles, do housework in seminaries, schools, rectories, abbeys, and convents, perform administrative, secretarial, and other office work, direct choirs, and work in libraries. In the field of publishing they do writing, editing, layout, art work, and printing.

Many of the above works are also carried on in the home and foreign missions.

Most congregations do a variety of work, with sometimes one sister or only a few in a particular activity. Often sisters will teach during the school months and do other work in the summer or whatever time they can spare. For instance, the Mother Seton Sisters of Charity have five full-time catechetical instructors and three hundred part-time. New congregations are founded to fill special needs, as the Sisters of St. Joan of Arc of Quebec, were begun in Massachusetts in 1914 because of the difficulty of obtaining good housekeepers for rectories; or they may take on new work as necessary, as when the Sisters of St. Philip Neri Missionary Teachers, among other congregations, recently took on the care of Cuban refugee children in Florida. A few congregations offer all their work for a specific cause—the Helpers of the Holy Souls are dedicated to the souls in purgatory, and the Franciscan Sisters of the Immaculate Conception and St. Joseph for the Dying to the dying sinners of each day.

Two congregations care for destitute cancer victims regardless of religion, nationality, or race: the Servants of Relief for Incurable Cancer, which has cancer homes in several cities, and the

Dominican Sisters of the Sick Poor, which also has a free home nursing service for the sick poor. Several congregations include running a boys' military academy among their activities. Visiting prisoners is part of the work of the Franciscan Capuchin Sisters of the Infant Jesus, and other communities. The Daughters of Charity of St. Vincent de Paul care for lepers at the National Leprosarium at Carville, Louisiana. Many communities have special centers for children. The Sisters of Charity of St. Augustine run the children's village of St. Vincent de Paul; the Sisters Servants of the Immaculate Heart of Mary, also known as the Sisters of the Good Shepherd of Quebec, care for disturbed and delinquent girls; the Sisters of St. Francis of Assisi of Penance and Charity have a school for potentially delinquent boys and also teach the deaf and the mentally retarded; and the Franciscan Sisters of Blessed Kunegunda perform office and domestic work at Father Flanagan's Boys' Town.

Girls sometimes ask if there is any opportunity for writing in the convent. Yes, there is plenty of opportunity, both occasional and frequent. Sisters write books and magazine articles and stories, poetry, promotional literature for their communities, schools and other institutions, and many congregations publish their own magazines. Several communities list writing as one of their apostolic works, including the Redemptoristine Nuns (contemplative) and the Dominican Congregation of Our Lady of the Sacred Heart, Grand Rapids. The Sisters, Servants of the Immaculate Heart of Mary, Monroe, Michigan, offer a consultation service for Catholic textbook publishers and collaborate in writing texts and producing religious film strips. The goal of the Pious Society, Daughters of St. Paul, is to bring Christ to the world by means of books, newspapers, magazines, films, TV, and radio.

You have probably heard the expression "Don't keep the faith—spread it." But keeping the faith is itself a problem in many areas with few priests or Catholic schools or in overcrowded sections of large cities. The Missionary Servants of the Most Blessed Trinity, with their motherhouse in Philadelphia, grew out of a lay apostolate movement in Brooklyn devoted to this work. The sisters labor in slums, in rural and mining areas, in the South, and in Puerto Rico. The Sisters of Service was founded in Toronto in 1922 because many immigrant Catholics in the prairies of Western Canada were without priests or parochial schools. Their initials are appropriately S.O.S., and in addition to meeting immigrants at the ports, they teach, operate rural hospitals, visit the sick in their homes, and run homes for girls in the larger cities. The Glenmary Home Mission Sisters work especially in non-Catholic areas in the South. The Maryknoll Sisters, who are well-known for their foreign missionary work (they seem to have taken the words, "Go, teach ye all nations," as personally applied to themselves) are also in the home missions working with Negroes, Puerto Ricans, Chinese, Japanese, and Mexicans.

The state of Alaska is still considered mission territory and in addition to the other congregations working there, the Oblates of Our Lady of the Snows, or the Eskimo Sisters, was founded by the Ursulines in 1954.

Nearly one-third of all Indians in the United States are Catholic. Many of the 285,000 Indians living on reservations are still suffering from hunger and inadequate shelter and the inability to find work. Teaching and helping them is part of the work of congregations of sisters in the United States and in Canada.

In the United States there are approximately 500,000 migrants, workers who stay in an area for a month or two, as long as the harvest lasts, usually living under very poor conditions, and then move on or return home. They need many kinds of help, including religious instruction, as their teaching is piecemeal and constantly interrupted, and there is often a language barrier. Among the congregations in this work are the Mission Sisters of the Holy Ghost who work with Mexican migrant workers.

Home visiting, such as that practiced by the Sisters, Home Visitors of Mary, brings a fruitful harvest in the return of lapsed Catholics and the gaining of converts. Parish census work is not merely a compilation of statistics but a form of home visiting, a means to seek out those in trouble. For instance, the Parish Visitors of Mary Immaculate, who do census work at the invitation of pastors, with their gentle and sympathetic manner of asking questions encourage strayed sheep to return to the Church. They also reunite families, promote the liturgy and family devotions, urge Catholics to join parish societies, and help immigrants, delinquents, and potential delinquents. In areas where it will facilitate their work, they also learn Spanish.

Foreign missionary work has always had its dangers and this is so today. Outright persecution and torture, confiscation of schools,

hospitals, etc., and expulsion of missionaries is still going on, and
not only in the Communist nations. The first act of a new nation
may be to drive out all foreigners, including missionaries, in an
excess of nationalism as a result of years of colonial oppression. Opposition may also spring from the dominant religion of a country.
Savagery still exists in some areas. Not long ago in *Worldmission* a
priest-missionary in Dutch New Guinea wrote matter-of-factly in
explaining a current situation, "In 1955, the people of the village
of Ajam killed and ate a rather large number of people from a
nearby village called Jipaer."

But for most missionaries the day-to-day trials are likely to be
closer to that of a Sister of Charity of Nazareth who in India was
faced with the problem of drinking, and appearing to enjoy, a native treat that looked like muddy water with wildlife, rather than
offend her hostess. Or they may suffer the frustrations inherent in
missionary work. A sister may have a cure for a rampant contagious
disease and find that the natives will refuse it because they are
afraid of medicine. Or their work may be hampered because local
customs make it nearly impossible for a convert to lead a Christian
life, as for instance when the cost of a legal marriage is so great
that many could not hope to afford it and turn to concubinage, or
where a girl's family can take her away from her husband and give
her to another.

Much of missionary work means going out to seek souls rather
than waiting for them to come to you, or as the Xavier Mission
Sisters put it, "Fuller Brush work." These sisters work in Japan
and an important part of their contact work consists in taking an
interest in everyone they meet, "the neighbor who wants to use the
telephone, the working girls who like to come to the sisters because
it 'makes their souls feel clean,' the neighborhood tots who come
to the convent parlor as soon as school lets out, the sales girl at
the market, the bus driver, and countless others. It means smiling
and talking to the child next to you whose lollipop is getting your
cloak all sticky. It means greeting the faces one meets on the way
to Mass. It means showing interest and admiration for progress
made in any field. Sincere interest in the individual brings the best
results and people sense in an instant whether one is genuine or
not."

Congregations which are not primarily missionary often send a
few sisters abroad and usually they must volunteer for this special

work. The Dominican Congregation of the Immaculate Conception, Great Bend, Kansas, sent six sisters to Africa, whose training
included a one-year licensed midwifery course.

In those congregations which were founded for missionary work
the activities are varied. The Franciscan Missionary Sisters for
Africa run elementary and high schools, schools of economics,
teach blind and handicapped children, instruct children and adults
in catechetics, care for homeless children, lepers, the incurable and
the aged, operate clinics, dispensaries and hospitals, visit homes
and villages, and train African sisters and nurses. Organizing native
sisterhoods is vital so that the work can eventually continue without outside help. Mother Mary of the Sacred Heart founded the
Missionary Sisters of Our Lady of the Angels in 1919 in Lennoxville, Quebec Province, because she had been working in China
and saw the great need for sisters to train native sisters and catechists there.

In the mission field there is abundant opportunity for those interested in medical work, including such congregations as the Medical Mission Sisters, founded in 1925 in Washington, D.C., by Dr.
Anna Dengel, and the Medical Missionaries of Mary. The Sisters
of St. Louis of Monaghan, Ireland, and the Society Devoted to
the Sacred Heart are training doctors and nurses for the missions.

Since their work is not self-supporting, the missionaries need a
great deal of help to carry on. The Missionary Sisters of St. Peter
Claver do not go on the missions themselves but raise money for
African missionaries by their writing and other work.

But what about the individual sister at home and on the missions? Even aside from an exciting life such as that of Sister Marie
Marquette, a Maryknoll nurse who spent nine years traveling by
canoe in the Amazon country treating the natives, there is plenty
of room for individual initiative and the display of special talents,
always, of course, under obedience. There is usually some special
quality added to the accomplishments of a sister because she is a
religious.

Sister Caroline of the California Institute of the Sisters of the
Most Holy and Immaculate Heart of the Blessed Virgin Mary was
teaching high school in California when she became very dis-
satisfied with the reading ability of her students. She asked her
superiors to let her teach first-graders instead, and not liking the
method for teaching reading that was used, gradually devised her

own. Her work was so successful that it received a good deal of
local attention and in 1959 she was asked to do a TV show which
brought her national acclaim. Even before that, a representative
of a large publishing company had told her, "I don't know how
you do it, but get it down on paper." Eventually her manuscript
was published under the title, *Breaking the Sound Barrier*. Perhaps
the most startling aspect of her method is the reasoning ability it
brings out in her young pupils, untapped by most teachers and
methods.

Sister Mary Corita of the above congregation teaches art at
Immaculate Heart College in Los Angeles. Her own paintings have
been hung at the Metropolitan Museum and the Museum of Modern Art in New York City, the Library of Congress in Washington, D.C., and in other collections. Her work is extremely modern
with such titles as "Pigeons on the Grass Alas." On the mission
front, Sister Pientia Selhorst of the Missionary Sisters of the
Precious Blood, teaches art in South Africa, leading her pupils
away from copying European art to an expression of their own
culture. In writing about the simplicity of the people, Sister said,
"Their way of life strikes me with its similarity to biblical customs.
One needs so little adaptation in preaching the Gospel to them—
they are so near the truth. One becomes a humble missionary in
contact with them."

Sister M. Inez Hilger, a Benedictine, is a mother superior in St.
Cloud, Minnesota, and also a university professor, an expert on
the American Indian, and the author of five books. Her study of
the Araucanian Indians in the Andes who still practice witchcraft
was sponsored by the Smithsonian Institution.

"Stop writing sweet stories and write something meaty," a professor told Sister Paschala, a Dominican who teaches at St. Catherine's Junior College near Louisville, and since she wanted to
make some money for the missions, she took the advice. The resulting story sold to *Ellery Queen's Mystery Magazine*. Sister Mary
Francis, the Poor Clare who wrote the article "What Do They Do
All Day?", couldn't go out to take lessons in playwriting because
she is a cloistered nun, so Dr. Natalie White from Notre Dame
University came to the monastery and taught her through the
grille. Sister's play, *La Madre*, about St. Teresa of Avila, was performed off-Broadway in New York and *The New York Times*
review said it was "capable of wringing tears from an atheist."

After the play closed, one of the actresses joined the Poor Clares. In the field of poetry, Sister Madeleva of the Sisters of the Holy Cross, who wrote the article "The Relaxed Grasp," and Sister Maris Stella of the Sisters of St. Joseph of Carondelet are both well known.

Unexpected assignments are often given to sisters. Sister Mary Cepha of the Parish Visitors of Mary Immaculate was suddenly appointed to teach religion on TV one summer. When she left for the convent, there had been no TV in her home and she didn't even know how to dial a set. But she performed nobly. Sister Mary St. Clara of the Sisters of Charity of the Blessed Virgin Mary conducted an award-winning cooking class on the radio.

Sisters are ingenious at discovering ways of making money, not for themselves but for their communities. Sister Mary Gilbert of the Sisters of the Holy Names of Jesus and Mary, who is head of the journalism department at Holy Names College, Spokane, thought she had at last found a way to pay off all the college debts when she persuaded her superiors to let her take a correspondence course in contest-winning. In an article in *Columbia* in which she wrote of her experiences with 25-words-or-less, she said, "Nuns should be experts at following rules. Their lives are built on them. . . . When the Simoniz Company sponsored a contest, I knew that I had to buy a can of paste wax, even though we didn't own a car to use it on. Didn't the rules say plainly that, although no labels were required, 'the purchase and use of a can of Simoniz Paste for Cars is essential to the preparation of an acceptable entry'?" Once again she had to do some persuading and she used the wax on her desk. Her ten-dollar prize, while not what she was hoping for, at least gave her a nice profit. In other contests she also won small money prizes and an electric coffee maker, unfortunately home-size rather than convent-size.

The articles that follow show but a few of the fields of work in which active and contemplative sisters are engaged.

There are other types of organizations for women, in addition to religious institutes, provided for in Canon Law. Some of these are easily confused with religious congregations, particularly the relatively new secular institutes which may or may not have community living and habits and are sometimes listed along with religious institutes. The members may refer to themselves as sisters

as do the Schoenstatt Sisters of Mary of the Catholic Apostolate
since they were founded in Europe where the term "sister" does
not necessarily mean "religious."

For an organization to be a true religious institute, that is, for
its members to be real sisters or nuns, the following requirements
must all be fulfilled:

1) Following the evangelical counsels.

2) Publicly taking vows of poverty, chastity, and obedience.
Vows are public when they are given before and accepted by an
ecclesiastical superior in the name of the Church. (In secular institutes a private vow of chastity is taken and there may be promises
or pledges or oaths of poverty and obedience.)

3) Living in community under the authority of a superior.

The life of a member of a secular institute is a life of total consecration to God, following the evangelical counsels, but in the world.
As far as the world is concerned, the goals of religious institutes
and secular institutes are the same—each aims to lead its neighbors
to a higher life. But one might say in general that members of religious institutes, by leaving the world, are pulling from without,
while secular institutes push from within. Secular institutes are
fairly new and were only recently recognized as having a special
canonical status, but they are growing fast all over the world. Because they might be of interest to readers of this book, even though
they do not strictly fall within its subject, there is an article about
them in this section and they are listed at the end of the book.
New institutes are constantly being recognized; they go through
diocesan and papal stages of approval just as religious institutes do.

A religious institute which is sometimes mistaken for a secular
institute is the Daughters of the Heart of Mary, founded in France
in 1790 in a time of religious persecution. The sisters wear modern
street clothes and some of them live and work in the world. Sisters
in a branch of the Congregation of Notre Dame de Sion also wear
modern dress and live and work outside the community. One of
the following articles describes the Little Sisters of Jesus who live
in small groups and support themselves by craftwork, working in
factories, or doing housework. They wear a uniform at work. Members of the Society Devoted to the Sacred Heart all live in community but are popularly known as "plainclothes sisters" since they
wear modern dress as they go about their work of making the Faith

known, restoring family unity, etc. These sisters and members of secular institutes seek out or make themselves accessible to those who would otherwise be difficult to reach.

Other types of organizations which might be of interest are: pious unions, which are associations of lay people or clergy to promote works of charity or special devotions, many of which may eventually become secular institutes, and which are also subject to Canon Law; Catholic Action groups, organizations of lay people with various religious aims; lay missionaries, who make promises to work in home and foreign missions for a definite period of time —one, two, or three years—and may renew the promises, or in some groups make lifetime promises; and Third Orders Secular, also called Tertiaries, whose members live in the world but are affiliated with a religious order and follow certain rules regarding prayer and action. These are also covered in Canon Law. On the other hand, Third Orders Regular are religious institutes, and so are Second Orders, which have the same founder and the same or a similar rule as a corresponding order of men, which is always the First Order. For instance, St. Francis of Assisi founded his order which became the First Order; he and St. Clare founded the Poor Clares, which became the Second Order. And there are Third Order Franciscans, both regular and secular.

Organizations in these categories may be found listed in the National Catholic Almanac, published annually by St. Anthony's Guild, Paterson, New Jersey.

The Teaching Sister

Robert T. Reilly

Lay persons see the teaching sister as a standard character without any individualities, peculiarities, secret hopes, problems, failings, or triumphs. They see her as "Sister" and think they have plumbed her depths in their compassionate and confused appraisal of her. They see her as helpless, sheltered, meek, unworldly, craving attention, imprisoned and mystically separated from the universe —a curious blend of saint and woman with the shortcomings of both.

To this distorted picture, the teaching sister has sometimes been an unwitting contributor. But much of it is mere fantasy or lack of communication.

Just who and what is the teaching sister?

First, like all segments of the population, she is a statistic. And she is coming to be viewed more and more in this light as pastors, superintendents, bishops, and parents clamor for her services. The Sister Superior, grimly insisting on the need for extended educational opportunity for her charges, hears that the school population is rising four times as fast as vocations to the sisterhood. She is concerned with the fact that less than 65 per cent of the Catholic boys and girls of elementary school age are now enrolled in Catholic schools. She knows this will grow worse—for six million pre-school Catholic children have already been born.

Nearly 80 per cent of Catholic educational institutions are elementary schools; 60 per cent of the available sister-teachers teach in them and 75 per cent of the total Catholic school enrollment studies here.

So the teaching sister is an important person—a woman as sought after as some of the storied heroines of old or some of the cinema ones of this century.

She can look back to the founding of the Ursuline Order in 1535 and trace the growth of the teaching orders from that historic event in the Counter-Reformation. Fifteen orders of teaching women originated during the next century and a half, and today this total has exceeded 250.

Some of the misapprehensions concerning the teaching sister go back to the early days. Ever conservative, the Church was reluctant to accept the idea of uncloistered religious women. And there were those who questioned the wisdom of educating women at all.

Many of the schools were of the convent type where it was rumored that all the sisters taught their sixteenth-century coeds was to stifle their natural desires and to neglect their bodies, which were "destined to serve as food for worms."

The Catholic school system, however, has outlived the attacks on its methods, its supposed antipathy toward science, its emphasis on the spiritual. Today's teaching sister mirrors both the fundamentals and the historic advances.

Her life is simple and she takes it for granted. She finds it difficult to imagine that this life could be so interesting to others.

Actually, her living conditions are on the upswing. Private rooms, while not universal, have become the standard thing; and more attention is given to both comfort and beauty in her surroundings.

The teaching sister has a good deal of recreation and is not a recluse. She reads a good deal and watches television. In fact, in a few convents, certain television programs have played occasional hob with the sacrosanct schedule of prayers.

Sisters, like other people, have a variety of hobbies. In every community there are the knitters, seamstresses, leather toolers, rosary makers, painters, cooks, gardeners, stamp collectors and even an occasional model-airplane builder. Sports like swimming, tennis, baseball, bowling, volleyball, and other games play an important part in their lives. And while they may deplore the cinema version of the bat-wielding religious, they will surely know some sisters who fit the portrait by desire or talent.

Again like women, they enjoy discussion periods. The favorite topic is the one common to most mothers—their children. Like mothers, their lives, too, are centered about their children. They retell the funny incidents that occur, repeat comments, poke fun at themselves. Rarely will they indulge in critical or disciplinary items at this time. Such topics are considered both uncharitable and not conducive to the sister's relaxation. They are saved for more serious and businesslike sessions.

Other conversation pieces are current news, the fine arts, educational subject matter, and religious questions. These are the topics of educated women and both "educated" and "women" need to be stressed.

Perhaps no other group has the collective sense of humor that pervades all aspects of convent life. Whether they are petitioning St. Anthony for a ride on a stormy night with "Tony, send a pony" or whether they are herding a live colt through a hospital ward to the chagrin of Mother Superior, the sister is a person of essential fun.

Sisters do not go around all day with folded hands and bowed heads. They drive station wagons, see movies, shop in department stores, and join in community singing. They can laugh about all their experiences—as well as about all the secret and mirth-provoking incidents that are part of their own community life. There is about them—particularly the younger sisters—a pixie quality which may be the result of their long association with precocious children—or with those not so precocious.

This association involves them for between eight and ten hours a day and is worked into a schedule that would shame a mother of eight.

The teaching sister arises between 5:00 and 5:30 A.M., dresses, goes to Mass and Communion, probably recites communal prayers and then breakfasts about 7 A.M. Household chores are next until the start of school (about 8 A.M.), and from that time forward she is continually on duty, both in and out of the classroom. After school there is time for some recreation and for paper work and other school-related duties. Supper follows with prayers either before or after, and then a brief period of recreation. After night prayers, the teaching sister spends her remaining waking hours in study and preparation for the next day. But midnight oil is not a household expense in the convents. The sisters ordinarily retire between 9 and 10 P.M.

On weekends, of course, the schedule varies, with hours for recreation and study being much longer. Many sisters are finding their day-to-day obligations so time-consuming that they must spend a good portion of Saturday and Sunday in detailed classroom preparation.

Naturally, her religious vocation is the central part of her existence. And this aspect of her calling is cause for much misunderstanding. The teaching sister emphasizes that she has no corner on sainthood and that every person has an equal chance at heaven and an equal responsibility to strive for it.

Her sacrifices are misunderstood and she is pitied for them even though similar traits are praised in courageous and selfless laymen. She points out wearily that all organizations have rules—the army, fraternities, even well-run families. Spectators should not be upset by the fact that she may not be able to eat publicly, or go out at night, or because she has her style of clothing prescribed for her.

Again, different values are set up for her. If a sister becomes ill, for example, outsiders will shake their heads and say, "She never should have entered the convent." On the other hand, the husband who would wish to dissolve his marriage because of a sick wife would be judged a cad.

Part of this error stems from the fact that many people today have no idea what sacrifice means. They grow up to think that love is selfish and that suffering is punishment.

For a sister, love is everything.

"A sister is a woman in love. And when a woman is in love, she overlooks the minor irritations of life. When a woman is secure in her love, she is happy. And the sister has this assurance every hour of every day."

She wants cooperation and understanding, not pity. Although she appreciates the cakes baked for her and the picnics planned for her, she laments the notion that prompts these benefits—the notion that she is basically unhappy.

"Why, they can't even imagine the joy we have in just being with our community. I've sometimes been anxious to terminate a vacation with my family so that I can return to my beloved companions."

Of course, some problems do exist—illness, overwork, personality conflicts, character weaknesses. There are mental and physical collapses and there are sisters who forsake the religious life. But these are the exceptions.

For most religious the convent is a happy place where laughter is spontaneous and dedication and sacrifice a commonplace. Theirs is not a prisoner's life demanding inhuman and exhausting labors with every act performed to the click of a cricket. Democracy and freedom prevail here, too, reflecting the type of society in which we live.

While customs may vary among orders and among sections of the United States, the basic elements of the vocation seem standard. In fact, most sisters are reluctant to dwell on the differences.

But there are some differences based on locale, rules of the order and the like. In the east, for example, rules tend to be more strict. A walk may be a mere turn around the yard, whereas in the middle and far west, the sisters may have only a time restriction on their sojourns. As one moves west, he is conscious of the order designations dropping away. A sister is no longer a Benedictine, a Dominican. She is just a sister. There are difficulties arising in urban communities that are not as serious in rural areas, and there are personal and clerical relationships which change conditions. But wherever she is, the teaching sister tries to reflect the times and the territory.

She is a professional person—an educator. She brings to her daily tasks a skill and devotion that would make her a good housewife, mother, a good businesswoman.

All religious houses either require a degree before a sister can teach or are moving toward this requirement. This is partly due to pressure from state authorities but the trend was there anyway. Some self-styled "rebels" among the superiors have stated that they would like to see a sister get her A.B. degree, teach for six or seven years, take two years out for graduate studies, and then return to the classroom. Education credits (many of which the sister regards as an inevitable nuisance) could be picked up in the summer months.

Chief requirements for a teaching sister (in addition to the vocation) would seem to be a love of children and the ability to influence them, plus understanding, firm kindness, and a sense of humor. She is the focal point of Catholic education—the one who embodies the Catholic philosophy of education and who creates the Catholic atmosphere and who produces the Catholic attitudes.

In her vocation she finds security.

"If I were teaching in a public school I would miss the solid foundation of the absolutes by which we teach. I don't see how you can motivate students without a grasp of the eternal and unchanging values. In the Catholic school system—even if you are teaching in a shack—you have the truth."

Today's teaching sister finds herself—like all of us—in an electronic, atomic, and chaotic world. More skilled than her predecessors, she finds her added skills more taxed.

Her biggest challenge is the understanding and the motivation of today's youth—from kindergarten through college. Her students are more worldly and more sophisticated than previous generations. They must be convinced that they are receiving a priceless heritage, something eternal and not passing. They must be given an enthusiasm for learning, a respect for law and order without a loss of freedom, a love of God. All of this must be made a living thing and must be presented to the student as a challenge.

The teaching sister has a deep concern for the religious well-being of her students, a concern that might profitably be imitated by numerous parents. She tries to make them see religious principles in depth and to teach them to live by them.

"Why is it that my students can often repeat the most perfect doctrine but can't live by it? They think the mere knowing is enough. How do we show them that the Catholic faith is a way of life?"

Discipline is not the problem it is elsewhere, and this is in spite of the fact that physical punishment—the ruler, the strap—are no longer used. One order's manual advises, "Consider the faults as infirmities. Then you will deal with the erring in loving forbearance."

Most sisters solve their disciplinary problems by never giving them a chance to happen. When they do occur, methods vary. One principal lets young male disputants go to the gym and don boxing gloves. She serves as referee and states that few fights get beyond the glove-lacing stage.

Others use conferences with students and with parents. The most effective solution, though, seems to be a thorough preparation which makes the class interesting, an outpouring of love and justice, and a quiet demand for respect.

One of the teaching sister's difficulties is that she is seldom able to get across to her pupils the humorous qualities she possesses. The student sees her "school-teacher face," a countenance which is awe-inspiring but mirthless.

A pastor comments that "sisters are often afraid to unbend for fear that discipline or respect will suffer. If they have this respect to start with, it does no harm to let little girls, particularly, see that a sister's life is a happy one. I even encourage an occasional sister vs. pupils snowball fight."

Yet, to the sister, the students are a limitless source of amusement. Whether they are asking her why she wears men's shoes or declaring that they want to be nuns because "Sister has the key to the Coke machine," they form one continuous Art Linkletter program.

One sister, displaying a biblical chart of which she was most proud, pointed to Adam and asked, "Who is this?" Her class chorused, "Tarzan."

Now there is material for the evening's recreation!

Most of the humor is in the little relationships between sister and pupil—the private thoughts comically expressed, the unexpected reactions, the mispronounced words.

Perhaps the failure to transfer this humor is natural. To the student, the sister seldom appears as a mere woman. She is always larger than life, and there is a mystery about her which is part physical (habit, bearing, education, etc.) but, in large measure, spiritual. The boys and girls sense this otherworldliness. It is only when sisters giggle or when they cry or when they are aged or senile that they seem more human. There is not the sympathetic bond between sister and layman that exists between priest and layman. The lay person can rather easily appreciate that a priest is a man pursuing a different vocation. His appraisal of the sister is more complex and less distinct.

Another major problem is the parents. Most disciplinary difficulties can be traced to them, as can most of the materialistic concepts. Sometimes the teaching sister feels that she is actually engaged in a struggle with the parents for the soul of the youngster.

She finds many contrary influences in some homes. Sister is

openly regarded as old-fashioned for the views she holds on dating, television, dress, and other fringe areas. There is even a long-distance debate on some of the hours the youngsters keep.

"Parents should greet some of these students on Monday morning," complains one veteran sister.

Some parents do not see discipline as an objective thing, as a part of character formation. They see it as something to be applied in individual and difficult cases. While they aver that they want the teacher to discipline their children—"try and do it!"

Parents are frequently unfair in what they expect of the teacher. They blame the school for the moral laxity in youth. Yet the sisters continue to dress modestly, to preach modesty, and to check immodest practices and dress in the classrooms. The sisters are blamed for dating habits and they can only ask in return, "Why is Mary allowed to go steady? Why is she permitted to go riding after school? Why is it that Johnny has the car to take Mary parking by the river?"

Often the teaching sister is at loggerheads with the parents as regards the spiritual life. She emphasizes daily Mass, frequent Communion. The parents treat this notion as if it were penance. Mother and father argue over the cut of clothes or about social life. They feel sixth graders should have dances. Sister says "no." Sister then becomes in their eyes a prude and a tyrant.

One published report on parental attitudes toward sisters showed that the parents looked upon them as "shy, reserved, frightened, flustered, defensive, nervous, patronizing and uncommunicative." They claimed it was hard to get in contact with the teacher.

Often the child is used as a go-between with the result that the message is garbled, producing more hostility or indifference. Regulations of religious congregations discourage communication with secular persons. And, too, many sisters feel that they can handle problems of conduct and application without bothering the parents.

Parents, too, are reluctant to "bother" the teachers and the contact is a stand-off. Often a parent by-passes the sisters and takes a complaint directly to the pastor. However, the practice of parent-teacher conferences is becoming widespread and is considered most effective by the sisters. One said she would rather eliminate report cards than do away with these conferences.

In spite of these shortcomings, the average Catholic parent is much more satisfied with the parochial school than is the non-Catholic parent with the public school system.

Among her other relationships, that with the lay teacher looms as important. Some few sisters feel that they are not getting the best lay teachers available because of the salary and the social deterrents. Most, however, would match their staffs with those of any public school.

They insist that the lay teacher must have equal status with the teaching sister but confess that the rule is not always followed. Often the slight is unintentional, such as the decision that is made at supper or in the community recreation room. But they love and respect the lay teachers and wish they had more of them. That they will have to have more is, of course, a statistical certainty.

"One thing is sure," says one sister. "Whenever people criticize our schools for having too many lay teachers, I ask them how many daughters they have sent to the convent."

The parish priest is closest to the teaching sister and the ideal pastor sees that she is respected, backed up on disciplinary problems, and consulted in any areas that relate to the school system.

"Most priests are a wonderful help. As a group, they are terrific. They can get out and get to the parents and they are usually most co-operative and appreciative."

"We try," says one pastor, "to put our sisters on a pedestal in this parish. Once there, the problems are minimal."

Other pastors try to provide in-service training for the sisters and they worry that they might be "killing off the sisters with hard work." They are coming to exclude the sister from many of the unreasonable services to the parish—sacristy duty, record keeping, choir, counting the collection.

Yet even the parish priest does not fully understand the teaching sister—just as no one can fully understand convent life without experiencing it. He is somewhat in awe of his sisters and of their efficient way of getting things done.

The sisters' contacts with various other publics are increasing. One important one is the contact with state education authorities. She feels that the state authorities, on the whole, have proved beneficial to the Catholic school system and that their demands have made the parochial schools better.

Absent from today's sister is much of the sentimental and quasi-religious activity—the thousand Hail Marys and the thirteen

Thursdays. Her teachings are more solid and her manner more direct. She is tolerant and understanding of other occupations and other faiths. She is concerned with the same educational problems as her lay confreres—slow learners, visual aids, fund drives, hot lunches, etc.

She is flesh and blood—because God builds his supernatural structure in human nature—and she is a member of a team striving to do the work of the Creator.

Lest you feel sorry for her, let us remember that today's sister is the most capable the Catholic Church has ever produced. She is better educated, more perceptive, just as religious, and twice as clever as the sister of the last century.

She is one of the most important women in any Catholic child's life—perhaps more important than will ever be realized. She is teacher, counselor, mother, father, confidante, spiritual advisor. She is a woman in love.

Sisters of the Bayous

M. F. Everett

When hurricane Flossie ripped through the bayou lands of southeast Louisiana in the fall of 1956, it left a trail of devastation in its wake: flooded homes and churches, drowned livestock, and total destruction of what had taken years to build up. As sun dawned on the grim scene, long before adequate communication was established or travel was safe, two Eucharistic Mission Sisters were on their way to stricken towns in a station wagon loaded with food and other necessities.

The fact that Flossie had torn out huge sections of the concrete highway didn't stop the sisters. If they couldn't go through, they went around. For they are trained to meet emergencies of any kind. Novices not only learn cooking, sewing, and other home crafts, but they are taught to operate machinery, fix flats, make auto repairs, and even pitch hay or do other farm work when occasion demands.

The nuns are often called Sisters of the Bayous, and they literally "paddle their own canoe" when visiting missions in Louisiana's swamplands. But they could also be called Sisters of the Desert because as the order grew it spread from the bayou country to the arid districts of the southwest.

It is significant that the Mission Sisters' first community life was in servant quarters. For the sisters are in every sense of the word servants—of God and man—teaching catechism to public school children and adults, visiting homes, taking census, collecting and distributing clothes for the needy, forming sodalities, training altar boys, conducting religious vacation schools, sponsoring retreats, and visiting the sick.

They have had a strange assortment of homes since their beginning: a small rented house, a one-room pool hall, a former "hobo hotel." Their present mother-house is a former mansion of a "magic soap king," and their novitiate an old farmhouse.

The founding of this flourishing community goes back to the early 1900's. In Amite, Louisiana, Catherine Bostick had been teaching catechism for some years when she was joined, in 1925, by Zoe Grouchy. While preparing to enter a contemplative order, they taught catechism, and cared for the sick and poor—often walking great distances in their work.

That year they helped prepare about two hundred persons for Confirmation. The late Archbishop John W. Shaw of New Orleans exhorted them to continue their work and promised them a car for traveling. This was a faithful model-T Ford, named Johnny I—the first of a long line of mission vehicles that have enabled the sisters to reach thousands of souls.

The young women frequently met with cold reception in their work. "Unless you wear a religious habit, your work will not succeed," a veteran missionary priest told them. So one evening they devised a habit out of bed sheeting, the only material available. From this model they made a garb of white wool, which was approved by the archbishop. Later it was suggested that this be changed to cotton—a wise move considering the humid heat of Louisiana and the scorching reaches of the desert.

Approval of the habit is considered the official date of the order's foundation: January 11, 1927. A few days later Catherine took the name of Sister Catherine and Zoe Grouchy became Sister Margaret. Thus their community life began in a tiny house, the servants' quarters behind Catherine's home in Amite. A month later they had to move to a small rented house. The following November they moved again, this time into a one-room pool hall in Albany, Louisiana.

Here they remained for eight years. Here, too, the first vows of the community, now grown to three, were taken on February 2, 1930. The three sisters pronounced vows "for life" on January 27, 1934, and the first novice received her habit.

By 1935 the community had grown to ten and outgrown the one-room house in Albany. Archbishop Joseph F. Rummel, who had just succeeded to the See of New Orleans after the death of Archbishop Shaw, made it possible for the nuns to move to New Orleans. The new mother-house had been a "hobo hotel" on the edge of the French Quarter and had been operated by the Society of St. Vincent de Paul for homeless transient men.

Many a time the sisters were awakened late at night by a thunderous rap on the door and a rough voice demanding shelter. Unpleasant for the sisters, of course, but imagine the surprise for the hobo on learning that his former stopping place was now occupied by nuns!

The Mission Sisters moved several more times before they finally found a suitable place for a novitiate—a seven-room farmhouse on 206 acres of land near Covington, Louisiana. This is across Lake Pontchartrain from New Orleans in the "ozone" belt of piney woods, just three miles from the Benedictine Abbey of St. Joseph.

The sisters did most of the repair work themselves. Sister Mary Magdalen was "foreman" and had only one helper at first. Then any sister who had a few days between religious vacation schools took a quick trip to the novitiate and wielded paintbrush, saw, or hammer. The sisters did over practically all the furniture, which was old and wobbly; patched and painted ceilings and walls, sanded and painted floors, and so on.

Our Lady and the angels were always at hand, they cheerfully said, and certainly help was given at times in unusual ways. There was, for instance, the second-hand tractor, with the name of Nellie Belle inscribed on the engine, that was such a help in cutting grass the first summer and then began to act up. Sister Francis, superior of the novitiate, decided that "if it had a more Christian name maybe it wouldn't give so much trouble." So she called it Isidore after the farmer saint, who was helped by angels with his plowing, and it behaved perfectly!

In the fall of 1954 the farmhouse novitiate was occupied by three sisters, six novices, and four postulants. Once again "growing pains" set in. One couldn't call it a vicious circle, for it is a work of divine charity, but it certainly has been a vexing cycle.

The sisters go out on the missions to bring souls to God. They pray for postulants so their work will grow. The postulants come and there is no place to put them. So they move to a larger place. More postulants come, and they are overcrowded again.

Within a year the novitiate was bursting at the seams. A new dormitory and chapel wing were needed. They would cost $100,000. The nuns had $14,000 on hand. How they did it, no one knows. Maybe through Our Lady and the angels—or more probably St. Joseph, to whom the nuns are devoted as their provider. At any rate the new building was dedicated in the fall of 1956 in honor of St. Joseph.

Surroundings are not always ideal. The sisters may teach catechism in a canvas tent with wooden boxes for chairs, at a gas station, in a school bus, on the front porch of a store, or outdoors. But there are many consolations: The sixteen-year-old bayou youth who could neither read nor write, but who had a cousin teach him prayers and who traveled miles of swamp to attend class so he could receive Communion; the woman dying of cancer who received the Sacraments and begged the priest to baptize her husband as she longed for him to receive grace too (he came into the Church later); First Communion for Spanish-speaking children (whose families live in terrible conditions while picking cotton in their "Okie and Arkie" existence) at a Mass celebrated in a Paulist trailer chapel, the first Mass the children had ever attended.

Two or more sisters stay at each of the permanent missions, and similar units are assigned to visit other missions for from one to several weeks, more often in the summer to conduct religious vacation schools, teaching catechism to children of itinerant Mexican workers and the like.

There are three permanent missions in the New Orleans Archdiocese and a number cared for from the mother-house. Two sisters are assigned to the archdiocesan headquarters of the Confraternity of Christian Doctrine, and others attend institutions such as the Crippled Children's hospital, the Home for Incurables, and a school for retarded children. Classes for deaf children are conducted in the mother-house (learning the sign language is included in the novices' course).

In the Diocese of Lafayette, Louisiana, there are three permanent missions and two sisters assigned to the diocesan CCD staff. In the Diocese of Tucson, Arizona, there are also three permanent missions with the sisters assisting part-time in diocesan CCD work.

The community works in six dioceses of the South and Southwest and are located in five states—Mississippi, Louisiana, Texas, New Mexico, and Arizona. The greatest number of vocations have come from Louisiana, but the order has received members from Arizona, Missouri, Michigan, Illinois, and as far away as Canada.

The formal title of the nuns is Missionary Servants of the Most Holy Eucharist of the Third Order of St. Dominic. This space-filling name indicates their original and continuing purpose and the fact that recently they were aggregated to the Dominican order in Rome.

Shepherdess of the Strayed

Brendan Mitchell, O.F.M.

The sister dressed in pure white with a blue cincture hanging from her waist and a silver heart on her breast has known, loved, and helped more graduates from broken homes, juvenile courts or plain and fancy slums than the average policewoman or social worker. For Mother Mary of St. Stanislaus, head of the Home of the Good Shepherd in New Orleans, has spent her adult lifetime as a member of what is without doubt the world's largest and most dedicated organization specializing in the reclamation of wayward girls and young women.

The Institute of the Good Shepherd to which Mother Mary of St. Stanislaus belongs is a congregation of nuns who conduct nearly four hundred refuges and institutions of correction of various types for girls and women on six continents. South America has 143 Good Shepherd Homes, and there are 149 in Western Europe. In English-speaking countries the Homes are designed especially for re-education of delinquent and so-called pre-delinquent girls. The sisters also conduct orphanages as well as "transitional homes" for young working women making an adjustment to social conditions. Strangely enough, too, in eleven countries they are entrusted by the governments with the difficult function of conducting women's prisons. The esteem in which secular authority holds their work of reclaiming twisted and tainted lives was spotlighted in 1954 when the French Government awarded the Cross of the Legion of Honor to Mother Mary of St. Ursula, Superior-General of the Institute, for the work achieved for bewildered, dislocated youth by her sisters during the war-torn years of that country.

The roots of the Good Shepherd tradition go back to another troublous time in France—the seventeenth-century period of religious decay—when St. John Eudes, a missionary priest working in the cities and towns, witnessing the tragedy of girls and young women led to corruption in a disrupted society, organized a small group of dedicated women to befriend and protect these hapless victims. At the beginning of the nineteenth century this Order of the Refuge, as it was then known, was reorganized and revitalized by another canonized saint—a woman whose genius and charity make her one of the truly great women of the last century, St. Mary Euphrasia Pelletier. It was then called the Institute of the Good Shepherd, and this amazing woman during her lifetime established 110 Good Shepherd Homes in Europe, Africa, India, Australia, and North and South America.

To emphasize their dedication toward wayward younger sisters, these nuns add a fourth to the three vows of poverty, chastity, and obedience customarily made in religious life. In a pledge that surely distinguishes them from any other group of social workers in the world, they vow also to give their best personal effort for the spiritual salvation of the girls and young women who come under their care.

"It's the power of grace and love that changes people," said Mother Mary of St. Stanislaus referring to this dedication. "Our foundress, St. Mary Euphrasia, was a great psychologist and teacher; she was years ahead of her time. She believed in using all the resources at one's command to help the girls and women. That's why we train our sisters at colleges outside our cloister in the scientific skills of counseling and teaching and invite the aid of trained lay helpers, psychologists, doctors, vocational guides. But nothing takes the place of God's grace and unmeasured love given in His name.

"When Gloria came to us, for instance, she was like a snarling, scratching, frightened little animal. She had run away from home, gotten involved with a couple of sailors, and at the age of fourteen her life seemed hopelessly tangled. Three years—and several bad moments—later, a lovely, gracious young woman emerged from the ugly shell of her scarred and twisted childhood. Today Gloria— and of course that isn't her real name—is happily married, the mother of three beautiful, well-trained children. Only the grace of God and patient love wrought a change like that—and all our sisters have seen it happen again and again."

The sisters are known to the girls by the title "Mother," a name that begets a badly needed attitude among youngsters who too often have missed the strength and profound love of their own mothers. Until recently, too, it was customary for a girl entering a Good Shepherd Home to be given a fictitious name, such as Gloria, Jeanne, or Cecilia, so that her stay in the correctional institution might remain anonymous.

"Recently, however," remarked Mother St. Stanislaus, "the girls and often their families don't seem concerned about anonymity any more. Perhaps it's a symptom of the times."

If your city is one of the fifty in the United States or Canada fortunate enough to have a Home of the Good Shepherd, the institution will probably be housed in a three- or four-story building in an inconspicuous part of town. It may be a modern structure, though the sisters have been unable to replace many of their older establishments. Its grounds are usually enclosed with a high wall, as much to exclude curious eyes as for any other reason, and probably the lower-floor windows facing the street are covered with heavy mesh wire to discourage truancy and outsiders from seeking forbidden entrance.

Most people look upon a Good Shepherd Home with an air of vague mystery. Public knowledge of this institution is too often limited to mention of it as a standard prop in confession or detective-type fiction—a stopping place somewhere in the career of a too vivid or tainted heroine. As a matter of fact, however, your local Community Chest, of which the Homes are frequently agencies, will usually issue a brochure telling you in detail and with illustrations how this refuge for delinquent and pre-delinquent girls helps to solve one of the community's most baffling problems.

In the impersonal, almost clinical, language of modern social science, this brochure describes the work of a center of re-education for girls from ten to seventeen years of age who are socially maladjusted, providing them with boarding school and vocational train-ing opportunities. It emphasizes that all the modern techniques of psychiatry, counseling, and supervision are employed. Augmenting the staff of perhaps fifteen nuns is a lay group of specially trained teachers, vocational directors, activity supervisors. The number of inmates—or "our girls" as the sisters call them—may be 150 in the average Good Shepherd Home in the United States, and they are of all races, creeds, and social strata.

In most cases in the United States the girls are remanded to the Good Shepherd Home by the authority of the juvenile courts or welfare agencies, though many are placed in the Home by parents or guardians. A minimum stay of one year is insisted on, though many remain longer voluntarily or at the insistence of parents and guardians. The viewpoint of the sisters is that the child has been confined not merely as a corrective penalty, but has been intro-duced to a calculated re-education program.

"Our concern," said Mother Mary of St. Stanislaus, "is to re-place the twisted and often unmoral habits of these children with new attitudes and wholesome habits of character—a process that can hardly be begun, much less accomplished, in a year.

"I think we have to be wary of that term 'juvenile delinquency,'" she continued. "It's too impersonal. It sounds too much like a disease, when really it involves personal failure. Moral wrong, whether it be stealing, running away, dope, or sex, is a terrifically personal matter—one's will is involved. Temptations and bad sur-roundings may be almost overwhelming. Our little girls are per-sons. Our work is to guide and train their wills, and to help and love them as persons, not to attack a vague generality called juvenile delinquency."

When a girl enters a Good Shepherd Home she is, according to her problem, segregated in one of two classes—those from ten to fifteen years of age, classed as pre-delinquents because they have been exposed to the contagion of evil conduct and shown tend-encies that haven't taken deep root; or the twelve- to seventeen-year-old group who have become involved in juvenile crime and have shown a bent of character toward wrongdoing.

Girls are then further grouped into smaller units to approximate as nearly as possible under limitations with youngsters of like age and traits that might characterize a family. In these smaller groups a girl lives under the care of a "mother"—one of the nuns and a trained lay worker to whom she may attach her loyalties and personal dependencies, and her "home" will be a designated cottage or dormitory.

Her school training will be in small classes with personal attention from the last elementary grades through high school. Since her later life will probably lack opportunity to pursue further formal education and she will rapidly be faced with the need to fit adequately into a domestic or working situation, training in home arts, home nursing, grooming, etiquette, and office and business procedure will be added. There will be plenty of play, in some instances a first-class gymnasium, or even a swimming pool. Her health will be regularly checked.

Integrating all of this, and suffusing it like a light which brings warmth and energy, a girl in a Good Shepherd Home will be taught, often for the first time, the truth of responsibility to God and of dependence upon Him for help in one's weakness. In hundreds of little ways garnered from her century-old, world-wide tradition, the Sister of the Good Shepherd will teach this girl how an act makes a habit, a habit a character, and a character a destiny. She'll learn that love is the greatest thing in the world, that God wants a little love in return—and that a little love given Him is what makes goodness.

What happens to "graduates" of Good Shepherd Homes?

Sisters so unworldly as to live what is called among Catholic religious orders the "cloistered" life—rarely leaving their convents except for university training or transferal from one house to another —are not so unwise after three hundred years of accumulated experience as to think their efforts yield perfect success.

Out of more than two thousand girls who have gone through one Home an impersonal report states that "85 per cent have done well after leaving the school." Sister Mary of the Angels, who has written a delightful teen-agers' life of St. Mary Euphrasia titled A Little White Shepherdess puts it this way:

"These youngsters have been thrown into problems no child should have—problems that are too big. They've been exposed to drunkenness, loose morals, crime. They've gulped great mouthfuls of foulness like a drowning person. Or they've been thrown, or allowed to wander, into a spiritual tar-pit till the evil clings to the crevices of their young souls. Alice has three stepmothers claiming her. Jane had been shunted around nine different foster homes.

Virginia never heard the name of God except in cursing. Yet when it's behind them, many of our girls marry happily. They come back to help us with the others. One has been named the 'foster mother of the year' in her community. Another has become a nun."

The mention of nuns recalls a flowering of Good Shepherd work which the sisters think of as among the fairest. Girls committed to a Good Shepherd Home may never join the Good Shepherd Sisters. But from the first days of the Good Shepherd apostolate the spirit of prayer and penitence lying at the heart of this great institute brought forth a group of co-workers of the institute known as the Magdalens. These are young women, many of them former inmates of the Homes, who have embraced a life of strict contemplative prayer as cloistered nuns in communities attached to some of the Good Shepherd Homes. They seek a closer union with God and offer their sacrifices and penances as a kind of spiritual blood transfusion against the sinfulness of a delinquent world. This vicarious prayer and penance as much as any part of the Good Shepherd idea gives a key to full understanding of what the Good Shepherd work is all about.

New Life for Modern Magdalenes

Antoinette Bosco

The young Dominican priest listened nervously as the heavy door closed behind him, the clanking of a lock assuring him once more that he was confined within prison walls. He reviewed his assignment mentally. In this September of 1864 he had been sent to preach a retreat to the women prisoners of the Maison Centrale at Cadillac-sur-Garrone, a building familiar to him for he had been born in this village.

The first woman he met was wild and unfriendly. "I am Father Lataste," he said. "And what is your name?"

She answered sullenly, "Angelique Jourdain."

Inwardly, Father Lataste wondered what he could do for these poor prisoners. "My God," he murmured to himself, "help me to show them Your love and mercy."

As he faced the 380 women for the first time, Father Marie-Jean-Joseph Lataste decided to use truth itself as his means to reaching them. He admitted the fact that they had shame and sorrow in their lives, but he told them that the past could be wiped away if only they loved God. Looking at them with his intense eyes, he said:

"What God loves above all is to be loved. Magdalene was forgiven much because she loved much. God does not ask us what we have been. He is concerned only with what we are."

In talk after talk he pounded home the same theme—God loves you. He came not to call the just, but to bring sinners to repentance. Father Lataste saw in these poor prisoners a picture of abandoned souls which he was to carry in his heart for the rest of his brief life.

New hope shone on the faces of the women when they heard him say, "Our Lord has given me a part of His Heart with which to love you. I would like to be the Hand of God to save you."

Could it be true that someone really cared for them? If there was such love in this world, and beyond, could they really find it? This remarkable priest, with his message of love instead of punishment and damnation, did reach them. At his Mass, 341 out of 380 inmates received Communion, a most unusual number.

Before he left the prison at Cadillac-sur-Garonne, several of the women told him that their most ardent wish was to be able to enter the religious life.

Father Lataste listened in anguish. Which convent would take these women when they were released? Even if they were to become saints, they would always bear the stigma of their prison record. Because of that, it would be hands-off as far as the existing religious communities were concerned.

Then, as he knelt in prayer before the Blessed Sacrament, the answer to the problem came clearly to Father Lataste. Could it be possible to found a new religious order—one in which good girls with fine reputations would welcome repentant girls, with their sin and shame forgotten, to be truly their sisters in the religious life, clothed in the same habit, bound by the same rules?

Father Lataste immediately set to work to win others to his idea. He put his thoughts down in writing in a brochure entitled *Les Réhabilities* and, fighting prejudices, quickly began to gain converts to his cause. In less than two years after his retreat at Cadillac, on August 14, 1866, the first House of Bethany was founded at Frasne in the Diocese of Besançon.

Three years later, at the age of thirty-seven, Father Lataste died. On his last Christmas on earth he had the joy of giving the habit of the Dominican Sisters of Bethany to Angelique Jourdain, the first inmate he had met at the Cadillac prison.

Today the Dominican Sisters of Bethany, Congregation of St.

Mary Magdalene, have six convents in France, three in Belgium, two in Switzerland, and one in Italy. The mother house is still in the Diocese of Besançon in France, at Montferrand-le-Chateau, Doubs. Richard Cardinal Cushing of Boston gave his blessing to the sisters, and their first foundation in the United States began in 1960 at Boston. Already several American girls have begun their vocation at Bethany.

This order is unusual to say the least. It is open to young women of excellent backgrounds and unsullied reputations, as are other religious communities; but at Bethany the door to admission is still open. For while other religious orders might receive pentitents as special cases, at Bethany a girl with a vocation can be accepted regardless of her past. She is received as an honored member of the community, given the same habit, title, honor, and rule.

The order's constitution states that Bethany is open to "every woman, who, having fallen in the past in whatever way and to whatever degree, being sincerely converted, and having proved her repentance, is resolved in her heart to give herself to God until death."

The essential aim of this congregation is to keep alive in the Church the same kind of penitent love which characterized St. Mary Magdalene. Ironically, when the world speaks of Mary Magdalene, her sins are remembered first. But when Christ spoke of Mary, she was the one who had "loved much." Christ Himself put the emphasis on love, and, if there was sorrow for sin because of love for Him, He not only forgave sins but He forgot them, too.

As clearly put by Father Raymond Neufeld (during a retreat which I was privileged to attend), Christ's forgiveness was complete and permanent. "Can you imagine Mary Magdalene coming up to Christ every other week, saying, 'Lord, did You really mean it?'?"

This Christlike spirit of forgiving and forgetting is the fragrance of Bethany. All that is important here is the present and the future, and the utmost discretion concerning the past history of those at Bethany is an obligation on all the sisters.

There are three ways in which girls may become a part of Bethany. First, there is the Pre-Bethany, a convent located in the clean and quiet open country. Here the life is more informal than in the religious life. It offers a great opportunity to those who need it to examine their lives, refresh themselves spiritually and become acquainted with the demands and joys of the religious life. It is actually a chance for women of all backgrounds to prepare themselves to enter the religious life.

One might almost say that life at Pre-Bethany is an indefinite retreat where a girl can travel at her own speed to the point where she can in peace make the choice either to stay with Bethany or to leave. As yet there is no Pre-Bethany in America, but the sisters hope to have one in a few years.

The next road to Bethany is the Dominican Third Order. The sisters in this group go through the regular phases of religious life —postulate, novitiate, and profession. They wear the same habit as the sisters who take vows, and they are together with them in worship, prayer, work, and recreation. But the religious exercises themselves are much less exacting for these tertiaries than for the religious, even though they live together within the cloistered convents.

This Third Order of Bethany offers a great advantage to women who otherwise might not have the discipline or stamina for the full religious life. In other words, if a woman has a real vocation to convent life but needs to progress a little more slowly in her spiritual formation, Bethany meets her more than halfway. She can become a tertiary, fulfilling her vocation to the religious life under a mildly exacting rule.

The third entry to Bethany is the canonical novitiate leading to religious profession for life with simple vows. Most of the girls of good background, who regard Bethany as an apostolate, enter the canonical novitiate. It should be made clear that a good reputation is not a prerequisite for this order, either for Pre-Bethany, the Third Order, or the canonical novitiate. Common sense dictates that a girl who has had a background of crime or sin will need more help and more time in her formation as a religious. But if a rehabilitated girl is ready for the full religious life she, too, enters the canonical novitiate.

No dowry is required of a girl seeking admission to Bethany. The sisters are poor, but they ask those who enter only for what they can afford. Art work is generally found for the sisters, such as printing cards and making Church linens and vestments, and they support themselves in this way. They are also helped by people like you and me who are "Friends of Bethany" and are able to send an annual contribution to the sisters.

How do the sisters spend their day? The life is that of a contemplative Dominican monastery, yet at the same time an apostolic life. The white habits of the Sisters of Bethany are often seen in prisons which two or three assigned sisters visit regularly with their message of hope that a new life is possible.

Within the convent the Divine Office, recited or sung in choir, is the framework of the day. The beginners take part in it progressively. As put by the sisters, "They love it, and the liturgy is the best school for converts."

The Blessed Sacrament is the center of their lives, and there is exposition three mornings a week in the Massachusetts convent. The rosary—which contains all the mysteries of salvation—is recited every day. There is also a special time set aside for meditation and sacred reading.

The sisters are silent during the work hours, but recreation brings the sounds of happy talk and play. A woman who had come from a long-term prison sentence once commented, "I don't understand how one can be so happy when one has suffered so much."

I am sure these words made Father Marie-Jean-Joseph Lataste very happy from his place in heaven where he watches over his dream-come-true on earth, the Convents of Bethany. Naturally the sisters pray constantly that their founder will someday be formally beatified by the Church. His cause was opened in the Diocese of Besançon in 1937, and is now in Rome.

Somewhere there may be a young woman reading this who has a fine reputation and character, an attraction to the religious life, and a desire to continue the work which Father Lataste began—that of helping her less fortunate sisters. She may find her vocation at Bethany.

Somewhere there may be a woman reading this who is abandoned or full of despair, homeless, or yearning for an answer to the why of her misery. There is consolation and hope for her at 19 Dartmouth Street, West Newton 65, Massachusetts, where she will find a home and, in Father Lataste's words, the "charity of Christ which erases all distances and all distinctions among the women of Bethany."

Sisters of the Forgotten

Vincent J. Giese

"Are you sure this is the place you want?" asked the cab driver.

I paid him and made my way up to the third floor, where the door to the parlor was ajar. On it were these simple words: "Jesus —Charity."

This was my first contact with the home of the Little Sisters of Jesus, more familiarly known as the Little Sisters of Charles de Foucauld. A simple, four-room apartment, known as their Fraternity, is the place where two Little Sisters of Jesus have settled quietly and obscurely to live a poor and humble life. Here they are trying to lead as closely as possible the hidden, humble existence of Nazareth.

Sister Marie Réjane greeted me at the door. It is her task to remain at home to look after the house and to look after Jesus in the Blessed Sacrament, hidden in the small chapel in the apartment. The Little Sisters are essentially contemplatives.

No matter how poorly the Little Sisters may be housed, one room is always converted into a chapel. They make of their Fraternity a Eucharistic Nazareth, with the tabernacle as its focus and center.

Sister Marie Réjane waited anxiously for her companion, Sister

Simone André, to return home from her job at the Lavelle Rubber Company, where she works daily at a kick press. The small factory is located in the neighborhood. Sister Simone André is the superior.

Sister Marie Réjane showed me the small chapel in their Fraternity. It is not completed as yet. The sister has been busy staining the wooden altar and platform on which the altar is built. Soon the Little Sisters will have the Blessed Sacrament present daily in their Fraternity for adoration. Mass will be celebrated at least one day a week in their chapel.

Sister Simone André returned home from her factory job at 5 P.M. She told me about their daily life.

"You will see, it is all very simple. It is not a complicated life at all. We say Lauds together in the morning, then we go to Mass at our parish church. At seven-thirty I must be at my place of work. After work we have an hour of adoration, then dinner. In the evening there is time for relaxation, for reading, for prayer. We end our day with Compline and a Gospel meditation. Then it is silence through the night."

During her lunch hour Sister Simone André slips away to church to pray. Each Little Sister spends an hour a day in adoration before the Blessed Sacrament. Likewise, one hour a week during the night. One day a month the Little Sisters attend a day of recollection. And, of course, there are retreats.

Preparations for the first foundation in the United States of the Little Sisters had been made well in advance. They had been granted permission on May 10, 1954, by His Eminence Samuel Cardinal Stritch to found a Fraternity in the Archdiocese of Chicago. This was preceded by a visit to Chicago in February, 1954, by Rev. René Voillaume, ecclesiastical superior of the Little Sisters. Father Voillaume is founder of the Little Brothers of Jesus and author of the recent book on their spirituality, *Seeds of the Desert: the Legacy of Charles de Foucauld* (Fides, Chicago).

Though the outlines of the new religious community were drawn up by Father Charles de Foucauld, the first Fraternity was not established until 1933, some eighteen years after his assassination in 1916 at the hands of the Touaregs in the Sahara Desert.

Charles de Foucauld (Brother Charles of Jesus), who had made a reputation for himself as a French explorer in Morocco, had become a Trappist monk, but received permission to leave the Trappists to work out the ideas for a new religious community. His search took him to Nazareth, where he spent two years as a kind of domestic servant. These were two years of silence and prayer. For hours at a time he would remain on his knees, motionless before the Blessed Sacrament. Whatever free time he had was spent meditating on the Scriptures and writing down his thoughts. His spirituality was direct, simple, strong. It was living constantly with Jesus—Jesus in the Eucharist and Jesus in the Gospel. Finally, he received permission from his bishop to isolate himself among the Touaregs at Tamanrasset, some 1,250 miles inside the Sahara Desert.

Father de Foucauld literally became a Touareg to the bottom of his soul among these people who knew no priests. His vocation, as he developed it, was to be *present* among them. His daily life, his whole way of living, even his dwelling place itself, were to help make him one with the Touaregs.

He decided that there must be no large Fraternities, but only small groups of three or four. He believed this would enable the Little Brothers and Little Sisters to lead a life of more marked poverty and also bring them closer to the people around them.

"It is even a good thing," he wrote, "to live alone in a place. One can thus have an influence, even without doing anything in particular, because one comes to belong and can make oneself so little and so easy to approach." Making oneself little and easy to approach—this was a program in itself.

Father de Foucauld remained convinced that it was his mission to found a double family of Little Brothers and Little Sisters, but he knew no disciples would come during his lifetime. "Jesus," he recorded, "wishes me to work for the establishment of this double family—in supplication, in self-immolation; by dying, by sanctifying myself, by loving Him . . ."

He was killed on December 1, 1916, by a band of Senoussis from the south of Tripolitania. Betrayed by one of his neighbors, dragged out of his house by ruthless force, he let them tie his hands behind his back as he knelt on the sands in front of his door. A few moments later a young Touareg shot him through the head.

Father de Foucauld left no final document to define the apostolic life of his double family. Certain directives, however, and rich spiritual ideas have been found among his papers. These can be outlined very simply:

1) He maintained the idea of small groups.

2) He insisted that adoration of the Blessed Sacrament be the central act of the day.

3) He insisted that his disciples undertake no regular ministry, nor have charge over any organized works, charitable or otherwise. They should, nevertheless, do all they can to bring the full truth to the surrounding population, wherever they are sent.

The new idea which he added to the principles of the Carthusians, Trappists, and Carmelites for example, was to have his religious actually "inserted" in small groups into the world of the poor, where they would share the hard life of that world.

The disciples of Brother Charles of Jesus have chosen to belong to the environment of the poor of the entire world. Belonging to the world of the poor involves the obligation of working for a living and not accepting alms. It likewise dictates the religious' choice of housing, food, care of illness, in fact, their whole manner of living. Everything must be in keeping with their love of the poor: everything must favor deep and easy contact with the poor. There is no need for them to talk or preach. Their very life as religious in the economic circumstances of the poor is a reminder of certain truths. It is in itself an object-lesson.

The Little Sisters learn from personal experience what repercussions the work of the poor, their housing and conditions of life, have on the spiritual life. Their own spirituality becomes better adapted to the real facts of the life of the poor. Thus they should be more able to help the poor pray and hope in Christ. At the same time, they are expected to work for the humanizing of living conditions wherever possible.

The fundamental rule is that they shall do everything in their power to live the evangelical counsels—the perfection of the Gospel life—under the conditions in which others have to lead their ordinary Christian lives.

In a world torn today by hatreds and racial divisions, all these oppositions among men must be met by an uprush of Christian love. This seems to be the source of the modern need for religious communities such as the Little Sisters and Little Brothers of Jesus.

Already Little Sisters and Little Brothers have gone among the Indians of South America, to Indochina, and to India. They have dedicated themselves to different working classes in Europe, such as miners, factory hands, deep-sea fishermen. Others have adopted certain Oriental rites—the Byzantine, the Coptic, the Syrian, the

Chaldean, and the Armenian. The lands of Islam have had Little
Brothers come to them to bear witness to friendship between
Christians and Moslems. Elsewhere they have entered into friendly
relations with Protestants. They have been accepted in Israel.

Father de Foucauld wished his disciples to consecrate themselves
preferably to areas forgotten or shunned, to minorities that are
neglected. Among those no one thinks of are the nomadic peoples.
Little Brothers and Little Sisters are living among the nomads of
the Sahara, in Algeria, among the gypsies in the south of France,
amidst the Fulla herdsmen in the north of the Cameroons and
the Touaregs in the Hoggar, with the Pygmies in the Belgian
Congo, among the lepers in Indochina.

In North America the Little Sisters have foundations in Vancouver, B.C., Montreal, Alaska, and now in Chicago, where the
Little Sisters find themselves inserted among the Negroes.

Fraternities of the Little Sisters are being established among the
few remaining Indians in South America, among the Bushmen of
South Africa, and among the primitive tribes of northern Australia. It will be for others to bring education and technical assistance
to all these peoples. It is the role of the Little Sisters and Brothers
to bring fraternal friendship by "being present," by "being inserted," by "disappearing in their environment."

Charity Is a Heavy Burden

Sister Maria del Rey of Maryknoll

In Chile the law requires that children wear a white pinafore to school. Our children at Buzeta come to school wrapped in sweaters fore and aft, with the white pinafore over all of it. It's not a bad idea. The children are sewed into their clothes in March and ripped out in September. The white pinafore keeps the multitudinous sweaters a little cleaner than they would be without it.

The Buzeta district of Santiago is a new section. So new that it's just a collection of huts and shacks and tumble-down lean-tos that people put up until they can afford something better. About the handsomest thing in the district is the St. John of God School, put up by the Maryknoll Fathers as the parish school and opened in March, 1953. About 650 children attend, the boys in the morning and the girls in the afternoon. Three of "ours" (as the Jesuits say) are staffing the school together with many lay teachers.

But we do not stay in the school. Our business is to penetrate into the homes—to bring to them the material and spiritual help they need. For this reason Sister Marian Therese took me on her rounds.

Sister is made of pioneer stuff. She comes of a large family in

Willow City, North Dakota. A registered nurse, she visits the homes in Buzeta.

Off the street, we ducked through a narrow alleyway and found ourselves in the most noisome court I ever saw. Some twelve years of mission life in Asia and Hawaii had prepared me for this, but it could not be surpassed for utter desolation. A number of haphazard shacks faced a single yard, indescribably dirty. A horse stood in a pile of manure in one corner; an ancient car, bereft of tires and much of its body, stood beside one of the huts. It looked like a long-dead monster, well-plucked by vultures. Three children under five stood near a puddle, blue with cold, for their little legs were bare and shivering. Their sore little noses needed wiping badly. Their hands were so chapped! A woman wrapped in a ragged sweater was hanging up clothes on the inevitable clothesline. Her hands were cracked with the cold. Several other women were puttering around their small wood fires, trying to cook in large tin cans or broken pots. Their wooden-soled shoes squooshed in and out and around a mush compounded of rubbish, garbage, and mud. It made one sick at heart to know that human beings have to live thus.

We were bound for Julita's house. The women were quick to help. "Right there, Madre!" they called, pointing to a lean-to holding itself up against the blank wall of a stable which faced another street.

Julita came out with the shouting. Her place was built like the traditional Christmas crib. Two walls were open to wind and rain. She had hung some dirty canvas from the corrugated tin roof to shut out some of it, but it was almost a useless gesture.

"Come in, come in!" she said, graciously as a queen, pulling aside the canvas to make an entry.

Benito—four years old—was lying in bed in a corner. He was wrapped in sweaters and wore no less than three woolen caps. His eyes were bright with fever. He was too sick to care much about anything outside his hot little body.

Julita was bundled in sweaters, too. On top was an apron with once pretty ruffles which had been washed beyond all hope of bright color. Her eyes moved anxiously from Sister to the child and back again. Then, mindful of her duties as hostess, she threw a stick of wood on the open brazier and fanned it into a flame.

She returned to the bedside and watched with her heart in her eyes.

Thanks be to God, Sister was able to look up with a cheerful smile. "He'll be all right in a few days, Julita," she said. "Just give him this, night and morning."

The other women crowded around the house. They had a few things to ask Sister, too. We had been in the district only a few months, then. It takes a while for neighbors to get to know you —and trust you.

It's not as easy as you think to gain the confidence of the poor. They have their standards. Oh, yes, they will swarm around and take your material aid and even—poor souls!—do a little bowing and scraping to please you. But you will not sweeten their bitter bread. Indeed, bitter bread is all the bitterer when it comes without love. The poor look through your eyes and read your soul.

St. Vincent de Paul, the great apostle of charity, knew the poor well. The movie of his life, *Monsieur Vincent*, quotes him: "You will soon learn that charity is a heavy burden to carry, heavier than the kettle of soup and the basket of bread—that you must keep your gentleness and your smile. It is not enough to give soup and bread; that the rich can do. You are the little servant of the poor, the maid of charity, always smiling and in good humor. They are your masters, terribly sensitive and exacting, as you will see. But, the uglier and dirtier they are, the more unjust and bitter, the more you must give them of your love.

"It is only because of your love—only your love—that the poor will forgive you the bread you give them."

For several months Buzeta's women had been watching us. They saw us leave the big school each morning and walk the four blocks to church. They stood by stolidly when we tried to make friends with their children. It was a red-letter day for us, the morning that first little ragamuffin ran across the muddy street shouting, "Madre! Madre!" running to throw herself into Sister's arms. From then on, Buzeta's tough characters began to soften. Like the folks from Missouri, they had to be shown.

The school helps a lot. You can form a bread line, or give out clothes, or run a clinic. Then poor people come to you, take what they need and go away. They are too involved with their own troubles to bother much about you. But in a school they are touched in their family loves. A sweater given to Juanito quietly because Sister noticed that Juanito was shivering in the school yard —ah, that's a different sweater than the one Mama got when she stood in line at the relief agency. Sister's personal love for Juanito has gone into it.

One by one the Juanitos and Juanitas have been led to the storeroom on the second floor and there outfitted with what they need. One by one the Julitas have had help for their sick little Benitos. One by one the poor women and children of Buzeta have come to realize that the Maryknoll padres and madres are there in Christ's name. And (which is the idea behind it all) they have found that God loves them each—each one, personally and intensely. In that lies happiness and security.

Glorifying God with a Camera

Sister M. Noemi Weygant, O.S.B.

A postulant who was told to bring her camera and darkroom equipment with her to the scholasticate has become a professional photographer at St. Scholastica Priory in Duluth. As Sister Noemi Weygant, O.S.B., she has been a member of the Professional Photographers of America Association since 1957 and is the winner of several distinguished awards.

In 1957 when she entered her "Cloister Walk" in the association's annual photographic competition and exhibit, she won an international award. Each successive year has brought her both state and national awards: twenty-six state and four national awards in five years. In 1961 her "Raindrop Gems," a 1960 national award winner, was chosen to hang in the International Exhibit at the Museum of Science and Industry in Chicago. Later this picture was purchased by *Turtox News* for its June, 1961, cover. When the magazine appeared, Stanford University at once requested the negative with permission to use the picture for a mural. She has had three public exhibits to date.

Except for her year as a novice, Sister Noemi's chief work in the community has been photography. With equipment provided by superiors who consider this work a special apostolate, she serves

Stanbrook High School, the College of St. Scholastica, and the priory, taking pictures for two yearbooks, the local and diocesan newspapers, and general publicity purposes. In addition to pictures for brochures, television programs, and vocational literature, she may be asked in a single day to provide a portrait of a sister for the priory, produce slides for the Cancer Research Department, catch a group of college students on their way to a music meet, and film a high school basketball team in action.

The pictures she most delights in producing, however, and the pictures that win her awards, are unscheduled. They bring into focus some hidden or half-revealed bit of splendor she discovers in the woods and fields of the convent grounds: a daisy deep in grass next to a wild strawberry; the sun striking one side of a shaded prickly thistle; or lamplike stamens on the floor of a wide-open lily. She knows that when she can capture the real character of a beautiful object, the picture will manifest something of God.

Sister Noemi says of her work:

> This morning I was outside again, seeking wonder with the camera, and discovered a tiny bloom in the rocks by the Sacred Heart shrine—a wild flower that I had never seen there before, yellow as the buttercup, but having velvet instead of waxy petals. There is not a year that I do not locate something new growing; or discover something gone.
>
> Nature does not remain the same, and conditions which favor a particular plant this year will be against it next year; nevertheless, she is always active, and we know that the same chemical and physical forces that spin the stars through space are also causing a wild cucumber vine to climb in the sun with mathematical precision, or a lichen to form in the shape of a camel in the damp, shady woodlands.
>
> The earth is "clothed with majesty and beauty, robed in light as in a mantle," sang David in praise of the Creator. This light is to me what a brush is to a painter, in my efforts to glorify God with a camera lens.
>
> While photography is considered "speedy," and I can turn out a print for a news release as rapidly as can any camera man, the type of picture in which I specialize, and with which I win awards, requires considerable time in the producing. I work from many angles, and use—or reject—a number of me-

chanical and artistic means at my disposal. This process goes on out in the field and inside the darkroom. Always the goal is that the finished picture will inspire those who view it with thoughts of God.

This objective has now become important as an apostolic work, because my pictures have hung in exhibits in Chicago, New York, and Washington, D.C.—large cities with large camera-minded audiences. Many who see them, I know, hardly know God at all; and few, indeed, are those who ever thought of taking pictures that manifest Him, although they may be masters in another type of propaganda picture. So when I go out-of-doors with the camera, it is always in the spirit of looking. And I ask God for seeing.

Once I have found an object to photograph, I seek its most distinguished feature, and then set out to emphasize it. This means stressing detail, texture, form, imagery, design, composition, color tone, or a combination of several. While I do not favor distortion, neither do I hold myself within the restrictions of realism, because sometimes a mood or a feeling can be better gained with the abstraction. Sharpness is retained only where it is advisable, for in my mind the blurring off of an object can be most desirable; and in color pictures, it is especially effective.

While I am aware that art can stir men into action with ugliness, and good can be accomplished by portraying life's inequities, I am not called to such campaigning, even when I find examples of it in nature. I hold to the ideal of beauty in every picture I complete.

In 1957, when the Professional Photographers of America Association announced its annual photographic competition and exhibit, I submitted a picture and won an international award, which was considered phenomenal by the association, merely because I was a sister, so prevalent is the idea that the religious life is antique and stifling. That within the walls of the vineyard of the Lord there was soil so rich and rewarding that one of its growers could bring forth such fruit, has presented a new concept of the religious life to many who never imagined there was such earth—on earth. It prompts them to ask questions, and intelligent ones, about the religious life and the Catholic Church. When I attend photography conventions, I depart believing my pictures have had an inspiring effect on others, in the way St. Benedict intended our works should influence society.

The Nuns Who Catch
Fishermen

Robert M. Debevec

A letter from Texas stated, "Using your lures, I recently caught three bass on three casts." A Michigan fisherman wrote, "Your lures have changed me from an unlucky fisherman into a lucky one." Hundreds of letters like these have been directed to a small group of cloistered nuns, only one of whom has ever fished in her life.

The Franciscan Nuns of the Most Blessed Sacrament live in the picturesque Sancta Clara monastery just outside Canton, Ohio. They manufacture and sell (what else?) St. Peter's fishing lures. Their trade-mark is an angel, Little Michael, complete with boots, fishing net, rod and reel, wings, and a halo.

For many years Sister Mary Angelica has been interested in establishing a monastery of perpetual adoration in the South. Since the South is only about 2 per cent Catholic, Sister realized she would have to have a source of income to keep it going. There would be very little local alms. Then one day, two years ago, she thought about fishing bait.

"We'll start with a few red worms," Sister suggested to her superior, Mother Mary Veronica, enthusiastically. "Soon we'll have a cellarful. The potential is practically unlimited." But the vision of a cellarful of an unlimited potential of worms made Mother Mary Veronica apprehensive, and the rest of the Community thoroughly shared her uneasiness. It was decided that Sister Angelica should look for a solution not quite so wriggly.

Sister pondered and prayed. Then one day she read that the first artificial fishing lure had been invented by a Benedictine nun many centuries ago. That was more than enough for Sister. Mother Superior and the rest of the Sancta Clara Community had no objections to keeping squirmless lures on the premises.

Sister Angelica dug out the name of a prominent fishing-lure manufacturer and explained the whole situation as well as she could in a letter. Then, one day, a package arrived at the convent. Out poured hundreds of tiny barbed hooks, feathers, spinners, propellers, shiny plastic bodies in assorted colors, eyelets, swivels, and some objects that looked suspiciously like small grass skirts. The Sisters looked at the conglomeration at first in awe, and then in dismay. Sister Julian tentatively picked up a small treble hook, studied it, and pricked her finger.

Luckily, there were instructions with the package. They didn't make much sense at first, but with patience, prayers, and strained eyes, objects began to emerge that looked like something a starving fish might snap at.

"But, oh," said one of the nuns later, "what a beating our fingers took!"

As completed lures began to stockpile, Sister Angelica realized that she had to begin thinking about the next step: how to sell them. A Jewish businessman came to her rescue.

"Direct-mail advertising might do the trick," he suggested. "It's a good place to start, anyway." He donated $100 "to get the good work started."

Sister Mary Raphael, the artist of the group, decided on the trade-mark of the angel, "Little Michael," and prepared a catalogue and circulars. Sister Angelica wrote to a "list" company and bought 2,500 names and addresses of fishermen at $19 per thousand. Envelopes were stuffed with circulars, addressed, $20 worth of postage was applied, and the project was then entrusted to Uncle Sam's postal employees.

In the words of Sister Angelica, "We waited and waited." Finally it happened. An order came in from Michigan for a $1 lure. The Sisters felt that this was only the beginning. They were right.

Another order soon came in from Minnesota for another $1 lure; but that was all.

"People are suspicious," the businessman explained to the disappointed nuns. "Fishing lures from sisters? It would probably be better if you could approach the fishermen through some other channel. Some way so that the whole idea wouldn't be such a shock."

This gave the enterprising Sister Angelica another idea. She sent one of the circulars to the editor of *Our Sunday Visitor* in Huntington, Indiana. He printed a short article on the unusual project. A few other papers picked up the item, and suddenly the gates burst open.

A TV station in North Carolina gave the sisters a plug. Reporters from papers all over the country began writing in for news and pictures. Orders (and checks) deluged the Canton post office. To date, business has shown no sign of letting up.

Each lure purchaser reaps a spiritual bonus, according to Sister Angelica. "With every order," she says, "the fisherman gets a fervent prayer that he will have big catches, and that he will be protected from accidents."

The letters received from enthusiastic purchasers show that the fishing lures are effective both ways. Two fishermen wrote that they never knew Catholics were so nice. Later they decided to take instructions in the Catholic faith.

The sisters spend eight hours a day in prayer, but they have so far managed to keep up with thousands of orders for the "Sonic Double Action Flash," "Double Trouble," "Sputnik the 3rd," and "Baby Jig-It." Only recently worms came back into the picture, too. The sisters make a very lifelike plastic wriggler as a new item in their line. St. Peter's lures come in fifteen assorted styles now. By next year, the sisters expect to expand to twenty.

Sister Mary Angelica has realized her goal of a convent in Birmingham, Alabama.

The Secular Institute

William B. Faherty

The secular institutes are the least understood of the many stirring developments in the modern Church. Few people have even heard of them. Those few quite frequently draw mistaken conclusions.

The Catholic public cannot be blamed for this. The secular institutes are new to the American scene. They often prefer to work in a hidden way and hesitate to answer forthright questions about their status. They defy many generalizations. Some things which can be said about one may not be true of another.

Most require no distinct uniform. Many groups do not live in common residence. Others, such as the members of the Rural Parish Workers of Christ the King may share common quarters. Some do not have an extensive routine of common prayer. Many institutes have members of only one sex. Opus Dei has independent sections for men and for women.

Some secular institutes, such as the Society of Our Lady of the Way (an Austrian-based organization of professional women, which only recently spread to the United States) allow their members to pursue their own professions. Others assign individual members to an area of the institute's distinct apostolate. The Caritas, a potential secular institute, for instance, began with a great con-

169

cern for race relations and set up its first center in a Negro parish in Louisiana. The Rural Parish Workers of Christ the King concentrate their efforts on rural problems in Missouri.

One cannot even state universally that the members of secular institutes are lay people. Some institutes have priest members. Some are composed exclusively of priests.

The only generalization possible is this: they are apostolic societies properly numbered among the states of perfection and governed by Pope Pius XII's apostolic constitution, *Provida Mater Ecclesia*, of February 2, 1947. The whole life of their members "must be turned toward the apostolate." This apostolate must "be faithfully practiced not only *in* the world, but as *of* the world and therefore with avowed aims, practices, forms and in places and circumstances corresponding to this secular condition"—to quote the words of Pope Pius XII.

The best way to understand secular institutes is to look at one of them in action. The Oblate Missionaries of Mary Immaculate will admirably serve this purpose. This institute had its start in North America. It is the fastest-growing in the world. It includes various sections which pursue its spirit in distinct ways. These diverse sections approximate features of the lives of members of most secular institutes.

The Oblate Missionaries began in Canada in July 1952 under the direction of Father Louis M. Parent, O.M.I. Within eight years one thousand members came from seventeen nationalities and staffed 102 apostolic centers in seven countries. American activities radiate from Minnesota, Texas, Connecticut, Massachusetts, Maine, Vermont, and Rhode Island.

The oblate interns take vows, live together in groups, and undertake a wide variety of assigned apostolic activities, such as health care, catechetics, social service, and sponsoring homes for employed women. The oblate externs take vows, wear no distinctive uniform, and live and work in their own respective professions and environments. (Some, incidentally, are widows taking care of their children.) The lay missionaries promise several years of their life to foreign missionary work and receive the necessary training for this task. The auxiliaries, who may be married people, promise to live the spirit of the institute without vows, special residence, or distinct apostolate.

This spirit shows itself in the performance of a chain of spiritual duties—prayer, Mass, Rosary, and the like—and of the five points of charity: (1) the practice of the presence of God, (2) the avoidance of unnecessary criticism, (3) the absence of the spirit of complaint, (4) the acceptance of all possible assignments, and (5) the radiance of peace and joy by word and example.

Both interns and externs dedicate their lives totally and permanently to God by vows of obedience, poverty, and chastity. In the practice of obedience the intern offers her life entirely to the direction of her superiors. The extern remains her own master in part, according to a precise rule of life determined for each one before vows.

The practice of poverty also differs slightly between the interns and the externs. While both retain the ownership of their possessions, the intern must have permission for all expenditures while those of the extern are controlled by arrangements with her superior.

When a young lady enters as an intern, she is assigned at once to a certain work or given an opportunity to further her professional training. She must learn to face squarely those everyday difficulties which put a barrier to her perfection. And so she spends her formal formation period within a framework of apostolic activity. She is trained not by going into the prayerful seclusion of some country place, but by working under guidance as an apostle "in the world."

The training period includes six months as an aspirant, two years as a probationer, and the first five years of vows. The vows are renewed annually, even though the spirit of her dedication endures permanently.

The rapid growth of the oblates may amaze some people. It does not astound those who know young people's zeal "for the apostolate." Often young women will visit an oblate center for a few days. They look over the life at close hand. Nine out of ten remark: "This is exactly what I've been looking for; but I never knew it existed."

Pope Pius XII knew that young people were as generous today as at any time in the past. He knew also that traditional forms of Christian life did not answer the aspirations of all. That's why he so wisely approved this new estate in the Church.

A greater understanding of secular institutes on the part of all

Catholics will help forestall criticism and misunderstanding. Much of it has been based on misinformation.

Secular institutes have been undergoing a crossfire of criticism. Some critics call the members "religious beatniks," nonconformists who refuse to adapt themselves to normal ways of Christian living. Others complain that they do not go "all the way," that is, into the convent.

The first charge has often been made, usually by students of Catholic women's colleges. On investigation it evidently stems from the actions and especially the attire of members of a potential secular institute who talked at their school. These individuals seemed to see a symbol of unworldliness in looking frumpy or dowdy. A more chic (while not expensive) uniform or a better choice of clothes and hair-do, plus a touch of make-up for the more pallid ones, would have forestalled this unnecessary disaffection. Perhaps a better understanding of the place of material things in God's plan might help all concerned.

The second charge is more widespread and at first glance more sensible. "If I want to dedicate my life to God," many individuals have declared, "I want no halfway stages. I will enter religious life."

The secular institute is no halfway stage, but a distinct way of life. Many single people wish to work for God, but still have responsibilities to their family which a religious cannot meet. Some may not have the physical health to live the routine of conventual life. Or still others may be high-strung individuals who would not make good at community living.

Some individuals wish to engage in a wider apostolic work than the rules of most religious institutes allow. They might see great opportunities for good in community organizational work, for instance. Others believe that the traditional religious garb sets barriers to the performance of certain apostolic activities.

Some individuals might wish to use their God-given talents and specific training in a particular field of influence. Specialization in this particular area might be incompatible with the rules of religious institutes. A journalist investigated the way of life of several religious congregations in her region. None had provisions for a journalist. A secular institute has much to offer such a person.

A secular institute gives a definite pattern of life, a framework in which to serve God. It offers the opportunity for a formal dedication of life. It gives an individual the support of associates similarly ideal-conscious.

The secular institutes, then, form a special adaptation of the evangelical counsels to the particular needs of the present day. They offer great mobility with a minimum of formality and routine. They present a life dedication without change of chosen profession. They offer a varied apostolate. Their potential influence is without horizon.

VII

Tradition and Adaptation

Tradition and Adaptation

Religious institutes for women have been with us for a long, long time, but today they are experiencing a new awakening, owing chiefly to the constant exhortations and entreaties of Pope Pius XII. The key words are adaptation and formation. An excellent book on what the place of the active sister should be in the modern world is *The Nun in the World* by Cardinal Suenens, Newman Press, Westminster, Maryland.

Essentially, adaptation is a return to the beginning of each congregation, not to the old ways but to the original spirit and fervor of the foundress. This does not mean change for the sake of change or a relaxation in the strictness of the life. Sisters are asked to study the life of their foundress in the context of the times and conditions in which she lived and her ideal for the institute, and to harmonize their work with the age they live in, doing away with outmoded, nonessential customs which may hinder the present work. In 1950 Pope Pius XII told a meeting of heads of religious and secular institutes and Catholic societies:

> Hence, if you wish to walk in the footsteps of your predecessors, act as they acted. Examine thoroughly the beliefs,

convictions, and conduct of your own contemporaries; and, if you discover in them elements that are good, proper, make these worthwhile features your own; otherwise you will never be able to enlighten, assist, sustain, and guide the men of your own time.

The first thing that comes to mind when we speak of adaptation is the redesigning of the sisters' habits, although this is only one aspect of the changes which are taking place. Pope Pius XII spoke more than once on this matter, saying for instance, "The religious habit must always express consecration to Christ; it is this which everyone expects and wants. For the rest, let the habit be appropriate and correspond to the needs of hygiene." He also urged that the habit be simple. Somehow, by the time this filtered down to the laity, many of us expected that overnight, sisters would switch to secular dress or something very like it.

There are some congregations which wear up-to-date uniforms or dresses from the more or less recent past, among them the Mission Sisters of the Holy Ghost, Missionary Servants of the Most Blessed Trinity, Sisters of Social Service, Sisters of Service, Society of Christ Our King, Sisters, Home Visitors of Mary, and the Medical Missionaries of Mary. The Society of Our Lady of Providence was founded in 1955 with the aim of following the directives of the Holy See on modernization and adaptation. Their habit is a gray jumper and a white blouse with a simple black veil.

But for the most part the changes are not drastic. The elaboration of pleats is going out of style, sleeves are becoming narrower, veils are simpler, habits are slightly shorter, and headdresses are losing that antiquated look. Ears and hair are in some cases coming into view with the elimination of tight headpieces, which can cause ear trouble and headaches. Also leaving the scene are those blinders around the face which can be such an aid to custody of the eyes but a hazard when driving and an obstacle in the classroom. Some congregations have special headgear used only for driving. Sisters are finding other means than pins, with the constant pricking they entail, to hold themselves together. Some of the old habits weigh ten or fifteen pounds. The new habits mean less time spent in washing and starching, and inexpensive lighter-weight synthetic material assures greater comfort in summer and in hot climates (many missionary sisters wear white in the tropics) besides being healthier and easier to work in.

This is not to say that all congregations have restyled their habits. Some are already simple, hygienic, and practical. And religious institutes are not known for making hasty decisions. A habit is expected to last for years and it must be in a style that will endure. (Some of the habits adopted in the thirties look stranger than those centuries old.) The material used should still be available in years to come and, what is often more difficult, in a matching shade.

But perhaps the greatest obstacle to change is tradition. A sister's habit is a symbol of her religious life; she learns to love it from the day she receives it in a special ceremony and she refers to it as the "holy habit." While some sisters in a convent may want to make changes, others consider any criticism of the habit a criticism of the religious life itself. And there is a feeling of "If it was good enough for those who went before us, it's good enough for us." This same fondness for tradition can be an obstacle to changes in external customs which may go back hundreds of years. However, Pope Pius XII said, "Tradition is something entirely different from mere attachment to an irretrievable past. . . . While progress means the mere act of marching forward step by step, looking into an uncertain future, tradition conveys the idea of an uninterrupted march forward, which progresses both serenely and in a vital manner in accordance with the laws of life, and which solves the agonizing dilemma between youth and old age."

The modern dress of some of the newer congregations is not likely to replace the older styles. Each is an aid to a particular type of work and spirit. The long robes are a symbol of unworldliness to the sister and also to the laity, and for most girls thinking of entering the convent they seem to be an asset rather than a deterrent. Since habits were often originally based on the dress of the poor people of the period, at one time the sisters were indistinguishable from other women, but I doubt that many of us would like to return to that. Many people prefer an obvious difference between the religious and the laity—when they meet a sister, they like to know it. However, there are some who will respond more easily to a sister in a long black gown, and others to someone in a dress closer to their own.

Sisters are also urged to carry the same spirit of simplicity over to their external customs. Girls can understand giving up the world, as can be seen by the growth of the cloistered orders, but this is not synonymous with going back in time to practices that had meaning only in the culture of centuries ago. If the novices as a group find certain practices hilarious (that is, if they laugh at the practices themselves rather than at their own mishaps in trying to follow them) or infantile rather than edifying, then it should be time to take a good look at them to see if there is a reason and a need for them. Religious life should be simple and direct, not a jumble of meaningless and anachronistic customs.

There is no reason why each congregation should have the same set of rules. They have different work and purposes and each has a particular spirit of its own which, rightly, they wish to keep. But if the rules on eating when away from the convent, for example, mean that a sister has to go hungry for a day at a time, then something obviously is wrong. And if the foundress used the quickest means of transportation available in her time, it is possible that today she would use a car or a plane when necessary to expedite her work.

Pope Pius XII advised teachers to be "so well versed in all with which young people are in contact, in all which influences them, that their pupils will not hesitate to say: 'We can approach the sister with our problems and difficulties; she understands and helps us.' "

The world is changing very fast, especially for young people. Even their parents have difficulty in keeping informed on what is happening to them and how it affects them. The sister by her years of training in the novitiate and her way of life quickly becomes far removed from worldly things. But since she is working in the world and aims to help the people in it (and to encourage vocations from it), she must somehow keep abreast of current customs and events if she wants to be effective. She may in many cases deplore the way things are, but if she wants to bring Christ to the world, she must be aware, as Christ clearly showed He was, of just what the problems are. If a sister from a middle-class background is teaching the poor or doing social work among them, she should learn exactly what it means to be poor in today's world. If she is working with Puerto Ricans or Indians, she should learn about their traditions and background.

While we're on this subject, it might be said that lay people should not be too quick to criticize the nuns. People can validly claim that the sisters are too mysterious, although many sister-writers are trying to remedy this situation, but they should remem-

ber that the difference in goal and way of life of today's religious
and seculars does not make communication easy. While the religious are trying to come to a better understanding of the lay world,
it would be well for lay people to try to learn more about the
sisters' before carping. The same can be said for many priests who
have no clear idea of what a sister is and who can do a great deal
of harm when a girl comes to them for vocational advice.

Not allowing sisters home visits is a constant complaint of families of religious, although many active congregations do allow the
sisters to visit for a day at a time once or several times a year, or
for a few days every few years. The trend is to an increase in this
practice for sisters not in strict enclosure. It may or may not be
entirely beneficial to the sisters themselves, but it is certainly an
act of charity to their parents, who have also given up a great deal,
and it can lead to better understanding. Another complaint often
heard is that the teaching sisters are not sociable enough. They
could do much good, it is said, by visiting the families of their
pupils in the evening and attending more parish functions. At present the rules in most convents do not allow this and it is difficult
with the little time at the disposal of the sisters. It is hoped that
the role of active sisters in the modern world will soon be clarified.
At present there is much discussion and controversy on this point.

Another change that is being discussed is the elimination of
the separate class of lay sisters (mostly found in contemplative
orders, although not all cloisters have them; they should not be
confused with extern sisters), or at least some of the differences in
habit, work, and prayer. While something of a class system still
exists, people like to pretend that it does not, and expect the sisters
to carry out democratic ideals in this respect. Most young women
are used to the idea of housework these days; if they have not
shared in it themselves, at least they have seen their mothers at
it. Illiteracy is rare in America, and there would seem to be no
reason for the lay sister to be restricted in her prayers to an endless routine of Our Fathers and Hail Marys. The role of the lay
sister varies from order to order. She may take her part in perpetual
adoration and meditation and some other elements of the religious
life of the institute, and there is certainly nothing wrong with
domestic work. But when lay sisters are treated as something entirely separate and apart, there is always a danger for the others
to look on them as inferiors or servants. More and more, choir

nuns are taking at least a share in the housework. It may be that in some of the strictest orders, such as the Trappistines, lay sisters are necessary, although the Poor Clares manage to do without them. Being a lay sister could be a good vocation for someone who wants the cloister without the Latin or whose health cannot stand up to the strict regime. However, the Recluse Missionaries of Jesus and Mary, contemplatives, recite the Divine Office in English most days and chant it in Latin on Sundays and feasts, and there are several orders to supply the need of a less strict regime in a cloistered life, as well as those of the mixed life which combine domestic work with contemplation. It is difficult to understand the need for a separate class of lay sisters in a few active congregations when most of them manage to treat their cooks and housekeepers as an integral and equal part of the community, even where they demand less of them in educational requirements for entrance.

The prayer schedule is being improved in many of the active congregations, bringing it more in line with the official prayer life of the Church. Instead of one of the little Offices in Latin or English, or instead of stringing together litanies and novenas and other community prayers, which added slowly over the years can become cumbersome but difficult to stop, many active congregations are now enthusiastically using "A Short Breviary For Religious and the Laity," an abbreviated form of the Divine Office in English which is published by The Liturgical Press, Collegeville, Minnesota. The same publisher has an English-Latin edition of the full Breviary, and Benziger Brothers, Inc. published a complete office in English. Sisters who formerly prayed in Latin often find that the English gives new life to their prayer, although the Latin is considered more beautiful for chanting and contributes to the universality of Church prayer. There is also a movement toward more variety and independence in books for spiritual reading and meditation, with each sister choosing her own instead of being limited to a community book, and this of course necessitates a good selection of books. Unfortunately many convents do not have much money for this purpose.

Good spiritual directors are often hard to come by and the sisters need excellent direction, not only in their early training, but throughout their lives. They have turned to modern means to solve this problem by having exceptionally good priest-directors record their talks and sending these records across the country.

Great stress is placed today on sister formation, or training for all the aspects of her life. Because the world is getting worldlier and more complex, the spiritual and professional training of the sisters is increasingly important. Sisters are becoming more involved in a world that is, as never before, opposed to the ideals by which they live. They must bring Christ to a society that fears fallout more than God, considers charity a cold and arid word, and rests its faith and hope on the dollar. Teachers and nurses must meet the state's higher standards for their professional training, the sisters are taking a greater part in professional organizations, their work involves greater responsibility and initiative, often entailing travel and the handling of money, and still they must conform to the spirit of religious obedience and poverty.

The sister must understand and be aware of her role as a woman, a Christian, a sister, an apostle, and a professional worker, and of how all these roles harmonize together to perfect each other, so that one aspect of her life will not draw her away from the others. In order to accomplish this, her formation or training must be careful and thorough. Otherwise, owing to exhaustion from overwork or the constant tension that her work may entail, with the resultant difficulty in keeping up her prayer-life, she may become cynical, lose her vocation, or settle for going through the motions and following the letter of her rule rather than its spirit. Her training must enable her to maintain a proper balance between her exterior and interior lives or she may become guilty of what Pope Pius XII called the "heresy of activity."

The demand for better training for teaching-sisters is nothing new. Throughout this century bishops have been urging it, and many communities set up their own training centers. Sisters began to teach during the week and attend school themselves on Saturdays and throughout the summer, some of them having physical or mental breakdowns in the process. But as the demand for higher training and the need for more and more sisters in the schools and hospitals increased, congregations found they could not begin to satisfy both. Sisters were sent out to teach without the proper training. Today the emphasis is on better all-round training at whatever financial sacrifice or temporary shortage of personnel on the job. Congregations are refusing to staff new schools and hospitals or, if necessary, are cutting down on present activities until adequately trained sisters are available.

But there is still too much overwork and too little pre-service training in many congregations, and sisters are often compelled for years to study evenings after a hard day's work or on week-ends and spend entire summers in taking courses and retreats. Since their work is of such importance, the quantity of work done should not be at the expense of quality. The sisters need time for prayer, for preparation of the next day's work, and for keeping their professional knowledge up to date. The vacation idea is gradually catching on, with some communities setting up special vacation areas where sisters can get a real rest and change. The sisters in the Society Devoted to the Sacred Heart spend their two-week vacation at the lake, fishing, swimming, and hiking.

The usual professional training today, received either before or while on the job, is the B.A. degree for elementary teachers, master's degree for some high school and many college teachers, with some college teachers receiving the Ph.D. Sister-nurses often obtain a B.Sc. degree and sometimes a master's. The formation program after the novitiate is often referred to as the juniorate.

Collaboration on a worldwide, national, and regional level has been a great aid to the sister formation movement and to adaptation. It has enabled superiors to get together to talk about their common problems and ways of solving them, to exchange information and ideas, to avoid competition and duplicated efforts, to work together effectively, and to combine their resources in setting up training centers. More and more new and expanded educational facilities are being provided.

Sisters from such areas as India, Burma, Peru, and Brazil are being given free training in teaching, nursing, science, and other professions at thirty Catholic colleges in the United States.

Regina Mundi is the name of a new pontifical institute for women in Rome, for members of religious orders and secular institutes and other women, with courses given in several languages. This school provides excellent training for those who will themselves be instructing sisters or novices or who will be teaching religion in high school and college.

Sisters studying at the Center of Intercultural Formation at Cuernavaca, Mexico, must wear secular clothes, since religious habits are forbidden in that area. This school, established by Monsignor Ivan Illich of New York in cooperation with Fordham University, is for lay and religious missionaries to Latin America and provides a rigorous training for rigorous work. The setting gives the students a better preparation for working and living in a completely different culture. The study of the language is intensive, and there are also courses in history, geography, and so on. The students work in the local slum areas as part of their training.

Information about the training in particular religious institutes can be found in the *Official Guide to Catholic Educational Institutions and Religious Communities in the United States,* which is published annually by the Catholic Institutional Directory Company, 370 Seventh Avenue, New York 1, New York, and sponsored by the Department of Education of the National Catholic Welfare Conference.

Since her goal is to become "another Christ," all of a sister's religious life is in a true sense a formation and it must be continued during all her years of work. To make sure that her active work does not overwhelm the spiritual side of her life, many congregations are introducing the tertianship. Sisters are brought back to the motherhouse after years on the missions (a mission in a sister's vocabulary is her working assignment, whether in her own country or abroad) and undergoes a sort of second novitiate or spiritual renewal. Many sisters, of course, do return to the motherhouse each summer for retreats, but this is something much more than a retreat.

A look at two congregations, one very new and the other over a hundred years old, will serve to exemplify some of the changes that are taking place.

The Congregation of the Divine Spirit, founded in 1955 in Pennsylvania, already has seventy sisters and many novices and postulants. The sisters wear a very modern outfit, even to their shoes, and their hair is also worn in a fashionable style. Their work includes teaching (one of their goals is to work in areas that have few parochial schools), nursing, social work, caring for the aged, catechetics, home visiting, and diocesan and college business administration. Their prayer is both mental and vocal. They receive their professional training at various colleges and universities. After five years they make an annual home visit. Older candidates are considered.

The Marist Missionary Sisters originated in France in 1845 as the first society of women dedicated solely to active service in the foreign missions. In 1922 they were established in the United

States, where they now have more than two hundred sisters. The Marists had already made some alterations in their habit just before the Pope's instructions in this matter but instead of taking it for granted that they had already complied, they reconsidered and made still more changes. The new black habit is simple and graceful and of a lighter-weight material. Thorough mission training is given at the novitiate and continued on the missions; teachers, doctors, dentists, nurses, medical technicians, and so on, receive their training at various colleges and schools; domestic workers take a course at the Fanny Farmer Cooking School; language courses are taken at the Berlitz School of Languages; and art instruction is taken by correspondence from the Famous Artists School. After as many as ten or twenty years on the missions, the sisters return from their posts for a six months' spiritual renewal at the motherhouse.

It has already been shown that adaptation and formation inspire new vocations to the religious life. But it would be a mistake to think that this will entirely solve the sister shortage. There is also a great shortage of secular nurses and teachers, with fewer girls entering these professions, and others leaving during or after their training. There have been many reasons offered for this condition, some of them the same as those given for the shortage of sisters, such as the emphasis today on material things and an unwillingness to give of oneself.

Adaptations have taken place, are taking place, and will continue to do so. New congregations will spring up, and a few old and stolid ones will die a slow death as they fail to get new recruits. Unfortunately others will also be in danger of facing this fate, since their work does not bring them into contact with likely candidates, and girls ordinarily choose an order with which they are familiar. The secular institutes, which have their own particular function, and the long hoped-for apostolate of the laity, when it comes to pass, will be complementary to, but not replacements of, the sisterhoods.

Much of the material in this book may indicate that the religious life is a hard life. And it is. It is a life of great sacrifice and a corresponding joy, of trials and the grace to meet those trials, and an enduring challenge. Perhaps the least of a sister's compensations is her assurance of constant care, food, clothing, and shelter, which become the responsibility of her order. But her daily sacrifice and self-denial seem bizarre in our age of comfort, luxuries, and the endless scramble after security and happiness. And yet no matter how desperately we chase after these elusive goals, most of us fail in our search. The nun on her knees in the cloister, the white-robed nursing sister, the black-robed sister behind the teacher's desk, the missionary at her post or in prison—all could tell us, and are trying to tell us, how to find what we are seeking, not from around us but from within.

A woman who enters the convent gives up marriage to become the bride of Christ; she gives up bearing children to become a mother to the world; she gives up her own possessions, will, and self to gain salvation for her soul and for ours.

Sister Formation

Robert A. Broenen

Plan-laden briefcases at their sides, topflight sister educators spent this past summer scurrying from motherhouse to campus to workshop session, talking up the latest developments and encouraging further advances in a movement which will one day touch the lives of every sister—and indirectly every Catholic school child—in the United States: the Sister Formation Movement.

The manifestations of its progress to date are many: new programs of study for young nuns—even whole campuses set aside solely to train sisters—are springing up; summer sessions in everything from spirituality to international affairs are attracting ever larger clusters of superiors, deans, and mistresses; a training period called the "juniorate" is becoming widespread in the 377 communities in the United States; some of the best theological and religious minds in the Church are expending their efforts to probe and improve sister training.

Yet the term Sister Formation still has a strange ring to millions of persons whose lives will be influenced by it, although it has stood as a name for an idea, a movement, and an organization for better than a half-dozen years.

Stated simply, Sister Formation is a nationwide campaign to

make sisters more saintly, skilled, and mature, and thereby more efficient in the face of ever greater demands on the Church unaccompanied by a commensurate increase in vocations.

The movement is best seen against the broad background of a world-wide drive to renovate and adapt all religious orders to modern times, as requested by the Holy See over ten years ago.

At that time Pope Pius XII voiced specific pleas for "excellence" of training for sisters in spirit, mind, and character, and that they equal or outstrip laymen in the secular fields in which they exercise their apostolate.

Addressing the General Congress on the State of Perfection, in December, 1950, he said: ". . . Catholic Sisters who nurse the sick . . . may at times be inferior to others in technical advantages, and we take this occasion to urge them not only to keep abreast of others in this matter but even to surpass them."

To the First International Convention of Teaching Sisters the following year he also spoke firmly: "Many of your schools are being described to me as being very good. But not all. It is our fervent wish that all endeavor to become excellent. This presupposes that your teaching sisters are masters of the subjects which they expound. See to it, therefore, that they are well trained. . . ."

The Church's great need of fully formed sisters is apparent. In education we see their importance to the Church's mission. In this age of the lay apostolate, how can the lay members of the Mystical Body of Christ be fully developed as apostles unless those who train them are spiritually, intellectually, and professionally trained to a high degree? And who, other than the parents, are to play a key role in training young Catholics to assume their full share in the Church's mission, if not the sisters?

Priests and brothers in education will readily concede that some 96,000 nuns have the major part in developing the mind and character of nearly five million young people in U.S. Catholic grade and high schools.

And if the products of these schools are to be zealous Christians and effective, integrated individuals, how much more so must the sisters who train them? Indeed, they must be "super-apostles," as one leader in the Sister Formation Movement has put it.

At the time the Holy See issued its mandate, sister training in the United States was less than ideal. In the teaching orders the growth of schools far outstripped the vocation gain; and sisters were by and large being sent to full-time teaching directly from the novitiate.

The practice was harmful to the sister in a number of ways, in turn lowering the efficiency of the school and the level of training of the pupils.

Professionally, the young nun suffered because she began teaching without attaining her bachelor's degree, which by today's state standards is considered minimal preservice training. She also faced the painful—and lengthy—summer-school road to her sheepskin.

Intellectually, the youthful sister lacked the broad training in liberal arts so helpful in seeing life in perspective—especially necessary for a nun, who must have a full appreciation of the social and apostolic character of her mission.

And spiritually, the recent novice, still in the formative and probationary period of her temporary vows, found her half-realized religious development challenged by the sudden return to secular cares and interrupted routine.

For some the sudden and serious test to their vocations was too great. For others the new tasks and trials tended to stunt their anticipated spiritual growth.

Further, a resulting dilemma was clear to major superiors: By pressing into service their small numbers of new sisters before they were fully formed, communities were lowering each nun's efficiency—when efficiency was the only likely means of compensating for paucity of number!

This was the challenge facing sister educators who pored over the Vatican's statements in the summer of 1952: to train their young members to excellence—as religious, as professional persons, as apostles—regardless of the cost to their communities' ongoing work.

The price would be high.

Such a program would mean taking their top-quality personnel from key jobs so they could plan and execute a "blue chip" training program for relatively small numbers of aspiring nuns. It would mean extending the formative full-time training period of the new religious, thus delaying the entry of new personnel into the communities' teaching, nursing, and social-work programs for one to three, maybe more, years. It would mean outlays of always scarce funds for training teachers, planning curricula, building facilities for such training.

But the challenge was met willingly, even eagerly. In fact, leading sister educators a decade before the Pope's plea had become concerned with the level of teacher training and, as a result of national studies, had by 1948 established a Teacher-Education section of the National Catholic Educational Association.

It was this section which provided the machinery necessary for implementing the Sister Formation Movement.

The history of the movement is short but packed with progress. Briefly traced, here is what has happened:

Studying Pope Pius' words that summer of 1952, several leading sister educators volunteered to complete an accurate, up-to-date survey of training for nuns across the nation.

Heading up the volunteer committee was the dynamic Sister Mary Emil, I.H.M., of Marygrove College in Monroe, Michigan.

Her group distributed a questionnaire to 377 major superiors in the United States, with disturbing results. Replies showed that of the 255 communities reporting, only 13 had programs in operation leading to the bachelor's degree. And 118 replied that they had neither educational facilities of their own to train their subjects nor easy access to such facilities in Catholic colleges!

Alarmed by such a state, the committee discussed the problem with Catholic school superintendents at the 1953 NCEA convention. They agreed to expand the committee and schedule regional conferences on the problems uncovered.

The following year, the NCEA gave official support and status to the movement by setting up its Committee on Sister Formation —an outgrowth of the survey committee—headed by Sister Mary Emil. That summer Operation Bootstrap, as some dubbed it, took itself up another hitch when Sister Mary Emil and an equally enthusiastic companion, Sister Ritamary Bradley, C.H.M., of Ottumwa Heights College, in Ottumwa, Iowa, took to the road to set up the regional conferences. Traveling some 25,000 miles, they thumped for the talks at about 150 communities.

Their trip paid off. The first round of Sister Formation Conferences was held in six regions of the United States during that fall and winter. In them, superiors, deans, and mistresses of novices sought to determine the mind of the Church in the formation of their members.

The outcome of their efforts was compiled into a volume by

Sister Ritamary, and the stage was set to build upon this progress with a new round of talks. So the next year the regional conferences analyzed the intellectual and spiritual elements they found essential for the training of young sisters.

By the summer of 1956 the conference leaders were ready to begin implementing the educational theory that was taking shape.

What took place at Everett, Washington, that summer now stands as a landmark in the short history of the Sister Formation Movement.

For three months fifteen sisters, each an expert in her field, plus a dozen part-time educational consultants, hammered out what they considered to be an ideal curriculum for the integrated training of sisters. The program was designed to blend in proper proportions a broad intellectual training and a specialized professional program, both unified and given apostolic meaning and motivation by an intensive spiritual development.

Two centers which would demonstrate the experimental curriculum were set up—one by the Sisters of Charity of Providence in conjunction with the University of Seattle, the other by the Sisters of St. Francis of Rochester, Minnesota, at St. Teresa's College in nearby Winona.

Results of the Everett workshop were discussed at the 1956–57 regional conferences, with an eye toward improving the proposed curriculum or adapting it to the missions and programs of varying communities.

The conferences took another major step forward the following year, when they concentrated their efforts on building up an understanding of the value of a juniorate program and how to administer it. The talks were built around a report by the Rev. Elio Gambari, S.M.M., a member of the Sacred Congregation for Religious. Father Gambari, who is an expert in the organization of religious communities of women, in this report stressed the obligatory character of juniorate training in the eyes of the Holy See.

These talks proved so successful that the Sister Formation committee urged Father Gambari to prepare an outline of a complete, integrated program for the spiritual formation of sisters all the way through the postulancy, novitiate, and juniorate.

The program he proposed formed the backbone of a summer course for mistresses of nuns in training, which was held at the two Sister Formation colleges.

In the 1958–59 talks the regional leaders turned their attention to a new area: How could they upgrade the level of spiritual and intellectual training of the thousands of sisters now in full-time service, many of them long past their formal training and their final profession?

More important than the details of the movement's history, however, are the human gains that have been made in this time.

Certainly the primary accomplishment of the Sister Formation Movement has been that it has created a nation-wide awareness among leaders of sister communities of the need to improve their members' training—and it has given them the confidence that comes from pursuing a common goal.

Concrete evidences of progress toward that goal are many.

The most obvious, and among the most significant, is the popularization of the juniorate period in sister training.

The juniorate has been praised by Arcadio Cardinal Larraona, secretary of the Sacred Congregation for Religious, as "the final achievement of a desire that had long been cherished by the Church, a guarantee to all sisters of a formation which would be integral and complete from every point of view—human, Christian, intellectual, professional, religious and apostolic."

The purpose of the juniorate is to provide several years of training after the novitiate to develop the spiritual principles the new sister has learned while bringing her to a high level of competence before she enters full-time service.

As Cardinal Larraona observed, "Formation and preparation for perpetual vows must be continued after the completion of the novitiate. The novitiate imparts a formation that is fundamental but of its very nature, incomplete. . . . There is need for the deepening and development of that quality of strength which even during a well-made novitiate has only begun to grow."

The 1957–58 conferences sought to fill in the broad outlines for a juniorate program for any community.

Generally it was agreed that each community should have its own juniorate if possible. If not, communities could pool their resources for a program together. The junior sisters should live and study apart from the professed community and the novices as well, to be free from unnecessary distractions and pressures. Classes should be conducted for junior sisters apart from lay students, even though many juniorate programs would operate in conjunction with colleges run by the community. "It is important," Cardinal Larraona observed in this regard, "that these studies be carried out in an atmosphere that is permeated with a supernatural spirit, so that the juniors come to realize that they are sister-students and not mere student-sisters." College-level courses in the juniors' major fields of service, such as teaching, nursing, or social work, would be conducted in the traditional sequence toward the bachelor's degree.

But the junior sisters' spiritual development would be primary during the two- or three-year period. Religious exercises similar to those for novices would continue. Spiritual guidance would be regular, with a mistress of junior sisters playing the all-important role of cultivating their development step by step through instruction, exhortation, and—above all—example.

A primary aim of the mistress would be to widen the apostolic outlook of the junior nuns. The human and spiritual needs of the world's people would be surveyed in the light of the doctrine of Christ's Mystical Body. The liturgy would be explored as the social implementation of one's individual spiritual life. The community's mission would be explained in relation to the whole work of the Church.

Such objectively oriented training, agree the experts, can go a long way toward dispelling a romanticized or self-centered view of one's vocation!

Another aim of the juniorate training is to develop in the recent novices a mature understanding of their vow of obedience, without which their human and apostolic effectiveness can be seriously impaired. Unquestioning submission to the order's rule is stressed in the novitiate. But the junior sister must be encouraged to cultivate her initiative and creativity, and exercise them within the limits of the community's rule. She must learn that initiative is simply the exercise of her practical intelligence, which, along with her will and all her other faculties, she has put at the disposal of God through her community.

And the two Sister Formation colleges which grew out of the Everett workshop are flourishing. A third Sister Formation college has been established at Normandy, Missouri. Marillac College, conducted by the Daughters of Charity of the St. Louis Province, was founded by Sister Catherine, D.C., who since their formal organization under the NCEA in 1957 has served as chairman of the Sister Formation Conferences. Marillac, like the Seattle college, is a co-operative effort, with sisters from fifteen different communities forming a faculty which teaches aspirants to different orders in a five-year program.

Nor is only the preservice sister's training benefiting; new attention is being focused on the problems of the teaching sister—her professional training, her general knowledge, her spiritual and mental health. And some communities have even gone beyond the inservice sister's problems, developing institutes and seminars for retired nuns to help them realize that they, too, have a useful part in the life of the community and the Church.

Many communities are now beginning to experience the effects of the juniorate training they have installed or revitalized in terms of those sisters' increased capabilities as teachers, nurses, and social workers. And a bonus benefit has been this: Among juniorate-trained sisters, a much smaller percentage are leaving the religious life before speaking their final vows—most likely because they better understand their vocation and are better equipped spiritually and professionally to pursue it.

This, of course, does something to ease the sister shortage. Furthermore, communities that have installed or improved a juniorate program have experienced a new flourishing of vocations. Apparently the promise of a more complete training is an allurement to capable young women and helps convince parents that their daughters' talents will be developed to the fullest in the religious life.

These, then, are some of the present gains in Sister Formation. What of its future?

Instrumental in guiding its program for the immediate future will be Sister Annette Walters, C.S.J., new executive secretary of the conferences. She succeeds Sister Emil, who has served three years in that capacity.

Sister Annette, chairman of the psychology department at the College of St. Catherine in St. Paul, Minnesota, has been active in the movement since 1954.

She spent the past summer canvassing the country, preparing for a new project in Sister Formation: a program for the graduate training of selected sisters, many of whom will then staff Sister Formation centers.

Nor will she neglect the basic program of perfecting the integrated spiritual and professional training of sisters throughout the United States.

The 377 communities of sisters in the United States have established the Sister Formation Program, she said, hoping "to use all their resources for the enrichment of America, increasing vocations and extending the Church's work of mercy throughout the world.

"Our goal is excellence," she says intently. "Nothing short of it."

West Point for Nuns

Edward Wakin

Hidden from traffic racing along Natural Bridge Road to and from the St. Louis airport, a streamlined, glass library occupies the site of an old baseball diamond in the middle of an unusual college success story. The library's glass walls, which slant inward like four playing cards resting on their sides, give away the story immediately, for visible inside are the students at Marillac College in suburban Normandy. They are all nuns, not from one religious order, but from twenty-five different orders, thirty-one states, and a few foreign countries.

Marillac (pronounced Maryac) regards itself as a West Point for nuns, a religious "service academy" where higher education is pursued for, of, and by nuns. The same spirit of unity that envelops future admirals and generals studying at their academies infects Marillac, though, of course, religious ideals replace patriotism as the guiding principle.

Most of all, Marillac is a nun's place, a shining, modern $5.5 million place on an 180-acre estate where college life is lived to its fullest in a nun's habit. In this sense Marillac is a college like any other, but it is also unique because of its position at the forefront of the Sister Formation Movement, which aims at improved training of nuns. Ultimately, some 170,000 U.S. nuns are involved in the consequences of the movement, as well as six million students in Catholic elementary and high schools who come under the influence of nuns in the classroom.

Marillac, aware of the stakes and its role, prizes its sudden success as a new college whose first degrees were awarded only four years ago. Yet, it already has achieved accreditation with highest commendation from the North Central Association of Secondary Schools and Colleges, the same prestige accreditation accorded undergraduate studies at Chicago or St. Louis Universities. Moreover, the Sacred Congregation for Religious in Rome has singled out the college for special praise.

Both accolades stem from Marillac's pursuit of excellence under the aegis of the Sister Formation Movement, which has come to the fore in the past ten years in response to directives from Pope Pius XII stressing the best possible training tailored for religious. Many orders established special college programs for their members, but the Daughters of Charity of St. Louis Province went a few giant steps further. They not only built Marillac for their own members but opened its classroom doors—free of charge—to religious communities throughout the country. Besides the twenty-five orders represented in the student body of 350, a cross-section of fifteen different orders have members on the faculty.

Both students and faculty are enthusiastic about Marillac's prevailing principle that nuns are best served by a special college integrating their development according to a four-fold formula embracing the spiritual, intellectual, social, and apostolic. In student terms, it is usually expressed by a sense of belonging; they are not left out, whether it's class discussions, student elections, or a school play. In faculty terms, it means teaching in terms of the particular needs of nuns; classes do not stray into examples, side issues, or discussions remote from a nun's life. In short, Marillac is a college with distractions and irrelevancies removed and with every part of the program directed to formation of the complete religious. Up close the Marillac atmosphere is noticeably serious and studious but not pretentious or bookish. The young nuns never forget their commitment, but they don't wear it self-consciously. They feel that the controlled environment at Marillac enables them to be natural about their special vocation, and from all appearances they remain college girls: feminine, exuberant, hard-working, and absorbed in the bits and pieces of college life—assignments, exams, extracurricular activities, faculty and campus idiosyncrasies.

The nun-students keep campus life whirling around intramural sports, student elections, club activities, and outings. (There was the time the Daughters of Charity got caught in the rain during a picnic and returned home with their soaring, starched bonnets drooping.) As one nun remarked, "We have practically everything except athletic scholarships and Saturday night dances."

The young nuns continually refer to the fact that they are not innocent bystanders as they would be in a college with lay students. They become student officers, perform in plays, and run the school newspaper, including the nun-photographer who leaps forward, camera in hand, and startles visiting lecturers with, "Hold it. Just one more." Before you can comment on all these aspects of collegiate life, you are faced repeatedly with the rhetorical question: "Would a nun ever become school president in another college?" Then it dawns on you that you never thought a nun would even be interested.

According to the college newspaper, which reflects student exuberance, "A Marillac student has the energy of IBM, the perseverance of a mosquito, the curiosity of a psychiatrist, the neatness of a pin, and the speed of a jet as she goes from one class to another in a single minute." A Daughter of Charity teaching sociology was more sober, describing Marillac students as typical American girls with middle-class backgrounds. They are realistic and avoid oversimplifying their approach to life. They retain their individual interests and personality and don't aspire to fit into any stereotyped version of a nun.

For Daughters of Charity, who comprise about two-thirds of the student body, Marillac provides a five-year program, with the novitiate year coming between freshman and sophomore years in the college. Students from other orders normally enter in their sophomore year and live off campus in their own juniorates under the supervision of a mistress. This enables the young nuns to maintain the distinctive spirit of their orders. Moreover, Marillac turns the nuns over to the rules of their respective orders every day between noon and three o'clock, producing a kaleidoscopic round of religious life manifested in twenty-five different ways.

Inside the college's shiny new classrooms, the students enjoy an unusual student-teacher ratio, an average of one teacher for every eight students. Twenty-seven of the forty-four faculty members are Daughters of Charity; over-all the faculty has earned degrees from fifty different colleges. According to the faculty, nun-students distinguish themselves by high academic motivation and lively class discussions.

Marillac's president, Sister Bertrande Meyers, who spelled out her dream of a special college for nuns in her doctoral thesis twenty years ago, emphasizes that Marillac is a school where the undesirable extremes of a nun's education are studiously avoided: being overprotected or ignored. Backing her up, the bulletin of the Sister Formation Movement has cited "the misguided kindness that has often led directors and teachers of sisters' summer sessions to make things just a little easier for 'the poor sisters.' " Moving her hands up and down in her characteristic way of making a point, Sister Bertrande speaks directly: "It isn't what I wear but what I do that merits respect. No sister goes out of here until she has earned her degree and learned that lesson."

Nothing sets off a flurry at Marillac like the composite charge that it is "raising hot-house plants by spoon-feeding nuns in an isolation booth off the main road." Sister Bertrande, who leads the attack on ivory towers for nuns, stresses regular and repeated student contacts with the community. Besides field trips which range from art museums to sewage plants, the nun-students do practice teaching, nursing, and welfare work throughout the St. Louis area. For good measure a parade of guests appears on campus, ranging from Slavic dancers and symphonic trios to lecturers on comparative religion who have covered Judaism, Lutheranism, Anglicanism, Presbyterianism, the Methodists, and the Baptists.

In the last analysis Marillac uses theology as its North Star. A student may earn a B.A. in history or English or a B.S. in biology, chemistry, physics, natural science, mathematics, psychology, sociology, or nursing. But in spirit, emphasis, and orientation, as well as required studies, the college program is kept on a straight course. As stated by the college catalogue and echoed by Sister Bertrande, philosophy and theology are "the strong undergirding for the sister's total formation, emphasizing theology as the unifying principle and the most potent means of integrating all the other elements of her formation."

The most compelling testimonials for Marillac's tailor-made education can't be hung on the wall. Yet its small number of nun alumnae have sent back good report cards from their graduate studies, testifying to the quality of the Marillac preparation. One chemistry graduate ran up a string of fourteen straight A's at De-Paul University. But their numbers are still small; there were thirty-six graduates in both 1959 and 1960, slightly more than fifty in 1961 and 1962. While the accrediting inspectors and the prefect of the Sacred Congregation for Religious have put their approbation on paper, it is the students who fill in the spaces between the lines with their enthusiastic remarks.

A faculty member might point out to the visitor that young nuns are being successfully trained elsewhere, but as far as the students are concerned there is no place like Marillac. They describe their reactions in the straightforward, natural talk of young ladies who know what they are about. And, invariably, they get around to the fact that Marillac is specially designed for them. Their remarks stand as the best summary of Marillac:

"I attended a girls' college as a religious for two years before coming here. As to having all nuns in the school, I just love the idea myself. In classes, we all have the same aim and the same purposes, and we're all going to face the same problems. The teachers can integrate everything and use examples from the religious life. At the same time, we are not so insulated that we don't know what's going on in the outside world."

"Here, we are getting the four-fold objective of the college—apostolic, intellectual, social, and spiritual, all integrated into a whole."

"It seems the big point here is that there is no separation between our intellectual and spiritual life."

Then two Marillac seniors looking ahead to postgraduation challenges add: "We go out of Marillac with gratitude and love and hope that we will do what we are supposed to do."

"People expect so much of you when you are from Marillac. It's going to be a bigger challenge."

Doffing the Bonnets

Sister M. Roberta, o.s.u.

"Gee, Sister, you got a crew cut!" That was only one of the startled (and startling) greetings that I had to face when my classes resumed after the Christmas holidays. I had to march into the classroom wearing the new coronet, or headpiece, which my community (the Ursulines of Paola in Kansas) had donned with the new year.

Our old bonnet, inherited from French peasant ancestry, was large and boxy; it framed the face with an old-world starchiness that many people liked. For us who wore it, it could be bothersome to sew in, though it was easy enough to wear. Our new coronet is simple, modest, "humble-looking."

The change of style itself has not been a difficult experience, but coming back to school in midterm with the New Look was a real trial by fire. Any nun who survived that ordeal deserves the Purple Heart.

I happened to meet one of our sophomores in a department store the Saturday before the close of the holidays. He is the kind of youngster who could shake the hand of a statue and get a friendly response. He did a double take; then, as we talked, he looked at the floor, above my head, to the left, to the right, but never directly at me. Finally I couldn't let him suffer any longer.

"Royce, you're a typical man!" I said. "For the first time in years I get a new hat, and you don't even notice."

"Oh, my gosh, is that it?" he exclaimed with considerable relief. "I thought you had forgotten something."

In our little community, Reverend Mother had wanted to be sure that every sister would be happy about any change in the habit. Among the sisters there was a wide range of points of view. The middle-youthful section of the community urged, designed, and hoped. The older sisters occupied various areas of opposition, from "I'll die in my holy habit" to "Well, show us some samples—if you dare."

The novices, who normally will wear the New Look longer than most of us, loved the habit they associated with their vocation, and were reluctant to change. Postulants were not consulted, but being postulants they voiced their hopes unasked: they wanted to be received into the "old habit," as it now was being called.

Committees, both lawfully appointed and self-appointed, got to work. Designs for headgear resembling poke bonnets, jockey caps, and beanies were produced, modeled, laughed over, and discarded. Finally Reverend Mother announced that there would be a "style show" to help us arrive at a decision. The date: the day after the end of summer retreat. Now we were getting somewhere.

Seven sisters modeled the new designs. Never were Powers models so scrutinized as these sisters were. Every so often one of the models would remove her headdress to let some sister with the "lean and hungry look" try it on. Then, to complete the test, a round-faced sister would model it, too.

Most of the entries were well made and withstood the test of being transferred from one head to another. To my chagrin, my brain child (a simple white band with balance of veil) fell ingloriously over the nose of Model No. 7.

The fashion show ended in voting and laughter, but there was still no action. The Ursulines, like Holy Mother Church, move slowly.

Then, at Christmas, came a letter from our superior. We would change with the new year, it said. A pattern had been chosen. It contained parts of all the best designs shown in August.

Everyone who could do so got home to the motherhouse for the holidays. The community room, festive with its huge fir tree emblazoned with lights and liturgical designs, had to take second place to the workshop. The measuring, cutting, punching, and fitting of the New Look was in full swing.

The hesitant oldsters no longer wished to die in their old bonnets. In fact, they were the first to wear the coronets into the refectory. One by one the last critics changed their minds as they felt the comfort of the simple veil. Each evening saw a longer row of sisters getting the "feel" of the new habit before actual community adoption.

Then, on New Year's Eve, came a beautiful admonition from our superior. "Tomorrow we will all appear on New Year's Day in our new headdress. May you wear it with joy and simplicity, and put aside any little woman's vanity that entered into the change. Let the change remind us that we must effect a change of heart also. We will do so by putting off the old self and putting on the new, by living every moment with Christ in His Mystical Body. As we worked together to make our new headdress, so may we continue to work during the year, selflessly pushing forward toward our common goal, the salvation of the souls of those entrusted to our care."

And so the new habit was blessed. We like it. In the new coronet no rain can melt us, no ironing can scorch us. And no amount of kidding can put the old one back on us. The only thing that can make us cringe is a "Hollywood" remark ("You remind me of that nun in—you know, she played with Bing Crosby"). We didn't want to look pretty-pretty.

The major hurdle still had to be cleared: wearing the coronet back to school. Some pastors jumped the gun and announced at Mass that "our sisters are still 'our sisters,' but they will come back after the holidays in a new garb." But for those of us who teach in a central high school there was no pastor to herald the change. We have had to face the curious, frank gaze of students who love us and feel appalling at home with us; to face that unforgettable greeting, "Sister, you got a crew cut!"

Index of Orders

T HE LIST which follows contains certain basic information plus other facts, where known, which might be of interest. There are undoubtedly many congregations in Canada and Mexico which were not discovered. In cases where congregations did not reply to requests for information, the few facts available are given.

There are several annual or frequently revised listings which would also be helpful. The *Official Guide to Catholic Educational Institutions*, Catholic Institutional Directory Company, Inc., 9 North Village Avenue, Rockville Centre, L.I., New York, is revised annually and gives the type of work, requirements, training, schools attended, whether the juniorate takes place before or during the time sister begins her apostolic work, etc. *The Guide to the Catholic Sisterhoods in the United States*, compiled by Rev. Thomas P. McCarthy, C.S.V., and published by the Catholic University of America Press, Washington 17, D.C., includes a picture of the habit as well as the work, requirements, etc., of each congregation. It is revised every few years. Both of these are inexpensive and can be obtained in Catholic bookstores. *The Official Catholic Directory*, a weighty volume which is found in many public libraries, is an annual directory published by P. J. Kenedy and Sons, 12 Barclay Street, New York City, and lists United States congregations within each diocese and in a general index. Canadian congregations are shown within each diocese but are not indexed. *The Ontario Catholic Directory*, published annually by the Newman Foundation of Toronto, 89 St. George Street, Toronto 5, Ont., Canada, lists the congregations in each diocese in the province of Ontario. Canadian congregations are also listed, for those who can read French, in *Le Canada Ecclésiastique*, published by Librairie Beauchemin Limitée, Montreal, P.Q., Canada. Secular institutes are described and listed in *New Vocations for Catholics*, a pamphlet published by America Press, 920 Broadway, New York 10, New York.

Parish pamphlet racks and local Catholic bookstores can provide booklets on sisters in a particular diocese. *These Sisters Serve New York*, for the New York Archdiocese, and *If You Really Love*, for the Cincinnati Archdiocese, are good examples. The latter, published by Geo. A. Pflaum, Publisher, Inc., includes information on the religious life. In Cincinnati and Dayton, Ohio, there are vocation centers with libraries where sisters are available for counselling.

A recent survey by *Divine Word Messenger* showed there were 983 Negro sisters in 109 religious communities. Most belonged to three congregations which were founded as Negro congregations, the Sisters of the Holy Family, Oblate Sisters of Providence, and Franciscan Handmaids of the Most Pure Heart of Mary. The first two, incidentally, were founded before the Emancipation Proclamation. However, a Negro girl should apply at any community she wishes to enter.

There are two communities which accept invalids or those in poor health. The Sisters of Jesus Crucified, primarily contemplative, accept the blind, the deaf, the bedridden, and those with heart disease and other ailments, who are not over thirty. The sisters receive excellent medical care but they do not pray for a cure or discuss their ailments except with the nursing sister and the prioress. The sisters help each other and each shares in the work (retreats for the sick, teaching retarded children, checking slides for the detection of cancer, housework) as far as she can, even if only for a few minutes a day. They accept suffering as their vocation but in a spirit of joy, not sadness. The Sisters of the Lamb of God, an active congregation, accepts the blind, crippled, polio and arthritis and cerebral palsy victims, and some with incurable cancer. There is no age limit. The Superior General, Mother Jeanne, is quoted as saying, "If a candidate had only six months to live, we would take her." In both congregations the illness must be neither mental nor contagious and the candidate, of course, must have a vocation to the religious life.

Communities accepting rehabilitated women (former prisoners, delinquents, etc.), are: Sisters Magdalens directed by Good Shepherd Sisters and Oblates of the Most Holy Redeemer; Dominican Sisters of Bethany; Dominican Sisters of Bethany, Congregation of

St. Mary Magdalene; Oblate Sisters of Misericordia; and Sisters of Seven Dolors, listed following Sisters of Our Lady of Charity of Refuge.

The titles of congregations in the list are as accurate as possible; wording of titles varies greatly from one reference source to another. There are also "popular" and "official" titles. The attempt here is to use the most well-known title for the main listing, and the titles are cross-indexed.

When writing to a congregation, the letter should be addressed to Reverend Mother Superior, name of congregation and open Dear Reverend Mother:

A

Adoratrices, see Sisters of Perpetual Adoration of the Blessed Sacrament of St. Mary of Guadalupe

Africa, see Franciscan Missionary Sisters for Africa; Our Lady of Africa, Missionary Sisters of

African, see Our Lady of Good Counsel, African Sisters of

Aged and Infirm, see Carmelite Sisters for the Aged and Infirm

Sisters of the Congregation of St. Agnes (C.S.A.) Founded in Wisconsin in 1858 by Rev. Caspar Rehrl. Pontifical, active, simple vows. 806 sisters. Teaching elementary and high school, college; hospitals, schools of nursing; care of aged and orphans; hospice for travelers; domestic work; missions in Nicaragua— schools and clinic. Ages 15-35, high school for postulate, one year college for novitiate. Aspirancy up to four years. Postulate one year, novitiate two years, juniorate four years. Black habit. Motherhouse: St. Agnes Convent, 390 E. Division St., Fond du Lac, Wisconsin.

Ancilla Domini Sisters, see Poor Handmaids of Jesus Christ

St. Andrew, see Sisters of the Cross

Angels, see Our Lady of the Angels, Missionary Sisters of

Sisters of St. Ann of Providence (S.S.A.) Founded in Italy in 1834; established in U.S. in 1952. Pontifical, active, simple vows. 20 sisters U.S., 1400 world. Teaching elementary school; retreats; catechetics; day nurseries; mission in India. Ages 15-30, high school. Postulate six to twelve months, novitiate two years. No lay sisters. Black habit. Motherhouse: Turin, Italy.

U.S. address: Mount St. Ann Retreat House, Ebensburg, Pennsylvania.

Sisters of St. Anne (S.S.A.) Founded in Vaudreuil, P.Q., Canada in 1848 by Mother Marie Anne Blondin to teach poor children in rural areas; established in U.S. in 1867. Pontifical, active, simple vows. 2208 sisters, 369 U.S. Teaching elementary and high school, academies, college, Indian schools, industrial, normal, and homemaking schools; hospitals, sanatoriums; homes for aged; missions in Alaska, Yukon Territory and Haiti. At least 16, high school. Postulate six months, novitiate one and a half years, juniorate three years. Black habit. Motherhouse: Mt. St. Anne, 1950 Provost St., Lachine, P.Q., Canada. Canadian provincialates: St. Anne's Academy, 835 Humboldt St., Victoria, B.C., Canada; 2450 St. Antoine St., Montreal, P.Q., Canada. U.S. provincialate: 22 Broad St., Marlboro, Massachusetts.

Missionary Servants of St. Anthony (M.S.S.A.) Founded in Texas in 1929 by Rev. Peter Baque and Mother M. Theresa to work among the poor. Diocesan, active, simple vows. 26 sisters. Home missions: teaching elementary school; nursing in general and maternity clinics; social work; home visiting; home for working girls; day nursery; home for aged and infirm priests; catechetics. The work is mainly among Latin Americans. Ages 17-30, high school education preferred. Aspirancy four years. Postulate six months, novitiate two years, juniorate six years. Black habit. Motherhouse: St. Anthony's Shrine, 100 Peter Baque Rd., San Antonio 9, Texas.

Congregation of Antonian Sisters of Mary, Queen of the Clergy (A.M.) Founded in Chicoutimi, Canada in 1904 by Rev. Elzear Delamarre; established in U.S. in 1932. Pontifical, active, simple vows. 291 sisters, 40 U.S. Domestic work in seminaries, colleges and rectories; teaching elementary school; care of orphans; home missions. Ages 16-30, ninth grade. Postulate six months, novitiate two years, juniorate one year. Motherhouse for Canada and U.S.: 927 Jacques-Cartier St. E., Chicoutimi, P.Q., Canada.

Sisters Auxiliaries of the Apostolate (A.A.) Founded in Alberta, Canada in 1903 by Rev. Francis Olszewski; relocated in U.S. in 1911. Diocesan, active, simple vows. 20 sisters. Teaching, especially poor children; teaching retarded children; care of aged; social work; domestic work and care of altars; conducting choirs; catechetics; home missions. Ages 16-35 preferred, high school education or business or domestic experience, R.N., P.N., or L.P.N. for nurses. Aspirancy one to two years, postulate six to twelve months, novitiate two years, juniorate three years. Black habit. Motherhouse: Sts. Peter and Paul Convent, 142 Maple Ave., Monongah, West Virginia.

Apostolate, see Blessed Sacrament, Sisters of the Apostolate of the; Catholic Apostolate, Sisters of the; Sacred Heart, Religious of the Apostolate of the

Little Sisters of the Assumption (L.S.A.) (Nursing Sisters of the Sick Poor) (Petites Soeurs de l'Assomption) Founded in France in 1865; established in U.S. in 1891. Pontifical, active, simple vows. 108 sisters U.S., world 2600. Nurse the sick poor regardless of race or religion and take over care of household; catechetics; missions in Africa, South America and New Zealand. Meditation, day hours of Divine Office in choir. Ages 17-35, high school education. Postulate six months, novitiate two years, juniorate six years. Black habit. Motherhouse: Paris, France. U.S. provincialate: 100 Gladstone Ave., Walden, New York. Novitiate also at Assumption Vale, Coopertown Rd., Haverford, Pennsylvania. Canadian address: 1626 St. Hubert St., Montreal 24, P.Q., Canada.

Missionary Sisters of the Assumption (M.S.A.) (Assumption Sisters) Founded in South Africa in 1850; established in U.S. in 1958. Pontifical, active, simple vows. Four sisters U.S., world 300. Teaching. Motherhouse: Cape Province, South Africa. U.S. address: St. John's Convent, Churchtown R.D. 2, Marietta, Ohio.

Oblate Sisters of the Assumption (O.A.) Founded in France in 1865; established in U.S. in 1956. Pontifical, active, simple vows. Six sisters U.S., world 650. Domestic work at a college. Foreign missions in Brazil and the Congo. To age 35. Postulate six months, novitiate two years, juniorate five years. U.S. address: Our Lady of Consolation Convent, Assumption College, 500 Salisbury St., Worcester, Massachusetts.

Religious of the Assumption (R.A.) Founded in France in 1839; established in U.S. in 1919. Pontifical, active and contemplative, simple vows. Eighty sisters U.S., 1500 world. Teaching elementary school, academies; convert instruction; retreats;

promoting Catholic Action; social work; domestic work; home missions; foreign missions in Africa and Far East. Full Divine Office in choir, daily adoration of Blessed Sacrament, contemplation. Ages 18-30, high school education or college preferred. Postulate nine months, novitiate one year, juniorate five years. Also lay sisters and auxiliary missionaries. Violet and white habit. Motherhouse: Paris, France. U.S. provincialate: Academy of the Assumption, Ravenhill, 3480 W. Schoolhouse Lane, Philadelphia 44, Pennsylvania.

Sisters of the Assumption of the Blessed Virgin Mary (A.S.V.) (Les Soeurs de l'Assomption de la Sainte Vierge) Founded in Canada in 1853 by Rev. John Harper (who was unable to find religious teachers for his parish schools); established in U.S. in 1891. Pontifical, active, simple vows. 2670 sisters, 305 U.S. Teaching elementary and high school, college, classical, commercial, and domestic science schools, schools of music; catechetics; domestic work; missions in Japan and Brazil. Ages 16-35, high school education. Postulate six months, novitiate two years, juniorate. Black habit. Motherhouse: Nicolet, P.Q., Canada. Canadian provincialates: 10765 Ninety-eighth St., Edmonton, Alta., Canada; St. Paul, Alta., Canada; Trois Rivières, P.Q., Canada; Sacred Heart Convent, Haileybury, Ont., Canada. U.S. provincialate and novitiate: Main St., Petersham, Massachusetts.

Assumption, see Mary of the Assumption, Daughters of

Atonement, see Franciscan Sisters of the Atonement

Missionary Sisters of St. Augustine (M.S.S.A.) (Missionary Canonesses of St. Augustine) Founded in India in 1897 by a Belgian missionary; established in U.S. in 1919. Pontifical, active, simple vows. 173 sisters U.S., 1234 world. Teaching elementary and high school; hospitals, dispensaries, leprosaria, maternity clinics, home nursing; care of children and aged; day nurseries; hostels; credit unions; social work centers; training native sisters in the missions. Foreign missions in India, Philippines, Formosa, Hong Kong, Congo, Ruanda-Urundi, West Indies, Virgin Islands; home missions in California and Texas. Ages 18-30, high school education. Postulate six months, novitiate two years. White habit, black veil. Motherhouse: Heverle, Belgium. U.S. and West Indies provincialate: St. John Berchmans Convent, 437 West Forty-seventh St., New York 36, New York. Novitiate in Albany.

Canonesses Hospitallers of St. Augustine (C.H.S.A.) Founded in
France *circa* 1155 by Sisters of St. Augustine from Palestine;
established in Canada in 1639 and founded the first Canadian
hospital, the Hôtel-Dieu de Quebec; Augustine Sisters of Canada federated in 1957. Pontifical, active and contemplative,
simple vows. 800 sisters. Hospitals, sanitoriums, schools of
nursing; care of aged and epileptics; mission in Paraguay. Ages
18-35. Postulate six to eight months, novitiate one and a half
to two years. Temporary vows annually for five years. White
habit, black veil; white veil while nursing. General novitiate:
2285, chemin St. Louis, Sillery, Quebec 6, P.Q., Canada.

St. Augustine, see also Charity of St. Augustine, Sisters of; Most
Holy Crucified, Sisters of the; St. Rita, Sisters of.

Augustinian Sisters (C.T.A.S.) Founded in Mexico City in 1932
by Mother J. M. Luisa Godeau; established in U.S. in 1958.
Diocesan, active, simple vows, 100 sisters, 12 in U.S. Teaching;
sanitoriums; homes for aged; domestic work in seminaries.
Ages 15-30, high school, some exceptions. Aspirancy six
months, postulate six months, novitiate one year. Black habit.
Motherhouse: Villa de Guadalupe, 4A de Garrido 40, Mexico
City, D.F., Mexico. U.S. address: St. Monica Seminary, Oco-
nomowoc, Wisconsin.

B

Baptistines, see Sisters of St. John the Baptist.

Sisters of the Order of St. Basil the Great (O.S.B.M.) (Basilian
Sisters) Pittsburgh Greek Rite. Originally founded in Capadocia in 358 A.D. by St. Basil the Great and his sister St. Macrina.
This community founded in U.S. in 1921 by Mother Macrina.
Pontifical, active, simple vows. 142 sisters. Teaching elementary and high school, academy; nursing; care of orphans and
aged women; catechetics; retreats; domestic work; publication
—*The Voice of Mt. St. Macrina*. Ages 16-30, high school education. Postulate six months, novitiate two years, juniorate one
year. Black habit. Motherhouse: Mt. St. Macrina Academy,
P.O. Box 1511, West National Pike, Uniontown, Pennsylvania.

Sisters of the Order of St. Basil the Great (O.S.B.M.) (Basilian
Sisters) Ukrainian Greek Rite. Founded in Capadocia in 358

A.D. by St. Basil the Great and his sister St. Macrina; established in U.S. in 1911 from Europe. Pontifical, active and contemplative, solemn vows. 150 sisters, 6 contemplative cloistered nuns. Teaching elementary and high school and college; care of orphans; catechetics; retreats; nursing; embroidering and sewing vestments; music; art; printing; library work; domestic work; publication—*Missionary*. Ages 15½-30, some exceptions, high school education. Aspirancy four years. Postulate six months, novitiate two years. Special training in Byzantine Rite. Black habit. Generalate: Rome, Italy. U.S. motherhouse: 710 Fox Chase Rd., Philadelphia 11, Pennsylvania.

Sisters of the Bayous, see Most Holy Eucharist, Missionary Servants of the.

Sisters of the Order of St. Benedict (O.S.B.) *Founded circa 529 A.D. in Italy by St. Benedict and his sister St. Scholastica. Now found throughout world with a total membership of approximately 20,000. First U.S. foundation in 1852. Benedictine oblates are somewhat similar to members of secular third orders. The oblates sometimes live within a monastery but they are not sisters or nuns.*

Benedictine Nuns of the Primitive Observance (O.S.B.) Independent U.S. priory founded in 1948 by Mother Benedict Duss, an American nun from the Benedictine Abbey of Jouarre, France. Pontifical, contemplative, minor papal enclosure, simple vows at present. 28 choir nuns and 5 oblates. Daily singing of Mass and Divine Office; study; domestic work; farming; painting; ceramics; printing; weaving; vestment making; book binding; stained glass work; wood carving; guest house. Age to 30; college education preferred for choir nuns; no age limits for oblates. Postulate one year, novitiate one and a half years, juniorate two years. Black habit. Regina Laudis Monastery, Bethlehem, Connecticut.

Benedictine Sisters (O.S.B.) Established in U.S. in 1931. Motherhouse: Bavaria, Germany. U.S. establishments:

St. Walburga Convent, Boulder, Colorado. Pontifical, contemplative, solemn vows. Fourteen sisters. Postulate nine to twelve months, novitiate one year, juniorate three years.

St. Therese Convent, P.O. Box 351, Canon City, Colorado. Active and contemplative. Eight sisters. Domestic work at an abbey. No training program in U.S.

Benedictine Sisters of Westmoreland County, % St. Vincent
Archabbey, Latrobe, Pennsylvania. Active and contemplative.
39 sisters, 1 oblate. Retreats. High school education preferred.
Aspirancy three months, postulate six months, novitiate one
year.

Benedictine Sisters (O.S.B.) Founded in France in 1883; established in U.S. in 1906. Pontifical, active and contemplative. 27
sisters, 2 oblates. Contemplation; teaching underprivileged
girls; retreats; domestic work; making vestments; baking altar
breads. Ages 15-35. Aspirancy one to four years. Postulate six
months, novitiate one year. U.S. motherhouse: St. Gertrude's
Monastery, St. Gertrude Rural Station, Covington, Louisiana.

Benedictine Sisters of Diocesan Jurisdiction (O.S.B.) Diocesan,
active, simple vows. Two independent motherhouses:

St. Scholastica Convent, Albert Pike and Rogers St., Fort
Smith, Arkansas. Founded in 1878. 310 sisters. Teaching elementary and high school, academy; nursing and related medical work; care of orphans; domestic work. Three years high
school education required unless candidate is beyond high
school age. Aspirancy three years. Postulate ten months, novitiate two years, juniorate three years.

Holy Name Convent, San Antonio, Pasco County, Florida.
Founded 1889. 58 sisters. Teaching elementary school, girls'
academy, boys' boarding school; nursing; retreats; catechetics;
domestic work; home missions. High school education. Postulate six months, novitiate one year, juniorate five years.

Benedictine Sisters of the Eucharistic King (O.S.B.) Founded in
the Philippines. Catechetics; home visiting. Motherhouse:
Vigan, Ilocas Sur, Philippines. U.S. headquarters: 420 S. San
Joaquin St., Stockton 2, California.

Benedictine Missionaries of Guadalupe of Christ the King
(O.S.B.) (Misioneras Guadalupanas de Cristo Rey Ordinis
Sancti Benedicti) Founded in Guadalupe, Mexico in 1930 by
Rev. Joseph Castillon Velasco and Mother Josephine Maria
Valencia; established in U.S. in 1948. 62 sisters in U.S. Teach-
ing elementary school, academies, colleges; catechetics; do-
mestic work at Benedictine abbeys, etc.; foreign missions.
Divine Office in choir. Ages 15-25, some exceptions to 30,
grade school education for choir and lay sisters. Black habit.

Motherhouse: Mexico City, Mexico. U.S. address: St. Benedict's Abbey, Maur Hill, Atchison, Kansas.

Benedictine Sisters of Saint Lioba (O.S.B.) Founded in Germany in 1920; established in Canada in 1951. Diocesan, active. 10 sisters in Canada, 400 world. Social work; domestic work. Ages 18-30, college education. Aspirancy six months, novitiate two years. Black habit. Motherhouse: Freiburg, Germany. Canadian address: Westminster Abbey, Mission City, B.C., Canada.

Benedictine Sisters of Perpetual Adoration (O.S.B.) Founded in U.S. in 1875 from Switzerland by Mother M. Anselma Felber and Abbot Forwin Conrad, O.S.B. Pontifical, contemplative, minor papal enclosure, simple vows. 270 sisters. Contemplation; Divine Office chanted in choir; perpetual adoration; writing, publishing magazine, *Tabernacle and Purgatory,* and booklets; correspondence apostolate; office work; making altar breads, linens, vestments; Eucharistic associations for laity; all share domestic work—no lay sisters. Ages 16-30, high school education preferred, no dowry necessary. Postulate six months, novitiate two years. Temporary vows annually for five years; usual vows plus Benedictine vows of stability and conversion of manners. Black habit. Motherhouse: Clyde, Missouri.

Benedictine Sisters of Pontifical Jurisdiction (O.S.B.) First U.S. foundation in 1852 at St. Mary's, Pennsylvania from St. Walburga's Abbey, Bavaria, Germany. This and subsequent foundations are now independent. There is no general motherhouse in the U.S. The individual motherhouses are grouped in three confederations. Applicant should apply to the specific motherhouse of her choice. Pontifical, active and contemplative, simple vows. Divine Office sung. Black habit.

1) Congregation of St. Scholastica. Erected 1922. 16 motherhouses in U.S. and 1 in Mexico.

Sacred Heart Convent, Cullman, Alabama. (1902) 121 sisters. Teaching elementary and high school, academy, junior college. High school education. Postulate nine months, novitiate one year, juniorate three years.

St. Lucy's Priory, 19045 E. Sierra Madre Ave., Glendora, California (1956) 73 sisters. Teaching elementary and high school; domestic work. Ages 16-30, high school education. Postulate six months, novitiate one year, juniorate three years.

St. Scholastica Convent, 7430 Ridge Blvd., Chicago 45, Illinois (1861) 197 sisters. Teaching elementary and high school, academy; retreats; summer camps; home missions; teaching the blind; baking altar breads. Ages 18-30, high school education preferred. Postulate ten months, novitiate one year, juniorate five years.

Sacred Heart Convent, Lisle P.O., Illinois (1895) 193 sisters. Teaching elementary school, academy, junior college; care of aged; domestic work. High school education. Aspirancy four years. Postulate one year, novitiate one year, juniorate five years.

Convent of Our Lady of Sorrows, Tinley Park, Illinois (1951) 28 sisters. Teaching elementary school; retreats; catechetics; domestic work. To age 30, high school education. Aspirancy three years. Postulate six months, novitiate one year, juniorate three years.

Mount St. Scholastica, Atchison, Kansas (1863) 588 sisters. Teaching elementary and high school, academy and colleges. Ages 17-30, high school education. Postulate six months, novitiate one year, juniorate five years.

St. Walburga Convent, 2500 Amsterdam Rd., Covington, Kentucky (1859) 251 sisters. Teaching elementary and high school, academy; nursing; catechetics; domestic work. Ages 16-35. Aspirancy one to four years. Postulate six months, novitiate one year, juniorate five years.

St. Scholastica Convent, 122 S. Massachusetts, Covington, Louisiana (1870) 94 sisters. Teaching elementary and high school, academy; catechetics; domestic work; mission in Colombia. Age 15, high school education. Aspirancy one to four years. Postulate one year, novitiate one year, juniorate five years.

St. Gertrude's Convent, Ridgely, Maryland (1857) 98 sisters. Teaching elementary and high school, special school, rural Sunday schools. Ages 17-35, high school education for prospective teachers. Postulate ten months, novitiate one year, juniorate five years.

St. Walburga Convent, 851 North Broad St., Elizabeth, New Jersey (1868) 215 sisters. Teaching elementary and high school, academies; hospital, school of nursing; domestic work. Postulate ten months, novitiate one year, juniorate five years.

St. Joseph's Convent, 2200 So. Lewis, Tulsa 14, Oklahoma (1879) 143 sisters. Teaching elementary and high school, boarding school and college; nursing; domestic work. Postulate nine months, novitiate one year, juniorate three years.

St. Benedict Convent, 345 E. Ninth St., Erie, Pennsylvania (1856) 176 sisters. Teaching elementary and high school, academy; girls' summer camp. Age 18, one and a half years high school. Postulate six months, novitiate one year, juniorate three years.

Mount St. Mary Convent, 4530 Perrysville Ave., Pittsburgh 29, Pennsylvania (1870) 188 sisters. Teaching elementary, high school, and academy. At least 16. Aspirancy four years. Postulate one year, novitiate one year, juniorate five years.

St. Joseph's Convent, 303 Church St., St. Mary's, Pennsylvania (1852) 116 sisters. Teaching elementary and high school; nursing; care of aged; domestic work. At least 16. Postulate six months, novitiate one year. Special aspirant classes held each summer—those who attend are under no obligation to enter the community.

St. Scholastica Convent, P.O. Box 905, Boerne, Texas (1911) 38 sisters. Teaching elementary and high school; nursing, care of aged. Ages 15-30, high school education. Postulate nine months, novitiate one year, juniorate five years.

St. Benedict's Convent, Bristow, Virginia (1868) 89 sisters. Teaching; nursing; domestic work. To age 30, high school education. Postulate six months, novitiate one year, juniorate five years.

2) Congregation of St. Gertrude the Great. Erected 1937. 10 motherhouses in U.S., 1 in Canada.

St. Gertrude's Convent, P.O. Box 185, Cottonwood, Idaho (1885) 154 sisters, 4 oblates. Teaching elementary school, academy and junior college; hospitals; nursing home; mission in South America. High school education preferred. Aspirancy. Postulate six months, novitiate one year, juniorate three to five years.

Our Lady of Grace Convent, 1402 Southern Ave., Beech Grove, Indiana (1957) 129 sisters. Teaching elementary, high school, and academy; domestic work; mission in Colombia. At least 17, high school education preferred.

Convent of the Immaculate Conception, Ferdinand, Indiana (1867) 363 sisters. Teaching elementary and high school, academy, college, school for retarded children; nursing; care of aged; domestic work; mission in Colombia. Ages 16-30, high school education. Postulate nine months, novitiate one year, juniorate five years.

Mount St. Benedict Convent, Crookston, Minnesota (1919) 276 sisters. Teaching elementary and high school, boarding school; nursing; care of aged; catechetics; domestic work; mission in Colombia. Aspirancy three and one-half years. Postulate six months, novitiate one year, juniorate three years.

Sacred Heart Convent, Fourteenth Ave. S.E., Minot, North Dakota (1910) 75 sisters. Teaching elementary, high school, academy, summer schools; hospital, nursing home; care of aged; catechetics; administration; domestic and office work; Indian mission; foreign missions in South America. Ages 16-30, high school education preferred. Aspirancy one to four years. Postulate six months, novitiate one year, juniorate five years.

Queen of Angels Convent, Mt. Angel, Oregon (1882) 146 sisters. Teaching elementary and high school, academy, college of education; nursing home; domestic work; catechetics. High school education. Postulate ten months, novitiate one year, juniorate five years.

Mother of God Priory, Pierre, South Dakota (1961) 135 sisters. Teaching elementary and high school; hospital, school of nursing; domestic work; social work; home for unwed mothers; administration; care of aged; mission in Colombia. Ages 17-35, high school education. Postulate six months, novitiate one year, juniorate three years.

St. Martin's Priory of the Black Hills, Rapid City, South Dakota (1889) 104 sisters. Teaching elementary and high school, academy; hospitals, school of nursing; catechetics; domestic work. Ages 16-30. Postulate nine months, novitiate one year, juniorate two years.

Sacred Heart Convent, Yankton, South Dakota (1880) 358 sisters. Teaching elementary and high school, college; hospitals, school of nursing; care of aged; office and domestic work; making liturgical vestments; catechetics; mission in Colombia. To age 30, high school education. Postulate six months, novitiate one year, juniorate four years.

St. Benedict's Convent, Rte. 1, Waunakee, Wisconsin (1897) 54 sisters. Teaching elementary school and academy; hospitals, maternity and infant home, school of nursing; domestic work.

Ages 15-35, high school education. Aspirancy four years. Postulate nine months, novitiate one year, juniorate three years. *Canadian motherhouse:* Box 1, Group 36, R.R. 1, Winnipeg, Man., Canada. Teaching; nursing.

3) Congregation of St. Benedict. Erected 1947. Seven motherhouses in U.S.

St. Mary's Priory, Nauvoo, Illinois (1874) 177 sisters. Teaching elementary and high school, academy; catechetics; domestic work. High school education. Postulate ten months, novitiate one year, juniorate three years.

St. Scholastica Priory, Kenwood Ave., Duluth 11, Minnesota (1892) 479 sisters. Teaching elementary and high school, college; nursing; care of orphans and aged; school for retarded girls; retreats; catechetics; administration; office and domestic work. To age 30, high school education, less for domestic workers. Aspirancy four years. Postulate six to ten months, novitiate one year, juniorate three years. Divine Office chanted in English.

St. Benedict's Priory, St. Joseph, Minnesota (1857) 987 sisters. Teaching elementary and high school, college; hospitals, schools of nursing and specialized medical work; care of aged; office and domestic work; catechetics; Indian missions in Minnesota; missions in Puerto Rico, Formosa, Japan, Bahamas. Ages 16-30, high school education. Aspirancy three months, postulate six months, novitiate one year, juniorate two to four years.

St. Paul's Priory, 301 Summit Ave., St. Paul 2, Minnesota (1948) 239 sisters. Teaching elementary and high school; care of orphans and aged; nursing; social work; catechetics; domestic work. Ages 16-30, high school education. Aspirancy three months, postulate six months, novitiate one year, juniorate three to five years.

Annunciation Priory, R.R. 2, Box 119, Bismarck, North Dakota (1947) 204 sisters. Teaching elementary and high school; nursing; care of aged; domestic work; catechetics. Aspirancy three to four years. Postulate six to nine months, novitiate one year, juniorate four to five years.

St. Placid Priory, 4600 Martin Way, Olympia, Washington (1952) 43 sisters. Teaching elementary and high school; domestic work. High school education. Postulate one year, novitiate one year, juniorate three years.

St. Bede's Priory, 1328 Wilson St., Eau Claire, Wisconsin
(1948) 105 sisters. Teaching elementary and high school,
junior college; hospital, nursing home; care of aged; domestic
work. To age 30. Aspirancy three to four years. Postulate six
months, novitiate one year, juniorate three years.

Missionary Benedictine Sisters (O.S.B.) Founded in Germany in
1885; established in U.S. in 1923. Pontifical, active, simple
vows. 85 sisters U.S.; 1,200 world. Teaching elementary and
high school, college; doctors, nurses, dentists, and technicians
for hospitals, dispensaries, maternity clinics, leprosariums; retreats; catechetics; domestic work; Winnebago Indian missions; foreign missions in South America, Philippines, Korea,
Portugal, Bulgaria, Africa. High school education for novitiate. Aspirancy four years. Postulate one year, novitiate one
year, juniorate three years. Black habit. General motherhouse:
Bavaria. U.S. motherhouse: Immaculata Convent, 1500 Norfolk Ave., Box 885, Norfolk, Nebraska.

Olivetan Benedictine Sisters (O.S.B.) Founded in Arkansas in
1887 by Mother M. Beatrice Rengli and a group of Swiss sisters from Benedictine community at Clyde, Missouri. Pontifical, active, simple vows. 185 sisters. Teaching elementary
and high school, boarding schools; hospitals, school of nursing;
hospice in Hot Springs; domestic work at seminary; catechetics;
care of aged; day nurseries. To age 30, some exceptions, no
dowry needed. Aspirancy one year, postulate six months, novitiate one year, juniorate five years. White habit. Motherhouse:
Holy Angels Convent, 223 E. Jackson Ave., Jonesboro, Arkansas.

Regina Pacis Benedictine Sisters (O.S.B.) Founded in Lithuania;
established in U.S. in 1957. Diocesan, active and contemplative, simple vows. 4 sisters U.S., world 50. Contemplation;
teaching; day nursery; retreats; catechetics; making vestments;
religious art. Ages 15-40, high school education preferred. Aspirancy six months, postulate six months, novitiate two years,
juniorate five to six years. U.S. address: 75 Wallace Rd., Bedford, New Hampshire.

Bernardine Sisters, see Franciscan Sisters of St. Bernardine of
Siena

Congregation of the Oblates of Bethany (C.O.B.) Founded in
France in 1902; established in U.S. in 1959. Diocesan, active

and contemplative, simple vows. 8 sisters in U.S. Contemplation and domestic work for all. Ages 17-35, high school education. Motherhouse: Paris, France. Canadian provincialate: Béthanie de St. Thérèse-de-l'Enfant Jesus, Pointe-du-Lac, P.Q., Canada (32 sisters). U.S. address: Regina Cleri Home, 4540 Lindell Blvd., St. Louis 8, Missouri.

Sisters of Bethany, Consolers of the Virgin of Dolors (C.V.D.) Founded in El Salvador in 1928; established in U.S. in 1949. Diocesan, active, simple vows. 23 sisters in U.S. Teaching; home for working girls; foster home; social work; domestic work. Ages 15-30, high school education preferred. Postulate six to twelve months, novitiate two years. Navy blue habit. Motherhouse: El Salvador. U.S. address: Mater Dolorosa Novitiate, 557 No. Mariposa Ave., Los Angeles 4, California.

Bethany, see Dominican Sisters of Bethany; Dominican Sisters of Bethany, Congregation of St. Mary Magdalene.

Bethlemite Sisters, see Daughters of the Sacred Heart of Jesus.

Oblate Sisters of the Blessed Sacrament (O.S.B.S.) Founded in South Dakota in 1935 by Rev. Sylvester Eisenman. Diocesan, active, simple vows. 15 sisters. Teaching and care of American Indians; office work. To age 30, high school education. Postulate six months, novitiate two years, juniorate five years. Motherhouse: St. Paul Indian Mission, Tekakwitha Convent, Marty, South Dakota.

Servants of the Blessed Sacrament (S.S.) Founded in France in 1858 by Blessed Peter Julian Eymard; established in U.S. in 1947. Pontifical, cloistered-contemplative, simple vows. 30 sisters in U.S., 61 Canada, 500 world. Contemplation, perpetual adoration; making vestments and altar linens. Choir nuns recite Divine Office, lay sisters do not. To age 25. Postulate six months, novitiate two years; temporary vow period three years. White habit. Motherhouse: Paris, France. U.S. vice-provincialate: Convent of the Blessed Sacrament, 101 Silver St., Waterville, Maine. Canadian address: Monastery of the Blessed Sacrament, Chicoutimi, P.Q., Canada.

Sisters of the Blessed Sacrament (S.B.S.) (Blessed Sacrament Sisters) Founded in Pennsylvania in 1891 to aid Indians and Negroes in the home missions by Mother M. Katherine Drexel at suggestion of Pope Leo XIII. Pontifical, active, simple vows. 548 sisters. Home missions in large cities, rural areas and Indian reservations: teaching in day and boarding, elementary and high schools, college, university; social work including home visiting; retreats; catechetics; publishing magazine; office and domestic work. Can use every type of talent. Ages 16-30, high school education. Postulate eleven months, novitiate two years, juniorate five years. Black habit. Motherhouse: St. Elizabeth's Convent, 1663 Bristol Pike, Cornwells Heights, Pennsylvania.

Sisters Servants of the Blessed Sacrament. Founded in Mexico in 1904 by Bishop Silviano Carrillo. Simple vows. 14 sisters in U.S. Teaching elementary and high school, commercial schools, college. Motherhouse: P.O. Box 480, Guadalajara, Jalisco, Mexico. U.S. address: 536 Rockwood Ave., Calexico, California.

Sisters of the Apostolate of the Blessed Sacrament (Eucharistic Mercedarians) 15 sisters in U.S. Teaching elementary school; home visiting; catechetics to public school children. Motherhouse: Mexico. U.S. address: Holy Family Convent, 2513 Nogales St., Corpus Christi, Texas.

Handmaids, Adorers of the Blessed Sacrament and of Charity Founded in Spain in 1855 by St. Mary Michael of the Blessed Sacrament. 4 sisters in U.S. Teaching. Motherhouse: Madrid, Spain. U.S. address: Sacred Heart Convent, 1217 Elgin Ave., Dos Palos, California.

Religious of the Blessed Sacrament and of Our Lady (O.S.S.) (Sacramentine Nuns) Founded in France in 1639 by Ven. Antony le Quieu, O.P.; established in U.S. in 1912. Pontifical, contemplative, minor papal enclosure, solemn vows. 182 nuns in world. Pray for the conversion of unbelievers and sinners; contemplation, Divine Office, perpetual adoration; making altar breads, altar linens and vestments; choir nuns assist with domestic work. To age 30, high school education for choir nuns. Postulate six months, novitiate one year. Black and white habit. Two independent monasteries:
Blessed Sacrament Monastery, 23 Park Ave., Yonkers, New York. 30 choir nuns, 5 lay sisters, 3 externs. Teaching in small academy; illuminating and painting.
Sacramentine Monastery of Perpetual Adoration, U.S. 31, Conway, Michigan. 12 choir nuns, 1 lay sister, 2 externs. Retreats; printing.

Blessed Sacrament, see also Incarnate Word and the Blessed Sacrament; Mercedaries of the Blessed Sacrament, Religious; Perpetual Adoration of the Blessed Sacrament; Most Blessed Sacrament.

Blessed Trinity, see Most Blessed Trinity, Missionary Servants of the.

Blessed Virgin, see St. Ursula of the Blessed Virgin, Society of the Sisters of.

Institute of the Blessed Virgin Mary (I.B.V.M.) (Ladies of Loretto) Founded in Belgium in 1609 by an English foundress; established in Canada in 1847 from Ireland; established in U.S. in 1892. Pontifical, active, simple vows. 513 sisters. Teaching elementary and high school, college, university; catechetics; religious correspondence courses. Ages 15-30, high school education preferred. Postulate six to twelve months, novitiate two years, juniorate five years. Black habit. American motherhouse: Loretto Abbey, Armour Heights, Toronto 12, Ont., Canada. U.S. novitiate: Loretto Convent, Wheaton, Illinois.

Institute of the Blessed Virgin Mary (I.B.V.M.) (Sisters of Loretto–Navan) Established in U.S. in 1954. Diocesan, active, simple vows. 10 sisters in U.S. Teaching elementary school. Motherhouse: Navan Co., Meath, Ireland. U.S. address: SS. Simon and Jude Convent, 6351 N. 27th Ave., Phoenix, Arizona.

Daughters of the Blessed Virgin Mary of the Immaculate Conception, see Sisters of Christian Charity.

Blessed Virgin Mary, see Assumption of the Blessed Virgin Mary, Sisters of the; Charity of the Blessed Virgin Mary, Sisters of; Dominican Sisters of Charity of the Presentation of the Blessed Virgin Mary; St. Francis of the Immaculate Conception of the Blessed Virgin Mary, Sisters of the Third Order of; Immaculate Conception of the Blessed Virgin Mary, Sisters of the; Most Holy and Immaculate Heart of the Blessed Virgin Mary, California Institute of the Sisters of the; Presentation of the Blessed Virgin Mary, Sisters of the.

Blue Sisters, see Sisters of the Holy Humility of Mary; Handmaids of Mary Immaculate.

Sisters of Bon Secours (S.B.S.) Founded in France in 1824 to care for the sick poor; established in U.S. in 1881. Pontifical, active, simple vows. 150 sisters in U.S., 800 world. Nursing and allied medical work in hospitals, convalescent homes, homes for crippled children, the aged, aged and infirm priests, the chronically ill; schools of nursing for sisters of this and other communities; missions in Africa. Ages 16-30, high school education preferred. Postulate six to eight months, novitiate two years, juniorate two years. Black and white habit, white habit on duty. Motherhouse: Paris, France. U.S. provincialate: Convent of Bon Secours, 2000 W. Baltimore St., Baltimore, Maryland.

Bridgettine Sisters (O.Ss.S.) (Order of Our Lady of the Most Holy Saviour) Founded in Sweden in 1346 by St. Bridget; revived in Rome, Italy, in 1911; established in U.S. in 1957. Pontifical, contemplative, semi-cloistered, simple vows. 6 sisters in U.S., 200 world. Contemplation, daily adoration; retreats; catechetics; guest house; making rosaries, vestments and altar linens. Pray for souls in Purgatory. Bridgettine Office based on Little Office of the Blessed Virgin. Ages 17-30, high school education. Postulate six months, novitiate one year, juniorate three years. Grey habit. Motherhouse: Rome, Italy. U.S. novitiate: Convent of St. Bridget, Vikingsborg, Darien, Connecticut.

Congregation of St. Brigid (C.S.B.) (Brigidines) Founded in Ireland in 1807; established in U.S. in 1953. Pontifical, active, simple vows. 16 sisters in U.S., 830 world. Teaching elementary schools. Age 16, high school education preferred. Postulate six months, novitiate two years. Motherhouse: Ireland. U.S. provincialate: St. Brigid's Novitiate, 5118 Loma Linda Dr., San Antonio 28, Texas.

C

Cabrini Sisters, see Missionary Sisters of the Sacred Heart of Jesus.

California Institute, see Most Holy and Immaculate Heart of the Blessed Virgin Mary, California Institute of the Sisters of the.

Daughters of Calvary (Hijas del Calvario) Founded in Spain in 1885. 3 sisters in U.S. Domestic work. Also located in Mexico. U.S. address: St. Joseph's Seminary, R. 2, Box 995, St. Charles, Illinois.

Capuchin Sisters, see Franciscan Capuchin Sisters of the Infant Jesus.

Carmelite Nuns of the Ancient Observance (O. Carm.) (Calced Carmelites) Second Order of Carmel. Founded in Holland in 1453 by Blessed John Soreth; established in U.S. in 1931 from Italy. Pontifical, contemplative, major papal enclosure, solemn vows. 31 sisters in U.S., 5,000 world. Contemplation, perpetual adoration, Divine Office chanted by choir nuns; making altar breads; mission correspondence. Pray especially for priests and religious. Postulate six months, novitiate one year, juniorate three years. Brown habit. Three monasteries:

Carmel of the Little Flower, St. Therese's Valley, Allentown, Pennsylvania. 25 nuns, 1 extern. Ages 15-28, high school.

Carmel of Mary, Wahpeton, North Dakota. 8 nuns, 2 externs. Ages 15-28, high school education, knowledge of Latin for choir nuns.

Carmel of St. Joseph and the Holy Child, 1 Carmelite Drive, Asheville, North Carolina. 9 nuns, 1 extern. Ages 15-25, high school education.

Carmelite Sisters for the Aged and Infirm (O. Carm.) Founded in New York City in 1929 by Cardinal Hayes and Mother M. Angeline Teresa to provide cheerful homes for middle-class aged. Pontifical, active, simple vows. 333 sisters. Care of aged. Ages 15-30, high school education or equivalent. Novitiate two years. Brown habit. Motherhouse: St. Teresa's Motherhouse, Avila on the Hudson, Germantown, New York.

Carmelite Sisters of Charity (Ca. Ch.) Founded in Spain in 1826 by St. Juana Joaquina de Vedruna; recently established in U.S. Pontifical, active, simple vows. 14 sisters in U.S., 3,000 world. Teaching; nursing; catechetics; missions in Puerto Rico. Ages 15-25, high school education. Postulate six months, novitiate two years, juniorate five years. Motherhouse: Spain. U.S. address: Our Lady of Grace Convent, 19950 Anita Ave., Castro Valley, California.

Carmelite Sisters of Corpus Christi (O. Carm.) Began as lay society (tertiaries) in England in 1908; established by foundress, Mother Mary Ellerker, in U.S. in Duluth, Minnesota, in 1920; now Carmelite Third Order Regular. Pontifical, active, simple vows. 64 sisters in U.S., 200 world. Chief aim is to work for the reunion of Christendom. Teaching elementary and high

school; convalescent homes for children; care of aged and retarded children; catechetics, convert instruction; family retreats; parish visiting; all types of social work; missions in British West Indies, British Guiana, and England; publication—
Corpus Christi Chronicle. Divine Office in choir. Ages 16-30,
some exceptions, high school education preferred, any race—
special need for Negro applicants. Postulate six months, novitiate two years, juniorate five years. Brown habit. Motherhouse: Port of Spain, Trinidad, B.W.I. U.S. vicariate: Corpus
Christi Carmel, 130 Highland Ave., Middletown, New York.
Novitiate also at Kearney, Nebraska.

Carmelite Sisters of the Divine Heart of Jesus (D.C.J.) Founded
in Holland in 1891 by Mother Maria Teresa; established in
U.S. in 1912 by the foundress. Pontifical, active and contemplative, semi-cloistered, rule of St. Teresa of Avila, simple
vows. 275 sisters in U.S., 1,000 world. Care of orphans and
aged; day nurseries; social work with families; missions in Nicaragua. Ages 16-30, high school education preferred. Aspirancy
two years. Postulate six months, novitiate two years, juniorate
five years. Brown habit. Motherhouse: Sittard, Holland. U.S.
provinces: St. Joseph's Provincialate, 1214 Kavanaugh Place,
Wauwatosa 13, Wisconsin; 8585 La Mesa Blvd., La Mesa,
California. Canadian provincialate: Carmel Heights, Erindale,
Ont., Canada.

Carmelite Sisters of St. Therese of the Infant Jesus (C.S.T.)
Founded in Oklahoma in 1917 by Mother Agnes Teresa Cav-
anaugh. Affiliated with Discalced Carmelite Order. Diocesan,
active, simple vows. 85 sisters. Home missions among the underprivileged, including Indians and Mexicans: teaching elementary and high school; day nurseries; care and teaching of
retarded children; care of aged; nursing; home visiting and
social work; catechetics; missions in Guatemala and Philippines. To age 30, some exceptions, high school education.
Postulate nine months, novitiate one year, juniorate six years.
Brown habit. Motherhouse: Villa Teresa, 1300 Classen Dr.,
Oklahoma City 3, Oklahoma.

Carmelite Sisters of the Third Order of St. Teresa (O.C.D.T.)
Founded in Mexico in 1904 by Mother Luisa Josefa; established in U.S. in 1927 by the foundress. Pontifical, active,
simple vows. 500 sisters, 96 in U.S. Teaching elementary and

high school, boarding school; nursing; care of orphans; catechetics; retreats; administration; office and domestic work; social work. Ages 15-30, high school education. Postulate six months, novitiate one year, juniorate four to six years. U.S. entrants remain in U.S. Brown habit. Motherhouse: Guadalajara, Mexico. U.S. provincialate: 920 E. Alhambra Rd., Alhambra, California.

Discalced Carmelite Nuns (D.C.) Second Order of Our Lady of Mt. Carmel. ("Discalced" means literally without shoes and refers to the fact that sandals are worn instead of regular shoes and stockings [see Mark 6:9].) Date of foundation of order uncertain. In 1562, in Spain, St. Teresa of Avila with St. John of the Cross began restoring the original rule to the Carmelite Order, which had grown lax even from the mitigated rule then in force. Established in U.S. in Maryland in 1790. Now more than sixty independent monasteries in U.S. and Canada. Applicant should write to the monastery of her choice. Pontifical, contemplative, major papal enclosure, solemn vows. More than 15,000 nuns in world. Contemplation, Divine Office in choir; meat not eaten, silent except for recreation. Supported by alms, making altar breads, vestments, linens, religious articles, art and writing. Average requirements: ages 17-30, high school education for choir nuns. Average training: postulate six months, novitiate one year, juniorate three years. Requirements and training vary slightly for lay and extern sisters. Brown habit. Monasteries alphabetized by state: *Carmelite Monastery*, 716 Fulton Rd., Mobile 18, Alabama (1943) 10 nuns.
Monastery of St. Teresa of Jesus, 7201 W. 32nd St., Little Rock, Arkansas (1950) 10 choir nuns, 2 externs.
Carmel of St. Teresa, 215 E. Alhambra Rd., Alhambra, California (1913) 15 choir nuns, 1 extern.
Carmelite Monastery of Christ the Exiled King, 68 Rincon Rd., Berkeley 7, California (1950) 11 nuns.
Carmelite Monastery of Our Lady and St. Therese, P.O. Box 17, Carmel by the Sea, California (1925) 22 choir nuns, 2 externs.
Carmel of St. Joseph, 3361 E. Ocean Blvd., Long Beach 3, California (1949) 18 choir nuns, 1 lay sister.
Carmel of the Holy Family and St. Therese, 2110 Stockton

Blvd., Sacramento, California (1935) 10 choir nuns, 1 extern.

Carmelite Monastery of the Trinity, 5158 Hawley Blvd., San Diego 16, California (1926) 19 nuns.

Carmelite Monastery of Cristo Rey, 721 Parker Ave., San Francisco 17, California (1928) 19 nuns.

Carmelite Monastery of the Infant Jesus, 1000 Lincoln St., Santa Clara, California (1908) 19 nuns.

Carmel of the Holy Spirit, 6138 So. Gallup St., Littleton, Colorado (1948) 15 nuns.

Carmelite Monastery, Coffee Bluff, Rte. 5, Box 256, Savannah, Georgia (1958) 7 nuns.

Monastery of Discalced Carmelites, River Rd. and Central, Des Plaines, Illinois (1959) 9 nuns.

Monastery of Discalced Carmelites, 2500 Cold Springs Rd., Indianapolis 22, Indiana (1922) 16 nuns.

Monastery of Discalced Carmelites, Allendale Rd., Terre Haute, Indiana (1947) 17 nuns.

Regina Coeli Monastery, Fourteenth St. and Central Ave., Bettendorf, Iowa (1911) 18 nuns.

Monastery of St. Michael, 3535 Wood Ave., Kansas City 2, Kansas (1954) 8 choir nuns, 2 externs.

Monastery of Discalced Carmelites, 1740 Newburg Rd., Louisville 5, Kentucky (1930) 29 choir nuns, 1 extern.

Monastery of Mary Mother of Grace, Carmel Ave., Lafayette, Louisiana (1936) 14 choir nuns, 4 externs.

Monastery of St. Joseph and St. Teresa, 1236 No. Rampart St., New Orleans 16, Louisiana (1877) 9 choir nuns, 3 lay sisters, 4 externs.

Carmelite Monastery, 1318 Dulaney Valley Rd., Towson, Baltimore 4, Maryland (1790) 21 nuns.

Discalced Carmelite Monastery, 61 Mt. Pleasant Ave., Roxbury, Boston 19, Massachusetts (1890) 13 choir nuns, 2 externs.

Monastery of Discalced Carmelites, 15 Mt. Carmel Rd., Danvers, Massachusetts (1959) 11 nuns.

Monastery of St. Therese of the Child Jesus, 16630 Wyoming Ave., Detroit 21, Michigan (1927) 15 choir nuns, 2 externs.

Carmelite Monastery, 1036 Valley Ave., N. W., Grand Rapids, Michigan (1916) 19 choir nuns, 4 externs.

Monastery of the Holy Cross, 317 E. B St., Iron Mountain, Michigan (1950) 12 choir nuns, 1 extern.

Monastery of the Infant Jesus of Prague, Silver Lake Rd., Rte. 5, Traverse City, Michigan (1950) 12 nuns.

Carmel of Our Lady of Divine Providence, 3890 De Montreville Rd., St. Paul 9, Minnesota (1952) 15 nuns.

Monastery of Our Lady of Mount Carmel and the Little Flower, 2155 Terry Rd., Jackson 4, Mississippi (1951) 10 nuns.

Carmelite Monastery, 9150 Clayton Rd., Clayton, St. Louis County 24, Missouri (1863) 17 choir nuns, 3 lay sisters, 3 externs.

Monastery of Our Lady of the Mountains, 2750 Thomas Jefferson Dr., Reno, Nevada (1954) 9 nuns.

Discalced Carmelite Monastery, 275 Pleasant St., Concord, New Hampshire (1946) 18 nuns.

Carmel of Mary Immaculate and St. Mary Magdalen, Carmel Rd., Mt. Carmel (Flemington P.O.), New Jersey (1949) 7 nuns.

Monastery of the Most Blessed Virgin Mary of Mt. Carmel, 189 Madison Ave., Morristown, New Jersey (1926) 12 nuns.

Discalced Carmelite Monastery, Mt. Carmel Rd., Santa Fe, New Mexico (1945) 12 nuns.

Monastery of Our Lady of Mt. Carmel, 745 St. John's Place, Brooklyn 16, New York (1907) 14 nuns.

Monastery of Discalced Carmelites, National Shrine of the Little Flower, 75 Carmel Rd., Buffalo 14, New York (1920) 18 choir nuns, 3 externs.

Carmelite Monastery, 1381 University Ave., New York 52, New York (1920) 19 choir nuns, 1 extern.

Monastery of Our Lady and St. Joseph, 1931 West Jefferson Rd., R.D. 2, Pittsford, New York (1930) 15 choir nuns, 1 extern.

St. Joseph's Monastery, 68 Franklin Ave., Saranac Lake, New York (1952) 14 choir nuns, 3 lay sisters.

Monastery of St. Teresa of Jesus, 428 Duane Ave., Schenectady 4, New York (1923) 14 choir nuns, 2 externs.

Carmel of the Most Holy Incarnation, Rte. 2, Mason Rd., Durham, North Carolina (1956) 6 nuns.

Carmel of the Holy Family, 3176 Fairmount Blvd., Cleveland Heights 18, Ohio (1923) 14 choir nuns, 2 externs.

Monastery of the Immaculate Heart of Mary, 2065 Barton Place, Columbus 9, Ohio (1947) 15 choir nuns, 3 externs.

Carmel of St. Joseph, 4200 No. Meridian Ave., Oklahoma City 12, Oklahoma (1939) 10 nuns.

Carmel of Maria Regina, Rte. 5, Box 1209, Eugene, Oregon (1957) 11 choir nuns, 1 extern.

Monastery of the Holy Family, 510 E. Gore Rd., Erie, Pennsylvania (1957) 6 nuns.

Carmel of St. Therese of Lisieux, Loretto, Pennsylvania (1927) 17 choir nuns, 2 externs.

Carmel of the Sacred Heart and of the Holy Face, Mt. Carmel, Elysburg, Pennsylvania (1953) 11 choir nuns, 2 externs.

Carmelite Monastery, Sixty-sixth Ave. and York Rd. (Oak Lane), Philadelphia 26, Pennsylvania (1902) 19 nuns.

Carmelite Monastery, Watson Ave. at Nayatt Rd., Barrington, Rhode Island (1930) 12 nuns.

Monastery of Discalced Carmelites, P.O. Box 2903, Dallas 21, Texas (1928) 12 nuns.

Monastery of the Most Holy Trinity, 1600 Sunset Terrace, Fort Worth, Texas (1958) 5 nuns.

Carmel of the Most Holy Trinity, 8040 Moline St., Houston, Texas (1958) 5 nuns.

Monastery of Discalced Carmelites, 1104 Kentucky Ave., San Antonio 1, Texas (1934) 19 nuns.

Carmel of the Immaculate Heart of Mary, 5714 Holladay Blvd., Salt Lake City, Utah (1952) 8 choir nuns, 2 externs.

Discalced Carmelite Monastery, R.F.D. 1, Box 42, Williston, Vermont (1950) 17 nuns.

St. Joseph's Monastery, 1808 Eighteenth Ave., Seattle 22, Washington (1908) 11 nuns.

Monastery of St. Teresa and St. John of the Cross, Carmel Rd., Wheeling, West Virginia (1913) 6 nuns.

Carmel of the Mother of God, Pewaukee, Wisconsin (1940) 17 nuns.

Canadian Monasteries:

St. Joseph's Monastery, 2 Lancaster St. E., Kitchener, Ont., Canada. 6 nuns.

Carmelite Monastery, Dolbeau, P.Q., Canada. 16 nuns. Founded in 1957 by Carmelites from Hanoi.

Carmelite Monastery, Ave. du Caress, Montreal, P.Q., Canada. 20 nuns.

Discalced Carmelite Tertiary Sisters of St. Theresa of Jesus Pontifical, active. 68 sisters in U.S. Domestic work at seminaries; catechetics. Motherhouse: Mexico City, Mexico. U.S. novitiate: Rte. 2, Box 971, Silsbee, Texas.

Congregation of Our Lady of Mount Carmel (O. Carm.) Founded in France in 1825 by Rev. Charles F. Boutelou; dispersed during 1830 Revolution and found refuge in New Orleans, Louisiana, in 1833. Pontifical, active, simple vows. 181 sisters. Teaching elementary, high and normal school; nursing. Ages 15-30, high school education, single and widowed. Postulate six months, novitiate two years, juniorate five years. Temporary vow period three years. Mount Carmel Motherhouse, 420 Robert E. Lee Blvd., New Orleans 24, Louisiana.

Institute of Our Lady of Mount Carmel (O. Carm.) Founded in Italy in 1854; established in U.S. in 1947. Pontifical, active and contemplative, simple vows. 19 sisters in U.S., 8 in Canada, 400 world. Domestic work in seminaries, etc. Ages 18-30, high school education. Aspirancy one year, postulate six to eight months, novitiate two years, juniorate one year. Motherhouse: Florence, Italy. U.S. headquarters: Carmelite Junior Seminary, Hamilton, Massachusetts. Canadian address: Mt. Carmel College, Niagara Falls, Ont., Canada.

Sisters of St. Casimir (S.S.C.) Founded in Pennsylvania in 1907 by Mother Maria Kaupas. Diocesan, active, simple vows. 480 sisters. Teaching elementary and high school, junior college; nursing; social work; care of aged; domestic work; missions in South America and Europe. Ages 16-35, high school education. Postulate six months, novitiate two years, juniorate five years. Black habit. Motherhouse: 2601 W. Marquette Rd., Chicago 29, Illinois.

Catechists, see Marian Society of Catechists.

St. Catherine, see Dominican Third Order.

Sisters of the Catholic Apostolate (C.S.A.C.) (Pallotine Sisters) Founded in Rome, Italy, in 1843 by St. Vincent Pallotti as part of an apostolate of priests, brothers, sisters and laity; established in U.S. in 1889. Pontifical, active, simple vows. 208 sisters in U.S., 1,000 world. Teaching elementary and high school, religious vacation schools; catechetics; care of orphans; day nurseries; summer camps; settlements; social work; census taking; domestic and office work. Ages 16-30, some exceptions, high school education. Postulate one year, novitiate two years, juniorate one year. Black habit. Motherhouse: Rome, Italy. U.S. provincialate: St. Patrick's Villa, Harriman, New York.

Society of Catholic Medical Missionaries, see Medical Mission Sisters.

Missionary Sisters of the Catholic Press, see Pious Society, Daughters of St. Paul.

Catholic, see St. Francis Xavier, Catholic Mission Sisters of.

St. Cecilia, see Dominican Third Order.

Cenacle, see Our Lady of the Retreat in the Cenacle, Congregation of.

Sisters of Charitable Instruction of the Holy Infant Jesus (H.I.J.) Third Order of St. Francis. Founded in France in 1662; established in U.S. in 1950. Pontifical, active, simple vows. 22 sisters in U.S., 2,000 world. Teaching elementary school; catechetics; missions in Thailand, Malaya, Japan. Ages 16-30, high school education. Postulate six months, novitiate two years, juniorate five years. Motherhouse: Paris, France. U.S. provincialate: Holy Infant Jesus Convent, Renier St., Colma, California.

Sisters of Charity, see Grey Nuns of Montreal.

Irish Sisters of Charity (I.S.C.) Founded in Ireland in 1815; established in U.S. in 1953. Pontifical, active, simple vows. 32 sisters in U.S., 900 world. Teaching elementary school; home for convalescents and retired women. Ages 16-40, high school education. Postulate six months, novitiate two years, juniorate three years. Black habit. Motherhouse: Dublin, Ireland. U.S. provincialate: St. Cornelius Convent, 3350 Bellflower Blvd., Long Beach 8, California.

Little Missionary Sisters of Charity (P.M.C.) Founded in Italy in 1915; established in U.S. in 1949. Pontifical, active, simple vows. 15 sisters in U.S., 1,500 world. Domestic work; nursing; teaching; retreats; home missions; only volunteers sent to foreign missions. Ages 15-35, eighth grade education. Postulate one year, novitiate two years. Temporary vow period ten years. Black habit. Motherhouse: Tortona, Italy. U.S. provincialate:

Immaculate Conception Convent, 120 Orient Ave., East Boston 28, Massachusetts.

Mother Seton Sisters of Charity (S.C.) (Sisters of Charity of Seton Hill) Founded at Altoona, Pennsylvania, in 1870 from Cincinnati foundation by Mother M. Aloysia Lowe. Pontifical, active, simple vows. 730 sisters. Teaching elementary and high school, college, school for the deaf; hospitals, convalescent home, school of nursing; foundling home; social work center for Negroes; catechetics; domestic work; missions in Korea. Ages 17-30, high school education. Postulate nine months, novitiate two years, juniorate five years. Black habit and cap. Motherhouse: St. Joseph Motherhouse, Seton Hill, Greensburg, Pennsylvania.

Vincentian Sisters of Charity (V.S.C.) Founded in U.S. in 1902 by Mother M. Emerentiana and a group of Sisters of Charity from Austria to serve European immigrants. Pontifical, active, simple vows. 379 sisters, 13 in Canada. Teaching elementary and high school; hospitals, nursing homes for convalescents and the incurable; catechetics; retreats; social work; hospital, clinic, elementary and high schools in Negro missions. Ages 16-35. Aspirancy four years. Postulate one year, novitiate two years, juniorate ten years. Black habit. Motherhouse: St. Vincent Hill, 8200 McKnight Rd., Pittsburgh 37, Pennsylvania. Canadian address: St. Catherine Laboure Convent, Hwy. 20, Fonthill, Ont., Canada.

Vincentian Sisters of Charity (V.S.C.) Founded in Bedford, Ohio, in 1928. Diocesan, active, simple vows. 144 sisters. Teaching elementary and high school; catechetics; nursing; domestic work. To age 30. Postulate six to twelve months, novitiate two years, juniorate three years. Motherhouse: Villa San Bernardo, 1160 Broadway, Bedford, Ohio.

Sisters of Charity of St. Augustine (C.S.A.) Founded at Cleveland, Ohio, in 1851 by Mother M. Bernardine and a group of Augustinian Sisters from France. Diocesan, active, simple vows. 363 sisters. Teaching elementary, academy, music and art schools; hospitals and schools of nursing; children's village of St. Vincent de Paul; homes for infants and unwed mothers; domestic work; social work. Ages 16-30, high school education. Postulate six months, novitiate two years, juniorate four to five years. Grey habit, black veil. Motherhouse: Mount Augustine, 5232 Broadview Rd., West Richfield, Ohio.

Sisters of Charity of the Blessed Virgin Mary (B.V.M.) Founded at Philadelphia, Pennsylvania, in 1833 by Mother Frances Clarke; motherhouse transferred to Iowa in 1843. Pontifical, active, simple vows. 2,333 sisters. Teaching elementary and high school, academies and colleges; missions in Colombia. Ages 18-30, high school education. Postulate six months, novitiate two years, juniorate five years. Black habit. Motherhouse: St. Joseph Convent, Mount Carmel, Dubuque, Iowa.

Sisters of Charity of Cincinnati (S.C.) Established from Maryland community in 1829, independent in 1852. Pontifical, active, simple vows. 1,478 sisters. Teaching elementary and high school, academies, boys' military academy, college, school for the deaf; hospitals, schools of nursing, cancer research clinic; care of orphans, including orphanage in Rome, Italy; infant home; day nurseries; social work centers; retreats; missions in Peru. Ages 16-30, high school education. Postulate eleven months, novitiate one year, juniorate three to five years. Black habit. Motherhouse: Mt. St. Joseph, Ohio. Elizabeth Seton Postulate, 431 Quincy, Pueblo, Colorado.

Sisters of Charity of St. Elizabeth (S.C.) Founded at Newark, New Jersey, in 1859 by Mother Mary Xavier Mehegan at the request of Bishop Bayley, nephew of Blessed Elizabeth Ann Seton. Pontifical, active, simple vows. 1,761 sisters. Teaching elementary and high schools, academies, commercial high schools and college, teaching exceptional children; hospitals, schools of nursing; care of orphans and aged; home for working women; domestic work; catechetics; missions in Florida and Virgin Islands. Ages 16-30, high school education. Postulate one year, novitiate one year, juniorate five years. Black habit. Motherhouse: Convent of St. Elizabeth, Convent, New Jersey.

Sisters of Charity of St. Hyacinthe, see Grey Nuns of St. Hyacinthe.

Sisters of Charity of the Immaculate Conception (S.C.I.C.) (Soeurs de la Charité de l'Immaculée-Conception) Founded in Canada in 1854 by Most Rev. Louis T. Connolly and Mother Mary Vincent Conway from the New York branch of the Sisters of Charity founded by Mother Seton. See also Sisters of Our Lady of the Sacred Heart. Pontifical, active, simple vows. 400 sisters. Teaching; nursing; care of aged and orphans; residence for girls; social work; catechetics; office, domestic, library, and sacristy work. Ages 17-30. Postulate ten to twelve months, novitiate two years. Temporary vow period five years. Black habit. Motherhouse: St. Vincent's Convent, 31 Cliff St., St. John, N.B., Canada.

Ivrea Sisters of Charity of the Immaculate Conception (S.C.I.C.) Founded in Italy in 1818; established in U.S. in 1961. Pontifical, active, simple vows. 16 sisters in U.S., 3,000 world. Teaching elementary school, day nurseries, domestic work at a seminary at present in U.S. Congregation also has an extern branch, Missionaries of Charity. Ages 15-30. Aspirancy one year, postulate six months, novitiate two years, juniorate five years. Black habit. Motherhuose: Ivrea, Italy. U.S. provincialate: Convent of the Immaculate Virgin of Miracles, R.D. 2, Mt. Pleasant, Pennsylvania.

Congregation of the Sisters of Charity of the Incarnate Word (C.C.V.I.) Founded in San Antonio, Texas, from Galveston in 1869 by Most Rev. C. M. Dubuis; became independent in 1870 because of the hardships and danger of travel between the two foundations; established in Mexico in 1922. Pontifical, active, simple vows. 1,060 sisters. Black habit.

Motherhouse: Incarnate Word Convent, 4515 Broadway, San Antonio 9, Texas. Perpetual adoration. Teaching elementary and high school, college; hospitals, schools of nursing; care of orphans; community center; domestic work; mission in Ireland. Ages 16-29, two years high school education. Aspirancy two years. Postulate nine months, novitiate two years.

St. Louis Province: Incarnate Word Convent, 2800 Normandy Dr., St. Louis 21, Missouri. 285 sisters. Teaching elementary and high school; nursing; care of orphans; social work; domestic work. Ages 15-30, three years high school education. Aspirancy one to three years. Postulate nine months, novitiate two years, juniorate five years.

Province of Mexico: Reforma # 8, Mexico 20, D.F., Mexico. 275 sisters. Hospitals, clinics; teaching in private schools and free schools for poor; home for girls.

Congregation of the Sisters of Charity of the Incarnate Word of Houston (C.C.V.I.) Founded originally in France in 1625 as a Third Order of the Order of the Incarnate Word and Blessed Sacrament; founded in Galveston, Texas, in 1866 by Most Rev. C. M. Dubuis; motherhouse transferred to Houston in 1925. Pontifical, active, simple vows. 456 sisters. Hospitals, schools of nursing; teaching elementary school; care of aged and orphans; teaching religion to retarded children; social work. To age 30, high school education. Postulate six to twelve months, novitiate two years, juniorate four to seven years. Black habit. Motherhouse: Villa de Matel, 6510 Lawndale Ave., Houston 23, Texas.

Sisters of Charity of the Infant Mary 3 sisters in U.S. Domestic work in a seminary. U.S. address: Infant Mary Convent, 218 Lighthouse Ave., Santa Cruz, California.

Sisters of Charity of St. Joan Antida (S.C.S.J.A.) Founded in France in 1799 by St. Joan Antida Thouret; established in U.S. in 1932. Pontifical, active, simple vows. 58 sisters in U.S., 10,000 world. Teaching elementary and high school; day nurseries; care of orphans and aged; nursing; social work centers; domestic work; foreign missions. No lay sisters. Ages 16-28, some exceptions, high school education. Aspirancy four years. Postulate six months, novitiate one year, juniorate two years. Grey and black habit. Motherhouse: Rome, Italy. Regina Mundi Provincialate, 8560 N. Seventy-sixth St., Granville, Milwaukee, Wisconsin.

Sisters of Charity of Leavenworth, Kansas (S.C.L.) Founded in 1858 in Kansas by Mother Xavier Ross. Originally part of Sisters of Charity of Nazareth, Kentucky. Pontifical, active, simple vows. 951 sisters. Teaching elementary and high school, and college; hospitals and schools of nursing; homes for infants, orphans, and aged; Negro missions. Ages 16-30, high school education. Postulate six months, novitiate eighteen months, juniorate two years. Black habit, white for nurses. Motherhouse: St. Mary's College, Xavier, Kansas.

Sisters of Charity of St. Louis (S.C.S.L.) Founded in France in 1803; now chiefly in Canada; established in U.S. in 1906. Pontifical, active, simple vows. 1,200 sisters, 58 in U.S. Teaching elementary and high school, academies, college; nursing; catechetics; retreats; missions in Haiti and Madagascar. Aspirancy two to three years. Postulate six months, novitiate two years. Black habit. Canadian provincialates: Rue St. Louis de France, Bienville, Levis Co., P.Q., Canada; St. Theresa's Convent, Medicine Hat, Alta., Canada. U.S. regionalate: Cheshire, Connecticut.

Daughters of Charity of the Most Precious Blood (F.C.P.S.)
Founded in Italy in 1872 to care for orphans; established in
U.S. in 1908. Pontifical, active, simple vows. 30 sisters in U.S.
Domestic work; day nursery. Ages 15-30, high school educa-
tion preferred. Black habit. Motherhouse: Rome, Italy. U.S.
address: 1482 North Ave., Bridgeport, Connecticut.

Sisters of Charity of Namur, Belgium Founded in Belgium in
1732. Canadian novitiate: Sorel, P.Q., Canada.

Sisters of Charity of Nazareth (S.C.N.) Founded in Kentucky in
1812 by Most Rev. John David and Mother Catherine Spald-
ing. Pontifical, active, simple vows. 1,584 sisters. Teaching
elementary and high school, academies and colleges; hospitals,
mental hospital, schools of nursing; care of orphans, infants
and aged; summer camps; domestic work; home missions;
teaching, hospital and leper clinic in India. Ages 16-30, some
exceptions, high school education. Postulate ten months, novitiate two years, juniorate two years. Entrance dates January
18, June 7, and September 24. Black habit, white cap. Motherhouse: Nazareth P.O., Nelson Co., Kentucky.

Sisters of Charity of Our Lady of Evron (S.C.E.) (Soeurs de la
Charité Notre Dame d'Evron) Founded in France in 1682;
re-established in 1903 in Evron after French Revolution; established in Canada in 1909. Active and contemplative. 78 sisters
in Canada, 700 world. Contemplation, Divine Office; hospitals,
school of nursing, home nursing; teaching; summer camps;
catechetics; domestic work; missions in Africa. Ages 15-30.
Postulate six months. Motherhouse: Evron, France. Canadian
provincialate: St. Mary's Convent, Box 100, Trochu, Alta.,
Canada.

Sisters of Charity of Our Lady of Mercy (O.L.M.) Founded in
South Carolina in 1829 by Bishop John England to care for orphans and slave children. Diocesan, active, simple vows. 86
sisters. Teaching elementary and high school, academy; hospitals, schools of nursing, clinic; care of orphans; social work
center; summer camps; catechetics; domestic work. Ages 16-30,
high school education. Postulate six to eleven months, novitiate
two years, juniorate three years. Black habit. Motherhouse:
P.O. Box 2111, Fort Johnson Rd., James Island, Charleston,
South Carolina.

Sisters of Charity of Our Lady, Mother of Mercy (S.C.O.L.M.)

Founded in Holland in 1832; established in U.S. in 1874. Pontifical, active, simple vows. 137 sisters in U.S., 5,000 world. Teaching elementary school and academy; nursing; care of aged; retreats; catechetics; domestic work. Ages 16-30, high school education or business or domestic experience. Aspirancy three years. Postulate six months, novitiate two years, juniorate five years. Black habit. Motherhouse: Tilburg, Holland. U.S. provincialate: Holy Family Convent, Baltic, Connecticut.

Sisters of Charity of Philadelphia, see Grey Nuns of the Sacred Heart.

Sisters of Charity of Providence (F.C.S.P.) (Sisters of Providence) Founded in Montreal in 1843 by Bishop Ignatius Bourget and Mother Emelie Gamelin; established in U.S. in 1854. (See also Sisters of Providence of St. Vincent de Paul.) Pontifical, active, simple vows. 3,435 sisters, 753 in U.S. Teaching elementary and high school, academy, school for Indians, normal school, maternal school, and college; hospitals, dispensaries, anti-TB dispensary, mental hospital, schools of nursing; interracial center; day nursery; care of aged and orphans; visiting the sick, poor and prisoners; home and kindergarten for deaf-mutes with 40 deaf-mute sisters in Montreal; depository for alms; domestic work; retreats; missions in Argentina. Ages 18-30, high school education. Postulate eleven months, novitiate two years, juniorate four years. Temporary vow period three years. Motherhouse: 2311 St. Catherine St. E., Montreal 24, P.Q., Canada. Canadian provincialates: Midnapore, Alta., Canada; Joliette, P.Q., Canada; St. Jean de Dieu (Gamelin P.O.), P.Q., Canada. U.S. provincialates: Providence Heights, Pine Lake, Issaquah, Washington; Mt. St. Joseph, 9 E. Ninth Ave., Spokane 3, Washington.

Sisters of Charity of Quebec, see Grey Nuns of Quebec.

Daughters of Charity of the Sacred Heart of Jesus (F.C.S.C.J.) (Les Filles de la Charité du Sacré-Coeur) Founded in France in 1823; established in U.S. in 1905. Pontifical, active, simple vows. 129 sisters in U.S., 2,100 world. Teaching elementary and high school, classical college; hospitals, sanitorium; domestic work; day nurseries; care of aged, foundlings, and orphans; catechetics; Negro missions, missions in South Africa. Ages 16-30. Postulate ten months, novitiate one year, juniorate two years. Black habit. Motherhouse: France. U.S. provincialate:

166 Main St., Colebrook, New Hampshire. Canadian provincialate: Bowen St. S., Sherbrooke, P.Q., Canada.

Sisters of Charity of Seton Hill, see Mother Seton Sisters of Charity.

Daughters of Charity of St. Vincent de Paul (D.C.) Founded in France in 1633 by St. Vincent de Paul and St. Louise de Marillac to help the poor; established in U.S. at Emmitsburg, Maryland, in 1809 by Blessed Mother Elizabeth Seton. First continuous uncloistered community for women in the Church and also the largest. Pontifical, active, simple vows. 45,000 sisters in world. No lay sisters. Blue habit. The white headpiece is often described as "wings" and has caused the sisters to be sometimes referred to as the "swallows of God." General motherhouse: Paris, France. Also located in Mexico. Under jurisdiction of superior general of the Lazarists. U.S. provincialates:

Eastern provincialate: St. Joseph Central House, Emmitsburg, Maryland. 1,298 sisters. Teaching elementary and high school, college; hospitals, mental hospitals, schools of nursing; homes for unmarried mothers; homes for children; care of aged; day nurseries; catechetics; retreats; domestic work; social work center; home missions; foreign missions in Bolivia. Ages 17-30, high school education. Postulate ten months, novitiate one and a half years, juniorate three years.

Western provincialate: Marillac Seminary, Normandy (St. Louis Co.) 21, Missouri. 1,363 sisters. Teaching elementary and high school, Marillac College for sisters; hospitals, mental hospitals, nursing in U.S. leprosarium, schools of nursing; care of aged, infants, orphans; home for working girls; day nursery; retreats; catechetics; social work and child guidance centers, settlements; missions in Puerto Rico, Japan and Formosa. Ages 16-35, high school education. Postulate six months, novitiate (called "seminary") one year, juniorate four years. Five years, including novitiate, before first vows.

Canadian French vice-provincialate: 613 Manning Ave., Toronto 4, Ont., Canada.

White Sisters of Charity of St. Vincent de Paul (W.S.C.) Founded in Yugoslavia in 1845; established in U.S. in 1955. Pontifical, active, simple vows. 15 sisters in U.S., 1,700 world. Domestic work in Franciscan seminaries; catechetics; nursing.

White habit. Motherhouse: Zagreb, Yugoslavia. U.S. address: Our Lady of Carey Seminary, Carey, Ohio.

Sisters of Charity of St. Vincent de Paul of Austria (C.S.V.P.) Founded in 1821 in Austria; established in U.S. *circa* 1935. Diocesan, active, simple vows. 33 sisters in U.S., 865 world. Domestic work in seminaries, care of aged at present. Ages 18-35, high school education. Postulate six months, novitiate two years. Motherhouse: Zams, Tyrol, Austria. U.S. provincialate: St. Joseph's Home for the Aged, 705 Clyman St., Watertown, Wisconsin.

Sisters of Charity of St. Vincent de Paul, Halifax (S.C.H.) Founded at Halifax, Nova Scotia, from Emmitsburg, Maryland, foundation in 1849; independent in 1856. Pontifical, active, simple vows. 1,615 sisters. Teaching elementary and high school, academies, normal school, schools for Indians, college; hospitals, schools of nursing; care of foundlings, orphans, and aged; day nurseries; social work centers; homes for working girls; missions in Bermuda. Ages 16-30, high school education. Postulate ten months, novitiate two years, juniorate five years. Temporary vow period six years. Entrance dates February 2 and September 8. Black habit. Motherhouse: Mt. St. Vincent, Rockingham Station, Halifax, N.S., Canada. U.S. provincialate: Resurrection-Ascension Convent, 85-18 Sixty-first St., Rego Park 74, New York.

Sisters of Charity of St. Vincent de Paul of New York (S.C.) Founded in New York in 1817 from Emmitsburg, Maryland, foundation; independent in 1847. Diocesan, active, simple vows. 1,368 sisters. Teaching elementary and high school, vocational and commercial schools, academies, junior college, college; teaching retarded children; hospitals, schools of nursing, clinics, mental hospital, convalescent home; children's homes, New York Foundling Hospital; day nursery; catechetics; retreats; missions in Bahamas. Ages 17-30, high school education preferred. Postulate one year, novitiate two years; juniorate varies. Black habit and cap. Motherhouse: Mount St. Vincent-on-Hudson. Two hundred-sixty-first St. and Riverdale Ave., New York 71, New York.

Charity, see Blessed Sacrament and of Charity, Handmaids, Adorers of the; Carmelite Sisters of Charity; Dominican Sisters of Charity of the Presentation of the Blessed Virgin Mary; Our

Lady of Charity of Refuge, Sisters of; see also Christian Charity; Divine Charity; Penance and Charity under Franciscan Third Order.

Missionary Sisters of St. Charles Borromeo (M.S.S.C.B.) (Scalabrini Sisters) Founded in Italy in 1895 by Bishop John Baptist Scalabrini; established in U.S. in 1941. Pontifical, active, simple vows. 37 sisters in U.S., 1,100 world. Domestic work; teaching elementary school; care of aged; retreats; social work; home and foreign missions. No lay sisters. Ages 15-30, eighth grade education. Postulate six months, novitiate two years. Motherhouse: Sao Paulo, Brazil. U.S. provincialate; Bishop Scalabrini Novitiate, 1414 N. Thirty-seventh Ave., Melrose Park, Illinois.

Little Sisters of Charles de Foucauld, see Jesus, Little Sisters of.

Dames de Chavagnes, see Ursulines of Jesus.

Sisters of Saint Chrétienne (S.S.Ch.) (Religious of the Holy Infancy of Jesus and Mary) Founded in France in 1807; established in U.S. in 1903. Pontifical, active, simple vows. 212 sisters in Canada and U.S., 1,100 world. Teaching; nursing; social work; retreats; catechetics; home missions; foreign missions in French Somalia, Africa, and Austria. Also located in Rumford, Mexico. Ages 17-30, eighth grade education. Aspirancy one to three years. Postulate 1 year, novitiate one year. Training schools in Canada, France, and Belgium. Black habit. Motherhouse: Metz, France. American provincialate: 3365 Rue Guimont, Giffard, Quebec 5, P.Q., Canada. U.S. aspirancy: Ste. Chrétienne Academy, 262 Loring Ave., Salem, Massachusetts.

Society of Christ Our King (C.R.S.) Founded in North Carolina in 1931 by Mother Teresa. Diocesan, active, simple vows. 6 sisters. Home missions in the spirit of recent social-action encyclicals: Catechetics; retreats; care of unwed mothers. Ages 14-30, eighth grade education. Habit: dress, coat and hat. Motherhouse: Lynn Regis, Box 1318, Danville, Virginia.

Missionary Sisters of Christ the King (M.C.R.) (Soeurs Missionnaires du Christ-Roi) Founded in Gaspé, Canada, in 1928 by Bishop Felix Ross and Mother Mary of the Sacred Heart. Pontifical, active and contemplative, simple vows. 203 sisters. Home missions among Indians: Teaching; nursing; social work; catechetics; hostel for girls; nursery. Foreign missions in

Japan and the Congo. No lay sisters. Contemplation. Divine
Office chanted in choir. Ages 18-30. Postulate six months, novitiate two years, juniorate two years. Temporary vow period
five years. Additional year of religious formation without
apostolic work four years after taking perpetual vows. White
habit. Motherhouse: 4730 Levesque Blvd. W., Chomeday,
Montreal, P.Q., Canada.

Sister-Servants of Christ the King (S.S.C.K.) Founded in North
Dakota in 1936 by Sisters Mary Rose and Carmelita. Diocesan,
active. 26 sisters. Domestic work; nursing; catechetics at summer schools and camps. Ages 16-35, high school education
preferred. Aspirancy four years. Postulate six to twelve months,
novitiate two years. Motherhouse: Loretto Convent, Mt. Calvary, Wisconsin.

Christ the King, see Benedictine Missionaries of Guadalupe of
Christ the King; and see Franciscan Third Order.

Sisters of Christ the Teacher (S.C.M.) Byzantine Greek Rite.
Founded in Pennsylvania in 1959 by Bishop N. T. Elko.
Diocesan, active, simple vows. 11 sisters. Teaching. To age
35, high school education. Postulate six months, novitiate one
year, juniorate three years. Motherhouse: 66 Riverview Ave.,
Pittsburgh 14, Pennsylvania.

Sisters of Christian Charity (S.C.C.) (Daughters of the Blessed
Virgin Mary of the Immaculate Conception) Founded in
Germany in 1849 to care for blind children; established in U.S.
in 1873. Pontifical, active, simple vows. 1,135 sisters in U.S.,
2,500 world. Teaching elementary and high school, academy,
junior colleges; office and domestic work; nursing; care of orphans; catechetics; retreats; social work; home missions. Ages
16-30, high school education. Aspirancy four years. Postulate
one year, novitiate two years, juniorate five to six years. Black
habit. Motherhouse: Rome, Italy. Eastern U.S. provincialate:
Mallinckrodt Convent, Mendham, New Jersey. Western U.S.
provincialate: Maria Immaculata Convent, Ridge Rd. at Walnut, Wilmettte, Illinois.

Missionary Sisters of Christian Charity (M.S.C.C.) Ukrainian
Byzantine Rite. Founded in Canada in 1946 by Very Rev.
Mark Romanovich, O.S.B.M. Diocesan, active, simple vows.
7 sisters. Social work; teaching; catechetics; visiting the sick
in homes, hospitals, mental hospitals; visiting prisons. Ages

15-35, to 40 with special permission. Postulate six months, novitiate two years. Temporary vow period four years. Navy blue habit, white in summer and for nursing, secular dress if necessary. Motherhouse: Box 180, 382 Main St. W., Grimsby, Ont., Canada.

Christian Charity, see St. Francis of Penance and Christian Charity, Sisters of; Franciscan Sisters of Christian Charity.

Christian Doctrine, see Our Lady of Christian Doctrine, Sisters of.

Religious of Christian Education (R.C.E.) Founded in France in 1817; established in U.S. in 1905. Pontifical, active, simple vows. 128 sisters in U.S., 500 world. Teaching elementary school, academies, junior college, teacher training school; office and domestic work; catechetics; missions in Dahomey, West Africa. To age 30, high school education. Postulate ten months, novitiate one year, juniorate three years. Black habit. U.S. regionalate: 130 Milton St., Milton 86, Massachusetts.

Cistercian Nuns of the Strict Observance (O.C.S.O.) (Trappistines) Founded in France in 1120; strict observance of rule adopted in 1664. Established in Canada in 1904, in U.S. in 1949. Pontifical, contemplative, major papal enclosure, solemn vows. The nuns live an austere life of prayer, silence, abstinence, and manual labor, including farming. Age 18, high school education. White and black habit for choir nuns. Motherhouse: France. Each monastery is autonomous, subject to Abbot General in Rome. Canadian monasteries: Monastery of Our Lady of Good Counsel, St. Romuald d'Etchemin, P.Q., Canada; Monastery of Our Lady of the Assumption, Rogersville, N.B., Canada. U.S. abbey: Mt. St. Mary's Abbey, Arnold St., R.F.D. Box 500, Wrentham, Massachusetts. 30 choir nuns, 27 lay sisters.

Cistercians of the Original Observance (S.O.Cist.) (Sacred Cistercian Order) (Cistercian Nuns) Founded in France in 1098 by St. Robert of Molesme; Swiss motherhouse founded in 1231; established in U.S. in 1958. Pontifical, contemplative, solemn vows. 5 choir nuns, 3 lay sisters in U.S., 4,123 members in world. Contemplation; making altar breads; farming; gardening; domestic work; needlework; retreats being planned. To age 30, some exceptions, high school or college education for choir nuns. Motherhouse: Frauenthal, Switzerland. U.S.

foundation: St. Ida's Convent, Rte. 1, Prairie du Sac, Wisconsin.

Missionaries of St. Clare of the Blessed Sacrament, see Poor Clare Missionary Sisters.

St. Clare, see also Poor Clare Nuns and Poor Clare Colettines.

Claretian Missionary Sisters, see Teaching Sisters of Mary Immaculate.

Missionary Sisters of St. Columban (S.S.C.) Founded in Ireland in 1922 to do missionary work in China, at the suggestion of Bishop Edward Galvin, founder of the Columban Fathers; established in U.S. in 1930. Pontifical, active, simple vows. 54 sisters in U.S., 275 world. Missions in Burma, Hong Kong, Korea, Philippines, South America: teaching; catechetics; nursing; domestic work; social work. Ages 17-30, high school education. Postulate six months, novitiate two years. Black habit; white habit in hot climates. Motherhouse: County Clare, Ireland. U.S. regionalate: St. Columban Novitiate, 950 Metropolitan Ave., Hyde Park 36, Massachusetts.

Consolata Missionary Sisters (M.C.) Founded in Italy in 1910; established in U.S. in 1954. Pontifical, active, simple vows. 17 sisters in U.S., 1,300 world. Teaching elementary school; nursing; social work; catechetics; missions in Africa and South America. Ages 17-30, high school education. Postulate one year, novitiate two years, juniorate five years. Motherhouse: Torino, Italy. U.S. provincialate: Belmont Rd., Belmont, Michigan.

Cordi-Marian Missionary Sisters (M.C.M.) Founded in Mexico in 1921 by Rev. Julian Collell and Mother Carmen Serrano; established in U.S. in 1926. Diocesan, active, simple vows. 151 sisters. Teaching elementary school; settlement house; catechetics; spreading good literature; missions in U.S. and Mexico. Ages 15-30, high school education preferred. Postulate eight months, novitiate two years. Novitiate in Mexico. Motherhouse: Cordi-Marian Villa, 78 W. Culebra Rd., San Antonio, Texas.

Corpus Christi, see Carmelite Sisters of Corpus Christi.

Daughters of the Cross (D.C.) Founded in Paris, France, in 1640 by Madame Marie de Villenueve and St. Francis de Sales; established in U.S. in 1855. Diocesan, active, simple vows. 93 sisters in U.S. Teaching elementary and high school; nursing; home missions. Ages 15-35, high school education. Aspirancy four years. Postulate nine months, novitiate two years, juniorate five years. Black habit. U.S. provincialate: St. Vincent's College, St. Vincent and Southern Aves., Shreveport 49, Louisiana.

Sisters of the Cross (F.C.) (Filles de la Croix dites Soeurs de St. André) Founded in France in 1804 by St. Andrew Fournet and St. Jeanne Bichier des Ages; established in Canada in 1905. Pontifical, active, simple vows. 111 sisters in Canada. Teaching elementary and high school, sewing schools; hospitals, dispensaries; care of orphans and aged; homes for girls in cities; catechetics; social work; foreign missions. Ages 16-35. Postulate six months, novitiate eighteen months. Black habit restyled in 1957, white habit in warm climates. Motherhouse: La Puye (Vienne) France. Canadian provincialate: Maison Sainte Croix, 275 Archibald Street, St. Boniface 6, Manitoba, Canada.

Cross, see Grey Nuns of the Cross; Our Lady of the Cross, Sisters of.

Sisters of Saints Cyril and Methodius (SS.C.M.) Founded in Pennsylvania in 1909 by Rev. Matthew Jankola to teach the children of Slovak immigrants. Diocesan, active, simple vows. 393 sisters. Teaching elementary and high school, academy; domestic work; care of orphans and aged; nursing; speech and reading clinics; catechetics; office and domestic work; gardening; journalism, art, music. Pray especially for the salvation of souls and the return of all separated brethren. Ages 16-30, high school education. Postulate six to nine months, novitiate two years, juniorate five years. Black habit. Motherhouse: Villa Sacred Heart, Danville, Pennsylvania.

D

Daughters of Divine Charity (F.D.C.) Founded in Austria in 1868; established in U.S. in 1913. Pontifical, active, simple vows. 2,500 in world. Black habit. Motherhouse: Vienna, Austria. Canadian address: Loretto Hall, 675 Devonshire Rd., Windsor, Ont., Canada. Home for working girls, school of music and kindergarten. U.S. provincialates:
St. Joseph Hill Academy, 850 Hylan Blvd., Arrochar, Staten

Island 5, New York. 231 sisters. Teaching elementary and high school, academy; rest home; homes for working girls; social work; catechetics; domestic work; missions in South America. Ages 14-25. Aspirancy four years. Postulate six months, novitiate two years, juniorate four years.

39 North Portage Path, Akron 3, Ohio. 32 sisters. Teaching elementary school; home for working girls; catechetics; domestic work; social work. Ages 14-24. Postulate six months, novitiate two years, juniorate seven years.

Divine Child, see Franciscan Missionary Sisters of the Divine Child.

Sisters of the Divine Compasssion (S.D.C.) Founded in New York City in 1886 by Msgr. T. S. Preston and Mother M. Veronica Starr. Diocesan, active, simple vows. 203 sisters. Teaching elementary and high school, academy, college. To age 25, some exceptions, high school education preferred. Postulate nine months, novitiate two years, juniorate three years. Black habit. Motherhouse: Good Counsel Convent, 52 N. Broadway, White Plains, New York.

Divine Heart, see Carmelite Sisters of the Divine Heart of Jesus; Reparation of the Divine Heart, Daughters of.

Oblate Sisters of Divine Love (R.D.A.) Founded in Italy in 1923; established in U.S. in 1947. 10 sisters in U.S. Teaching elementary school. Ages 15-25, some exceptions. Aspirancy. After final profession the sisters are called "Mother." Black habit. U.S. address: St. Clare of Assisi Convent, 2118 Hone Ave., Bronx, New York.

Pious Disciples of the Divine Master (P.D.M.) Founded in Italy in 1924; established in U.S. in 1948. Pontifical, active and contemplative, simple vows. 39 sisters in U.S., 1,500 in world. Perpetual adoration; liturgical apostolate; domestic work in seminaries, etc. Also located in Mexico. Ages 14-25, eighth grade education. Aspirancy six months, postulate one year, novitiate one year, juniorate five years. Motherhouse: Alba, Italy. U.S. provincialate: 3700 Cornelia Ave., Fresno, California.

Divine Motherhood, see Franciscan Missionaries of the Divine Motherhood.

Sisters of Divine Providence (C.D.P.) Founded in Germany in 1851; established in U.S., in Pennsylvania, in 1876. Pontifical, active, simple vows. 833 sisters in U.S., 1,600 world. Black habit. U.S. provincialates:

Providence Heights, 9000 Babcock Blvd., Allison Park, Pennsylvania. 633 sisters. Teaching elementary and high school, academies, extension college, junior military academy; hospitals, schools of nursing; home for boys; domestic work; missions in Puerto Rico. Age 16, high school education. Aspirancy four years. Postulate six to twelve months, novitiate two years.

Box 2, Rte. 80, Kingston, Massachusetts. 79 sisters. Teaching elementary and high school, teacher training school; catechetics; domestic work. Age 16, high school education. Postulate six months, novitiate two years, juniorate three years.

Mount Providence, 8351 Florissant Rd., Normandy 21, Missouri. 121 sisters. Teaching elementary and high school; nursing; home missions. Ages 15-30, two years high school education. Aspirancy two to three years. Postulate six to twelve months, novitiate two years, juniorate five to six years.

Sisters of Divine Providence of San Antonio, Texas (C.D.P.) Founded in France in 1762 by Blessed John Martin Moye; established in U.S. in 1866. (See also Missionary Catechists of Divine Providence, below.) Pontifical, active, simple vows. 722 sisters. Teaching elementary and high school, college, graduate school of social work; hospitals, clinics; home for working girls; club for underprivileged girls; catechetics; office and domestic work; missions in Mexico. Ages 15-30. Aspirancy until high school graduation. Candidacy three months, postulate six months, novitiate one year, juniorate three years. Black habit. Motherhouse: Our Lady of the Lake Convent, 515 S.W. Twenty-fourth St., San Antonio 7, Texas.

Missionary Catechists of Divine Providence (M.C.D.P.) Founded in 1930 as a filial society of the Sisters of Divine Providence of San Antonio, Texas, above. 62 sisters. Catechetics; home visiting; clinics. To age 30, some exceptions, high school education. Aspirancy. Candidacy one to two years, postulate six months, novitiate one year, juniorate one year. Temporary vow period four years. Black habit. Motherhouse: St. Andrew's Convent, 2318 Castroville Rd., San Antonio 37, Texas.

Sisters of Divine Providence of Kentucky (C.D.P.) Founded in France in 1762 by Blessed John Martin Moye; established in U.S. 1889. Pontifical, active, simple vows. 461 sisters in U.S. Teaching elementary and high school, academies, university, schools for Negroes; nursing; care of infants, orphans, and aged; homes for working girls; domestic work in seminaries; office work; teaching and nursing in primitive sections in the Kentucky mountains. Ages 14-30. Aspirancy varies, postulate six months, novitiate one year, juniorate four years. No lay sisters. Black habit. Motherhouse: Moselle, France. U.S. provincialate: St. Anne Convent, Melbourne, Kentucky.

Daughters of the Divine Redeemer (D.D.R.) Founded in Alsace-Lorraine in 1849 by Ven. Mother Mary Eppinger; established in U.S. in 1912. Pontifical, active, simple vows. 156 sisters in U.S., 5,000 world. Teaching elementary school and academy; nursing; domestic work; care of aged; administration. To age 30, high school education. Aspirancy three and a half years, postulate six months, novitiate two years, juniorate five years. Black habit. Motherhouse: Rome, Italy. U.S. provincialate: St. Joseph's Convent, R.D. 1, Box 357, 356 Rock Run Rd., Elizabeth, Pennsylvania.

Sisters of the Divine Saviour (S.D.S.) (Salvatorian Sisters) Founded in Italy in 1888; established in U.S. in 1895. Pontifical, active, simple vows. 391 sisters in U.S., 2,200 world. Teaching elementary and high school, junior college; hospitals, schools of nursing; care of orphans and aged; domestic work in seminaries; home missions; foreign missions in Ceylon, Formosa, Tanganyika, the Congo, Jordan, Israel, Colombia, Brazil and Spain. To age 30, high school education. Postulate six months, novitiate two years, juniorate three years. Temporary vow period six years. Motherhouse: Rome, Italy. U.S. provincialate: St. Mary's Convent, 3516 W. Center St., Milwaukee 10, Wisconsin.

Congregation of the Divine Spirit (C.D.S.) Founded in Pennsylvania in 1955 by Archbishop John Gannon in response to the plea of Pope Pius XII for the adaptation and renovation of religious institutes. Diocesan, active, simple vows. 70 sisters. Home missions; teaching elementary school; nursing; catechetics; care of aged; social work; census taking and home visiting; administration at a college and diocesan offices. Meditation, Divine Office planned. Ages 18-35, older considered. Candidacy four months, postulate eight months, novitiate two years, juniorate four years. Home visit after three years, annual visit after five years. Habit: Grey skirt and jacket, navy hat. Hair worn in modern style. Motherhouse: Domus Pacis, 409 W. Sixth St., Erie, Pennsylvania.

Dominican Nuns of the Second Order of Perpetual Adoration (O.P.—Order of Preachers) Founded in 1206 in France by St. Dominic. Although this is a second order, it was actually founded by St. Dominic before the men's order. The nuns are sometimes referred to as Preacheresses. Established in U.S. in 1880. Pontifical, contemplative, major papal enclosure, solemn vows. 3,000 in world. Austere life, meat not eaten, rising at midnight to pray, etc. Prayer and sacrifice are offered for the salvation of souls and for the work of the Dominican friars. Perpetual adoration, Divine Office sung. Embroidering vestments and church linens; sewing habits for Dominican friars; arts and crafts; illumination on parchment; translating books; printing and bookbinding; office work. To age 30, high school education, some knowledge of Latin desirable. Postulate six to twelve months, novitiate one year, juniorate three years. White habit, black veil. Fourteen independent monasteries, alphabetized by state:

Monastery of the Angels, 1977 Carmen Place, Los Angeles 28, California. 25 nuns, 1 extern sister.

Corpus Christi Monastery, Oak Grove Ave., Menlo Park, California. 40 nuns, 4 externs.

Monastery of Our Lady of Grace, North Guilford, Connecticut. 34 nuns, 3 externs.

Monastery of the Mother of God, 1430 Riverdale St., West Springfield, Massachusetts. 43 nuns, 2 externs.

Monastery of the Blessed Sacrament, 9704 Oakland Ave., Detroit 11, Michigan. 29 nuns, 3 externs.

Monastery of St. Dominic, Thirteenth Ave. and So. Tenth St., Newark 3, New Jersey. 37 nuns, 3 externs.

Monastery of Our Lady of the Rosary, Rosary Shrine, Morris and Springfield Aves., Summit, New Jersey. 22 choir nuns, 6 lay sisters, 4 externs. Perpetual rosary.

Monastery of the Immaculate Conception, 714 New Scotland Ave., Albany, New York. 22 nuns, 4 externs.

Monastery of Our Lady of the Rosary, 335 Doat St., Buffalo, New York. 42 nuns, 2 externs.

Monastery of Mary the Queen, 1310 W. Church St., Elmira, New York. 16 nuns.

Corpus Christi Monastery, Lafayette Ave. and Barretto St., Hunt's Point, Bronx, New York. 45 nuns, 4 externs.
Monastery of the Holy Name, 3020 Erie Ave., Hyde Park, Cincinnati, Ohio. 15 nuns, 1 extern.
Monastery of the Infant Jesus, 1501 Lotus Lane, R.F.D. 4, Box 1190, Lufkin, Texas. 26 nuns, 2 externs.
Canadian monastery: Monastery of Our Lady of the Rosary, Berthierville, P.Q., Canada.

Dominican Sisters of the Perpetual Rosary (O.P.) Founded in France in 1880 by Rev. Damien Saintourens, O.P.; established in U.S. in 1891 by the founder. Diocesan, contemplative-cloistered, simple vows at some monasteries, solemn vows at others. Perpetual rosary day and night, contemplation, Divine Office chanted in choir. Making altar breads, rosaries, vestments, altar linens, spiritual bouquets; embroidering; painting; typing and filing. Ages 16-30, high school education. Average training: Postulate six to twelve months, novitiate one year, juniorate three years. Black and white habit. Each monastery is independent.
Dominican Nuns of Perpetual Rosary and Perpetual Adoration, Monastery of St. Jude, Marbury, Alabama. 9 nuns.
Dominican Nuns of the Perpetual Rosary, 720 Maiden Choice Lane, Catonsville 28, Maryland. 14 nuns.
Dominican Nuns of the Perpetual Rosary, Monastery of the Perpetual Rosary, Haddon and Euclid Aves., Camden 3, New Jersey. 15 nuns, 3 extern sisters.
Monastery of the Dominican Sisters of the Perpetual Rosary, Fourteenth and West Sts., Union City, New Jersey. 37 nuns.
Dominican Nuns of the Perpetual Rosary, Monastery of the Perpetual Rosary, 802 Court St., Syracuse 8, New York. 10 nuns, 1 extern.
Monastery of the Immaculate Heart of Mary, 1834 Lititz Pike, P.O. Box 1125, Lancaster, Pennsylvania. 19 nuns.
St. Dominic's Monastery, 3000 South Ave., La Crosse, Wisconsin. 17 nuns.
Convent of the Dominican Sisters of the Perpetual Rosary, 217 No. Sixty-eighth St., Milwaukee 13, Wisconsin. 18 nuns, 1 extern.
Sisters of the Third Order of St. Dominic. *Originally founded in Prouille, France, in 1206 by St. Dominic. Each congregation*

is independent, affiliated with the Order of Preachers but with no central motherhouse. Dominican habit is white with black veil.

Dominican Sisters of Bethany (O.P.) Founded in France in 1866 by Father Lataste; Netherlands congregation independent in 1923; established in Canada in 1955. Pontifical, active, and contemplative, simple vows. 21 sisters in Canada, 13 U.S., 720 world. Rehabilitation of girls and women; visiting and teaching at prisons; homes for girls in Chicago and Miami; care of Cuban refugee children in Miami; missions in Caribbean. A great variety of talents can be used—apiarists and artists, ballet teachers and bookkeepers, chemists and contemplatives, and many more. Divine Office chanted. Ages 16-35, high school education preferred. Aspirancy one year. Postulate six months, novitiate two years, juniorate five years. Temporary vow period five years. Rehabilitated women are given an opportunity to become full members of the congregation. White habit. Motherhouse: Venlo, Netherlands. American regionalate: R. R. 2, Lambeth, Ont., Canada.

Dominican Sisters of Bethany, Congregation of St. Mary Magdalene (O.P.) Founded in France in 1866 by Father Lataste; established in U.S. in 1960. Pontifical, contemplative, semi-cloistered, simple vows. 6 sisters U.S., 530 world. Contemplation, Divine Office in choir; sewing vestments; artwork; a few sisters visit women in prisons. The purpose of the congregation is the rehabilitation of ex-prisoners and other penitents, making the religious life possible for them as well as other members. There are also tertiary sisters, members of the Third Order of Bethany, in which the training and life are less exacting although they wear the same habit and work and pray together with the canonical sisters. Tertiary sisters may enter the canonical novitiate if they so wish and are considered ready by their superiors. To age 35. Postulate nine months, novitiate two years, juniorate five years. For tertiary sisters length of training varies according to the needs of each sister. No dowry required. Motherhouse: France. International Juniorate in Rome. U.S. novitiate: 19 Dartmouth St., West Newton 65, Massachusetts.

Dominican Congregation of St. Catherine de Ricci (O.P.) Founded in New York in 1880 by Mother Maria de Ricci Smith, a young convert, to conduct retreats and offer laywomen an opportunity for deeper religious development. Pontifical, active, simple vows. 164 sisters. Retreats; catechetics; teaching in academies; homes for working girls and retired women; hospices for women; social work; missions in Cuba. Ages 16-30, some exceptions, high school education. Postulate six months, novitiate two years, juniorate three years. Motherhouse: Convent of Mary, Queen of All Saints, 2850 No. Providence Rd., Media, Pennsylvania.

Dominican Congregation of St. Catharine of Siena (O.P.) Founded in Kentucky in 1822 by Rev. Samuel T. Wilson. First U.S. community of Dominican Sisters. Pontifical, active, simple vows. 807 sisters. Teaching elementary and high school, academies, colleges; nursing; missions in Puerto Rico. High school education preferred. Postulate one year, novitiate one year, juniorate three years. Motherhouse: St. Catharine of Siena Convent, St. Catharine P.O., Kentucky.

Dominican Congregation of St. Catherine of Sienna (O.P.) Founded in Massachusetts in 1891 by Mother Mary Sheridan. Diocesan, active, simple vows. 141 sisters. Teaching elementary and high school, academy; domestic work; catechetics; day nursery. At least 16, high school education for prospective teachers. Postulate one year, novitiate two years, juniorate three years. Motherhouse: St. Catherine's Convent, 37 Park St., Fall River, Massachusetts.

Dominican Sisters of St. Catherine of Sienna (O.P.) Founded in Portugal in 1866; established in U.S. in 1911; independent congregation in 1952. Pontifical, active, simple vows. 127 sisters. Nursing; teaching elementary school; care of aged; catechetics. Recite Divine Office daily. Ages 15-30, high school education preferred. Postulate six to twelve months, novitiate one year, juniorate four years. Motherhouse: St. Catherine of Sienna Convent, 3556 Seventh Ave., Kenosha, Wisconsin.

Dominican Congregation of St. Catherine of Siena, South Africa. Founded in South Africa in 1890; established in U.S. in 1955. Pontifical, active, simple vows. 16 sisters in U.S., 351 world. Teaching elementary school; domestic work; catechetics; missions in South Africa. Age 16, eighth grade education. Motherhouse: Oakford, Natal, Union of South Africa. U.S. address: Dominican Convent, 2659 Homestead Rd., Santa Clara, California.

Dominican Congregation of St. Cecilia (O.P.) Founded in Ten-

nessee in 1860 by sisters from the Congregation of St. Mary
of the Springs, then in Somerset, Ohio. Pontifical, active, simple vows. 153 sisters. Teaching elementary and high school,
academy, junior college; care of orphans; catechetics; home
missions. Ages 16-30, high school education. Postulate six
months, novitiate one year, juniorate three years. Motherhouse: St. Cecilia Convent, Eighth Ave. N. and Clay St.,
Nashville 8, Tennessee.

**Dominican Sisters of Charity of the Presentation of the Blessed
Virgin Mary** (O.P.) (Sisters of the Presentation) Founded
in France in 1684; established in U.S. in 1906. Pontifical, active, simple vows. 35 sisters in U.S., 4,600 world. Hospital,
school of nursing; care of aged; mission in Africa. Ages 17-35,
high school education. Postulate six months, novitiate two
years. Motherhouse: Tours, France. U.S. provincialate: St.
Ann's Hospital, 795 Middle St., Fall River, Massachusetts.

Dominican Sisters of the Holy Guardian Angels (O.P.) (Soeurs
Dominicaines des Saints-Anges-Gardiens) Founded in Yugoslavia in 1905; established in Canada in 1953. Diocesan, semi-
contemplative, simple vows. 26 sisters in Canada, 301 in world.
Teaching, works of charity. Postulate six months, novitiate
one year, juniorate three years. Entrance dates: March 25,
September 25. Motherhouse: Yugoslavia. Canadian novitiate:
361 rue Moore, Sherbrooke, P.Q., Canada.

Congregation of the Immaculate Conception, see Dominican Sisters of the Sick Poor.

Dominican Sisters of the Immaculate Conception (O.P.) Founded
in Poland in 1929. Diocesan, active, simple vows. 27 sisters
in U.S. Teaching; nursing in convalescent homes. Ages 16-30.
Postulate six to twelve months, novitiate one year. Temporary
vow period three years. Motherhouse: Biala Nizna, Poland.
U.S. provincialate: 9000 W. Eighty-first St., Justice, Illinois.

Dominican Sisters of the Infant Jesus (O.P.) (Soeurs Dominicaines de l'Enfant-Jesus) Founded in Canada in 1887. Nursing. Motherhouse: 615 S. Cyrille St., Quebec, P.Q., Canada.

Dominican Oblates of Jesus (D.O.J.) Founded in Spain in 1946;
recently established in U.S. Diocesan, active and contemplative, simple vows. 15 sisters in U.S., 46 world. Domestic work;
catechetics; social work. To age 33, high school education.
Aspirancy one year, postulate six months, novitiate two years,

juniorate six years. Motherhouse: Madrid, Spain. U.S. delega-
tion: LaSallette Seminary, 475 Oak Ave., Cheshire, Connecticut.

Dominican Congregation of St. Mary (O.P.) Founded in New Orleans in 1860 by Mother Mary John Flanagan and a group
of Dominican Sisters from Ireland. Pontifical, active, simple
vows. 218 sisters. Teaching elementary and high, public school,
college; nursing. Ages 16-30, high school education. Aspirancy
four years. Postulate nine months, novitiate one year, juniorate
three years. Motherhouse: St. Mary's Convent, 7214 St.
Charles Ave., New Orleans 18, Louisiana.

Dominican Congregation of St. Mary of the Springs (O.P.)
Founded in Somerset, Ohio, in 1830 by sisters of the Congregation of St. Catharine of Siena, St. Catharine, Kentucky.
Called St. Mary of the Springs because of the springs on the
motherhouse property. Pontifical, active, simple vows. 698 sisters. Teaching elementary and high school, academies, colleges; nursing; domestic work; catechetics; home missions.
Ages 17-30, some exceptions, high school education for prospective teachers. Postulate ten months, novitiate two years,
juniorate five years. Motherhouse: St. Mary of the Springs
Convent, Columbus 19, Ohio.

**Dominican Mission Sisters, Congregation of Our Lady of the
Rosary** (O.P.) Founded in Chicago in 1955 by Rev. Jordan
Aumann, O.P. Diocesan, active, simple vows. 34 sisters. Home
missions: social work; visiting and aiding the aging; catechetics
for the Spanish-speaking; publication—*Veritas;* foreign missions in Ecuador, Peru, and Chile—teaching elementary
school, catechetics; clinic. Ages 18-40, high school education,
widows accepted, any race or nationality. Postulate one year,
novitiate one year, juniorate three years. Two temporary vow
periods of three years each. Motherhouse: 5017 S. Greenwood
Ave., Chicago, Illinois, 60615.

Dominican Congregation of the Most Holy Name of Jesus (O.P.)
Founded in California in 1850 by Mother Mary of the Cross
from a convent in Paris, France. Pontifical, active, simple
vows. 326 sisters. Teaching elementary, high school, and college; nursing; administration; office and domestic work; Divine Office chanted. To age 30, some exceptions, high school
education. Postulate six months, novitiate one year, juniorate

three years. Motherhouse: Dominican Convent, San Rafael, California.

Dominican Congregation of the Most Holy Rosary (O.P.) Founded in Wisconsin in 1847 by Very Rev. S. C. Mazzuchelli, O.P. Pontifical, active and contemplative, simple vows. 1,951 sisters. Contemplation; teaching elementary and high school, academies, colleges, Institute of Pius XII, a graduate school of fine arts in Florence, Italy; nursing; office and domestic work; catechetics in rural areas; playground supervision in public parks; Negro missions; foreign missions in Bolivia. Ages 16-30. Postulate one year, novitiate one year, juniorate three years. Temporary vow period three years. Motherhouse: St. Clara Convent, Sinsinawa, Wisconsin.

Dominican Sisters of Nancy, France, see Dominican Sisters of the Roman Congregation.

Congregation of Our Lady of the Rosary, see Dominican Mission Sisters.

Dominican Congregation of Our Lady of the Rosary (O.P.) Founded in New York City in 1876 by Mother Catherine Antoninus Thorpe. Diocesan, active, simple vows. 818 sisters. Teaching elementary and high school, teachers' college, secretarial schools; children's homes; day nursery; settlement house; women's hospice; summer camp; catechetics; office work; missions in West Pakistan. Ages 18-30, high school education preferred. Postulate eight months, novitiate one year, juniorate five years. Motherhouse: St. Agnes Convent, Sparkill, New York.

Dominican Congregation of Our Lady of the Sacred Heart (O.P.) Founded in Illinois in 1873 by sisters from the Congregation of St. Catharine of Siena, St. Catharine, Kentucky. Pontifical, active, simple vows. 619 sisters. Teaching elementary and high school; hospitals and convalescent home; care of orphans and aged; domestic work; administration; care of sacristies; catechetics; rural missions. Ages 16-30, high school education. Aspirancy three months, postulate six months, novitiate one year, juniorate three years. Motherhouse: Sacred Heart Convent, 1237 W. Monroe St., Springfield, Illinois.

Dominican Poor School Sisters of Penance (O.P.) Founded in Germany in 1852; established in U.S. in Helena, Montana in 1925. Diocesan, active, simple vows. 113 sisters in U.S.,

1,000 world. Teaching elementary and Indian mission boarding schools; hospitals and nursing homes; domestic work; home
missions; foreign missions in Ghana, Africa. Ages 16-30. Postulate one year, novitiate one year, juniorate four years. Motherhouse: Rhein, Germany. U.S. provincialate: Our Lady of the
Valley Convent, Kettle Falls, Washington.

Dominican Sisters of the Roman Congregation (O.P.) (Dominican Sisters of Nancy, France.) Founded in France in 1853;
established in U.S. in 1904. Pontifical, active and contemplative, simple vows. 132 sisters in U.S., 1,300 world. Contemplation for all; teaching elementary and high school, academies;
domestic work; retreats; missions in Brazil and Japan. Ages
17-30. Postulate one year, novitiate one year, juniorate five
years. Motherhouse: Rome, Italy. U.S. regionalate: St. Dominic's Institute, 200 Ivy St., Brookline 46, Massachusetts.

Dominican Sisters of the Rosary (O.P.) (Soeurs Dominicaines du
Rosaire) Founded in Canada in 1902. Teaching; care of orphans. Motherhouse: Trois-Rivières, P.Q., Canada.

Dominican Congregation of St. Rose of Lima (O.P.) Founded
in Pennsylvania in 1923 by Mother Mary DeSales. Diocesan,
active, simple vows. 115 sisters. Teaching elementary and high
school; nursing in convalescent home; catechetics; domestic
work. Little Office of the Blessed Virgin. Ages 15-30, high
school education. Aspirancy three years. Postulate six months,
novitiate two years, juniorate up to six years. Motherhouse:
St. Joseph Convent, 775 W. Drahner Rd., Oxford, Michigan.

Dominican Congregation of St. Rose of Lima, see Relief for Incurable Cancer, Servants of.

Dominican Rural Missionaries (O.P.) Founded in France in 1932
for the evangelization of rural areas; established in U.S. in
1951. Pontifical, active, simple vows. 11 sisters in U.S., 450
world. Rural missions: catechetics; social work; nursing; foreign missions in Africa. Also located in Canada. Ages 18-30,
high school education. Postulate one year, novitiate two years,
juniorate varies. Motherhouse: Flavigny, Côté d'Or, France.
U.S. headquarters: Our Lady of the Bayous Convent, 1318
So. Henry St., Rte. 1, Box 12A, Abbeville, Louisiana.

Dominican Congregation of the Sacred Heart (O.P.) (Sisters of
Penance) Founded in Galveston, Texas, in 1882 by Mother
M. Agnes Magevney from the Congregation of St. Mary of

the Springs, Columbus, Ohio. Pontifical, active, simple vows. 356 sisters. Teaching elementary and high school, academies, college; residences for women; domestic work; catechetics. Ages 16-35, high school education. Postulate nine months, novitiate one year, juniorate five years. Motherhouse: Sacred Heart Convent, 6501 Almeda Rd., Houston 21, Texas.

Dominican Sisters of the Sick Poor, Congregation of the Immaculate Conception (O.P.) Founded in New York City in 1879 by Mother Mary Walsh. Affiliated with Dominican Order in 1910. Diocesan, active, simple vows. 150 sisters. Free home nursing of the sick poor and family rehabilitation without regard to race or religion; House of Calvary Hospital in New York City for indigent cancer patients; publication— *Sick Poor*. Interested girls may spend a weekend at one of the convents. Girls may volunteer as nurse's aides and secretaries. Also offers three months residency of professional volunteers from 21-30-years-old. Ages 16-30, high school education. Postulate one year, novitiate one year, juniorate three years. Motherhouse: Queen of the Rosary Convent, P.O. Box 231, Mariandale, Ossining, New York.

Dominican Third Order, see also: Marian Society of Catechists; Maryknoll Sisters; Missionary Servants of the Most Holy Eucharist; Servants of Relief for Incurable Cancer.

Sisters of the Third Order of St. Dominic. *The following congregations were founded directly or indirectly from the Convent of the Holy Cross in Ratisbon, Bavaria, which was founded in 1233:*

Adrian Dominicans, see Congregation of the Most Holy Rosary.

Congregation of St. Catherine of Sienna (O.P.) Founded in Wisconsin in 1862 by Mother Maria Benedicta Bauer, Prioress of the Convent of the Holy Cross, Ratisbon, Bavaria. Pontifical, active, simple vows. 619 sisters. Teaching elementary and high school, college, elementary and high school in Negro mission; domestic work; nursing; care of aged; hospice; home for women; catechetics. Ages 13 (for aspirancy) to 30, some exceptions, high school education. Aspirancy four years. Postulate six to twelve months, novitiate two years, juniorate two years. Motherhouse: Convent of St. Catherine of Sienna, 1209 Park Ave., Racine, Wisconsin.

Congregation of St. Dominic (O.P.) Founded in Blauvelt, New York, in 1878 by Mother Mary Sammon of the Congregation of the Most Holy Rosary; independent of New York City house in 1890. Diocesan, active, simple vows. 495 sisters. Teaching elementary and high school, college, school for blind children; care of orphans; home for convalescent children; Catholic Center for the Blind, New York City; summer camp for girls; hospital and schools in Jamaica, B.W.I. Ages 16-25, high school education. Postulate ten months, novitiate one year, juniorate three years. Motherhouse: Convent of St. Dominic, Western Hwy., Blauvelt, New York; or write Vocation Directress, 1960 University Ave., Bronx 53, New York.

Congregation of the Holy Cross (O.P.) Founded in Brooklyn in 1853 by Mother Josepha from the Convent of the Holy Cross in Ratisbon, Bavaria. Diocesan, active, simple vows. 1,560 sisters. Teaching elementary and high school, academies, commercial schools, schools of music and art, normal school, college; hospitals, schools of nursing; care of aged; summer camps; boys' home; retreats; catechetics; office and domestic work; missions in Puerto Rico. Ages 18-25, some exceptions, high school education. Postulate one year, novitiate one year. Motherhouse: Queen of the Rosary Convent, Albany Ave., Amityville, New York.

Congregation of the Holy Cross (O.P.) Founded in Washington in 1890 from Dominicans of the Most Holy Rosary, New York City; independent in 1923. Pontifical, active, simple vows. 177 sisters. Teaching elementary and high school; nursing; catechetics in rural areas. To age 30, high school education. Postulate nine months, novitiate two years, juniorate two years. Motherhouse: Rosary Heights, P.O. Box 280, Edmonds, Washington.

Congregation of the Immaculate Conception (O.P.) Founded in Kansas in 1902 from the Congregation of the Holy Cross, Brooklyn, New York. Pontifical, active, simple vows. 277 sisters. Teaching elementary and high school, college; hospitals, school of nursing; catechetics; missions in Africa. Ages 15-30, two years high school education. Aspirancy two years. Postulate nine months, novitiate two years, juniorate six years. Motherhouse: Immaculate Conception Convent, 3600 Broadway, Great Bend, Kansas.

Congregation of the Immaculate Heart of Mary (O.P.) Founded in Ohio in 1887 by the Congregation of the Sacred Heart of Jesus, Caldwell, New Jersey; independent in 1929. Diocesan, active, simple vows. 237 sisters. Teaching elementary and high school, academy; teaching the deaf; nursing; day nursery; social work; office and domestic work; catechetics; summer camp; music, art; making altar breads; home missions. Ages 16-30. Aspirancy three years. Postulate one year, novitiate one year, juniorate three and a half years. Motherhouse: Our Lady of the Elms, 1230 West Market St., Akron 13, Ohio.

Congregation of the Most Holy Rosary (O.P.) (Adrian Dominicans) Founded in Traverse, Michigan, in 1877 by Dominican Sisters of the Congregation of the Holy Cross, Amityville, New York; independent in 1923. Pontifical, active, simple vows. 2,327 sisters. Ages 16-30. Postulate six to twelve months, novitiate one year, juniorate five years.

Motherhouse: Adrian, Michigan. 181 sisters. Teaching elementary school, academy, and colleges.

Holy Cross Province, 190 W. Cliff Dr., Santa Cruz, California. 202 sisters. Teaching elementary and high school; nursing.

St. Rose of Lima Province, 807 N. Flagler Dr., West Palm Beach, Florida. 315 sisters. Teaching elementary and high school, academies; home for working women; catechetics; missions in Puerto Rico, West Indies, Dominican Republic, Peru.

St. Dominic Province, 701 Geneva Rd., St. Charles, Illinois. 583 sisters. Teaching elementary and high school, academy, junior military academy; summer camp; catechetics.

Immaculate Conception Province, 8549 Greenfield Rd., Detroit 28, Michigan. 604 sisters. Teaching elementary and high school; domestic work.

St. Catherine of Siena Province, 9740 McKinney Ave., Detroit 24, Michigan. 442 sisters. Teaching elementary and high school; care of aged; summer camps; social work.

Congregation of the Most Holy Rosary (O.P.) (Dominican Sisters of Newburgh) Founded in New York City in 1859 by Mother Mary Augustine from the Congregation of the Holy Cross, then in Brooklyn. Pontifical, active, simple vows. 599 sisters. Teaching elementary and high school, academies, sisters' college; catechetics; day nursery; social work; office and domestic work; missions in Puerto Rico. Ages 16-35, some exceptions, high school education. Postulate six to nine months, novitiate one year, juniorate two years. Entrance date August 30. Motherhouse: Mt. St. Mary on the Hudson, New-burgh, New York.

Dominican Sisters of Newburgh, see Congregation of the Most Holy Rosary.

Congregation of Our Lady of the Sacred Heart (O.P.) Founded in Traverse City, Michigan, in 1871 by Mother Mary Aquinata Fiegler from the Congregation of the Most Holy Rosary, Newburgh, New York. Pontifical, active, simple vows. 831 sisters. Teaching elementary and high school, academies, college, public elementary and high school; hospitals, sanitorium; care of orphans; domestic work; catechetics; religious correspondence school; social work; library work; writing; administration; office work; missions in Guatemala. Ages 16-30, high school education for prospective professional workers. Aspirancy one to four years. Postulate six to nine months, novitiate one year, juniorate three years. Motherhouse: 2025 E. Fulton St., Grand Rapids 3, Michigan.

Congregation of the Queen of the Holy Rosary (O.P.) Founded in San Francisco in 1876 by Mother M. Pia Backes from the Congregation of the Holy Cross, Amityville, New York; independent in 1890. Pontifical, active, simple vows. 549 sisters. Teaching elementary and high school, teachers' college for sisters; children's homes; missions in Mexico. Ages 18-30, high school education. Postulate nine months, novitiate one year, juniorate three years. Motherhouse: Queen of the Holy Rosary College, Mission San Jose, California.

Congregation of the Sacred Heart of Jesus (O.P.) Founded in New Jersey in 1872 from the Congregation of the Holy Cross, Amityville, New York. Diocesan, active, simple vows. 550 sisters. Teaching elementary and high school, academies, college; domestic and office work; nursing; administration. Ages 16-30, high school education. Aspirancy four years. Postulate one year, novitiate one year, juniorate two years. Motherhouse: Mt. St. Dominic, Caldwell, New Jersey.

Congregation of St. Thomas Aquinas (O.P.) Founded in Washington in 1888 by Mother Mary Thomasina from the Congregation of the Sacred Heart of Jesus, Caldwell, New Jersey. Pontifical, active, simple vows. 216 sisters. Teaching elementary and high school, military academy, junior college; rural missions; catechetics; domestic work. Also maintains a house for candidates in Ireland. Ages 16-30, high school or equivalent education preferred. Aspirancy to high school graduation. Postulate six to eleven months, novitiate two years, juniorate five years. Motherhouse: Marymount, 423 E. One hundred fifty-second St., Tacoma 44, Washington.

Sisters of St. Dorothy (S.S.D.) Founded in Italy in 1834 by Blessed Paula Frassinetti; established in U.S. in 1911. Pontifical, active, simple vows. 95 sisters in U.S., 2374 world. Teaching elementary school and academy; social work centers; domestic work; visiting prisons; forming Catholic Action groups; retreats; catechetics; missions in Brazil and Africa. Ages 17-30, high school education for prospective teachers, grade school for lay sisters. Aspirancy two months, postulate one year, novitiate two years, juniorate three years. Black habit. Motherhouse: Rome, Italy. U.S. provincialate: Villa Fatima, 26 County St., Taunton, Massachusetts.

E

Sisters of St. Elizabeth (S.S.E.) Third Order of St. Francis. Founded in Wisconsin in 1931 by Mother M. Elizabeth and Mother M. Agnes. Diocesan, active, simple vows. 21 sisters. Nursing chronically ill women. Older women as well as young women urged to apply. Postulate six months, novitiate one year. Brown habit, black veil. Motherhouse: St. Elizabeth's Convent, 745 N. Brookfield Rd., Brookfield, Wisconsin.

St. Elizabeth, see Charity of St. Elizabeth, Sisters of; Grey Sisters of St. Elizabeth; see also Franciscan Third Order.

Eskimo Sisters, see Oblates of Our Lady of the Snows.

Little Missionaries of the Eucharist (P.M.E.) Founded in Naples, Italy, in 1922; established in U.S. in 1957. Diocesan. 7 sisters in U.S. Motherhouse: Italy. U.S. address: St. Theresa House, 50 Brown Ave., Roslindale, Boston, Massachusetts.

Eucharistic, see Franciscan Missionary Sisters, Eucharistic.

Eucharistic King, see Benedictine Sisters of the Eucharistic King.

Eucharistic Mercedarians, see Sisters of the Apostolate of the Blessed Sacrament.

Eucharistic Mission Sisters, see Missionary Servants of the Most
Holy Eucharist.
Eucharistic Missionary Sisters of St. Theresa 38 sisters in U.S.
Domestic work in seminaries. Motherhouse: Mexico City.
U.S. address: St. Joseph Convent, Conception, Missouri.

F

Faithful Companions, see Jesus, Society of the Sisters, Faithful
Companions of.
Felician Sisters (C.S.S.F.) (Congregation of Sisters of St. Felix of
Cantalice of the Third Order of St. Francis) Founded in Po-
land in 1855 by Ven. Mother Mary Angela Truszkowska;
established in U.S. in 1874 in Wisconsin. Pontifical, active,
simple vows. 4,100 sisters in U.S., 4,900 world. Ages 15-30, high
school or college education. Aspirancy four years. Postulate
one year, novitiate one year, juniorate six years. Brown habit.
Motherhouse: Rome, Italy. Seven provinces in U.S., one in
Canada, each with novitiate.
Our Lady of the Angels Province, 1335 Enfield St., Enfield,
Connecticut. 432 sisters. Teaching elementary school, academy, normal school; catechetics; domestic work; nursing;
missions in Brazil.
Mother of Good Counsel Province, 3800 W. Peterson Ave.,
Chicago 45, Illinois. 739 sisters. Teaching elementary and high
school, junior college, Negro mission school; domestic work;
catechetics; nursing; care of aged and orphans; social work;
home missions; missions in Brazil and France.
Presentation of the Blessed Virgin Mary Province, 36800
Schoolcraft Rd., Livonia, Michigan. 751 sisters. Teaching elementary and high school, academy, college, mission schools
including Negro missions, teaching mentally handicapped;
domestic work; social work; nursing; day nurseries; care of orphans; catechetics; missions in Brazil and Germany.
Immaculate Conception Province, So. Main St., Lodi, New
Jersey. 607 sisters. Teaching elementary and high school,
junior college; domestic work; nursing; care of orphans; catechetics; missions in Brazil.
Immaculate Heart of Mary Province, 600 Doat St., Buffalo 11,
New York. 806 sisters. Teaching elementary and high school,

academies, college, school for retarded; catechetics; social work; home missions; nursing; day nurseries; home for working girls; care of orphans; care of handicapped and retarded children; psychiatric clinics; missions in Canada, Brazil and France. Publication—*Ave Maria*, in Polish.

Assumption of the Blessed Virgin Mary Province, Assumption Villa, Monument Rd., Ponca City, Oklahoma. 170 sisters. Teaching elementary and high school, Negro mission school; catechetics; nursing; domestic work; social work; protective institution.

Our Lady of the Sacred Heart Province, 1500 Woodcrest Ave., Coraopolis, Pennsylvania. 333 sisters. Teaching elementary and high school; catechetics; domestic work; nursing; missions in Brazil.

Canadian provincialate: Holy Name of Mary Convent, 1315 Mississauga Rd. W., Port Credit, Ont., Canada. Teaching elementary and evening schools; catechetics; day nurseries; social work; care of sacristies.

Religious Teachers Filippini (M.P.F.) Founded in Italy in 1692 by St. Lucy Filippini; established in U.S. in 1910. Pontifical, active. 596 sisters in U.S., 1,476 world. Teaching elementary school, academy, high school, college; congregation specializes in teaching music; catechetics; missions in Canada, Brazil, England, Switzerland. Ages 15-30. Aspirancy. Postulate one year, novitiate three years. Motherhouse: Rome, Italy. American provincialate: Villa Walsh, Morristown, New Jersey. Canadian address: St. Anthony of Padua Convent, 830 Barton St., E., Hamilton, Ont., Canada. (5 sisters.)

Regular Canonesses of the Five Wounds of Our Saviour (C.R.C.P.) (Chanoinesses Régulières des Cinq-Plaies du Sauveur) Founded in France in 1856; established in Canada in 1895. Diocesan, active, simple vows. 73 sisters. Teaching; nursing; care of aged; mission in Brazil. To age 30, high school education. Aspirancy varies, postulate six months, novitiate two years, juniorate five years. Black and white habit. Motherhouse: 210 Kenny St., St. Boniface, Man., Canada.

Foot of the Cross, see Loretto at the Foot of the Cross, Sisters of.

Foreign Mission Sisters of St. Dominic, see Maryknoll Sisters.

Franciscan Nuns of the Most Blessed Sacrament (F.SS.S.) Founded in France in 1854; established in U.S. in 1921. Pontifical, contemplative, major papal enclosure, solemn vows. 40 nuns and 5 externs in U.S., 400 world. Contemplation, perpetual adoration, Divine Office chanted; baking altar breads, study, art, music; making fishing lures at Canton convent. Ages 17-30, older considered; 2 years high school education. Average training: Postulate six months, novitiate one year, juniorate six years. Brown habit. Motherhouse: Troyes, France. Write to: St. Paul Shrine, 4108 Euclid Ave., Cleveland 3, Ohio. Monasteries also in Canton and Portsmouth, Ohio, Washington, D.C. and Birmingham, Alabama.

Second Order of St. Francis, see Poor Clare Nuns and Poor Clare Colettines.

Third Order of St. Francis. *The following are independent congregations:*

Daughters of St. Francis of Assisi (D.S.F.) Founded in Hungary in 1892; established in U.S. in 1946. Pontifical, active, simple vows. 16 sisters in U.S., 800 world. Nursing in hospitals and private homes. Ages 15-30, high school education. Postulate six months, novitiate two years. Temporary vow period three years. U.S. provincialate: St. Joseph Motherhouse, 507 N. Prairie St., Lacon, Illinois.

Congregation of the Sisters of the Third Order of St. Francis (O.S.F.) Founded in Indiana in 1851 by Rev. F. J. Rudolf and Mother Theresa Hackelmaier, a Franciscan sister from Austria. Pontifical, active, simple vows. 834 sisters. Teaching elementary and high school, academies, college, schools in Negro missions; domestic work; social work; nursing; care of orphans; Crow Indian missions; missions in New Guinea. Ages 18-30, high school education. Aspirancy one to four years. Postulate six months, novitiate two years, juniorate three years. Black habit. Motherhouse: Immaculate Conception Convent, Oldenburg, Indiana.

Missionary Sisters of the Third Order of St. Francis (O.S.F.) (Peekskill Sisters) (Grey Franciscan Sisters of Peekskill) Founded in Italy in 1860; established in U.S. in 1865. Pontifical, active, simple vows. 441 sisters in U.S. Teaching elementary and high school, academy, business schools, college; homes for children; day nurseries; catechetics; missions in Bolivia. Ages 16-30, high school education. Postulate one year, novitiate one year. Grey habit, black veil. Motherhouse: Rome,

Italy. U.S. provincialate: Mount St. Francis, 250 South St., Peekskill, New York.

Sisters of St. Francis (O.S.F.) Founded in Chicago in 1908 by Mother M. Alphonse Liguori; moved to Wisconsin in 1916. Diocesan, active, simple vows. 27 sisters. Catechetics; nursing; care of aged and orphans; domestic work; visiting the poor and sick in their homes. To age 35. Aspirancy. Postulate six months, novitiate two years. Brown habit, black veil; white habit for nursing. Motherhouse: St. Francis Convent, 1107 E. Orchard Beach Lane, Rice Lake, Wisconsin.

Sisters of the Third Order of St. Francis (O.S.F.) Founded in Illinois in 1877 by Archbishop John L. Spaulding and Mother M. Frances Krasse and sisters from Germany. Pontifical, active, simple vows. 339 sisters. Hospitals, schools of nursing; rehabilitation of polio victims and other handicapped; care of aged. Ages 15-35, high school education preferred. Aspirancy one to two years. Postulate six to twelve months, novitiate two years, juniorate six years. Two three-year periods of temporary vows. Motherhouse: St. Francis Convent, 616 N. Glen Oak Ave., Peoria, Illinois.

Sisters of the Third Order of St. Francis (O.S.F.) Founded in Missouri in 1894 by Mother Mary Augustine Giesen. Pontifical, active, simple vows. 126 sisters. Hospitals, schools of nursing; teaching high school; retreats; catechetics. Age 15-30. Postulate six months, novitiate two years. Black habit. Motherhouse: Mount Alverno Convent, Maryville, Missouri.

Sisters of the Third Order of St. Francis (O.S.F.) Founded in New York in 1859 by Rev. Pamphilus da Magliano, O.F.M., and Mother M. Teresa O'Neill. First U.S. community to send missionaries to foreign countries. Pontifical, active, simple vows. 937 sisters. Teaching elementary and high school, academies, colleges; hospitals, schools of nursing; homes for working girls; rest homes; care of aged; social work center; catechetics; home missions; publication—*Zeal*; foreign missions in Brazil and Jamaica. Ages 15-30, high school education. Postulate ten months, novitiate one year, juniorate one year. Temporary vows annually for six years. Motherhouse: St. Elizabeth's Motherhouse, Allegany, St. Bonaventure P.O., New York.

Sisters of the Third Order of St. Francis (O.S.F.) Founded in

Buffalo in 1861 from Philadelphia foundation. Pontifical, active, simple vows. 412 sisters. Teaching elementary and high school; hospitals, college of nursing; care of aged and orphans; domestic work; catechetics; home missions; missions in Puerto Rico. Perpetual adoration at motherhouse. Ages 16-30, high school education. Postulate six to ten months, novitiate two years, juniorate three years. Black habit. Motherhouse: St. Mary of the Angels Convent, 400 Mill St., Williamsville 21, New York.

Hospital Sisters of St. Francis (O.S.F.) Founded in Germany in 1844; established in U.S. in 1875. Pontifical, active, simple vows. 786 sisters in U.S., 3,646 world. Hospitals, sanitorium, dispensary, school of nursing; administration; accounting; domestic work; care of aged, foundlings, unwed mothers; kindergarten; catechetics; teaching health and liturgical music; nursing and visiting poor in homes and public institutions; respond to war and emergency calls for nurses; home missions on Indian reservations and in the Ozarks; missions in Japan— hospitals, TB sanitorium, novitiate. Perpetual adoration at motherhouse. Little Office of the Blessed Virgin. Ages 18-30, some exceptions, high school education. Aspirancy one to four years. Postulate one year, novitiate two years, juniorate two to four years. Black habit, white for nurses. Motherhouse: Westphalia, Germany. U.S. provincialate: St. Francis Convent, P.O. Box 42, Springfield, Illinois.

School Sisters of St. Francis (O.S.F.) Founded in Austria in 1850; established in U.S. in 1924. Pontifical, active, simple vows. 61 sisters in U.S., 850 world. Teaching elementary and high school; nursing; care of aged; domestic work. Ages 18-30, some exceptions, high school education. Aspirancy three years. Postulate six to ten months, novitiate one year, juniorate varies. Black habit. U.S. provincialate: La Verna Heights, Savannah, Missouri.

School Sisters of St. Francis (O.S.F.) Founded in Austria in 1842; established in U.S. in 1913. Pontifical, active, simple vows. 221 sisters in U.S., 660 world. Teaching elementary and high school; catechetics; retreats; directing choirs. Ages 15-27. Aspirancy three years. Postulate six months, novitiate one year, juniorate five years. Black habit. U.S. provincialate: Mt. Assisi

Academy, 934 Forest Ave., Bellevue, Pittsburgh 2, Pennsylvania.

School Sisters of St. Francis (O.S.F.) Founded in Austria in 1723; established in U.S. in 1931. Pontifical, active, simple vows. 31 sisters in U.S., 250 world. Teaching elementary school; catechetics; care of children and aged; day nurseries; domestic work. Ages 14-30, over 30 by special permission, eighth grade education. Aspirancy one to three years. Postulate six months, novitiate two years, juniorate seven years. Black habit. Motherhouse: Vienna, Austria. U.S. provincialate: Sancta Maria Convent, P.O. Box 906, Panhandle, Texas.

School Sisters of St. Francis (O.S.F.) Founded in Wisconsin in 1874 by Mothers M. Alexia and M. Alfons, sisters who left Germany because of religious persecution. Pontifical, active, simple vows. 2,747 sisters. Teaching elementary and high school, school of music, college; hospitals, sanitoriums, school of nursing; domestic work; catechetics; home missions; foreign missions in Costa Rica and Honduras. To 30, high school education. Aspirancy four years. Postulate one year, novitiate two years, juniorate two to six years. Motherhouse: St. Joseph Convent, 1501 S. Layton Blvd., Milwaukee 15, Wisconsin. Provinces in Rockford, Illinois, and Omaha, Nebraska.

Poor Sisters of St. Francis Seraph of the Perpetual Adoration (O.S.F.) Founded in Germany in 1863; established in U.S. in 1875. Pontifical, active, simple vows. 940 sisters in U.S., 2,300 world. Ages 16-30, some exceptions. Aspirancy four years. Postulate six to twelve months, novitiate two years, juniorate three years. Brown habit, black veil. Motherhouse: Westphalia, Germany. U.S. provincialates:

St. Francis Convent, Mt. Alverno, Box 377, Mishawaka, Indiana. 543 sisters. Teaching elementary and high school, college; hospitals, schools of nursing; domestic work; home for boys; home missions; missions in Philippines.

St. Joseph Convent, Mt. St. Francis, P.O. Box 1059, Colorado Springs, Colorado. 397 sisters. Teaching elementary and high school, junior college, college; hospitals, schools of nursing; domestic work; care of aged and orphans; home missions.

Franciscan Missionary Sisters for Africa (O.S.F.) Founded in Africa in 1910 by Mother Mary Kevin; established in U.S. in 1953. Pontifical, active, simple vows. 9 sisters in U.S., 232 world. Foreign missions in Africa: catechetics; teaching elementary and high school, normal schools, schools of economics, schools for blind and handicapped children; care of orphans, aged, incurably ill, and lepers; doctors and nurses for general and maternity hospitals, clinics, dispensaries; nursing schools; visiting homes and villages; training African nurses and candidates for African community of the Little Sisters of St. Francis; publication—*Daystar*. Ages 18-30, some exceptions, high school education. Postulate six months, novitiate two years. Brown habit. Motherhouse: County Louth, Ireland. U.S. novitiate: Immaculate Heart of Mary Convent, 172 Foster St., Brighton 35, Massachusetts.

Franciscan Sisters of the Atonement (S.A.) (Graymoor Sisters) Founded in 1898 in New York as an Anglican community by Episcopalian Minister Paul James Francis, who also founded an order for men, and Mother Lurana Mary Francis. The community prayed for Christian unity and the founder also began the Church Unity Octave, which was later approved by the Vatican. In 1909 the founder and the two communities he founded entered the Church and the former minister became a priest. Pontifical, active. 391 sisters. Teaching kindergarten and elementary school; settlement houses; day nurseries; catechetics; correspondence school; summer camps; retreats; care of orphans and aged; guest houses; clinics; social work; conducting the Rosary League; publication—*Candle*; home missions; missions in Canada, Japan, Ireland and Italy. Ages 17-30, high school education. Postulate six to eight months, novitiate one year, juniorate five years. Grey-brown habit. Motherhouse: St. Francis Convent, Graymoor, Garrison P.O., New York.

Franciscan Sisters of Baltimore City (O.S.F.) Founded in England in 1868; established in U.S. in 1881. Pontifical, active, simple vows. 97 sisters in U.S., 200 world. Work mostly among Negroes. Teaching elementary, high, normal school, schools of special education; catechetics; care of orphans; visiting the poor and sick; home missions. Ages 16-30, some exceptions, high school education. Postulate six to twelve months, novitiate two years, juniorate three years. Black habit. Motherhouse: Convent of Our Lady and St. Francis, 2226 Maryland Ave., Baltimore 18, Maryland.

Franciscan Sisters of St. Bernardine of Siena (C.S.B.) (Bernardine

Sisters) Founded in Pennsylvania in 1894 by Mother Mary Veronica from community founded in Poland in 1457. Pontifical, active, simple vows. 1,070 sisters. Ages 16-30, high school or college education desirable. Aspirancy one to four years. Postulate six to eleven months, novitiate one year, juniorate varies. No lay sisters. Publication—*The Bernardine*. Brown habit, black veil. Motherhouse: Maryview, 647 Spring Mill Rd., Villanova, Pennsylvania. Foreign missions in Brazil and Liberia. U.S. provincialates:

Villa Maria, Sky Meadow Dr., North Stamford, Connecticut. 201 sisters. Teaching elementary school; hospital, school of nursing; care of orphans; retreats; domestic work.

Rosary Glen, 27405 West Ten Mile Rd., Farmington, Michigan. 192 sisters. Teaching elementary and high school; nursing; care of aged; domestic work.

Mount Alvernia, Reading, Pennsylvania. 512 sisters. Teaching elementary and high school, college, nursery school, reading clinic; homes for children; nursing; retreats; domestic work.

Franciscan Sisters of Blessed Kunegunda (O.S.F.K.) Founded in Chicago in 1894 by Mother Mary Theresa Dudzik. Pontifical, active, simple vows. 385 sisters. Teaching elementary and high school; hospitals, dispensary, school of nursing; care of aged; day nurseries; home for working girls; domestic work and bookkeeping at Boys' Town; care of retarded boys; catechetics; librarians; organists; sacristans; making vestments. Ages 16-30, high school education. Aspirancy one to three years. Postulate six months, novitiate two years, juniorate five years. Temporary vows renewed annually for five years. Brown habit. Motherhouse: 2649 N. Hamlin Ave., Chicago 47, Illinois.

Franciscan Sisters of the Blessed Virgin Mary of the Angels, see Franciscan Sisters of Our Lady of the Holy Angels.

Franciscan Sisters of Calais (O.S.F.) Founded at Calais, France, in 1854; established in U.S. in 1913. Pontifical, active, simple vows. 41 sisters in U.S., 1,000 world. Hospitals, school of nursing. Ages 17-35. Black habit. Motherhouse: Descres, France. U.S. provincialate: Our Lady of the Lake, Baton Rouge, Louisiana.

Sisters of St. Francis of Christ the King (O.S.F.) Founded in Austria in 1864; established in U.S. in 1909. Pontifical, active, simple vows. 161 sisters in U.S., 1,200 world. Teaching elementary school and academy; nursing; care of orphans and aged; day nursery; domestic work. Ages 16-30, high school education. Postulate six months, novitiate one year, juniorate three years. Black habit. Motherhouse: Rome, Italy. U.S. provincialate: Mount Assisi Convent, 1600 Main St., Lemont, Illinois.

Franciscan Sisters of Christian Charity (O.S.F.) Founded in Wisconsin in 1867 by Mothers M. Gabriel Gramlich and M. Odelia Wahl. Pontifical, active, simple vows. 1,044 sisters. Teaching elementary and high school, college, Indian boarding school, music conservatory; hospitals, schools of nursing; domestic work; care of aged. Ages 16-30, high school education. Aspirancy four years. Postulate six months, novitiate one year, juniorate five years. Black habit. Motherhouse: Holy Family Convent, Rte. 1 (Alverno), Manitowoc, Wisconsin.

Conventuals of the Third Order of St. Francis, see Sisters of St. Francis of the Mission of the Immaculate Virgin.

Franciscan Missionary Sisters of the Divine Child (F.M.S.D.C.) Founded in Buffalo, New York, in 1927 by Bishop William Turner to teach catechetics to children who would otherwise receive no religious instruction. Diocesan, active, simple vows. 84 sisters. Home missions; teaching; catechetics; social work; parish census work; reclaiming fallen-away Catholics. Ages 17-35, high school education. Postulate one year, novitiate two years, juniorate five years. Grey-brown habit. Motherhouse: Regina Coeli Acres, 6380 Main St., Williamsville 21, New York.

Franciscan Missionaries of the Divine Motherhood (F.M.D.M.) Founded in England in 1935; established in U.S. in 1962. Pontifical, active and contemplative, simple vows. 8 sisters in U.S., 400 world. Teaching elementary school at present in U.S. Work of congregation includes medical work, child care, etc., in home and foreign missions. Divine Office in choir. Ages 16-30. Postulate six months, novitiate two years, juniorate five years. White habit. Motherhouse: Surrey, England. U.S. postulate: Holy Spirit Convent, Highland Dr., East Greenbush, New York.

Sisters of St. Elizabeth of the Third Order of St. Francis (O.S.E.) Founded in Aix-la-Chapelle in 1622; established in Canada in 1911. Pontifical, active, simple vows. 118 sisters. Hospitals, school of nursing; teaching; care of aged; domestic work in seminaries, etc. Ages 15-30, some exceptions. Aspirancy varies. Postulate six months, novitiate two years, juniorate three years. Brown habit. Motherhouse: P.O. Box 567, Humboldt, Sask., Canada.

Franciscan Sisters of St. Elizabeth (F.S.S.E.) Founded in Italy in 1862; established in U.S. in 1919. Pontifical, active, simple vows. 62 sisters in U.S., 500 world. Nursing; day nurseries; care of orphans; domestic work; catechetics; missions in Panama. Ages 16-30, high school education preferred. Postulate six months, novitiate two years. Grey habit, black veil. Motherhouse: Naples, Italy. U.S. provincialate: 185 Parkhurst St., Newark 5, New Jersey.

Eucharistic Franciscan Missionary Sisters (M.E.F.) (Misioneras Eucaristicas Franciscanas) Founded in Mexico City in 1943 by Mother Gemma de Jesus Aranda; established in U.S. in 1959. Pontifical, active, simple vows. 7 sisters. Perpetual adoration. Home visiting; day nurseries; home for women and women with infants; will soon open a house for Latin American sisters in Rome, Italy. Ages 17-30, high school education. Aspirancy six months, postulate six months, novitiate one year, juniorate five years. White habit. Motherhouse: Francisco Sosa 29, Mexico City, D.F., Mexico. U.S. address: Jeanne d'Arc Hall, 2263 S. Harvard Blvd., Los Angeles 18, California.

Franciscans of Glen Riddle (O.S.F.) (Glen Riddle Sisters) Founded in Philadelphia in 1855 by Ven. John N. Neumann, C.SS.R. First U.S. Franciscan sisterhood. Pontifical, active, simple vows. 1,719 sisters. Teaching elementary and high school, academies, commercial schools; hospitals, schools of nursing; domestic work; care of orphans and aged; catechetics; Negro and Indian missions; missions in Puerto Rico and Ireland. Ages 18-30, high school education. Postulate eleven months, novitiate two years. Motherhouse and Eastern novitiate: Convent of Our Lady of the Angels, Glen Riddle P.O., Pennsylvania. Western novitiate: Convent of Our Lady of the Angels, 0858 S.W. Palatine Hill Rd., Portland 19, Oregon. Provincialates also in Philadelphia, Pennsylvania; Trenton, New Jersey; and Baltimore, Maryland.

Gray Franciscan Sisters of Peekskill, see Missionary Sisters of the Third Order of St. Francis.

Sisters of St. Francis of the Holy Cross (O.S.F.) Founded in Wisconsin in 1874 by Rev. Edward Daems. Diocesan, active, simple vows. 163 sisters. Teaching; catechetics; administration; domestic work; care of aged. Ages 15-30, high school education. Aspirancy three years. Postulate one year, novitiate two years, juniorate varies. Black habit. Motherhouse: St. Francis Convent, Rte. 1, Green Bay (Bay Settlement), Wisconsin.

Sisters of St. Francis of the Holy Family (O.S.F.) Founded in Germany in 1864; community came to U.S. in 1875 during religious persecution in Europe. Pontifical, active, simple vows. 927 sisters. Teaching elementary and high school, academy, college; nursing; domestic work; care of orphans and aged; home for working girls; catechetics; summer religious schools; Negro mission. Perpetual adoration at motherhouse. Ages 15-30, high school education. Aspirancy one to four years. Postulate eleven months, novitiate two years, juniorate two years. Brown habit, black veil. Motherhouse: Mount St. Francis, Dubuque, Iowa.

Franciscan Hospitaller Sisters 6 sisters in U.S. Teaching elementary school. Motherhouse: Portugal. U.S. address: Five Wounds School, 1390 Five Wounds Lane, San Jose, California.

Franciscan Sisters of the Immaculate Conception (O.S.F.) Founded in Illinois in 1893. Diocesan, active, simple vows. 54 sisters. Hospitals, convalescent homes, school of nursing; care of children and aged; catechetics. Ages 16-32. Postulate six months, novitiate two years, juniorate six years. Temporary vow period three years. Motherhouse: St. Mary of the Angels Convent, 1000 Thirtieth St., Rock Island, Illinois.

Franciscan Sisters of the Immaculate Conception (O.S.F.) Originally part of the Missionary Franciscan Sisters of the Immaculate Conception founded in Minnesota in 1873 by Mother Mary Ignatius Hayes; reorganized into a separate diocesan community in 1891 when their mission was destroyed by fire while the foundress was ill in Rome and could not be reached. Diocesan, active, simple vows. 461 sisters. Teaching elementary and high school, junior college for sisters; hospitals, schools of nursing; care of aged; care of retarded and disturbed children; catechetics; domestic work; missions in Peru. Ages 16-30, high school education or equivalent. Novitiate two years. Brown habit, black veil. Motherhouse: St. Francis Convent, Little Falls, Minnesota.

Franciscan Sisters of the Immaculate Conception (O.S.F.) Founded in Germany in 1856; established in U.S. in 1936. Pontifical, active, simple vows. 50 sisters in U.S., 500 world. Teaching; nursing; social work; domestic work; catechetics; retreats. Ages 17-30, high school education except for domestic workers. Candidature six to twelve months, postulate six months, novitiate one year, juniorate being established. Black habit. Motherhouse: Germany. U.S. provincialate: Mount of the Immaculate Conception, North Davis Rd., East Aurora, New York.

Sisters of St. Francis of the Immaculate Conception (O.S.F.) Founded in Missouri in 1888 by Mother Mary Pacifica Forrestal; moved to Illinois in 1890. Diocesan, active, simple vows. 148 sisters. Teaching; social work; care of orphans and aged; homes for working girls; domestic work; catechetics. Ages 16-30, high school education. Aspirancy one to four years. Postulate eleven months, novitiate two years. Temporary vow period five years. Black habit. Motherhouse: Immaculate Conception Convent, 2408 W. Heading Ave., Peoria 5, Illinois.

Franciscan Missionary Sisters of the Immaculate Conception (O.S.F.) Founded in Mexico in 1874 by Rev. Refugio Morales, O.F.M.; established in U.S. in 1927. Pontifical, active, simple vows. 63 sisters in U.S., 913 world. Teaching elementary school; catechetics; retreats; nursing; care of aged, orphans, and underprivileged girls; children's recreation center; visiting the sick poor in their homes and in county hospitals; home missions; foreign missions in Central America. Ages 16-30, high school education. Postulate six months, novitiate two years, juniorate three years. Motherhouse: Mexico. U.S. novitiate: 1332 Griffith St., San Fernando, California.

Missionary Franciscan Sisters of the Immaculate Conception (O.S.F.) Founded in Belle Prairie, Minnesota, in 1873 by Mother Mary Ignatius Hayes. Pontifical, active, simple vows. 850 sisters. Teaching elementary and high school, Italian school, college; social work; domestic work; care of orphans; parish visiting; catechetics; Negro missions in the South; foreign missions in Egypt, Australia and New Guinea. Novitiates also in Australia, Rome and Ireland. Ages 16-30, high school education preferred. Postulate six months, novitiate two years. Brown habit, black veil. Motherhouse: Rome, Italy. U.S. provincialate and novitiate: 20 Manet Rd., Chestnut Hill 67, Newton, Massachusetts. Provincialates also in Belle Prairie, Minnesota, and Union City, New Jersey. Canadian novitiate: 5690 Blvd. Rosemont, Montreal P.Q., Canada.

Sisters of the Third Order of St. Francis of the Immaculate Conception of the Blessed Virgin Mary (O.S.F.) Founded in Kentucky in 1868 by Abbot Benedict Berger. Pontifical, active, simple vows. 311 sisters. Teaching elementary and high school, academy, junior college; hospitals, school of nursing; administration and office work; catechetics; domestic work; homes for working girls; care of aged; missions in British West Indies. Ages 16-30, high school education. Postulate nine months, novitiate two years. Black habit. Motherhouse: Mount St. Clare Convent, Bluff Blvd. and Springdale Dr., Clinton, Iowa.

Franciscan Sisters of the Immaculate Conception and St. Joseph for the Dying (O.S.F.) Founded in California in 1919 by sisters who were forced to leave their community in Rome, Italy, during World War I. Diocesan, active, simple vows. 26 sisters. Teaching elementary school; domestic work; nursing in convalescent home; care of orphans; office work; catechetics. The sisters offer their lives for the salvation of dying sinners. Ages 17-30, high school education preferred. Postulate six months, novitiate one year. Brown habit, black veil. Motherhouse: St. Joseph Convent, Church St., Monterey, California.

Sisters of St. Francis of the Immaculate Heart of Mary (O.S.F.) Founded in Bavaria in 1241, fifteen years after the death of St. Francis; probably the oldest Third Order Franciscan sisterhood in existence. Established in U.S. in 1913. Pontifical, active, simple vows. 193 sisters in U.S., over 2,000 world. Teaching elementary school, academy; nursing; domestic work; care of aged; administration and office work; catechetics; making vestments; farming. Ages 14-30, high school education. Aspirancy four years. Postulate six months, novitiate one year, juniorate five years. Temporary vow period three years. Black habit. Motherhouse: Dillingen, Bavaria. U.S. provincialate: Hankinson, North Dakota.

Sisters of the Third Order of St. Francis of the Immaculate Virgin Mary, Mother of God (O.S.F.) Founded in Pittsburgh in 1866 from the Buffalo community. Pontifical, active, simple vows. 579 sisters. Teaching elementary and high school; hospitals, schools of nursing, dispensaries; office and domestic work; catechetics; care of aged and convalescents; missions in Puerto Rico. Ages 16-30, high school education. Aspirancy four years. Postulate one year, novitiate one year, juniorate five years. Black habit. Motherhouse: St. Francis Convent, 146 Hawthorne Rd., Millvale P.O., Pittsburgh 9, Pennsylvania.

Franciscan Capuchin Sisters of the Infant Jesus (O.Cap.) (Capuchin Sisters) Founded in New Jersey in 1927. Affiliated with the Order Friars Minor Capuchin in Rome. Diocesan, active, simple vows. 138 sisters. Teaching elementary and high school; day nurseries; care of orphans; summer camp; catechetics; retreats; social work; parish visiting; visiting sick and prisoners; home missions. Ages 15-30, high school education preferred. Postulate six months, novitiate one year. Brown habit. Motherhouse: Mount St. Francis, Ringwood, New Jersey.

Franciscan Missionaries of St. Joseph (F.M.S.J.) Founded in England in 1883; established in U.S. in 1952. Pontifical, active, simple vows. 16 sisters in U.S., 370 world. Domestic work; catechetics; missions in Borneo and Africa—teaching, nursing, social work, catechetics. Ages 16-30, high school education. Postulate six to nine months, novitiate one and a half years, juniorate five years. Motherhouse: Staffordshire, England. U.S. novitiate: Mount St. Joseph Novitiate, 1903 New Scotland Rd., Slingerlands, Albany, New York.

Franciscan Sisters of St. Joseph (Hermanas Franciscanas de San Jose) Founded in Mexico City in 1956 by Mother Maria de San Jose Vera; established in U.S. in 1960. Pontifical, active, simple vows. 225 sisters, 35 in U.S. Domestic work in seminaries. Age 15, grade school education. Postulate one year, novitiate one year. Brown habit. Motherhouse: Avenida Revolucion 431, San Pedro de los Pinos, Mexico 18, D.F., Mexico. U.S. address: St. Paul's College, Fourth St. and Lincoln Rd., N.E., Washington 17, D.C.

Franciscan Sisters of St. Joseph (F.S.S.J.) Founded in New Jersey in 1897 by Very Rev. Hyacinth Fudzinsky, O.F.M.Conv., and Mother Mary Colette Hilbert and Charity Sisters of St. Charles Borromeo from Poland. When the latter congregation found it necessary to recall its foreign missionaries, these sisters remained at the urging of U.S. clergy and laity. Pontifical, active, simple vows. 502 sisters. Teaching elementary and high school, academy, junior college for sisters; hospitals, care of chronically ill and convalescents, schools of nursing and allied skills; care of aged; catechetics; Negro missions. Ages 14-30. Aspirancy four years. Postulate six to twelve months, novitiate two years, juniorate three years. Black habit. Motherhouse: Immaculate Conception Convent, 5286 S. Park Ave., Hamburg, New York.

Oblate Franciscan Sisters of St. Joseph Founded in Canada in 1929 by Marie Anne Lavallée and Germain Marie des Noyers, O.F.M. Nursing, teaching. Novitiate: 11430 Bois de Boulogne, Montreal, P.Q., Canada.

Sisters of St. Joseph of the Third Order of St. Francis (S.S.J.) Founded in Wisconsin in 1901 by Mothers Mary Felicia and Mary Clara. Pontifical, active, simple vows. 1,226 sisters. Ages 15-30, high school education. Aspirancy in each province three to four years. Postulate six months, novitiate two years, juniorate one year. Temporary vows annually for five years. Motherhouse: St. Joseph Convent, 107 S. Greenlawn Ave., South Bend 17, Indiana. 12 sisters. Missions in Puerto Rico. Provincialates:

Immaculate Conception Convent, Bartlett Rd., Bartlett, Illinois. 340 sisters. Teaching elementary and high school, junior college for sisters; nursing.

Marymount Convent, 12215 Granger Rd., Garfield Heights 25, Ohio. 503 sisters. Teaching elementary, high, mission school; nursing.

St. Joseph Convent, Maria Drive, Stevens Point, Wisconsin. 353 sisters. Teaching elementary and high school, college for sisters; nursing; catechetics.

Sisters of St. Francis of the Martyr St. George (O.S.F.) Founded in Germany in 1869 during an epidemic of typhoid fever; established in U.S. in 1923. Pontifical, active, simple vows. 51 sisters in U.S., 2,200 world. Nursing; caring for aged and chronically ill; domestic work; foreign missions in East Africa; teaching elementary and high school also planned in future. Little Office of the Blessed Virgin. Ages 16-30, some exceptions. Postulate eight months, novitiate two years, juniorate three years. Temporary vows renewed annually for at least three years. Entrance dates in February and July. Black habit.

Motherhouse: Hanover, Germany. U.S. vice-provincialate: St. Anthony's Novitiate, 2120 Central Ave., Alton, Illinois.

Franciscan Missionaries of Mary (F.M.M.) (Les Franciscaines Missionaires de Marie) Founded in India in 1877; established in U.S. in 1904. Subject to the minister general of the Friars Minor. Pontifical, active, simple vows. 351 sisters in U.S., 10,500 world. Cardiac and general hospital, hospital for handicapped children, care of convalescent children; teaching elementary school, domestic science school; day nurseries; care of orphans and aged; temporary shelters for children; homes for working girls; summer camps; missionary sewing circles; shrine of perpetual adoration; retreats; catechetical and missionary work among Navaho Indians in Arizona; publication —*Far Away Missions;* teaching and nursing in foreign missions, training native sisters. Also located in Mexico. Daily adoration. Ages 18-30. Those between 30 and 40 may be received as associate members. Aspirancy. Postulate six months, novitiate two years, juniorate three to six years. White habit. Motherhouse: Rome, Italy. U.S. provincialate: 225 E. Forty-fifth St., New York 17, New York. Holy Family Novitiate, 399 Fruit Hill Ave., N. Providence 11, Rhode Island. Canadian novitiates: 180 Grande Allée, Quebec, P.Q., Canada; Rigaud, P.Q., Canada.

Little Franciscan Sisters of Mary (P.F.M.) Founded in Massachusetts in 1889 by Rev. Ambroise Fafard; motherhouse later moved to Canada. Pontifical, active, simple vows. 658 sisters, 127 in U.S. Hospitals, sanitorium; teaching; care of aged and orphans; office and domestic work. Ages 16-35. Aspirancy two to three years. Postulate six months, novitiate two years. Brown habit. Motherhouse: Baie St. Paul (Charlevoix), P.Q., Canada.

Sisters of St. Mary of the Third Order of St. Francis (S.S.M.) Founded in Missouri in 1872 by Mother Mary Odilia Berger and other sisters who had to leave France during the Franco-Prussian war. Pontifical, active, simple vows. 545 sisters. Nursing and allied skills in hospitals, schools of nursing; office and domestic work; foreign missions. Ages 17-35, high school education. Postulate one year, novitiate two years, juniorate three years. Temporary vow period five years. Black habit. Motherhouse: St. Mary of the Angels Convent, 1100 Bellevue Ave., St. Louis 17, Missouri.

Congregation of the Third Order of St. Francis of Mary Immaculate (O.S.F.) (Franciscan Sisters of Mary Immaculate) Founded in Illinois in 1865 by Mother M. Alfred Moes and Very Rev. Pamfilo da Magliano, O.F.M. Pontifical, active, simple vows. 771 sisters. Teaching elementary and high school, college; home missions; domestic work; social work; office work; care of orphans, mentally retarded girls, and aged; catechetics; care of sacristies. Ages 16-26, high school education. Aspirancy four years. Postulate eleven months, novitiate two years, juniorate five years. Motherhouse: St. Francis Convent, 520 Plainfield Ave., Joliet, Illinois.

Franciscan Sisters of Mary Immaculate (O.S.F.) Founded in Ecuador in 1888 by sisters from Switzerland; moved to Colombia because of revolution in Ecuador; established in U.S. in 1932. Pontifical, active, simple vows. 88 sisters in U.S., 700 world. Teaching elementary and high school; domestic work; nursing; making vestments; missions in Panama. To age 30, some exceptions, high school education. Aspirancy four years. Postulate six to twelve months, novitiate two years, juniorate one year. Brown habit, black veil. Motherhouse: Pasto, Colombia. U.S. provincialate: St. Francis Convent, Box 5664, Amarillo, Texas.

Sisters of the Third Franciscan Order Minor Conventuals (O.S.F.) Founded in New York in 1860 by Mother M. Bernardine from the Philadelphia foundation. Pontifical, active, simple vows. 547 sisters. Teaching elementary and high school, normal school; hospitals, schools of nursing; domestic work; care of aged; catechetics; retreats; guest house in Rome, Italy; missions in Hawaii—teaching, nursing, care of lepers. Ages 16-30, high school education. Postulate nine months, novitiate two years. Black habit. Motherhouse: St. Anthony Convent, 1024 Court St., Syracuse 8, New York.

Sisters of St. Francis of the Mission of the Immaculate Virgin (Conventuals of the Third Order) (O.S.F.) Founded in New York in 1893 from Philadelphia foundation. Diocesan, active, simple vows. 227 sisters. Teaching elementary and high school, academy; hospitals and school of nursing; care of orphans; day nursery. Ages 16-30, high school education. Postulate six months, novitiate two years, juniorate. Black habit. Motherhouse: Immaculate Conception Convent, Hastings on Hudson 6, New York.

Franciscan Handmaids of the Most Pure Heart of Mary (F.H.M.) Founded in Georgia in 1917 as a Negro congregation by Rev. Ignatius Lissner and Mother M. Theodore. Diocesan, active, simple vows. 76 sisters. Teaching elementary school; home missions; visiting the sick; camps; day nursery; census taking and social work. To age 35, high school education preferred. Postulate six months, novitiate two years, juniorate one year. Motherhouse: Handmaids of Mary Convent, 15 W. One hundred twenty-fourth St., New York 27, New York.

Franciscan Sisters of Our Lady of Good Counsel Founded in Spain in 1896. 14 sisters in U.S. Domestic work in seminaries. Motherhouse: Madrid, Spain. U.S. address: c/o Divine Word Seminary, 26581 State Rte. 65, Perrysburg, Ohio.

Franciscan Sisters of Our Lady of the Holy Angels (B.M.V.A.) (Franciscan Sisters of the Blessed Virgin Mary of the Angels) Founded in Germany in 1863; established in U.S. in 1923. Pontifical, active, simple vows. 42 sisters in U.S., 1,300 world. Divine Office in Latin. Ages 16-30, some exceptions to 35. Elementary school education. Postulate eight months, novitiate two years. Temporary vow period five years. Entrance dates January 6 and September 8. Nursing; care of aged; office and domestic work; social work. Brown habit, black veil. Motherhouse: Rhine, Germany. U.S. provincialate: St. Mary's Home, 1925 Norfolk Ave., St. Paul 16, Minnesota.

Sisters of St. Francis of Our Lady of Lourdes (O.S.F.) Founded in Ohio in 1916 by Mother M. Adelaide from Rochester, Minnesota, foundation. Pontifical, active, simple vows. 493 sisters. Teaching elementary and high school; hospitals and convalescent home; catechetics. To age 30. Aspirancy four years. Postulate six months, novitiate two years, juniorate four years. No dowry. Brown habit, black veil. Motherhouse: 6832 Convent Blvd., Sylvania, Ohio.

Sisters of the Third Order of St. Francis of the Congregation of Our Lady of Lourdes (O.S.F.) Founded in Minnesota in 1877 by Mother Mary Alfred Moes from Joliet, Illinois, foundation. Pontifical, active, simple vows. 880 sisters. Teaching elementary and high school, college; hospitals, sanitorium, schools of nursing; care of aged and convalescents; catechetics; retreats; missions in Colombia. Ages 16-30, high school education. Postulate six to eleven months, novitiate two years, juniorate varies. Community's College of St. Teresa is a Sister Formation demonstration center. Brown habit, black veil. Motherhouse: Assisi Heights, Rochester, Minnesota.

Franciscan Sisters of Our Lady of Perpetual Help (O.S.F.) Founded in St. Louis, Missouri, in 1901 by Mothers M. Solana Leczna, M. Ernestine Matz, and M. Hilaria Matz. Pontifical, active, simple vows. 314 sisters. Teaching elementary and high school; nursing; domestic and sacristy work; care of aged; catechetics; retreats; Negro and Indian missions; missions in Thailand. Ages 15-30, high school education except for domestic workers. Aspirancy four years. Postulate six months, novitiate two years, juniorate three years. Entrance dates: February 2 and August 2. Brown habit, black veil. Motherhouse: Villa St. Joseph, 201 Brotherton Lane, (Ferguson) St. Louis 35, Missouri.

Franciscan Missionary Sisters of Our Lady of Sorrows (O.S.F.) Founded in China in 1936 by Bishop R. Palazzi; motherhouse established in U.S. in 1949 by these Chinese sisters and four American sisters from the Missionary Sisters of St. Francis. Diocesan status under the Society for the Propagation of the Faith; active, simple vows. 50 sisters. Home and foreign missions; teaching elementary school; social work; domestic work; retreats; catechetics; missions in Hong Kong and Formosa. Ages 17-30, high school education. Postulate six months, novitiate two years, juniorate three years. Black habit. Motherhouse: 16535 S.W. Tualatin Valley Hwy., Beaverton, Oregon.

Sisters of St. Francis of Assisi of Penance and Charity (O.S.F.) Founded in Wisconsin in 1849 by Mother Aemiliana Duerr from Germany. Pontifical, active, simple vows. 934 sisters. Teaching elementary and high school, academy, college, schools for deaf and retarded, the underprivileged, and predelinquent boys; educational clinics; care of orphans and aged; social work; catechetics; domestic work. Ages 16-32. Aspirancy two years. Postulate one year, novitiate two years, juniorate two years. Black habit. Motherhouse: St. Francis of Assisi Convent, 3221 S. Lake Dr., Milwaukee 7, Wisconsin.

Sisters of the Third Order of St. Francis of Penance and Charity (O.S.F.) Founded in Ohio in 1869 by Rev. Joseph Bihn and Mother Francis Schaefer, a widow, and her two daughters, to care for children left homeless by the Civil War. Pontifical, active, simple vows. 211 sisters. Teaching elementary and high school; nursing; care of aged and orphans; hostel; domestic work. Ages 14-30, high school education. Aspirancy three years. Postulate six to twelve months, novitiate two years, juniorate five years. Brown habit, black veil. Motherhouse: St. Francis Convent, 200 St. Francis Ave., Tiffin, Ohio.

Sisters of St. Francis of Penance and Christian Charity (O.S.F.) Founded in Holland in 1835; established in U.S. in 1874. Pontifical, active, simple vows. 797 sisters in U.S., 5,000 world. Ages 18-30, high school education. Postulate six to twelve months, novitiate two years, juniorate varies. Contemplation, Divine Office chanted. Brown habit, black veil. Motherhouse: Rome, Italy. U.S. provincialates:

Mount Alverno, 3910 Bret Harte Dr., P.O. Box 1028, Redwood City, California. 211 sisters. Teaching elementary and high school, academy; nursing; domestic work; social work; office work and administration; retreats.

Marycrest, 2851 W. 52nd Ave., Denver 21, Colorado. 150 sisters. Teaching elementary and high school, academies; hospitals, school of nursing; catechetics; domestic work; Indian missions in South Dakota. Aspirancy four years.

Seminary of Our Lady of the Sacred Heart, 4421 Lower River Rd., Stella Niagara, New York. 436 sisters. Teaching elementary school, junior military academies, high school, commercial high school, academies, college; nursing; care of infants and orphans; domestic work; retreats; Negro mission; foreign missions in Java and Bali, Indonesia, and Tanganyika, East Africa.

Sisters of St. Francis of Perpetual Adoration (O.S.F.) Founded in Missouri in 1893 by Mother Mary John Hau from Switzerland as a possible refuge for the Swiss community during a time of unrest in that country. The Swiss congregation was founded in 1424. Diocesan, active, simple vows. 58 sisters. Teaching elementary and high school; care of orphans; domestic work. Perpetual adoration at motherhouse. Ages 15-30, high school education preferred. Postulate seven months, novitiate one year, juniorate five years. Brown habit, black veil. Motherhouse: St. Francis Convent, University and Prewitt Sts., Nevada, Missouri.

Sisters of the Third Order of St. Francis of Perpetual Adoration
(F.S.P.A.) (Franciscan Sisters of Perpetual Adoration)
Founded in Wisconsin in 1849 by Franciscan Tertiaries from
Bavaria. Pontifical, active, simple vows. 1,176 sisters. Teaching
elementary and high school, college; Negro and Indian mis-
sions; domestic work; hospitals, schools of nursing and practical
nursing; care of orphans and aged; social work; missions in
Guam and El Salvador. Perpetual adoration. Ages 15-30, high
school education for postulate. Aspirancy one to four years.
Postulate six months, novitiate two years, juniorate five years.
Black habit. Motherhouse: St. Rose Convent, 912 Market St.,
La Crosse, Wisconsin.

Franciscan Sisters of the Poor (S.F.P.) Founded in Germany in
1845; established in U.S. in 1858. Pontifical, active (contemplative branch in Western province), simple vows. 549 sisters
and 6 contemplative sisters in U.S., 2,650 world. Interested
girls are invited to visit for a weekend or retreat. Brown habit,
black veil. Motherhouse: Rome, Italy.

Eastern U.S. province: Mount Alverno Convent, 20 Grand St.,
Warwick, New York. 230 sisters. Hospitals, schools of nursing;
catechetics; retreats; care of aged; domestic work; home missions; missions in Brazil. Ages 16-30. Postulate six months, novitiate two years, juniorate five years.

Western U.S. province: St. Clare Convent, 60 Compton Rd.,
Hartwell, Cincinnati 15, Ohio. 319 sisters, 6 contemplatives.
Hospitals, nursing home, schools of nursing; social work; domestic work; teaching; foreign missions. Ages 16-30, high
school education preferred. Aspirancy four years. Postulate
nine months, novitiate two years, juniorate five years.

Sisters of St. Francis of the Providence of God (O.S.F.) Founded
in Pittsburgh, Pennsylvania, in 1922 from Millvale, Pennsylvania, community by Msgr. M. L. Krusas. Diocesan, active,
simple vows. 281 sisters. Teaching elementary and high school,
academy; nursing; catechetics; domestic work; home missions;
teaching and novitiate in Brazil. Ages 17-30, high school education. Aspirancy three years. Postulate one year, novitiate one
year, juniorate three years. Motherhouse: St. Francis Convent,
Grover and McRoberts Rds., Pittsburgh 34, Pennsylvania.

Franciscan Sisters of the Sacred Heart (O.S.F.) Founded in Germany in 1866; community moved to U.S. in 1876 because of

religious persecution. Pontifical, active, simple vows. 475 sisters. Hospitals, schools of nursing; domestic work; teaching elementary and high school; care of aged and orphans. Ages 16-30. Postulate one year, novitiate two years, juniorate five years. Motherhouse: 372 N. Broadway, Joliet, Illinois.

Franciscan Sisters, Daughters of the Sacred Hearts of Jesus and Mary (O.S.F.) Founded in Germany in 1859; established in U.S. in 1872. Pontifical, active, simple vows. 400 sisters in U.S.; 2,500 world. Hospitals, home nursing, school of nursing; teaching elementary and high school; care of orphans; homes for working girls; social work; missions in Brazil. To age 40, high school and higher education desirable. Aspirancy three years. Postulate one year, novitiate two years, juniorate three years. Brown habit, black veil. Motherhouse: Westphalia, Germany. U.S. provincialate: Our Lady of the Angels Convent, P.O. Box 166, Wheaton, Illinois.

Franciscan Third Order, see also: Sisters of Charitable Instruction of the Holy Infant Jesus; Sisters of St. Elizabeth; Felician Sisters; Grey Sisters of St. Elizabeth; Glenmary Home Mission Sisters; Mothers of the Helpless; Servants of the Holy Infancy of Jesus; Missionary Sisters of the Immaculate Conception of the Mother of God; Sister Servants of Mary Immaculate; Sisters of Mercy of the Holy Cross; Missionary Sisters of Our Lady of the Angels; Sisters of St. Philip Neri Missionary Teachers; Poor Clare Missionary Sisters; Sisters of the Sorrowful Mother.

Oblate Sisters of St. Francis de Sales (O.S.F.S.) Founded in France in 1866 to provide homes for working girls; established in U.S. in 1951. Pontifical, active, simple vows. 12 sisters in U.S., 700 world. Teaching elementary and high school; retreats; catechetics; social work; home and foreign missions. Especially devoted to working with young workers. Ages 16-35, high school education preferred. Postulate one year, novitiate one year, juniorate five years. Temporary vow period four years. Black habit. Motherhouse: Troyes, France. U.S. address: Villa Aviat Convent, Childs, Maryland.

Catholic Mission Sisters of St. Francis Xavier (S.C.M.S.) (Xavier Mission Sisters) Founded in Michigan in 1946 by Edward Cardinal Mooney to serve as missionaries in India and Japan, lands evangelized by St. Francis Xavier. Diocesan, active, simple vows. 11 sisters. Catechetics, home visiting, teaching, nursing, dispensaries, social work in villages and rural areas in Japan and India. Publication—*Mission Digest*. Ages 17-30, high school education. Aspirancy (in Japan) one year, postulate six months, novitiate two years, juniorate five years. White habit, black veil. Motherhouse: Convent of St. Francis Xavier, 35750 Moravian Dr., Fraser, Michigan.

G

Sisters del Giglio 4 sisters in U.S. Domestic work in a seminary. U.S. address: % St. Hyacinth Seminary, Granby, Massachusetts.

Glen Riddle Sisters, see Franciscans of Glen Riddle.

Glenmary Home Mission Sisters (Home Mission Sisters of America) Third Order of St. Francis. Founded 1941-1952 at Glendale, Ohio, by Very Rev. W. Howard Bishop, founder of the Glenmary Fathers and Brothers. Diocesan, active, simple vows. 93 sisters. Home missions: social work; catechetics including radio and TV; home nursing; teaching; assist Glenmary Fathers in rural missions; publication—*Kingship*. Ages 16-30, high school or college education or professional training desirable. Postulate nine months, novitiate one year, juniorate five years. Grey habit, black veil. Motherhouse: 4580 Colerain Ave., Cincinnati 23, Ohio.

Good Counsel, see Our Lady of Good Counsel; Franciscan Sisters of Our Lady of Good Counsel.

Good Shepherd Sisters of Quebec, see Sisters, Servants of the Immaculate Heart of Mary.

Good Shepherd Sisters (R.G.S.) (Religious of Our Lady of Charity of the Good Shepherd) Originated from Sisters of Our Lady of Charity of Refuge founded by St. John Eudes in France in 1641; established as a separate congregation in France in 1835 by St. Mary Euphrasia Pelletier; established in U.S. in 1843 at Louisville, Kentucky. Pontifical, active and contemplative, minor papal enclosure, simple vows. 1,086 sisters in U.S. plus Sisters Magdalens, 10,000 in world. The congregation's chief work is the care and training of disturbed and problem girls, which involves teaching, nursing, social work, domestic work, etc. Teaching, care of orphans, and catechetics in Philippines and Hong Kong. Also direction of cloistered communities of Sisters Magdalens, women who desire to make reparation for past mistakes. Those wishing information about these communities should write to any Good Shepherd provincialate. To age 35, high school education. Postulate six months, novitiate two years, juniorate five years. Fourth vow of zeal for souls. White habit, black veil. Motherhouse: Angers, France. Seven provinces in U.S., two in Canada:

Good Shepherd Convent, 1500 S. Arlington Ave., Los Angeles 19, California. 26 sisters. Serves as novitiate also for foreign missions.

Good Shepherd Convent, Mount and Hollins Sts., Baltimore 23, Maryland. 79 sisters, 53 Sisters Magdalens.

Good Shepherd Convent, 931 Blair Ave., St. Paul 4, Minnesota. 149 sisters, Sisters Magdalens.

Good Shepherd Convent, 3801 Gravois Ave., St. Louis 16, Missouri. 192 sisters, 104 Sisters Magdalens.

Mount St. Florence, Maple Ave., Peekskill, New York. 339 sisters, 232 Sisters Magdalens.

Our Lady of the Woods, Girls Town of America, N. Bend Rd., Cincinnati 16, Ohio. 200 sisters, 165 Sisters Magdalens.

Good Shepherd Convent, Tekakwitha Hills, 8550 Verree Rd., Philadelphia 11, Pennsylvania. 101 sisters, 64 Sisters Magdalens.

Good Shepherd Convent, Quinpool Rd., Halifax, N.S., Canada.

Good Shepherd Convent, 9465 Blvd., Gouin W., Pierrefonds, Montreal, P.Q., Canada.

Graymoor Sisters, see Franciscan Sisters of the Atonement.

Grey Nuns of the Cross (S.G.C.) Founded in Ottawa, Canada, in 1845 by Mother Elizabeth Bruyere and Grey Nuns of Montreal; established in U.S. in 1857. Pontifical, active, simple vows. 1,783 sisters, 185 in U.S. Teaching elementary, high and normal school, university; hospitals, sanitoriums for the incurable; care of orphans and aged; domestic work; office work and administration; farming; Indian mission in James Bay; foreign missions in Brazil, Africa, and Japan. Ages 16-30, high school education.

Postulate six months, novitiate one and a half years. Purple habit, black veil. Motherhouse: 9 Bruyere St., Ottawa 2, Ont., Canada. Canadian provincialates: Maison Provinciale Notre-Dame-du-Rosaire, Ste.-Madeleine, Cap-de-la-Madeleine, P.Q., Canada; St. Marie Provincialate, 86 Ignatius St., Sudbury, Ont., Canada. U.S. provincialate: St. Joseph Provincialate, 25 Fairmount St., Lowell, Massachusetts; novitiate at Framingham, Massachusetts, and Church Point, Louisiana.

Grey Nuns of St. Hyacinthe (S.G.S.H.) (Sisters of Charity of St. Hyacinthe) Founded at St. Hyacinthe, Canada, in 1840 by R. P. Edouard Crevier and Grey Nuns of Montreal; established in U.S. in 1878. Pontifical, active, simple vows. 802 sisters, 220 in U.S. Hospitals, care of disabled, visiting the sick and dying; care of orphans and aged; home for retired priests; social work; farming; missions in Haiti and Brazil. Ages 18-35, eighth grade education. Postulate six months, novitiate two years. Motherhouse: Hôtel Dieu, St. Hyacinthe, P.Q., Canada.

Grey Nuns of Montreal (S.G.M.) (Soeurs Grises de Montréal) (Sisters of Charity) Founded in Montreal, Canada, in 1738 by Blessed Marguerite d'Youville; established in U.S. in 1855. Pontifical, active, simple vows. 8,000 sisters, 198 in U.S. Hospitals, sanitoriums, convalescent home, TB sanitarium, radium institute, schools of nursing; care of orphans, retarded children, and aged; institutions for the blind; social work; domestic work; office work; academy and Indian mission school. Postulate six months, novitiate two years, juniorate three years. Grey habit. Motherhouse: General Hospital of the Grey Nuns, 1190 Guy St., Montreal 25, P.Q., Canada. Canadian provincialates: St. Alberta, Alta., Canada; 151 Despins St., St. Boniface, Man., Canada; Hôtel Dieu, Nicolet, P.Q., Canada. U.S. provincialate: Grey Nuns Provincial House, 10 Pelham Rd., Lexington 73, Massachusetts.

Grey Nuns of Quebec (S.C.Q.) (Sisters of Charity of Quebec) (Soeurs de la Charité de Quebec) Founded in Quebec, Canada, in 1849 by Mother Marie-Anne-Marcelle Mallet and Grey Nuns of Montreal; established in U.S. in 1890. Pontifical, active, simple vows. 1,924 sisters, 90 in U.S. General, mental, and TB hospitals, sanitorium for nervous diseases and alcoholism; care of orphans and aged; teaching, school for retarded; French orphanages and home for aged in Massachusetts; foreign missions in Japan. Postulate one year, novitiate one year, juniorate two years. Motherhouse: Rue d'Estimauville, Giffard 5, P.Q., Canada.

Grey Nuns of the Sacred Heart (G.N.S.H.) (Sisters of Charity of Philadelphia) Established in U.S. in 1857 by Grey Nuns of Montreal; independent congregation in 1923. Pontifical, active, simple vows. 488 sisters. Teaching elementary and high school, academies, normal school, college; hospitals, schools of nursing; domestic work; care of orphans and aged. Ages 16-30, high school education. Postulate ten months, novitiate twenty-six months, juniorate five years. Sand-color habit, black veil. Motherhouse: 7500 West Ave., Philadelphia 26, Pennsylvania.

Grey Sisters of St. Elizabeth Third Order of St. Francis. Founded in Germany in 1842; established in U.S. in 1923. Pontifical. 13 sisters in U.S., over 5,000 in world. Domestic work in Redemptorist seminaries in U.S. Ages 16-30, no dowry necessary. Training in Germany, no novitiate in U.S. Black habit, grey cloak. Motherhouse: Reinbek District, Hamburg, Germany. U.S. residence: Mount St. Alphonsus, Esopus, New York.

Grey Sisters of the Immaculate Conception (G.S.I.C.) Founded in Canada in 1926 by the English speaking houses of the Grey Nuns of Montreal. Pontifical, active, simple vows. 358 sisters. Teaching elementary and high school, university, schools of music; hospitals, schools of nursing; Chinese mission in Vancouver, B.C.; care of aged; teaching, nursing, and catechetics in missions in Bahamas, B.W.I., and Dominican Republic. Ages 17-30. Postulate ten months, novitiate two years. Entrance date: September. Grey habit, white for work in hospitals, homes for aged, and foreign missions. Motherhouse: 700 Mackay St., Pembroke, Ont., Canada.

Guadalupan Catechist Sisters (Hermanas Catequistas Guadalupanas) (H.C.G.) Founded in Mexico in 1921 by Bishop Jesus Maria Echovarria; established in U.S. in 1950. Diocesan, active, simple vows. 200 sisters, 20 in U.S. Teaching; visiting homes and hospitals; retreats; catechetics; home missions. Ages 15-30, grade school education. Aspirancy one year, postulate six months, novitiate two years, juniorate three years. Training in U.S. and Mexico. Motherhouse: Saltillo, Coah., Mexico. U.S. address: 7815 Somerset Rd., San Antonio, Texas.

Sisters of Guadalupe (O.L.G.) (Hermanas Oblatas Lasalianas Guadalupanas) Founded in Mexico City in 1946 by Brother Juan Fromental, F.S.C., and Maria de la Luz Lopez, O.S.F. Diocesan, active, simple vows. 150 sisters, 51 in U.S. Domestic work in schools and seminaries; catechetics; foreign missions. Age 14, eighth grade education. Aspirancy six months, novitiate two years, juniorate one year. Spanish-speaking community, training in Mexico. Motherhouse: Mexico City. U.S. address: % St. Mary's College, Winona, Minnesota.

Guadalupe, see Benedictine Missionaries of Guadalupe of Christ the King; Perpetual Adoration of the Blessed Sacrament of St. Mary of Guadalupe, Sisters of; Sacred Heart and Our Lady of Guadalupe, Missionaries of the.

H

Health of the Sick, see Mary, Health of the Sick, Daughters of.

Daughters of the Heart of Mary (D.H.M.) Founded in France in 1790 at a time when religious could not live in community, wear habits, or operate openly as religious. This accounts for the fact that this religious congregation displays some of the characteristics of a secular institute; established in U.S. in 1851. Pontifical, active, simple vows. 398 sisters in U.S., 5,000 world. Teaching elementary and high school, academy; school for deaf, hearing conservation center; nursing in clinics; social work; catechetics; retreats; homes for infants and girls; students' hostel; Indian missions in U.S.; foreign missions in Ethiopia, Pakistan, India and Japan. Also located in Mexico. Ages 17-35. Aspirancy one to two years. Postulate one year, novitiate two years, juniorate two years. Habit: modern dress, not uniform. Many members live and work outside the community but follow the same Rule. Motherhouse: Paris, France. U.S. provincialate: 103 E. Twentieth St., New York 3, New York. Canadian address: 160 Patterson St., Sudbury, Ont., Canada.

Help, see Our Lady of Help, Sisters of.

Mothers of the Helpless (M.D.) Third Order of St. Francis. Founded in Spain in 1873; established in U.S. in 1916. Pontifical, active, simple vows. 26 sisters in U.S., 2,500 world. Teaching; domestic work; day nursery; catechetics; missions in Puerto Rico. Ages 15-30, high school education. Postulate six months, novitiate two years, juniorate five years. Motherhouse: Valencia, Spain. Novitiate also in Mexico. U.S. provincialate: San Jose Day Nursery, 432 W. Twentieth St., New York 11, New York. St. Joseph Novitiate, 157 Piermont Ave., Nyack, New York.

Holy Angels, see Franciscan Sisters of Our Lady of the Holy Angels.

Sisters of the Holy Child Jesus (S.H.C.J.) Founded in England in 1846 by Mother Cornelia Connelly, an American convert; established in U.S. in 1862. Pontifical, active, simple vows. 530 in U.S., 950 world. Ages 17-25, some exceptions, high school education. Postulate nine months, novitiate twenty-seven months. Black habit, white habit for missionaries. Motherhouse: Rome, Italy. U.S. provincialates:

Convent of the Holy Child Jesus, Westchester Ave., Rye, New York. 195 sisters. Teaching elementary and high school, academies; domestic work; administration.

Convent of the Holy Child Jesus, 1341 Montgomery Ave., Rosemont, Pennsylvania. 335 sisters. Teaching elementary and high school, academies, college; administration; domestic work; missions in Africa.

Holy Cross Sisters, see Sisters of Mercy of the Holy Cross.

Sisters of the Holy Cross (C.S.C.) Founded in Le Mans, France, in 1841; established in U.S. in 1843. Pontifical, active, simple vows. 1,526 sisters in U.S., 1,700 world. Teaching elementary and high school, academies, colleges; nursing; care of orphans; summer camp; Negro mission; missions in East Pakistan and Brazil. Ages 16-30, high school education preferred. Postulate ten months, novitiate two years, juniorate five years. Black habit. Motherhouse: St. Mary's Convent, Box V-2, Notre Dame, Indiana. Provincialates: St. Mary of the Wasatch, Salt Lake City 8, Utah; 3720 Miami Rd., South Bend 14, Indiana; 10701 Rockville Pike, Rockville, Maryland.

Sisters of the Holy Cross and of the Seven Dolors (C.S.C.) (Soeurs de Ste. Croix et des Sept-Douleurs) Founded in Le Mans, France, in 1841 by the founder of the Holy Cross Fathers; established in Canada in 1847; established in U.S. in 1881. Pontifical, active, simple vows. 514 sisters in U.S., 2,300 world. Teaching elementary and high school, academies, college; catechetics; farming; missions in Haiti and East Pakistan. Age 16, high school education preferred. Postulate six months, novitiate one year, juniorate five years. No lay sisters. Motherhouse: 815 Blvd. S. Croix Ville, St. Laurent, Montreal 9, P.Q., Canada. Canadian provincialates: 8321 One hundred-twelfth St., Edmonton, Alta., Canada; 245 Laurier Ave. E., Ottawa 2, Ont., Canada. U.S. provincialate: St. George Manor, 357 Island Pond Rd., Manchester, New Hampshire.

Holy Cross, see under Dominican Third Order; St. Francis of the Holy Cross, Sisters of; Marianites of Holy Cross, Sisters.

Sisters of the Holy Faith (S.H.F.) Founded in Ireland in 1856; established in U.S. in 1953. Pontifical, active, simple vows. 27 sisters in U.S. Teaching elementary and high school. Motherhouse: Dublin, Ireland. U.S. address: St. John of God School, 13817 Pioneer Blvd., Norwalk, Los Angeles Co., California.

Sisters of the Holy Family (S.S.F.) Founded in New Orleans in 1842 as a Negro community by Henrietta Delisle and Juliette Gaudin. Pontifical, active, simple vows. 349 sisters. Teaching elementary and high school, academy, De Lisle Institute (Sister Formation); care of orphans and aged; day nursery; domestic work; home missions; foreign missions in British Honduras. Ages 15-30, high school education. Postulate six months, noviti-ate two years. Black habit. Motherhouse: Holy Family Convent, 6901 Chef Menteur Hwy., New Orleans 26, Louisiana.

Sisters of the Holy Family (S.H.F.) Founded in San Francisco in 1872 by Archbishop Alemany, Msgr. Prendergast and Mother Dolores Armer to teach religion to children who otherwise would receive no religious instruction. Pontifical, active, simple vows. 429 sisters. Catechetics for public school children and retarded children; family welfare; day nurseries; retreats for high school students and families of retarded children; training catechists; college courses in religion for lay teachers; missions in Hawaii. Ages 18-30, high school education. Postulate one year, novitiate one year, juniorate three years. Black habit. Motherhouse: Holy Family Motherhouse, Box 3248, Mission San Jose, California.

Little Sisters of the Holy Family (P.S.S.F.) (Institut des Petites Soeurs de la Sainte-Famille) Founded in Canada in 1880 by Mother Marie-Leonie and Mother Camille Lefebvre of the

Sisters of the Holy Cross; established in U.S. in 1900. Pontifical, active, simple vows. 1,131 sisters, 145 in U.S. Domestic
work in seminaries, bishops' residences, colleges, etc. Ages
15-30, ability to read and write French or English. Postulate
six months, novitiate two years. Black habit. Motherhouse:
Mont Sainte-Famille, 1820 Ouest rue Galt, Sherbrooke, P.Q.,
Canada.

Holy Family Sisters of Bordeaux (S.S.F.B.) (Soeurs de la Sainte-
Famille de Bordeaux) (Sisters of Hope) Founded in France
in 1820; established in Canada in 1901. Pontifical, active (one
convent of contemplative sisters in France), simple vows. 200
sisters in Canada, 4,435 world. Nursing, including nursing the
sick poor in their homes; teaching; social work with the poor
and the blind. Postulate nine months, novitiate two years,
juniorate five years. Black habit. Canadian provincialate: 1374
West Pine Ave., Montreal 25, Canada.

Sisters of the Holy Family of Nazareth (C.S.F.N.) Founded in
Rome, Italy, by Ven. Mother Mary Frances Siedliska in 1875;
established in U.S. in 1885. Pontifical, active, simple vows.
1,581 sisters in U.S., 2400 world. Black habit. Motherhouse:
Rome, Italy. U.S. provincialates:
Sacred Heart Provincialate, 353 No. River Rd., Des Plaines,
Illinois. 616 sisters. Teaching elementary and high school, college; hospitals, school of nursing; social work; catechetics;
health resort. Ages 15-30, some exceptions, high school education and two years college preferred. Aspirancy one year, postulate one year, novitiate two years, juniorate five to seven years.
Immaculate Heart of Mary Provincialate, Villa Immaculata,
Sound Ave., Riverhead, L.I., New York. 263 sisters. Teaching
elementary and high school; catechetics; care of orphans. Ages
15-30, some exceptions. Aspirancy three years. Postulate six to
twelve months, novitiate two years, juniorate six years.
Immaculate Conception Provincialate, Grant and Frankford
Aves., Torresdale, Philadelphia 14, Pennsylvania. 329 sisters.
Teaching elementary and high school, academy, college; nursing; domestic work; office work and administration; catechetics;
care of orphans; missions in Puerto Rico and Australia. Ages
15-30, some exceptions, eighth grade education. Aspirancy
three years. Postulate six to twelve months, novitiate two years,
juniorate six years.

St. Joseph's Provincialate, 285 Bellevue Rd., Pittsburgh 29, Pennsylvania. 373 sisters. Teaching elementary and high school, academy; nursing; care of orphans and aged; social work. Ages 15-30, some exceptions. Aspirancy two years. Postulate six to twelve months, novitiate two years, juniorate six years.

Holy Family, see St. Francis of the Holy Family, Sisters of.

Daughters of the Holy Ghost (F.S.E.) (White Sisters) Founded in France in 1706; established in U.S. in 1902 during religious persecution in France. Pontifical, active, simple vows. 553 sisters in U.S., 3,500 world. Teaching elementary and high school, academy, college; care of the sick in their homes and in hospitals; homes for working girls; day nurseries; care of aged; catechetics; Negro missions in Alabama; foreign missions in Africa and Chile; teaching in Greenfield Park, P.Q., Canada; also located in Mexico. Ages 16-30, high school education. Postulate nine months, novitiate one year, juniorate three years. No lay sisters. White habit redesigned in 1954. Motherhouse: France. U.S. provincialate: Holy Ghost Provincial House, 72 Church St., Putnam, Connecticut.

Mission Sisters of the Holy Ghost (M.S.) Founded in Cleveland, Ohio, in 1923 by Most Rev. Joseph Schrembs. Diocesan, active, simple vows. 13 sisters. Home missions: catechetics; social work; home visiting and parish census; clinic, nursing the sick poor; center for the Spanish speaking; domestic work; missions to Mexican migrants in Michigan. Ages 18-30, high school education. Novitiate one year. Blue dress and hat which may be restyled from time to time. Motherhouse: Missiondell, 1030 N. River Rd., Saginaw, Michigan.

Sisters of the Holy Ghost (C.H.G.) Founded in Pennsylvania in 1913 by Bishop F. Regis Canevin. Pontifical, active, simple vows. 139 sisters. Teaching elementary and high school; nursing; care of aged; domestic work. Aspirancy two to three years. Postulate six months, novitiate two years. Black habit. Motherhouse: Holy Ghost Convent, 5246 Clarwin Ave., Pittsburgh 29, Pennsylvania.

Sisters of the Holy Ghost (C.S.Sp.) Founded in Rome, Italy, in 1890; established in U.S. in 1929 by Mother Mary Josephine, the foundress. Diocesan, active, simple vows. 16 sisters. Care of aged, domestic work. To age 30, to 35 by dispensation, high school education preferred. Postulate six months, novitiate two years, juniorate three years. Black habit. Motherhouse: 10102 Granger Rd., Garfield Heights, Cleveland 25, Ohio.

Sister Servants of the Holy Ghost and Mary Immaculate (S.H.G.) Founded in San Antonio in 1888 by Mother Mary Margaret Healy-Murphy to bring Catholicism to Negroes in the South. Pontifical, active and contemplative, simple vows. 278 sisters. Teaching; catechetics; care of aged and infirm; missions and a house of studies in Ireland for European candidates. Age 15, high school education. Aspirancy three years. Postulate nine months, novitiate one year. Black habit. Motherhouse: Convent of the Holy Ghost and Mary Immaculate, 301 Yucca St., San Antonio 3, Texas.

Sister Servants of the Holy Ghost of Perpetual Adoration (S.Sp.S.de A.P.) (Pink Sisters) Founded in Holland in 1896; established in U.S. in 1915. Pontifical, contemplative, major papal enclosure, simple vows. 30 sisters in U.S., 383 in world. Contemplation, perpetual adoration, Divine Office in Latin. Pray particularly for priests and the propagation of the faith. Ages 18-30, high school education or equivalent. No lay sisters. Pink habit, white veil. Motherhouse: Steyl, Holland. U.S. convents: Convent of Divine Love, 2212 Green St., Philadelphia 30, Pennsylvania; Mount Grace Convent, 1438 E. Warne Ave., St. Louis 7, Missouri; Adoration Convent, 2630 Exposition Blvd., Austin 3, Texas.

Holy Guardian Angels, see Dominican Sisters of the Holy Guardian Angels.

Servants of the Holy Heart of Mary (S.S.C.M.) Founded in France in 1860; established in U.S. in 1889. Pontifical, active, simple vows. 180 sisters in U.S., 1,100 world. Teaching elementary and high school, academy, business college; hospitals, schools of nursing; homes for working girls; Negro mission; catechetics; retreats; administration; office and domestic work. Ages 16-30, some exceptions, high school education. Postulate six months, novitiate two years, juniorate five years. Black habit. Canadian provincialate: 37 Ave. des Cascades, Beauport, P.Q., Canada. Novitiate: Villa St. Joseph, Montreal, P.Q., Canada. U.S. provincialate: St. Mary Hospital, 192 S. Fifth Ave., Kankakee, Illinois.

Sisters of the Holy Hearts of Jesus and Mary (Ss.Cc.J.M.)

Founded in France in 1853; established in Canada in 1891. Pontifical, active and contemplative, simple vows. 300 sisters in Canada, 600 world. Teaching elementary and high school; care of aged; residence for retired women. Age 16, high school education. Postulate six months, novitiate two years. Temporary vows annually for five years. Black habit. Motherhouse: Paramé, France. Canadian provincialates: 390 St. Louis St., Joliette, P.Q., Canada; Boulevard-des-Prairies, Laval-des-Rapides, P.Q., Canada.

Sisters of the Holy Humility of Mary (H.H.M.) (Blue Sisters) Founded in France in 1854 by Abbé John Joseph Begel and Antoinette Pottier; in 1864 because of religious persecution entire congregation and founders moved to U.S. Pontifical, active, simple vows. 539 sisters. Teaching elementary and high school; hospitals and schools of nursing; home and school for crippled children; domestic and office work; catechetics; missions in Latin America. Ages 16-30, high school education. Postulate ten months, novitiate two years, juniorate five years. Dark blue habit, black veil. Motherhouse: Villa Maria Convent, Villa Maria, Pennsylvania.

Servants of the Holy Infancy of Jesus. Third Order of St. Francis. Founded in Germany in 1855; established in U.S. in 1929. Pontifical, active, simple vows. 76 sisters in U.S. Domestic work in seminaries; nursing home; social work; visiting the sick poor; care of infants; missions in Zululand. Ages 17-30. Novitiate one year. Black habit. Motherhouse: Wuerzburg, Germany. U.S. provincialate: Villa Maria, P.O. Box 708, 641 Somerset St., North Plainfield, New Jersey.

Religious of the Holy Infancy of Jesus and Mary, see Sisters of St. Chretienne.

Holy Infant Jesus, see Charitable Instruction of the Holy Infant Jesus, Sisters of.

Sisters of the Holy Names of Jesus and Mary (S.N.J.M.) Founded in Canada in 1843 by Mother Marie Rose Durocher; established in U.S. in 1859. Pontifical, active, simple vows. 4,000 sisters, 1,645 in U.S. Choir and lay sisters. Black habit. Motherhouse: 1420 Mount Royal Blvd., Outrement, Montreal, P.Q., Canada. 860 sisters. Teaching elementary school, academies, schools of domestic science and agriculture, college; farming; missions in Basutoland, South Africa and South

America. Canadian provincialates: St. Emelie's Academy, 4837 Adam St., Montreal, P.Q., Canada; Longueuil, P.Q., Canada; L'Epiphanie, P.Q., Canada; St. Mary's College, Crescentwood, Winnipeg 9, Man., Canada; St. Mary's Academy, Windsor, Ont., Canada. U.S. provincialates:

Convent of the Holy Names, P.O. Box 907, Los Gatos, California. 463 sisters. Teaching elementary and high school, college; nursing; missions in Peru. Ages 15-30, high school education. Postulate eleven months, novitiate one and a half years, juniorate five years.

Convent of the Holy Names, 1061 New Scotland Rd., Albany 8, New York. 259 sisters. Teaching elementary school and academies; catechetics; nursing; domestic work; missions in Africa. Ages 16-30, high school education. Postulate six months, novitiate one and a half years, juniorate five years.

Convent of the Holy Names, Marylhurst, Oregon. 397 sisters. Teaching elementary and high school, colleges; day nursery; care of orphans; social agency for dependent children; missions in Basutoland, South Africa. Ages 15-30, high school education. Novitiate one and a half years, juniorate two to three years.

Convent of the Holy Names, N. 1114 Superior St., Spokane 2, Washington. 408 sisters. Teaching; nursing; domestic work; missions in South Africa. Ages 15-30, high school education. Postulate eleven months, novitiate two years, juniorate two years.

Holy Rosary, see Our Lady of the Holy Rosary.

Helpers of the Holy Souls (H.H.S.) Founded in France in 1856 by Blessed Mary of Providence; established in U.S. in 1892. Pontifical, active, simple vows. 140 sisters in U.S., 1,500 world. Nursing; social work; home visiting; domestic work; catechetics; publication—*The Harvest*; missions in Japan, Formosa, Hong Kong and Africa. Also located in Mexico. Work and prayers offered for the souls in purgatory. Ages 18-30, some exceptions, high school education. Postulate nine months, novitiate two years, juniorate varies. Temporary vow period six years. Black habit and cape. Motherhouse: Paris, France. U.S. provincialate: 303 W. Barry Ave., Chicago 14, Illinois. Canadian novitiate: Granby, P.Q., Canada.

Missionary Sisters, Servants of the Holy Spirit (S.Sp.S.) Founded in Holland in 1889; established in U.S. in 1901. Pontifical, active, simple vows. 389 sisters in U.S., 4,650 in world. Teaching elementary and high school; hospitals, school of nursing; domestic work in seminaries; care of aged; office work; catechetics in rural areas; retreats; Negro missions; publication— *The Master's Work*; foreign missions in Africa, Far East and Australia. Ages 18-30, high school education preferred. Aspirancy one to four years. Postulate six months, novitiate two years, juniorate six years. Blue habit. Motherhouse: Rome, Italy. U.S. provincialate: Convent of the Holy Spirit, Techny, Illinois.

Religious of the Holy Union of the Sacred Hearts (S.U.S.C.) Founded in France in 1826; established in U.S. in 1886. Pontifical, active, simple vows. 453 sisters in U.S., 1,500 world. Ages 17-30, high school or college education preferred. Aspirancy four years. Postulate ten to eleven months, novitiate two years. Black habit. Generalate: Rome, Italy.

Immaculate Heart Provincialate, 492 Rock St., Fall River, Massachusetts. 245 sisters. Teaching elementary and high school, college; nursing; domestic work; home missions; missions in Africa.

Sacred Heart Provincialate, 1 Main St., Groton, Massachusetts. 208 sisters. Teaching elementary and high school; domestic work; missions in Cameroons, Africa.

Holy, see also Most Holy.

Home Mission Sisters of America, see Glenmary Home Mission Sisters.

Home Visitors, see Mary, Sisters, Home Visitors of.

Sisters of Hope, see Holy Family Sisters of Bordeaux.

Hospital Sisters of St. Francis, see Franciscan Third Order.

Hospitaller, see Franciscan Hospitaller Sisters.

Hospitallers, see St. Augustine, Canonesses Hospitallers of.

Hotel Dieu Sisters, see Religious Hospitallers of St. Joseph.

Congregation of the Sisters of the Humility of Mary (C.H.M.) Founded in 1870 in U.S. when part of the congregation, Sisters of the Holy Humility of Mary, H.H.M., moved westward. Pontifical, active, simple vows. 400 sisters. Teaching elementary and high school, college; hospital and school of nursing; homes for dependent children; catechetics; domestic work. Ages 15-30, older by dispensation, high school education. Postulate nine months, novitiate two years, juniorate three years. Black habit, white for nurses. Motherhouse: Convent of the Humility of Mary, Ottumwa, Iowa.

I

Immaculata Sisters, see Missionary Sisters of the Immaculate Conception of the Mother of God.

Little Servant Sisters of the Immaculate Conception (S.S.M.I.) Founded in Poland in 1850; established in U.S. in 1926. Pontifical, active (3 contemplative sisters), simple vows. 32 sisters in U.S., 6,000 world. Teaching; home nursing; domestic work; refuge house; care of aged; catechetics; retreats; home missions; foreign missions in Africa. Ages 15-30, high school education preferred, nurses' training helpful. Postulate six months, novitiate two years. Blue habit. Motherhouse: Poland. U.S. provincialate: St. Joseph's Home, 184 Amboy Ave., Woodbridge, New Jersey.

Missionary Sisters of the Immaculate Conception (M.I.C.) Founded in Canada in 1902 by Mother Marie du Saint Esprit; first Canadian missionary congregation; established in U.S. in 1946. Pontifical, active, simple vows. 911 sisters, 11 in U.S. Teaching; hospitals, dispensaries; care of orphans and aged; social work; catechetics; retreats; Chinese mission in Ottawa. Foreign missions in Bolivia, Chile, Guatemala, Peru, Haiti, Philippines, Japan, Formosa, Africa, Madagascar, Italy. High school education. Postulate six months, novitiate two years, juniorate three years. No lay sisters. White habit. Motherhouse: Côté des Neiges, 2900 St. Catherine's Rd., Montreal 26, P.Q., Canada. U.S. postulate: Our Lady Queen of Missions Retreat House, 207 Pleasant St., Marlboro, Massachusetts.

Sisters of the Immaculate Conception (C.I.C.) Founded in Louisiana in 1874 by Rev. Cyprian Venissat, who needed sisters to teach in his parish. Diocesan, active, simple vows. 36 sisters. Teaching elementary and high school; domestic work. Ages 16-35, high school education preferred. Aspirancy four years. Postulate six months, novitiate two years, juniorate four years. Black and blue habit. Motherhouse: Immaculate Conception Convent, 3037 Dauphine St., New Orleans 17, Louisiana.

Sisters of the Immaculate Conception (R.C.M.) Founded in Spain in 1892; established in U.S. in 1960. Pontifical, active, simple vows. 11 sisters in U.S., 1,000 world. Teaching. Age 18, high school education. Aspirancy. Postulate six months, novitiate one year, juniorate three years. White and blue habit. Motherhouse: Madrid, Spain. U.S. novitiate: Our Lady of Perpetual Help Convent, Harvard and Ninth Sts., Clovis, California.

Sisters of the Immaculate Conception (S.I.C.) (Soeurs de l'Immaculée) Founded in Italy in 1876; established in Canada in 1951. Pontifical, active, simple vows. 20 sisters in Canada. Domestic work; teaching. Age 17. Postulate six months, novitiate two years. Temporary vow period five years. Blue habit. Motherhouse: Genoa, Italy. Canadian provincialate: École Ste. Thérèse, Manneville, Abitibi, P.Q., Canada.

Sisters of the Immaculate Conception of the Blessed Virgin Mary (M.I.C.) Founded in Lithuania in 1918; established in U.S. in 1936. Diocesan, active, simple vows. 47 sisters in U.S., 17 in Canada. Teaching; nursing; care of children and aged; home for girls; day nurseries; summer camp; publishing; domestic work; catechetics; retreats. Ages 15-30, some exceptions, high school education preferred, ability in nursing, teaching, domestic work, music. Postulate six months, novitiate one year. Generalate at Mariampole, Lithuania, suppressed by Communist government. U.S. motherhouse: Immaculate Conception Convent, R.F.D. 2, Putnam, Connecticut. Canadian novitiate: Pont Viau, P.Q., Canada.

Missionary Sisters of the Immaculate Conception of the Mother of God (S.M.I.C.) (Immaculata Sisters) Third Order of St. Francis. Founded in Brazil in 1910 by Conceptionist nuns; motherhouse established in U.S. in 1922. Pontifical, active, simple vows. 143 sisters in U.S., 732 world. Teaching elementary school and college; nursing; care of orphans and aged; domestic work; catechetics; publication—*Mission Horizons*; Indian and Negro missions; teaching elementary and high school, normal schools and college, hospitals, dispensaries, and care of orphans in Africa, Bolivia, Brazil, Formosa and Germany. Ages 17-30, high school or equivalent education. Postulate six months, novitiate two years, juniorate five years. No lay sisters.

Any race or nationality. Blue and white habit, black veil. Motherhouse: Maria Immaculata Convent, P.O. Box 39, Middleville, New Jersey.

Immaculate Conception, see Charity of the Immaculate Conception, Sisters of; Charity of the Immaculate Conception, Ivrea Sisters of; Dominican Third Order; Franciscan Third Order; Grey Sisters of the Immaculate Conception; Mary of the Immaculate Conception, Daughters of; Providence and of the Immaculate Conception, Sisters of.

Daughters of the Immaculate Heart of Mary (I.H.M.) Founded in Ohio in 1952 by Mothers M. Joan and M. Canisius. Diocesan, active, simple vows. 5 sisters. Teaching high school and academy; domestic work. Postulate six months, novitiate two years. Motherhouse: Immaculate Heart of Mary Convent, Box 2077, Wintersville, Steubenville P.O., Ohio.

Sisters, Daughters of the Immaculate Heart of Mary (I.H.M.) Founded in Spain in 1848; established in U.S. in 1915. Pontifical, active, simple vows. 86 sisters in U.S. Teaching elementary and high school; social work; home missions. Ages 15-30. Aspirancy three years. Postulate six months, novitiate two years, juniorate three years. Motherhouse: Barcelona, Spain. U.S. provincialate: Immaculate Heart Academy, 35 E. Fifteenth St., Tucson, Arizona.

Sisters of the Immaculate Heart of Mary, see California Institute of the Sisters of the Most Holy and Immaculate Heart of the Blessed Virgin Mary.

Sisters, Servants of the Immaculate Heart of Mary (S.C.I.M.) (Good Shepherd Sisters of Quebec) Founded in Canada in 1850 by George Manly Muir and Genevieve Fitzbach Roy; established in U.S. in 1882. Pontifical, active, simple vows. 1,491 sisters, 228 in U.S. Teaching elementary school, academies, normal schools, classical school, home economics and industrial schools; care of foundlings, orphans and aged; hospital for unmarried mothers; domestic work; catechetics; retreats; home for wayward girls; reform school; missions in Basutoland and Madagascar. Age 15, high school education. Postulate one year, novitiate one year, juniorate two years. Black habit. Motherhouse: 74 rue Lachevrotière, P.Q., Canada. Canadian provincialate: Chicoutimi, P.Q., Canada. U.S. provincialate: Bay View, Saco, Maine.

Sisters, Servants of the Immaculate Heart of Mary (I.H.M.)
Founded at Monroe, Michigan, in 1845 by Rev. Louis Florent
Gillet. Pontifical, active, simple vows. Now three independent
communities:
St. Mary Convent, 610 W. Elm Ave., Monroe, Michigan. 1,599
sisters. Teaching elementary and high school, academy, college,
boys' military academy; domestic work; nursing; Pius XII Re-
source Center, which provides religion courses on elementary
and high school levels, consultation service for religious text
publishers, collaborates on religious texts and filmstrips; missions in Puerto Rico. Ages 16-28. Postulate nine months, novitiate two years; juniorate two years. Temporary vow period five
years. Blue habit; white in Puerto Rico.
Immaculate Heart of Mary Convent, Marywood, Scranton 9,
Pennsylvania. 1,168 sisters. Teaching elementary and high
school, academy, boys' industrial school, college; hospital,
children's hospital, school of nursing; catechetics; care of orphans. Ages 16-30, high school education. Postulate nine
months, novitiate two years, juniorate three years. Blue habit.
Villa Maria, West Chester, Pennsylvania. 2,064 sisters. Teaching elementary and high school, academy, normal school, college, demonstration schools for teacher-training, teaching blind
and slow-learners; catechetics; day nurseries; social work; missions in Chile and Peru. To age 30, high school education.
Postulate nine months, novitiate two years. Blue habit.
Immaculate Heart, see under Dominican Third Order; St. Francis of the Immaculate Heart of Mary, Sisters of; St. Rita of
the Immaculate Heart, Daughters of; Sacred Heart of Jesus
and the Immaculate Heart of Mary, Missionary Catechists of
the; Visitation of the Congregation of the Immaculate Heart
of Mary, Sisters of the.
Immaculate Virgin, see St. Francis of the Mission of the Immaculate Virgin, Sisters of.
Immaculate Virgin Mary, see St. Francis of the Immaculate Virgin Mary, Mother of God, Sisters of the Third Order of.
Congregation of the Incarnate Word and the Blessed Sacrament
(I.W.B.S.) Originally founded in Roanne, France, in 1625;
established in U.S. in 1852; this congregation formed in 1939
when three independent convents of the Sisters of the Incarnate Word and the Blessed Sacrament (V.I.) united under a

motherhouse at Victoria, Texas. Pontifical, active, simple vows. 233 sisters. Teaching elementary school, academies; catechetics; nursing; domestic work. Also in Mexico. Age 14, high school education. Aspirancy three years. Postulate eleven months, novitiate one year, juniorate four years. White and red habit, black veil. Motherhouse: Nazareth Convent, 105 W. Church St., Victoria, Texas.

Sisters of the Incarnate Word and the Blessed Sacrament (V.I.) Founded in 1625 in France; suppressed during French Revolution, reestablished in 1832; established in U.S. in 1852; originally cloistered, cloister lifted in 1913. Active, simple vows. Applicants should have an interest in teaching, domestic work, sewing, music, or office work. White and red habit, black veil. Three independent motherhouses:

Incarnate Word Convent, 6618 Pearl Rd., Parma Heights, Cleveland 30, Ohio. Diocesan. 75 sisters. Teaching elementary school and academy; domestic work. Ages 15-30, high school education. Aspirancy three years. Postulate one year, novitiate two years, juniorate three years.

Incarnate Word Convent, 4600 Richmond Rd., Bellaire, Texas. Pontifical. 159 sisters. Teaching elementary and high school, academy. Age 15, high school education. Aspirancy three months, postulate six months, novitiate two years.

Incarnate Word Convent, 2930 So. Alameda, Corpus Christi, Texas. Pontifical. 129 sisters. Teaching elementary school, academies, college; domestic work. Age 15, high school education. Postulate six months, novitiate two years, juniorate three years.

Incarnate Word, see Charity of the Incarnate Word.

Incurable, see Relief for Incurable Cancer, Servants of.

Sisters of the Infant Jesus (C.I.J.) (Nursing Sisters of the Sick Poor) Founded in Brooklyn in 1905 by Mother Marie Antoinette of the Sisters of the Infant Jesus founded in France in 1835. Diocesan, active, simple vows. 190 sisters. Nursing the sick poor regardless of race or religion in their homes and in a hospital; social work; catechetics; care of sacristies; teaching religion to normal and exceptional children; office and domestic work; missions in Nassau. Ages 18-30, high school education. Postulate one year, novitiate one year, juniorate three years. Black habit. Motherhouse: Convent of the Infant Jesus, 439 Henry St., Brooklyn 31, New York.

Sisters of the Infant Jesus (C.I.J.) (Soeurs de l'Enfant-Jesus) Founded in France in 1835. Teaching, nursing. Canadian provincialate: Rivière-du-Loup, P.Q., Canada.

Infant Jesus, see Carmelite Sisters of St. Therèse of the Infant Jesus; Dominican Sisters of the Infant Jesus; Franciscan Capuchin Sisters of the Infant Jesus.

Infant Mary, see Charity of the Infant Mary, Sisters of.

J

Daughters of Jesus (F.I.) Founded in Spain in 1871; established in U.S. in 1950. Pontifical, active, simple vows. 32 sisters in U.S., 1,200 world. Teaching; missions in Chile, Bolivia, Philippines, Far East. Ages 15-30, high school education. Postulate six months, novitiate two years, juniorate six years. Black habit. Motherhouse: Rome, Italy. U.S. vice-provincialate: St. Egbert's Convent, 1705 Evans St., Morehead City, North Carolina.

Daughters of Jesus (F.J.) Founded in France in 1834; established in U.S. in 1904. Pontifical, active, simple vows. 470 sisters in Canada and U.S., 3,000 world. Teaching; hospitals, schools of nursing; care of aged; home missions; domestic work. Ages 16-30, high school education preferred. Postulate eight months, novitiate two years. Motherhouse: France. American provincialates: Maison St. Joseph, 9040 Eighty-fourth Ave., Edmonton, Alta., Canada; Trois-Rivières, P.Q. Canada. U.S. address: St. Joseph's Hospital, Lewiston, Montana.

Little Sisters of Jesus (Petites Soeurs de Jesus) (Hermanitas de Jesus) (Little Sisters of Charles de Foucauld) Founded in the Sahara in 1939 by Little Sister Magdeleine of Jesus; established in U.S. in 1952. Diocesan, active and contemplative, simple vows. 16 sisters in five U.S. convents, 900 world. The Little Sisters earn their own living by manual work and live a contemplative life in small groups, among the very poor and the outcast. This is a religious institute; see also the listing for Jesus-Caritas, a potential secular institute which is also based on the spirituality of Father de Foucauld. Ages 16-30. Postulate one year, novitiate one year. White habit, blue veil, also blue cotton uniform, sandals. Motherhouse: Le Tubet, France. North American Central House: 700 Irving St. N.E., Washington 17, D.C. Novitiate: 1235 Third Ave., Fairbanks, Alaska. Canadian address: 4148 Ave. Hôtel de Ville, Montreal, P.Q., Canada. Mexican address: Allende 103 (Antes 55), Villa de Guadalupe, Mexico 14, D.F., Mexico.

Society of the Sisters, Faithful Companions of Jesus (F.C.J.) Founded in France in 1820 by Ven. Marie Madeline de Bonnault d'Houet; established in U.S. in 1896. Pontifical, active. 72 sisters in U.S.; 1,000 world. Teaching; retreats; catechetics. High school education. Postulate six months, novitiate two years, juniorate varies. Black habit. Motherhouse: Paris, France. U.S. provincialate: St. Joseph's Convent, Columbus St., Fitchburg, Massachusetts. Canadian provincialate: Calgary, Alta., Canada.

Jesus, see Dominican Oblates of Jesus.

Poor Handmaids of Jesus Christ (P.H.J.C.) (Ancilla Domini Sisters) Founded in Germany in 1851; established in U.S. in 1868. Pontifical, active, simple vows. 585 sisters in U.S., 3,227 world. Teaching elementary and high school, college; hospitals and schools of nursing; care of orphans and aged; catechetics; domestic work. Ages 18-30. Aspirancy four years. Postulate six to twelve months, novitiate two years, juniorate two to three years. Black habit. Motherhouse: Germany. U.S. provincialate: Ancilla Domini Convent, Donaldson, Indiana.

Sisters of Jesus Crucified (C.J.C.) Founded in France in 1930 to make religious life possible for ill or physically handicapped women; established in U.S. in 1955. Pontifical, contemplative, minor papal enclosure, simple vows. 25 sisters and 2 oblates in U.S., 250 world. No lay sisters. Oblate sisters live in community but are not bound by enclosure, wear grey habit, no age limit. All races and nationalities. Contemplation; Divine Office chanted; retreats for the sick; cytology labs for the early detection of cancer; teaching retarded children. All members work as far as their abilities allow. Ages 20-30, high school education or equivalent. Postulate six months, novitiate two years, juniorate five years. Applicants in good health are also accepted. Those with nervous or mental disorders or contagious diseases not admitted. White habit, black veil. Motherhouse: Brou, France. U.S. priories: Regina Mundi Priory, Devon, Pennsylvania; St. Paul's Priory, Newport, Rhode Island.

Poor Sisters of Jesus Crucified and the Sorrowful Mother (C.J.C.)

Founded in Pennsylvania in 1921 by Rev. Alphonsus, C.P., to work among Lithuanians in the U.S. Diocesan, active, simple vows. 112 sisters. Teaching elementary school; nursing; catechetics; retreats; care of aged; domestic work; home missions. Ages 15-30, high school education. Aspirancy one to four years. Postulate eleven months, novitiate two years, juniorate six years. Black habit. Motherhouse: Our Lady of Sorrows Convent, 261 Thatcher St., Brockton 54, Massachusetts.

Recluse Missionaries of Jesus and Mary (R.M.J.M.) Founded in Montreal, Canada, in 1941; established in U.S. in 1951. Diocesan, contemplative, simple vows. 60 sisters, 17 in U.S. Contemplation, perpetual adoration, perpetual rosary. Divine Office recited in vernacular on weekdays and in Latin on Sundays and feasts, High Mass sung daily; study; domestic work. No lay sisters. A few sisters in each monastery do active work—catechetics, social work, parish census, retreats, visiting the sick. Ages 16-35, high school education preferred. Postulate six to twelve months, novitiate two years. Temporary vows annually for five years. Interested girls may spend a few days at Louisiana monastery making a private retreat; group visits also welcome. Make reservations in advance. Grey habit. Motherhouse: 14130 W. Gouin Blvd., Rivière-des-Prairies, P.Q., Canada. Canadian monastery: St. Jerome, P.Q., Canada. U.S. monastery and novitiate: Monastery of the Assumption, Rte. 1, Box 170, Abbeville Hwy., Lafayette, Louisiana.

Religious of Jesus and Mary (R.J.M.) Founded in Lyons, France, in 1818; established in U.S. in 1877. Pontifical, active, simple vows. 2,236 in world. Ages 15-30, high school education. Postulate six months, novitiate two years, juniorate one to two years. Also located in Mexico. Little Office of the Blessed Virgin. Black habit. Motherhouse: Rome, Italy.

Eastern U.S. provincialate: Convent of Jesus and Mary, 8910 Riggs Rd., Hyattsville, Maryland. 309 sisters. Teaching elementary and high school; catechetics; residence for women; missions in India and Pakistan.

Western U.S. provincialate: 1401 West Yandell Blvd., El Paso, Texas. 66 sisters. Teaching elementary school and commercial academy; domestic work; residences for women; catechetics; missions in Colombia and India.

Canadian provincialate: Sillery, P.Q., Canada. Teaching elementary school, academies, domestic science school and normal school; missions to Cree Indians in Manitoba.

Servants of Jesus and Mary (S.J.M.) Founded in Canada in 1894 by Rev. Alexis-Louis Mangin and his housekeeper, Mother Marie-Zita de Jésus. Pontifical, contemplative, simple vows. 170 sisters. Perpetual adoration; making altar breads and vestments; Divine Office in Latin for choir sisters; Little Office of the Immaculate Conception in vernacular for lay sisters. Ages 16-30 for choir sisters, 16-35 for lay sisters. Postulate six months, novitiate two years, juniorate three years. White habit, blue cape. Motherhouse and novitiate: 210 Laurier St., Hull, P.Q., Canada.

Missionaries of Jesus, Mary and Joseph (M.J.M.J.) Founded in Spain in 1939 to work exclusively among the poor; established in U.S. in 1956. Diocesan, active, simple vows. 29 sisters in U.S., 150 world. Social work; catechetics; domestic work. Ages 15-35. Postulate nine months, novitiate one and a half years, juniorate six years. Motherhouse: Madrid, Spain. U.S. provincialate: 810 Antelope St., Corpus Christi, Texas.

Oblates of Jesus the Priest (O.J.S.) (Oblatas de Jesús Sacerdote) Founded in Tlalpán, Mexico, in 1937 by Rev. Felix Rougier; established in U.S. in 1950. Diocesan, active and contemplative, simple vows. 50 sisters in U.S. Domestic work in seminaries; prayers offered for priests and priestly vocations. Age 15, grade school education. Aspirancy six months, postulate six months, novitiate two years, juniorate one year. White and black habit. Motherhouse: Mexico City 22, Tlalpán, D.F., Mexico. U.S. address: 314 E. King's Hwy., San Antonio 12, Texas.

St. Joan Antida, see Charity of St. Joan Antida, Sisters of.

Institute of St. Joan of Arc of Ottawa (S.J.A.) (Institut Jeanne d'Arc) Founded in Canada in 1919 by Mother St. Thomas Aquinas Branda; established in U.S. in 1923. Diocesan, active, simple vows. 142 sisters in Canada, 8 in U.S. Homes for working girls and students; teaching elementary school and commercial courses; domestic work; social work. To age 30, some exceptions. Postulate six months, novitiate two years. Black habit. Motherhouse: Institut Jeanne d'Arc, 360 Kenwood Ave., Ottawa 3, Ont., Canada. U.S. address: St. Aloysius School, Newburyport, Massachusetts.

Sisters of St. Joan of Arc of Quebec (Soeurs de Ste. Jeanne d'Arc) Founded in Massachusetts in 1914 by Rev. Marie Clement Staub, A.A., because he saw the difficulty American priests had in finding competent housekeepers. Diocesan, active, simple vows. 290 sisters in Canada and U.S. Domestic work in rectories, bishops' residences, seminaries, etc. Ages 16-30, seventh grade education. Postulate six months, novitiate two years. Motherhouse: 1681 Chemin St. Louis, Bergerville 6, P.Q., Canada.

Catechist Missionary Sister of St. John. Diocesan. 7 sisters. Catechetics. St. John Bosco Convent, Taylor, Texas.

Sisters of St. John the Baptist (C.S.J.B.) (Baptistines) Founded in Italy in 1875 to care for orphans; established in U.S. in 1906. Pontifical, active, simple vows. 204 sisters in U.S., 1,300 world. Teaching elementary and high school, college; domestic work; nursing; care of aged and orphans; catechetics; retreats; office work; day nursery; guest homes; social work; summer camps; missions in Africa and South America. Ages 15-30, high school education preferred. Aspirancy four years. Postulate ten months, novitiate one year. Black habit. Motherhouse: Rome, Italy. U.S. provincialate: St. John Convent, Anderson Hill Rd., White Plains, New York. Canadian address: Infant Jesus Convent, 52 Colbourne St., Hamilton, Ont., Canada.

St. John Bosco, see Salesian Sisters of St. John Bosco.

Little Daughters of St. Joseph (L.D.S.J.) (Les Petites Filles de St. Joseph) Founded in Canada in 1857 by Rev. Antoine Mercier and Rose de Lima Dauth as a community devoted to the spiritual and temporal welfare of the clergy and seminarians; established in U.S. in 1931. Pontifical, active, simple vows. 11 sisters in U.S. Domestic work in seminaries; making vestments; care of sacristies. Ages 15-30, some exceptions, any nationality. Black habit. Motherhouse: 2333 W. Sherbrooke St., Montreal 25, P.Q., Canada. U.S. address: Convent of St. Thomas the Apostle Seminary, Kenmore, Washington.

Little Missionaries of St. Joseph (Petites-Missionnaires de Saint-Joseph) Founded in Canada in 1925 by Brother Louis Gareau, C.S.V. Diocesan, active, simple vows. 42 sisters. Manual work in religious institutions. Ages 18-20, eighth or ninth grade education. Postulate six months, novitiate two years, juniorate three years. Motherhouse: Ste. Marcelline, Cté. Joliette, P.Q., Canada.

Oblate Sisters of St. Joseph (O.S.J.) Founded in 1959 in Pittsford, Vermont, as a potential secular institute by Jean T. Polworth (now Sister Jean) and Very Rev. John A. Lynch; potential religious institute in 1963. Diocesan, active, simple vows. 1 sister. Service to aged; at present visit the aged in their homes, hospitals, and nursing homes; plan to establish a "noninstitutional" residence in which the retired can maintain their dignity and independence since conventional homes for the aged and nursing homes do not meet the needs of many aged persons in today's society. Ages 21-35. Grey street-length habit. Motherhouse: Marydawn, Pittsford, Vermont.

Religious Daughters of St. Joseph (F.S.J.) (Josephite Sisters) Founded in Spain in 1875; recently established in U.S. Pontifical, active. 18 sisters in U.S., 1,300 world. Teaching, nursing. Ages 15-30. Postulate six months, novitiate two years, juniorate one year. Motherhouse: Gerona, Spain. Mexican provincialate: Francisco I Madero #3, Tiacopac, San Angel, Mexico, D.F., Mexico. U.S. address: St. Julia School, 3100 Lyons Rd., Austin 2, Texas.

Religious Hospitallers of St. Joseph (R.H.S.J.) (Religieuses Hospitalières de St. Joseph) (Hôtel Dieu Sisters) Founded in France in 1636; established in Montreal, Canada, in 1659 by Miss Jeanne Mance, who had founded Montreal's Hôtel Dieu Hospital; established in U.S. in 1894 in Winooski, Vermont. Pontifical, active, simple vows. 1,700 sisters, 120 in U.S. Hospitals, TB sanatoriums, leprosariums, schools of nursing; teaching elementary school, academies and college; care of aged; social work; retreats; domestic work in hospitals; missions in Peru and West Africa. Ages 18-35, tenth grade education. Postulate six months, novitiate one and a half years, juniorate two years. Black habit. Motherhouse: 251 W. Pine Ave., Montreal 18, P.Q., Canada. Provincialates: Ville Marie, 2450 Ste. Catherine Rd., Montreal 26, P.Q., Canada (389 sisters); R.R. #3 Collins Bay, Kingston, Ont., Canada (976 sisters, English-speaking); Vallee-Lourdes, West Bathurst, N.B., Canada (376 sisters). U.S. addresses: Bishop de Goesbriand Hospital, Burlington, Vermont; Fanny Allen Hospital, Winooski, Vermont.

Servants of St. Joseph (S.S.J.) Founded in Spain in 1874; established in U.S. in 1957. Pontifical, active. 10 sisters in U.S. Domestic work; nursery. Motherhouse: Madrid, Spain. U.S. address: St. Joseph Nursery School, 201 S. Spring St., Falls Church, Virginia.

Sisters of St. Joseph of St. Augustine, Florida (S.S.J.) Diocesan, active, simple vows. 263 sisters. Teaching elementary and high school, junior college for sisters, schools for handicapped children; nursing; care of orphans, aged, and unwed mothers; catechetics; missions in Puerto Rico. Ages 17-35, high school education. Postulate six months, novitiate one and a half years, juniorate six years. Motherhouse: St. Joseph Convent, 241 St. George St., St. Augustine, Florida.

Sisters of St. Joseph of Bourg (C.S.J.) Founded in Le Puy, France, in 1650; independent congregation in 1824; established in U.S. in 1855; established in Canada from Crookston in 1941. Pontifical, active, simple vows. 394 sisters, 1,200 world. Black habit. Motherhouse: Bourg, France.

St. Joseph Provincialate, 1200 Mirabeau Ave., New Orleans 22, Louisiana. 199 sisters. Teaching elementary and high school; Newman Club instructors; nursing; care of orphans; summer camps; home for working girls; visiting prisons; catechetics; social work; Negro and rural missions; missions in Central America. Ages 15-30, high school education. Postulate nine months, novitiate two years, juniorate five years.

St. Joseph Provincialate, Marywood Rd., Crookston, Minnesota. 140 sisters. Teaching elementary and high school, academy; nursing; domestic work; catechetics; social work; Negro and Indian missions; teaching in Rainy River, Ont., Canada. Age 16. Postulate nine months, novitiate two years, juniorate five years.

St. Joseph Provincialate, 6532 Beechmont Ave., Cincinnati 30, Ohio. 55 sisters. Teaching; social work; domestic work; administration. To age 30, high school education. Postulate nine months, novitiate two years.

Sisters of St. Joseph (C.S.J.) *Canadian congregations. Originally founded in Le Puy, France, in 1650. Black habit, white for nurses. Each motherhouse is independent.*

Sisters of St. Joseph of Hamilton. Founded in 1852. Diocesan, active, simple vows. 338 sisters. Hospitals, schools of nursing; teaching elementary and high school; social work; care of aged, and emotionally disturbed children; Indian mission. At least 16. Postulate six to twelve months, novitiate two years, juniorate three years. Motherhouse: P.O. Box 155, Hamilton, Ont., Canada.

Sisters of St. Joseph of London. 485 sisters. Hospitals, schools of nursing; teaching, schools of music; homes for children. Motherhouse: 1486 Richmond St. N., London, Ont., Canada.

Sisters of St. Joseph of Pembroke. Founded in 1921. Pontifical, active, simple vows. 173 sisters. Nursing; teaching elementary and high school, academies; nursing; teachers' college; care of aged and orphans. Ages 16-30, high school education, some exceptions. Postulate six to ten months, novitiate two years, juniorate five years. Motherhouse: St. Joseph's-on-the-Lake, P.O. Pembroke, Ont., Canada.

Sisters of St. Joseph of Peterborough. Founded in 1890. 200 sisters. Teaching elementary school, academy; hospitals, school of nursing; care of aged. Motherhouse: Mount St. Joseph, Monaghan Rd., Peterborough, Ont., Canada.

Sisters of St. Joseph of Sault Ste. Marie. Founded in 1937. 381 sisters. Pontifical, active, simple vows. Teaching elementary school, academy, colleges; hospitals, schools of nursing; care of orphans and aged; missions in Guatemala and Bahamas, B.W.I. Age 17, high school education preferred. Postulate six to twelve months, novitiate two years, juniorate five years. Motherhouse: St. Joseph's College, Harriet St., North Bay, Ont., Canada.

Sisters of St. Joseph of Toronto. Founded in 1851 by Msgr. de Charbonnel. Teaching kindergarten, elementary and high school, college; hospitals, hospital for chronically ill, schools of nursing; children's village; students' residence. Motherhouse: Morrow Park, 3377 Bayview, Willowdale, Ont., Canada.

Sisters of St. Joseph of St. Hyacinthe. Founded in 1877 by Bishop Louis Zéphirin Moreau. Teaching elementary and high school, domestic science school, school for Indians; farming. Motherhouse: St. Hyacinthe, P.Q., Canada.

Sisters of St. Joseph of St. Vallier. Founded in France in 1683; established in Canada in 1903. Pontifical, active, simple vows. 440 sisters. Teaching elementary school, academy; nursing; missions in Haiti. Ages 17-35. Postulate six months, novitiate

two years, juniorate two years. Motherhouse: 560 Chemin
Ste-Foy, Quebec 6, P.Q., Canada.

Sisters of St. Joseph of Carondelet (C.S.J.) Founded in Le Puy,
France, in 1650; Lyons community reestablished in 1806 after
the French Revolution in which some of the sisters were guil-
lotined and others imprisoned; established in U.S. in 1836 at
Carondelet, now part of St. Louis, Missouri. Pontifical, active,
simple vows. 4,620 sisters. Black habit. General motherhouse:
St. Joseph's Generalate, 2307 S. Lindbergh Blvd., St. Louis
31, Missouri.

St. Mary's Provincial House, 11999 Chalon Rd., Los Angeles
49, California. 888 sisters. Teaching elementary and high
school, academies, college; hospitals, sanitarium; care of orphans and deaf children; missions in Hawaii, Japan and Peru.
High school education. Postulate one year, novitiate two years,
juniorate two years.

St. Theresa's Convent, 712 North School St., Honolulu 17,
Hawaii (vice-province). 43 sisters assigned from other provinces. Teaching elementary school; nursing; catechetics; missions in Japan. Hawaiian entrants trained at Los Angeles
provincialate.

St. Joseph's Provincial House, 1890 Randolph Ave., St. Paul
16, Minnesota. 1,341 sisters. Teaching elementary and high
school, academies, college; hospitals, schools of nursing; school
for exceptional children; care of infants; missions in Hawaii,
Japan and Peru. High school education. Postulate eleven
months, novitiate two years, juniorate two years.

St. Joseph Provincial House, 6400 Minnesota Ave., St. Louis 11,
Missouri. 1,386 sisters. Teaching elementary and high school,
academies, colleges; hospitals, schools of nursing; care of orphans and deaf children; home for the friendless; catechetics;
home missions; missions in Japan and Peru. Age 16, high
school education. Postulate eleven months, novitiate two
years, juniorate five years.

St. Joseph's Provincial House, 90 Overlook Ave., Latham,
New York. 1,005 sisters. Teaching elementary and high school,
college; hospital, school of nursing; care of orphans; catechetics; missions in Hawaii, Japan and Peru. To age 35. Postulate eleven months, novitiate two years, juniorate two years.

Sisters of St. Joseph. *The following nineteen communities, alphabetized by state, were founded directly or indirectly from the foundation at Carondelet. With the Carondelet congregation, these communities include over 17,300 sisters, or almost one-tenth of the sisters in the U.S. (The total world membership of all congregations of the Sisters of St. Joseph is over 35,000.) Each of the following motherhouses is independent. Not included in this group are those communities which came to the U.S. from the French motherhouses in Bourg, Chambery, Le Puy, and Lyons later than the Carondelet foundation. Black habit.*

Sisters of St. Joseph or Orange, California (C.S.J.) Founded in California in 1912 by Mother Bernard Gosselin. Pontifical, active, simple vows. 484 sisters. Teaching elementary and high school, college; nursing; office work; administration; catechetics; home visiting; missions in San Francisco's Chinatown; teaching and nursing in Hawaii, Solomon Islands, New Guinea. Foreign missionaries must volunteer. High school education. Aspirancy. Postulate one year, novitiate two years, juniorate four years. Motherhouse: 380 So. Batavia St., Orange, California.

Sisters of St. Joseph of La Grange, Illinois (C.S.J.) Founded in Illinois in 1899. Diocesan, active, simple vows. 282 sisters. Teaching elementary school and academies. Ages 18-30, high school education preferred. Aspirancy four years. Postulate six to eleven months, novitiate two years, juniorate varies—includes time required for Bachelor's degree. Motherhouse: Our Lady of Bethlehem Convent, 1515 W. Ogden Ave., La Grange Park, Illinois.

Sisters of St. Joseph of Tipton, Indiana (C.S.J.) Founded in 1888 by Mother M. Gertrude Moffit. Diocesan, active, simple vows. 162 sisters. Teaching elementary and high school, academy, teaching retarded children; hospitals, convalescent homes, school of nursing; catechetics; retreats; care of aged; work with migrants. To age 35, high school education. Postulate six months, novitiate two years. St. Joseph Motherhouse: R.R. 5, Tipton, Indiana.

Sisters of St. Joseph of Concordia, Kansas (C.S.J.) Founded in Kansas in 1883. Pontifical, active, simple vows. 616 sisters. Teaching elementary and high school, academy, college; hospitals, schools of nursing; care of orphans and aged; social work; domestic work; home missions; missions in Brazil. Age 16, high school education preferred. Aspirancy four years. Postulate ten months, novitiate one year, juniorate five years. Motherhouse: Nazareth Motherhouse, Thirteenth and Washington Sts., Concordia, Kansas.

Sisters of St. Joseph of Wichita, Kansas (C.S.J.) Founded in Kansas in 1888. Pontifical, active, simple vows. 458 sisters. Teaching elementary and high school, college; hospitals, dispensary, schools of nursing; care of aged; day nursery; social work; domestic work; catechetics; missions in Japan. Ages 15-35, high school education. Aspirancy 1 year, postulate six months, novitiate two years, juniorate three years. Motherhouse: Mt. St. Mary's Convent, 3700 East Lincoln St., Wichita 18, Kansas.

Sisters of St. Joseph of Boston, Massachusetts (C.S.J.) Founded in Massachusetts in 1873. Diocesan, active, simple vows. 1,758 sisters. Teaching elementary and high school, academies, colleges, secretarial schools, school for deaf and aphasic children; care of aged and aged blind women; homes for working girls; nursing; catechetics. Ages 16-35. Postulate nine months, novitiate two years. Motherhouse: 444 Centre St., Milton 86, Massachusetts.

Sisters of St. Joseph of Springfield, Massachusetts (C.S.J.) Founded in Massachusetts in 1883. Diocesan, active, simple vows. 721 sisters. Teaching; nursing. Ages 16-30, high school education. Motherhouse: St. Joseph Convent, 62 Elliot St., Springfield, Massachusetts.

Sisters of St. Joseph of Nazareth, Michigan (S.S.J.) Founded in 1889. Pontifical, active, simple vows. 800 sisters. Teaching elementary and high school, academy, college; hospitals, schools of nursing; care of orphans; domestic and office work. High school education preferred. Postulate ten months, novitiate two years, juniorate three years. Motherhouse: Nazareth Convent, Nazareth, Michigan.

Sisters of St. Joseph of Brentwood, New York (C.S.J.) Diocesan, active, simple vows. 1,827 sisters. Teaching elementary and high school, academies, teaching deaf, blind and retarded children, colleges; nursing; missions in Puerto Rico. Ages 17-35, high school education. Postulate nine months, novitiate two years, juniorate three years. Motherhouse: St. Joseph's Convent, Brentwood, L.I., New York.

Sisters of St. Joseph of Buffalo, New York (S.S.J.) Founded in 1854. Pontifical, active, simple vows. 420 sisters. Teaching elementary and high school, academy, teachers' college, schools for the deaf and exceptional children, St. Joseph College for the Deaf in Buffalo; nursing; care of infants and aged. To age 30, high school education preferred. Postulate ten months, novitiate two years, juniorate five years. Motherhouse: Mt. St. Joseph, 2064 Main St., Buffalo 8, New York.

Sisters of St. Joseph of Rochester, New York (S.S.J.) Founded in 1854. Pontifical, active, simple vows. 860 sisters. Teaching elementary and high school, college, teachers' college, school for exceptional children; hospitals, schools of nursing; care of aged and orphans; catechetics; social work; Negro mission. To age 35, high school education. Postulate ten months, novitiate two years, juniorate varies. Motherhouse: Nazareth Convent, 4095 East Ave., Rochester 10, New York.

Sisters of St. Joseph of Watertown, New York (S.S.J.) Founded in 1881. Diocesan, active, simple vows. 156 sisters. Teaching elementary and high school, college, music conservatory; care of orphans; social work; domestic work. Ages 16-35, high school education preferred. Postulate nine and a half months, novitiate two years, juniorate three years. Motherhouse: 362 West Main St., Watertown, New York.

Sisters of St. Joseph of Cleveland, Ohio (C.S.J.) Founded in Ohio in 1872 by Mother St. George Bradley. Diocesan, active, simple vows. 370 sisters. Teaching elementary school and academies; domestic work; catechetics; social work. Postulate six to twelve months, novitiate two years, juniorate six years. Motherhouse: St. Joseph Convent, 3430 Rocky River Dr., Cleveland 11, Ohio.

Sisters of St. Joseph of Erie, Pennsylvania (C.S.J.) Founded in 1860. Diocesan, active, simple vows. 411 sisters. Teaching elementary and high school, academy, college; care of aged and orphans; protectorate; day nursery; catechetics. Ages 18-30, high school education. Postulate ten months, novitiate two years, juniorate five years. Motherhouse: Villa Maria, 819 West Eighth St., Erie, Pennsylvania.

Sisters of St. Joseph of Philadelphia, Pennsylvania (S.S.J.) Founded in 1847. Pontifical, active, simple vows. 2,327 sisters. Teaching elementary and high school, academies, college, industrial school, schools for deaf mutes and for retarded children; society for Catholic mothers. Ages 17-30, high school education. Postulate six months, novitiate two years, juniorate five years. Motherhouse: Mt. St. Joseph Convent, Chestnut Hill, Philadelphia 18, Pennsylvania.

Sisters of St. Joseph of Pittsburgh, Pennsylvania (S.S.J.) Pontifical, active, simple vows. 594 sisters. Teaching elementary and high school, academies; hospital, school of nursing; domestic work; retreats; catechetics; administration; home missions. To age 30, high school education. Aspirancy four years. Postulate eleven and a half months, novitiate two years, juniorate three years. Motherhouse: St. Joseph Convent, Baden, Pennsylvania.

Sisters of St. Joseph of Rutland, Vermont (S.S.J.) Founded in 1873. Diocesan, active, simple vows. 147 sisters. Teaching elementary and high school, commercial school; catechetics. Ages 17-35, high school education. Motherhouse: Mt. St. Joseph, Rutland, Vermont.

Sisters of St. Joseph of Wheeling, West Virginia (S.S.J.) Founded in 1853. Diocesan, active, simple vows. 256 sisters. Teaching elementary and high school; hospitals, schools of nursing; care of orphans. To age 35, high school education. Postulate one year, novitiate two years, juniorate five years. Motherhouse: Mt. St. Joseph, Pogue Run Rd., Wheeling, West Virginia.

Sisters of St. Joseph of Superior, Wisconsin (C.S.J.) Founded in 1907. Diocesan, active, simple vows. 60 sisters. Teaching elementary school academy; nursing; catechetics. Ages 15-30, three years high school education. Postulate eight months, novitiate two years. Motherhouse: Nazareth-on-the-Lake Convent, 1412 E. Second St., Superior, Wisconsin.

Sisters of St. Joseph of Chambery (C.S.S.J.) Founded in France in 1650; established in U.S. in 1885. Pontifical, active, simple vows. 410 sisters in U.S., over 4,000 in world. Teaching elementary and high school; hospitals, schools of nursing; care of orphans; catechetics; missions in India, Pakistan and Wales. To age 35, high school education. Postulate six months, novitiate two years, juniorate five years. Motherhouse: Rome, Italy.

U.S. provincialate: Convent of Mary Immaculate, 27 Park Rd., West Hartford 7, Connecticut.

Sisters of St. Joseph of Cluny (S.J.C.) Founded in France in 1807 by Blessed Anne-Marie Javouhey. Pontifical, active, simple vows. 53 sisters in U.S., 3,600 world. Teaching; nursing; social work; domestic work; catechetics; home and foreign missions. To age 30. Postulate six months, novitiate two years. Blue and black habit. Motherhouse: Paris, France. U.S. provincialate: Mary Immaculate Queen Novitiate, Brenton Rd., Newport, Rhode Island.

Sisters of St. Joseph of Le Puy, France (S.S.J.) Founded in 1650 in Le Puy, France; established in U.S. in 1902. Diocesan, active, simple vows. 111 sisters in U.S., 700 world. Teaching elementary and high school, normal school; catechetics; home missions. Ages 18-35. Postulate eleven months, novitiate two years, juniorate five years. Motherhouse: Le Puy, France. U.S. provincialate: St. Teresa's Convent, 2501 S. Main St., Fall River, Massachusetts.

Sisters of St. Joseph of Lyons, France (S.S.J.) Founded in France in 1650; established in U.S. in 1906. Pontifical, active, simple vows. 117 sisters in U.S., 1,637 world. Teaching elementary and high school; catechetics; nursing; social work; missions in Mexico, India, Egypt and Lebanon. Ages 18-30, high school education. Postulate six months, novitiate two years. Mother-house: Lyons, France. U.S. provincialate: 277 Minot Ave., Auburn, Maine.

Sisters of St. Joseph of St. Mark (S.S.J.S.M.) Founded in Alsace-Lorraine in 1845; established in U.S. in 1937. Diocesan, active, simple vows. 71 sisters in U.S., 700 world. Nursing; care of aged; domestic work in seminaries, etc. Ages 17-30, some exceptions. Postulate six months, novitiate two years, juniorate six years. Black habit. Motherhouse: France. U.S. provincialate: 21750 Chardon Rd., Euclid 17, Ohio.

Sisters of St. Joseph of Napa, California, see Sisters of St. Joseph of the Sacred Heart.

Sisters of St. Joseph of Newark (C.S.J.) (Sisters of St. Joseph of Peace) Founded in England in 1888; established in U.S. in 1888. Pontifical, active, simple vows. 741 sisters in U.S., 865 world. Teaching elementary and high school; hospitals, schools of nursing; care of and teaching blind children; teaching retarded children; homes for working girls; children's village;

catechetics; retreats; domestic work; social work; office work; publication—*The Orphans' Messenger and Advocate of the Blind;* missions in Alaska, Philippines, Ireland, England, Scotland; schools and a hospital in Nelson, Rossland, and Trail, N.B., Canada. Ages 15-30, high school education preferred. Aspirancy one year, postulate ten months, novitiate two years, juniorate five years. Entrance date: September 12. Black habit. Motherhouse: Mount St. Joseph, Glendola Rd., Spring Lake, New Jersey. Mount St. Mary's Provincialate, 1655 Killarney Way, Bellevue, Washington. St. Michael's Provincialate, Englewood, New Jersey.

Sisters of St. Joseph of Peace, see Sisters of St. Joseph of Newark.

Sisters of St. Joseph of the Sacred Heart (C.S.J.) (Sisters of St. Joseph of Napa, California) Founded in Australia in 1866; established in U.S. in 1950. Diocesan, active, simple vows. 5 sisters in U.S. Nursing and allied work. Motherhouse: Sydney, Australia. U.S. address: 2100 Jefferson St., Napa, California.

St. Joseph, see Carmelite Sisters of St. Joseph; see Franciscan Third Order.

Josephite Sisters (Hermanas Josefinas) Founded in Mexico in 1872 by Cesarea Esparza y Davalos and Father Joseph Velaseca; established in U.S. *circa* 1950. Over 1,000 sisters. Teaching; nursing; domestic work in seminaries; missions in Nicaragua. Ages 15-30. Temporary vow period five years. Black habit. Motherhouse: Mexico City, Mexico. U.S. address: % St. John's Seminary, 222 East Mitchell St., San Antonio 10, Texas.

Josephite Sisters, see also Religious Daughters of St. Joseph.

K

Kunegunda, see Franciscan Sisters of Blessed Kunegunda.

L

Sisters of the Lamb of God (A.D.) Founded in France in 1945; established in U.S. in 1958. Diocesan, active, simple vows. 5 sisters in U.S., 160 world. Social work; taking over care of household when the mother is ill; teaching kindergarten planned. Accept physically handicapped and those in good health, regardless of race. No age limit, no educational requirements, all talents used. Postulate ten months, novitiate two years. White habit, blue veil and cape for outdoors. Motherhouse: Brest, France. U.S. provincialate: Our Lady of Hope Convent, 1516 Parrish Ave., Owensboro, Kentucky. U.S. novitiate planned soon.

St. Lioba, see Benedictine Sisters of St. Lioba.

Ladies of Loretto, see Institute of the Blessed Virgin Mary.

Sisters of Loretto—Navan, see Institute of the Blessed Virgin Mary.

Sisters of Loretto at the Foot of the Cross (S.L.) Founded in Kentucky in 1812 by Rev. Charles Nerinckx, a Belgian missionary; oldest U.S. community originating without foreign affiliation. Pontifical, active, simple vows. 1,113 sisters. Teaching elementary and high school, colleges; office and domestic work; librarians; nursing; missions in Bolivia. Ages 18-30, high school education. Postulate eight and a half months, novitiate two years, juniorate two years. Black habit. Motherhouse: Loretto Motherhouse, Nerinx P.O., Kentucky. Provincialates: 470 E. Lockwood Ave., Webster Groves 19, Missouri; 3001 So. Federal Blvd., Loretto P.O., Denver, Colorado; 1101 W. Thirty-ninth St., Kansas City 11, Missouri.

Sisters of St. Louis of Monaghan, Ireland (S.S.L.) Founded in France in 1842; established in U.S. in 1949. Pontifical, active, simple vows. 110 sisters in U.S., 800 world. Teaching elementary and high school; nurses and doctors are now being trained for missions in Africa. Ages 15-30, education—two years of high school. Motherhouse: Monaghan, Ireland. U.S. regionalate: Louisville Convent, 22300 Mulholland Dr., Woodland Hills, California.

St. Louis, see Charity of St. Louis, Sisters of.

Sisters of the Love of God (R.A.D.) (Hermanas del Amor de Dios) Founded in Spain in 1864; established in U.S. in 1958. Pontifical, active, simple vows. 37 sisters in U.S., 2,000 world. Teaching; nursing; social work among the Spanish-speaking; domestic work; catechetics; home missions. Also located in Puerto Rice and Mexico. Ages 15-28. Postulate six months, novitiate two years, juniorate two years. Motherhouse: Zamora,

Spain. U.S. novitiate: St. Anthony Convent, Main St., Matta-poisett, Massachusetts. Canadian address: % Brothers of the Christian Instruction Provincial House, St. Anthony (Parent), N.B., Canada (4 sisters, domestic work).

Sisters of the Love of Jesus (Soeurs de l'Amour de Jésus) Founded in Canada in 1937. Nursing. St. Mary's Priory, 567 Goldstream Ave., Victoria, B.C., Canada.

M

Mantellate, see Mary, Mantellate Sisters, Servants of; Servants of Mary.

Marian Sisters (M.S.) Founded in Nebraska in 1954 by two sisters from Czechoslovakia. Diocesan, active, simple vows. 25 sisters. Teaching elementary school; care of orphans; catechetics; social work; office and domestic work. Divine Office in English. Ages 16-30, high school education. Postulate six months, novitiate one year, juniorate five years. Temporary vow period five years. Home visits allowed every two years after profession. Grey habit, black veil. Motherhouse: Box Z, Waverly, Nebraska.

Marian Society of Catechists (M.S.C.) Third Order of St. Dominic. Founded in Louisiana in 1954 by Most Rev. Charles P. Greco. Diocesan, active, simple vows. 4 sisters. Catechetics, home missions. Ages 15-35, high school education preferred. Aspirancy one to three years, postulate six to twelve months, novitiate two years, juniorate five years. Motherhouse: St. Margaret's Convent, P.O. Box 176, Boyce, Louisiana.

Marianist Sisters, see Congregation of the Daughters of Mary Immaculate.

Sisters Marianites of Holy Cross (M.S.C.) Founded in Le Mans, France, in 1841; established in U.S. in 1843. Pontifical, active, simple vows. 364 sisters in U.S., 650 world. Black habit. Motherhouse: Le Mans, Sarthe, France. U.S. provincialates: *Marianite Provincialate,* 4123 Woodland Dr., New Orleans 14, Louisiana. 276 sisters. Teaching elementary and high school; nursing; domestic work; catechetics. Ages 16-35, high school education or equivalent. Postulate eleven months, novitiate two years, juniorate two years.

Our Lady of Princeton Convent, Great Rd., Princeton, New Jersey. 88 sisters. Teaching elementary school, academy; nursing; missions in Canada (9 sisters), Pakistan and Haiti. Ages 15-35, high school education. Postulate six months, novitiate two years, juniorate three years.

Marist Missionary Sisters (S.M.S.M.) (Missionary Sisters of the Society of Mary) Founded in France in 1845-1857 by Ven. Jean Claude Colin, S.M., to aid Marist Fathers working among primitive people in Oceania; established in U.S. in 1922. First community of women formed solely for foreign missionary work. Pontifical, active, simple vows. 246 in U.S., 750 world. Missions in Hawaii; Samoa; Fiji; Tonga; Wallis-Futuna; New Caledonia; New Hebrides; North and South Solomons; Chatham Island, New Zealand; Jamaica; Algeria and Dakar; Lima, Peru. Schools, maternity centers, dispensaries, hospitals, leprosy and tuberculosis sanatoriums, catechetics, social work, domestic work, caring for sacristies, training native sisters, publication—*Marist Missions*. Ages 17½-30, high school education. Postulate six months, novitiate two years, juniorate twelve years. Motherhouse: Rome (Castelgondolfo), Italy. U.S. regionalate: 62 Newton St., Waltham 54, Massachusetts.

St. Mark, see St. Joseph of St. Mark, Sisters of.

Sisters of St. Martha (C.S.M.) Founded in Canada in 1916 by Bishop Henry O'Leary. Pontifical, active, simple vows. 148 sisters in Canada, 10 in U.S. Hospitals, schools of nursing; teaching elementary and high school; welfare centers; care of aged, orphans, and unwed mothers; residence for students; domestic work. Black habit. Motherhouse: Mount St. Mary's, 141 Mt. Edward Rd. Charlottetown, Prince Edward Island, Canada. U.S. address: St. Martha's Residence, 294 Mt. Prospect Ave., Newark, New Jersey.

Sisters of St. Martha (C.S.M.) Founded in France in 1643; established in Canada in 1900. 460 sisters. Nursing; teaching; parish social work; welfare bureaus; care of orphans; domestic work in seminaries, universities, etc.; retreats; guest house. Motherhouse: Bethany, Antigonish, N.S., Canada.

Sisters of St. Martha of St. Hyacinthe (S.S.M.S.H.) Founded in Canada in 1883 by Canon Jean-Remi Ouellette and Eleanore

Charron; established in U.S. in 1929. Diocesan. 180 sisters in
Canada, 37 in U.S. Domestic work in schools, seminaries, rectories, etc. In work and prayer the sisters emulate both Martha
and Mary. Ages 15-30, knowledge of French helpful. Postulate
six months, novitiate two years. Temporary vow period three
years. Black habit. Motherhouse: St. Joseph de Hyacinthe, St.
Hyacinthe, P.Q., Canada. U.S. postulate: La Salette Seminary,
Enfield, New Hampshire.

Martyr St. George, see Sisters of St. Francis of the Martyr St.
George.

Ladies of Mary, see Daughters of Mary and Joseph.

Missionary Sisters of Mary (M.M.) (Xaverian Missionary Sisters
of Mary) Founded in Italy in 1945; established in U.S. in
1954. Diocesan, active, simple vows. 10 sisters in U.S., 180
world. Teaching; nursing; domestic work; mission in Japan at
present. Community plans missionary work in Africa and Brazil also. Ages 15-30, high school education. Aspirancy one year,
postulate one year, novitiate two years. Motherhouse: Parma,
Italy. U.S. address: St. Joseph's Convent, N. Main St., Petersham, Massachusetts.

Missionary Sisters of the Society of Mary, see Marist Missionary
Sisters.

Servants of Mary (Servite Sisters) *The Third Order of Servites
was originally founded in Italy* circa 1305 *by St. Juliana Fal-
conieri, niece of one of the founders of the Servite Order for
men.*

Servants of Mary (O.S.M.) (Servite Mantellate Sisters) (Third
Order of Servites) Founded in France in 1840 by Sister Marie
Barbe Guynot; established in England in 1864; established in
U.S. in 1893 from England; established in Canada in 1953
from French province. Pontifical, active, simple vows. 238 sisters in U.S., 26 Canada, 566 world. Teaching elementary and
high school; domestic work. To age 35, high school education.
Postulate one year, novitiate one year. Temporary vow period
five years. Black habit. Motherhouse: London, England. U.S.
provincialate: Our Lady of Sorrows Convent, Seventy-fourth
and Military Aves., Omaha 4, Nebraska. Canadian novitiate:
360 Galt Est., Sherbrooke, P.Q., Canada. No set age or education requirements. Aspirancy varies, postulate six to twelve
months, novitiate twelve to eighteen months.

Servants of Mary (O.S.M.) (Servite Sisters) (Third Order of Servites) Founded in Austria in 1894; established in U.S. in 1952. Pontifical, active. 6 sisters in U.S. Nursing convalescents. To age 36. Postulate six months, novitiate one year. Black habit. Motherhouse: Vienna, Austria. U.S. address: Marian Home, Sublimity, Oregon.

Servants of Mary (O.S.M.) (Servite Sisters) (Third Order of Servites) Founded in U.S. in 1912. Diocesan, active, simple vows. 175 sisters. Teaching elementary and high school, colleges; hospitals, convalescent home; care of aged; catechetics; domestic work; home missions. High school education preferred. Aspirancy four years. Postulate six to twelve months, novitiate one year, juniorate six years. Black habit. Motherhouse: Our Lady of Sorrows Convent, Ladysmith, Wisconsin.

Mantellate Sisters, Servants of Mary (O.S.M.) (Servite Mantellates) (Third Order of Servites) Founded in Italy in 1861; established in U.S. in 1916. Pontifical, active, simple vows. 82 sisters in U.S., 1,600 world. Teaching elementary and high school, academy; social work; home for girls; day nurseries; domestic work; catechetics; retreats; home missions; foreign missions in Spain and South Africa. Ages 15-30, some exceptions, high school education. Aspirancy four years. Postulate six months, novitiate two years. Black habit. Motherhouse: Rome, Italy. U.S. provincialate: Our Mother of Sorrows Convent, 13811 S. Western Ave., Blue Island, Illinois.

Sisters, Home Visitors of Mary (H.V.M.) Founded in Detroit in 1949 by Edward Cardinal Mooney and Rt. Rev. John C. Ryan. Diocesan, active, simple vows. 16 sisters. Catechetics; home visiting; returning lapsed Catholics to the faith; recruiting converts, particularly Negroes; teaching homemaking and home nursing; recreation programs. Ages 16-30, high school education. Postulate nine months, novitiate two years, juniorate four years. Navy blue dress, hat and coat. Motherhouse: Holy Family Convent, 356 Arden Park, Detroit 2, Michigan.

Sisters Servants of Mary (S.M.) Founded in Spain in 1851 by Blessed Mother Soledad Torres Acosta; established in U.S. in 1914. Pontifical, active, simple vows. 104 sisters in U.S., 2,584 world. Home nursing; residence for working girls; Spanish settlement; catechetics; lay sisters do domestic work. Ages 16-30, high school education preferred. Postulate six months, noviti-

ate two years. Black habit. Motherhouse: Rome, Italy. U.S.
provincialate: 800 N. Eighteenth St., Kansas City 2, Kansas.
Novitiate: 3779 W. Gonzales Rd., Oxnard, California.

Mary, see Antonian Sisters of Mary, Queen of the Clergy, Congregation of; Dominican Third Order; Franciscan Third Order;
Medical Missionaries of Mary; Perpetual Adoration of the
Blessed Sacrament of St. Mary of Guadalupe, Sisters of; Reparation of the Congregation of Mary, Sisters of.

Daughters of Mary of the Assumption (F.M.A.) (Filles de Mariede-l'Assomption) Founded in Canada in 1922 by Archbishop
Louis Melanson. Pontifical, active, simple vows. 272 sisters.
Teaching; domestic work in bishops' residences; missions in
Philippines. At least 16, tenth grade education, age 18 and
high school education preferred. Postulate six months, novitiate two years. Temporary vow period five years. Black and
white habit redesigned in 1962. Motherhouse: Mount Maria,
Arran St., Campbellton, N.B., Canada.

Daughters of Mary, Health of the Sick (F.M.S.I.) Founded in
New York in 1935 by Rev. Edward F. Garesche, S.J. Diocesan,
active, simple vows. 28 sisters. Nursing; catechetics; social
work; home missions; catechetics, home nursing and dispensary
and training native nurses and catechists in Okinawa. This is a
missionary community with future plans to extend its mission
fields. All mission activities are engaged in *except* teaching elementary and high school. Publication—*Daughters of Mary,
Health of the Sick*. Ages 17-30, high school education. Postulate six months, novitiate two years, juniorate three years. No
lay sisters. Blue habit, white for missions. Motherhouse: Vista
Maria, Cragsmoor P.O., Ulster Co., New York.

Daughters of Mary Help of Christians, see Salesian Sisters of St.
John Bosco.

Congregation of the Daughters of Mary Immaculate (F.M.I.)
(Marianist Sisters) Founded in France in 1816 by the founder
of the Marianist Fathers; established in U.S. in 1949 from
Spain. Pontifical, active, simple vows. 22 sisters in U.S., 525
world. Teaching; catechetics; retreats; residence for college
students. At least 16, high school education preferred. Postulate six to twelve months, novitiate two years, juniorate at least
three years. Black habit. Motherhouse: Paris, France. U.S. pro-

vincialate: Our Lady of the Pillar Convent, 251 W. Ligustrum Dr., San Antonio 28, Texas.

Daughters of Mary Immaculate (F.M.I.) Founded in Spain in 1876 to help and protect working girls; established in U.S. in 1954. Pontifical, active, simple vows. 21 sisters in U.S., 2,700 world. Social work; retreats; catechetics; homes for working girls and students; home missions; foreign missions in India. Also located in Mexico. Eighth grade education for lay sisters, high school for choir sisters. Postulate six months, novitiate two years, juniorate one year. Motherhouse: Rome, Italy. U.S. provincialate: Villa Maria, 719 Augusta St., San Antonio 4, Texas.

Handmaids of Mary Immaculate (A.M.I.) (Blue Sisters) Founded in Montana in 1952 by Mother Mary Stanislaus. Diocesan, active and contemplative, simple vows. 8 sisters. Catechetics, teaching; home visiting among Blackfeet Indians. Ages 18-35, college education preferred. Postulate six months, novitiate two years, juniorate five years. Blue, brown, and white habit. Motherhouse: % Carroll College, Helena, Montana.

Minim Daughters of Mary Immaculate (C.F.M.M.) Founded in Mexico in 1886 by Archdeacon Pablo de Anda; established in U.S. in 1926. Pontifical, active, simple vows. 450 sisters, 43 in U.S. Teaching elementary school and academy; nursing; care of infants and aged; domestic work; missions. Ages 15-30, eighth grade education. Black habit. Motherhouse: 20 de Enero 909, Leon, Guanajuato, Mexico. U.S. novitiate: St. Joseph's Novitiate, Box 636, Nogales, Arizona.

Parish Visitors of Mary Immaculate (P.V.M.I.) Founded in New York City in 1920 by Mother Mary Teresa Tallon. Diocesan, active and contemplative, simple vows. 138 sisters. Assist parish priests by missionary and charitable work to families: parish census and home visiting; visiting jails, courts and hospitals; helping family members to return to the Church and to take part in parish activities and organizations; contacting social welfare organizations on behalf of the needy; teaching religion; guiding delinquents and pre-delinquents; promoting family devotions and the Liturgy; strengthening weak and broken families; helping immigrants; apostolate to the Spanish-speaking; publication—*The Parish Visitor*; contemplation, vocal prayer. Ages 16-30, high school education. Postulate six months, novitiate two years, juniorate four years. Black habit. Motherhouse: Marycrest Convent, Box 535, Monroe, New York. Central Mission House: St. Joseph's Convent of the Sacred Heart, 328 W. Seventy-first St., New York, New York.

Sisters Servants of Mary Immaculate (S.S.M.I.) Byzantine Greek Rite. Founded in Western Ukraine in 1892; established in Edmonton, Canada, in 1902; established at Stamford, Connecticut in 1935. Pontifical, active, simple vows. 85 sisters in U.S., 1,500 world. Teaching elementary and high school, academies, evening schools, school of music; nursing; social work; day nurseries; care of aged and orphans; catechetics in rural areas; retreats; domestic work. Ages 15-35. Postulate six months, novitiate two years, juniorate three years. Navy blue habit, black veil. Motherhouse: Rome, Italy. Canadian provincialates: Christ the King Convent, 5 Austin Terrace, Toronto, Ont., Canada. Mount Mary Immaculate Novitiate, Ancaster, Ont., Canada. U.S. provincialate: Home of Divine Providence, 209 W. Chestnut Hill Ave., Philadelphia 18, Pennsylvania.

Sister Servants of Mary Immaculate (S.S.M.I.C.) Third Order of St. Francis. Founded in Poland in 1876; established in U.S. in 1952. Pontifical, active, simple vows. 19 sisters in U.S., 2,500 world. Teaching; nursing home; day nursery; domestic work; social work. To age 30, eighth grade. Postulate six months, novitiate two years. Motherhouse: Poland. U.S. provincialate: Immaculate Conception Convent, 1220 Tugwell Rd., Catonsville 28, Maryland.

Teaching Sisters of Mary Immaculate (R.M.I.) (Claretian Missionary Sisters) Founded at Santiago de Cuba in 1855 by St. Anthony Claret and Mother M. Antonia Paris; established in U.S. in 1957. (See also Institute of Daughters of the Immaculate Heart of Mary under secular institutes, also founded by St. Anthony Claret.) Pontifical, active, simple vows. 10 sisters in U.S., 1,000 world. Teaching; domestic work. Ages 16-30, eighth grade. Aspirancy four years. Postulate six months, novitiate two years, juniorate three years. Motherhouse: Barcelona, Spain. U.S. headquarters: 714 Monroe St., N.E., Washington 17, D.C.

Mary Immaculate, see also Franciscan Third Order; Holy Ghost and Mary Immaculate, Sister Servants of the; Most Blessed Sacrament and Mary Immaculate, Missionary Sisters of the;

Sacred Heart and Mary Immaculate, Oblate Missionaries of the; Salesian Missionaries of Mary Immaculate.

Daughters of Mary of the Immaculate Conception (C.F.M.) Founded in Connecticut in 1904 by Msgr. Lucian Bojnowski to care for orphans. The first members were sodalists from his parish. Pontifical, active, simple vows. 174 sisters. Teaching elementary school and academy, remedial reading clinic; care of orphans and aged; domestic work; homes for working girls and immigrants; hospital, nursing home; children's camp; catechetics. Blue habit, black veil. Ages 15-30, high school education preferred. Postulate six months, novitiate two years, juniorate three years. Motherhouse: Immaculate Conception Convent, Osgood Ave., New Britain, Connecticut.

Daughters of Mary and Joseph (D.M.J.) (Dames de Marie) (Ladies of Mary) Founded in Belgium in 1817; established in U.S. in 1926. Pontifical, active, simple vows. 116 sisters in U.S., 600 world. Teaching elementary and high school, teaching retarded children; retreats; domestic work. Ages 16-30, high school education. Postulate one year, novitiate two years, juniorate two years. Black and blue habit. Motherhouse: Brussels, Belgium. U.S. provincialate: 12935 San Vicente Blvd., Los Angeles 49, California.

Daughters of St. Mary of Leuca. Founded in Italy in 1938; established in U.S. in 1948. Pontifical, active, simple vows. 13 sisters in U.S., 370 world. Domestic work at present in U.S. Congregation's primary work is the care of orphans and foundlings. Also located in Canada. Age 16. Postulate six months, novitiate two years. Motherhouse: Leuca, Italy. U.S. address: 564 Dodge St., Buffalo 8, New York.

Sisters of St. Mary of Namur (S.S.M.N.) Founded in Namur, Belgium, in 1819; established in U.S. in 1863; established in Canada in 1886. Pontifical, active, simple vows. 429 sisters in U.S., 1,000 world. Black habit. Motherhouse: Namur, Belgium. Provincialates:

Mount St. Mary Provincialate, 3756 Delaware Ave., Kenmore 17, New York. 235 sisters. Teaching elementary and high school; catechetics; Negro mission; missions in Africa. Ages 18-30, high school education preferred. Postulate one year, novitiate two years, juniorate four years.

Our Lady of Victory Provincialate, 3300 S. Hempill St., Fort

Worth 10, Texas. 194 sisters. Teaching elementary and high school; domestic work; missions in Africa. Ages 15-30, high school education. Postulate nine to eleven months, novitiate two years, juniorate four years.

Convent of Our Lady of Good Counsel, 207 Bayswater Ave., Ottawa, Ont., Canada. Teaching elementary school, academies. Novitiate: St. Anne's Convent, St. Eugene, Ont., Canada.

Little Company of Mary, Nursing Sisters (L.C.M.) Founded in England in 1877 to nurse the sick and pray for the dying and the dead; established in U.S. in 1893. Pontifical, active, simple vows. 118 sisters in U.S., 1,000 world. Nursing and allied work; missions in Argentina. Little Office of the Blessed Virgin in choir. No lay sisters. Ages 18-30, high school education. Postulate six months, novitiate two years, juniorate at least three years. Black habit, blue veil; white for nursing. Motherhouse: Rome, Italy. U.S. provincialate: Convent of the Maternal Heart, 9350 So. California Ave., Evergreen Park 42, Illinois.

Sisters of St. Mary of Oregon (S.S.M.O.) Founded in Sublimity, Oregon, in 1886 by Archbishop William H. Gross. Pontifical, active, simple vows. 233 sisters. Teaching elementary and high school, academy; catechetics; sacristans; domestic and office work; nursing. Age 15, high school education except domestic workers. Aspirancy four years. Postulate ten months, novitiate two years, juniorate three to six years. Each applicant is trained in the field of her interest. Black habit. Motherhouse: St. Mary of the Valley Convent, 4440 S. W. One hundred forty-eighth Ave., Beaverton, Oregon.

Company of Mary, Our Lady (O.D.N.) (Order of Notre Dame) Founded in France in 1607 by St. Joan de Lestonnac; established in U.S. in 1926. Pontifical, active and contemplative, solemn vows. 104 sisters in U.S., 5,000 world. Teaching elementary school and kindergartens; catechetics; home missions; missions in Japan and Africa. Ages 16-35, high school education preferred. Postulate six months, novitiate two years, juniorate five years. Black habit. Motherhouse: Rome, Italy. U.S. provincialate: Company of Mary Novitiate, 16791 E. Main St., Santa Ana, California.

Sisters of St. Mary of the Presentation (F.S.M.) Founded in France in 1828; established in U.S. 1903 because of religious persecution in France. Pontifical, active, simple vows. 165 sisters in U.S. Teaching elementary and high school, academies; hospitals, school of nursing; domestic work; care of aged; social work; missions in Africa. Ages 16-30, eighth grade education. Aspirancy one to two years. Postulate six to nine months, novitiate two years, juniorate three years. Temporary vows for two three-year periods. Motherhouse: France. U.S. regionalate: St. Catherine Convent, Valley City, North Dakota. St. Margaret's Novitiate, Spring Valley, Illinois. Canadian novitiate: Grande-Baie, P.Q., Canada.

Daughters of St. Mary of Providence (D.S.M.P.) Founded in Italy in 1872 to work among the poor, abandoned, and mentally handicapped; established in U.S. in 1913. Pontifical, active, simple vows. 90 sisters in U.S., 1,500 world. Teaching, including schools for retarded; nursing; care of aged and infirm; social centers. To age 30. Postulate six months, novitiate two years. Temporary vow period five years. Black habit and cape. Motherhouse: Como, Italy. U.S. provincialate: St. Mary of Providence Institute, 4200 N. Austin Ave., Chicago 34, Illinois.

Society of Mary Reparatrix (S.M.R.) Founded in France in 1857; established in U.S. in 1908. Pontifical, contemplative, semi-cloistered, simple vows. 105 sisters in U.S., 2,200 world. Contemplation; choir nuns recite Divine Office; daily adoration; encouraging lay adorers; retreats for laywomen; catechetics; missions in Africa and Palestine. Community's purpose is to make reparation to Our Lord through Mary. Also located in Mexico. Novitiate two and a half years. White and blue habit, blue veil for choir nuns, white for lay sisters. Motherhouse: Rome, Italy. U.S. provincialate: Convent of Mary Reparatrix, 14 E. Twenty-ninth St., New York 16, New York. Novitiate: 17330 Quincy Ave., Detroit 21, Michigan. Canadian novitiate: St. Laurent, P.Q., Canada.

Maryknoll Sisters (O.P.) (Foreign Mission Sisters of St. Dominic) Third Order of St. Dominic. Founded at Maryknoll, New York, in 1912 by Mother Mary Joseph Rogers for foreign mission work. Pontifical, active (contemplative branch). 1,316 sisters. Teachers, catechists, doctors, nurses, social workers, office workers, domestic workers, writers, editors, artists, photographers; home missions, including Hawaii; foreign missions in Marshall Islands, Caroline Islands, Philippines, Tanganyika,

Ceylon, Hong Kong, Japan, Korea, Taiwan, Canal Zone, Guatemala, Panama, Chile, Bolivia, Peru, Nicaragua and Mexico. 20 sisters in contemplative branch which was begun in 1932. One year after high school graduation to age 30. Postulate nine months, novitiate two years, juniorate varies. Grey habit, black veil; white habit in tropics. Motherhouse and novitiate: Maryknoll, New York. Other novitiates: Ladycrest, Topsfield, Massachusetts; R. R. 1, Box 82, Valley Park, Missouri.

Medical Mission Sisters (S.C.M.M.) (Society of Catholic Medical Missionaries) Founded in Washington, D.C., in 1925, with the help of Father Michael A. Mathis, C.S.C., by Dr. Anna Dengel, who was carrying on the work begun by Dr. Agnes McLaren who had seen the need for sister-doctors and nurses in missionary lands. Diocesan, active, simple vows. 349 sisters in U.S., over 700 in world. Doctors, nurses, pharmacists, technicians, etc., for hospitals, dispensaries, maternity and child welfare centers, leprosariums, and for training medical workers, in India, Pakistan, Africa, South Vietnam, Philippines, Venezuela and home missions. Also journalists, promotional workers, office workers, bookkeepers, and domestic workers. Publication—*The Medical Missionary*. Ages 17-30, some exceptions, high school or college education; professional training desirable but not necessary. Postulate ten months, novitiate two years, juniorate one to five years. Grey habit, blue veil. Generalate: Rome, Italy. U.S. motherhouse: 8400 Pine Rd., Philadelphia 11, Pennsylvania.

Medical Missionaries of Mary (M.M.M.) Founded in Ireland and Africa in 1937 in response to the appeal of Pope Pius XI for missionaries trained as doctors and nurses; established in U.S. in 1950. Pontifical, active, simple vows. 265 sisters in U.S., 436 world. Nurses, doctors, all types of medical workers, and social workers for nursing lepers and mothers and children, marriage training centers, teaching domestic science, and office work in Africa, Formosa, Nyasaland and Italy. Ages 17-35. Postulate six months, novitiate two years, juniorate—time needed to finish training. Temporary vows renewed annually for five years. Motherhouse: County Louth, Ireland. U.S. provincialate: 1 Arlington St., Winchester, Massachusetts.

Mercedarian Missionaries of Berriz (M.M.B.) (Formerly titled Missionaries of Our Lady of Mercy) Founded in Spain in 1218 by St. Peter Nolasco; originally cloistered, converted to a missionary institute in 1926; established in U.S. in 1946. Pontifical, active and contemplative, simple vows. 72 sisters in U.S. Missions in South Pacific Islands—teaching, catechetics, dispensaries, home visiting; care of aged and home for girls in U.S. Also located in Mexico. Contemplation, Divine Office. To age 26, high school education for choir sisters, less for lay sisters. Postulate six months, novitiate two years, juniorate five years. White habit, black veil for choir sisters, white veil for lay sisters. Motherhouse: Berriz, Spain. U.S. vice provincialate: 918 E. Ninth St., Kansas City 6, Missouri.

Mercedarian Missionary Sisters (Religiosas Mercedarias Misioneras) Founded originally in Spain in 1265 by St. Maria de Carvello; restored in 1860. 3 sisters in U.S. Domestic work in a seminary. Motherhouse: Barcelona, Spain. U.S. address: Divine Word Seminary, Bordentown, New Jersey.

Mercedarians, see Missionary Sisters of Our Lady of Mercy.

Religious Mercedaries of the Blessed Sacrament 5 sisters in U.S. Teaching elementary school. Motherhouse: Mexico City. U.S. address: St. Joseph's School, Barstow, California.

Daughters of Mercy, see Daughters of Our Lady of Mercy.

Sisters of Mercy (R.S.M.) Founded in Ireland in 1831 by Mother Mary Catherine McAuley; first established in U.S. in 1843 in Pittsburgh. Active, simple vows. Approximately 30,000 sisters in world. Black habit. The following are independent motherhouses:

Convent of Our Lady of Mercy, Rte. 3, Box 3216, Auburn, California. Pontifical. 122 sisters. Teaching elementary and high school; nursing. High school education. Aspirancy. Novitiate two and a half years, juniorate five years.

College of Our Lady of Mercy, 2300 Adeline Dr., Burlingame, California. Pontifical. 437 sisters. Teaching elementary and high school, college for sisters; hospitals, nursing homes, schools of nursing; catechetics; administration; care of aged; family guidance in emotional and mental illnesses. To age 30, high school education. Postulate one year, novitiate two years, juniorate five years.

St. Joseph Convent, 160 Farmington Ave., Hartford 5, Connecticut. Pontifical. 737 sisters. Teaching elementary and high school, academies, college; care of foundlings, orphans and aged; catechetics; retreats; domestic work. High school education. Postulate six to twelve months, novitiate two years, juniorate three years; six-week tertianship ten years after profession.

Sacred Heart Convent, 1330 Elmhurst Dr., Cedar Rapids, Iowa. Pontifical. 258 sisters. Teaching elementary and high school, college; hospitals, school of nursing; domestic work; care of aged; office work. Ages 15-35, high school education. Postulate ten months, novitiate two years, juniorate three years.

St. Joseph's Convent, 605 Stevens Ave., Portland 5, Maine. Pontifical. 356 sisters. Teaching elementary and high school, junior college for sisters, college; teaching blind children; hospitals, school of nursing; domestic work; care of orphans and aged; catechetics; home missions. High school education for prospective teachers. Postulate nine months, novitiate two years, juniorate five years.

St. Gabriel's Convent, 46 High St., Worcester 8, Massachusetts. Pontifical. 142 sisters. Teaching elementary school, school for exceptional children; catechetics; care of emotionally disturbed boys; home for working girls; home missions. Ages 18-30, high school education. Postulate ten months, novitiate two years, juniorate five years.

Our Lady of Mercy Motherhouse, 435 Union St., Windham, New Hampshire. Pontifical. 440 sisters. Teaching elementary and high school, college; hospital, school of nursing; care of aged and orphans; home for working girls; publication—*Magnificat.* High school education. Postulate nine months, novitiate two years, juniorate three years.

Mount St. Mary Motherhouse, U.S. Hwy. 22 and Terrill Rd., North Plainfield, New Jersey. Pontifical. 581 sisters. Teaching elementary and high school, academies, college; nursing; catechetics. Postulate eleven months, novitiate two years, juniorate three years.

Convent of Mercy, 634 New Scotland Ave., Albany, New York. Pontifical. 377 sisters. Teaching elementary and high school, college for sisters; hospital, school of nursing; catechetics. To age 30, high school education. Postulate ten months, novitiate two years, juniorate five years.

St. Francis Convent, 273 Willoughby Ave., Brooklyn 5, New

York. Diocesan. 480 sisters. Teaching elementary and high school, academy, teaching blind children; nursing; care of orphans; social work; catechetics including instruction of retarded; domestic work; missions in Canal Zone. High school education. Aspirancy four years. Postulate six months, novitiate two years, juniorate three years.

Mount Mercy Motherhouse, 625 Abbott Rd., Buffalo 20, New York. Pontifical. 408 sisters. Teaching elementary and high school, academy, junior college for sisters; general hospitals, hospitals for chronically ill, schools of nursing; home for working girls; domestic work; catechetics; retreats; teaching, nursing, and catechetics in missions in Mindanao, Philippines. Ages 17-35. Postulate ten months, novitiate two years, juniorate three years.

Our Lady of Mercy Motherhouse, 1437 Blossom Rd., Brighton Station, Rochester 10, New York. Pontifical. 403 sisters. Teaching elementary and high school, junior college, college for sisters, reading laboratory; hospital, school of nursing; domestic work; catechetics. To age 30, high school education. Postulate ten to twelve months, novitiate two years, juniorate five years.

Sacred Heart Convent, Belmont, North Carolina. 207 sisters. Teaching elementary and high school, academy, junior college, junior military academy; hospitals, nursing home for brain-damaged children, schools of nursing; care of retarded children and orphans; catechetics; home missions; missions and novitiate in Guam. High school education or equivalent. Postulate six to twelve months, novitiate two years, juniorate three years.

Mercyhurst, P.O. Box 1249, 501 E. Thirty-eighth St., Erie, Pennsylvania. Pontifical. 214 sisters. Teaching elementary and high school, academies, college; nursing; home for working women; catechetics; domestic work. High school education. Postulate ten months, novitiate two years, juniorate five years.

Mater Misericordiae, 515 Montgomery Ave., Merion, Montgomery Co., Pennsylvania. Pontifical. 547 sisters. Teaching elementary and high school, academies, vocational school, junior college, schools for retarded children; hospitals, schools of nursing; home for working girls; social work; missions in India. High school education. Postulate six months, novitiate two years, juniorate five years.

St. Mary Convent, 3333 Fifth Ave., Pittsburgh 13, Pennsylvania. Pontifical. 493 sisters. Teaching elementary and high school, academies, college; hospitals, school of nursing; care of orphans; social work; domestic work; missions in Puerto Rico. High school education. Postulate six to twelve months, novitiate two years, juniorate three years.

Mount St. Mary, 100 Mansfield Ave., Burlington, Vermont. 179 sisters. Teaching elementary and high school, academy, college; summer camp for girls; domestic work; catechetics; retreats. High school education. Postulate ten months, novitiate two years, juniorate five years.

Sisters of Mercy of the Holy Cross (S.C.S.C.) (Holy Cross Sisters) Third Order of St. Francis. Founded in Switzerland in 1856; established in U.S. in 1912. Pontifical, active, simple vows. 114 sisters in U.S.; 9,000 world. Teaching; nursing; domestic work; catechetics; home missions; Divine Office chanted in English. Ages 18-25, high school education. Aspirancy two years. Postulate nine months, novitiate one year, juniorate six years. Black habit, white for nurses. Motherhouse: Switzerland. U.S. provincialate: Holy Cross Convent, Merrill, Wisconsin.

Sisters of Mercy of Ireland (R.S.M.) Founded in Ireland in 1831 by Mother Catherine McAuley. The following congregations, all teaching elementary school, have their motherhouses in Ireland.

Sisters of Mercy of Ireland. 14 sisters in U.S. Holy Spirit School, 2725 Fifty-fifth St., San Diego 5, California. Blessed Sacrament School, 74462 Palm Vista Dr., Twentynine Palms, California.

Sisters of Mercy of Ardee, Ireland. 4 sisters. Ascension School, Eau Gallie, Florida.

Sisters of Mercy of Birr, Ireland. 10 sisters. Nativity School, Biloxi, Mississippi.

Sisters of Mercy of Carrick-on-Suir, Ireland. 13 sisters. St. John's Convent of Mercy, 11154 San Pablo Ave., El Cerrito, California.

Sisters of Mercy of Clonakilty, Ireland. 5 sisters. Sacred Heart School, 6416 One hundred third St., Jacksonville, Florida.

Sisters of Mercy of Drogheda, Ireland. 7 sisters. Teaching and catechetics. Ages 17-30, high school education. Postulate seven months, novitiate two years, juniorate three years. Training in

Ireland. Holy Infant Convent, New Ballwin Rd., Ballwin, Missouri.

Sisters of Mercy of Dublin, Ireland. 4 sisters. St. James School, Gadsden, Alabama.

Sisters of Mercy of Dundalk, Ireland. 5 sisters. Holy Family School, 1304 Garland St., Mobile, Alabama.

Sisters of Mercy of Enniskillen, N. Ireland. 10 sisters. Immaculate Conception School, 4501 W. Second Ave., Hialeah, Florida.

Sisters of Mercy of Gort, Ireland. 4 sisters. St. Teresa's School, Ojibway St., Titusville, Florida.

Sisters of Mercy of Kells, Ireland. 7 sisters. St. Clare's School, Essex, Maryland.

Sisters of Mercy of Kinsale, Ireland. 7 sisters. St. Vincent Ferrer's School, 715 N. E. Eighth Ave., Delray Beach, Florida.

Sisters of Mercy of Limerick, Ireland. 17 sisters. St. Pius X School, 217 S. Sage Ave., Mobile, Alabama. St. Mary's School, Rockledge, Florida.

Sisters of Mercy of Loughrea, Ireland. 4 sisters. St. Finnbarr's School, 415 Edna St., San Francisco 12, California.

Sisters of Mercy of Navan, Ireland. 14 sisters. Our Lady of Lourdes School, 1428 N. Halifax Ave., Daytona Beach, Florida. San Jose School, 3619 Toledo Rd., Jacksonville 7, Florida.

Sisters of Mercy of Skibbereen, Ireland. 5 sisters. St. Joan of Arc School, Boca Raton, Florida.

Sisters of Mercy of Trim, Ireland. 9 sisters. Our Lady of Mt. Carmel School, 175 W. White Horse Pike, Berlin, New Jersey.

Sisters of Mercy of Tullamore, Ireland. 8 sisters. 2959 Babb St., Costa Mesa, California.

Sisters of Mercy of Wexford, Ireland. 7 sisters. St. Peter's School, De Land, Florida; Epiphany School, Lake City, Florida.

Sisters of Mercy of St. John's, Newfoundland (R.S.M.) Founded in Ireland in 1831 by Mother Catherine McAuley; established in Newfoundland in 1842. Pontifical, active, simple vows. 346 sisters. Teaching elementary and high school, academies; nursing the sick in their homes and in a hospital; care of aged and orphans; visiting public institutions such as hospitals, penitentiaries, etc.; mission in Peru. Postulate six to ten months, novitiate two years, juniorate three years. Black habit, white in Peru. Motherhouse: Convent of Our Lady of Mercy, St. John's, Newfoundland, Canada.

Sisters of Mercy of the Union in the United States (R.S.M.) Founded in Ireland in 1831 by Mother Catherine McAuley; first established in the U.S. in 1843; this congregation formed by a union of U.S. motherhouses in 1929. Pontifical, active, simple vows. 6,626 sisters. Ages 16-30, high school education. Postulate eleven months, novitiate two years, juniorate three years. Black habit. General motherhouse: Sisters of Mercy Generalate, 10000 Kendale Rd., Bethesda P.O., Washington 14, D.C. Provincialates:

10024 S. Central Park Ave., Chicago 42, Illinois. 1,021 sisters. Teaching elementary and high school, college; hospitals, sanatorium, schools of nursing; homes for working girls; care of aged; missions in Peru.

Holy Family Convent, 5707 Smith Ave., Mt. Washington, Baltimore 9, Maryland. 539 sisters. Teaching elementary and high school, college, teachers' college; hospitals, convalescent homes, schools of nursing; care of orphans and aged.

8200 West Outer Dr., Detroit 19, Michigan. 637 sisters. Teaching elementary and high school, college; hospitals, sanatoriums, schools of nursing; care of aged.

Our Lady of Mercy Convent, 2039 No. Geyer Rd., St. Louis 31, Missouri. 813 sisters. Teaching elementary and high school, junior college; hospitals, schools of nursing; day nursery; care of underprivileged girls and aged; home for working girls; retreats.

Maryview, 1901 So. Seventy-second St., Omaha 14, Nebraska. 702 sisters. Teaching elementary and high school, college; hospitals, school of nursing; care of aged and orphans; home for working girls; missions.

Mt. Mercy-on-Hudson, Dobbs Ferry, New York. 388 sisters. Teaching elementary and high school, college; hospitals, school of nursing; care of orphans and aged; homes for working girls; summer camps.

2301 Grandview Ave., Cincinnati 6, Ohio. 806 sisters. Teaching elementary and high school, college, commercial school, art school; hospitals, schools of nursing; care of orphans and aged; homes for working girls; vacation home for girls; missions in Jamaica, B.W.I.

Villa St. Teresa, Dallas, Pennsylvania. 829 sisters. Teaching elementary and high school, junior college, college; hospitals, leprosarium, schools of nursing; care of orphans; home for working girls; catechetics; missions in British Guiana.

Convent of Mercy, R.D. 3, Cumberland, Rhode Island. 884 sisters. Teaching elementary and high school, colleges, schools for exceptional children; care of orphans; missions in Honduras and British Honduras.

Mercy, see Our Lady of Mercy.

St. Methodius, see Saints Cyril and Methodius, Sisters of.

Minim, see Mary Immaculate, Minim Daughters of.

Sisters of Misericorde (S.M.) (Misericordia Sisters) Founded in Montreal, Canada in 1848 by Bishop Ignace Bourget and Mother de la Nativite (Marie Cadron-Jette) to help unwed mothers and infants; established in U.S. in 1887. Pontifical, active, simple vows. 409 sisters, 105 in U.S. Hospitals, nursing homes, TB sanatoriums, schools of nursing; care of unwed mothers and infants; care of orphans; domestic and office work; retreats; missions in Africa; directing Oblate Sisters of Misericordia—(see the following). Ages 16-30, some exceptions, high school education. Postulate six months, novitiate one and a half years, juniorate three years. Temporary vow period five years. Black habit. Motherhouse: 12435 Ste. Croix St., Cartierville, Montreal 9, P.Q., Canada. U.S. novitiate: Misericordia Novitiate, 288 South Ave., Beacon, New York.

Oblate Sisters of Misericordia. A congregation of repentant women under the direction of the Sisters of Misericorde. Write to motherhouse or U.S. novitiate of Sisters of Misericorde for information.

Missions, see Our Lady of the Missions, Sisters of.

Montfort Sisters, see Daughters of Wisdom.

Sisters of the Morsel for the Poor. Catechetics to public school children. Motherhouse: Mexico City, Mexico. U.S. address: Our Lady of Guadalupe Convent, San Bernardino, California.

Missionary Sisters of the Most Blessed Sacrament and Mary Immaculate (Misioneras del Santísimo Sacramento y María Inmaculada) Founded in Spain in 1896; established in U.S. in 1960. Pontifical, active and contemplative, simple vows. 5

sisters in U.S., 280 world. Social work, catechetics, home visiting among the Spanish speaking. Ages 16-30, ninth grade education at least, high school preferred. Aspirancy varies, postulate six months, novitiate two years, juniorate three years. Blue and white habit. Motherhouse: Madrid, Spain. U.S. address: Convent of Mary Immaculate, 473 Pine St., Bridgeport, Connecticut.

Most Blessed Sacrament, see Franciscan Nuns of the Most Blessed Sacrament.

Missionary Servants of the Most Blessed Trinity (M.S.B.T.) Founded in Alabama in 1912, growing out of a lay organization begun by Very Rev. Thomas A. Judge, C.M., in Brooklyn in 1909, who also founded the Missionary Servants of the Most Holy Trinity for priests and brothers. Pontifical, active, simple vows. 522 sisters. Home missions among the abandoned of all races in large cities, rural and mining areas, and the South: visiting the sick in homes and hospitals; teaching; nursing; catechetics; retreats; working with clubs, Scouts, etc.; census taking; settlement houses; welfare bureaus; fostering the Missionary Cenacle Lay Apostolate; missions in Puerto Rico. Ages 18-30, high school education. Postulate one year, novitiate one year, juniorate two years. Entrance dates February 11 and August 5. Black habit, coat and hat. Motherhouse: Blessed Trinity Missionary Cenacle, 3501 Solly St., Philadelphia 36, Pennsylvania.

Nuns of the Most Holy Cross and Passion of Our Lord Jesus Christ, see Passionist Nuns.

Sisters of the Most Holy Cross and Passion of Our Lord Jesus Christ, see Passionist Sisters.

Sisters of the Most Holy Crucified (S.S.C.) Founded in Italy in 1840; established in U.S. in 1948. Affiliated with the Order of Hermits of St. Augustine. Pontifical, active, simple vows. 21 sisters in U.S., 1,000 world. Domestic work at present. Ages 15-30. Postulate one year, novitiate two years. Black habit. Motherhouse: Rome, Italy. U.S. address: Bishop Scalabrini Home for the Aged, 860 N. Quidnesset Rd., North Kingstown, Rhode Island.

Missionary Servants of the Most Holy Eucharist (O.P.) (Eucharistic Mission Sisters) (Sisters of the Bayous) Third Order of St. Dominic. Founded in Louisiana in 1927 by Mothers M.

Catherine Bostick and M. Margaret Grouchy. Diocesan, active, simple vows. 62 sisters. Home missions in the South and Southwest: visiting the sick and poor; census taking; catechetics for public school children and adults; retreats; summer religious schools; moderating discussion clubs and sodalities; social work; training lay apostles. Divine Office in English. The sisters live in mission centers in groups of two and three. Ages 16-30, high school education preferred. Postulate eleven months, novitiate two years, juniorate five years. White cotton habit, black or white veil depending on climate. Motherhouse: 3453 Magazine St., New Orleans 15, Louisiana.

California Institute of the Sisters of the Most Holy and Immaculate Heart of the Blessed Virgin Mary (I.H.M.) (Sisters of the Immaculate Heart of Mary) Founded in Spain in 1848; established in U.S. in 1871; California foundation became separate institute in 1924. Pontifical, active, simple vows. 563 sisters. Teaching elementary and high school, academy, college; general and convalescent hospitals; retreats; publication— *Magnificat*; missions in U.S. and Canada. Ages 16-30, high school education. Postulate eight months, novitiate one year. Blue-violet habit, black veil. Motherhouse: Immaculate Heart Convent, 5515 Franklin Ave., Los Angeles 28, California. Canadian address: Sisters of the Immaculate Heart of Mary, Sacred Heart School, 866 McKenzie Ave., Victoria, B.C., Canada—13 sisters, teaching elementary, industrial and Indian school.

Most Holy Name of Jesus, see Dominican Congregation of the Most Holy Name of Jesus.

Daughters of the Most Holy Redeemer (D.M.H.R.) Founded in Germany in 1866 as a branch of the Daughters of the Divine Redeemer which was founded in 1849; established in U.S. in 1924. Diocesan, active, simple vows. 126 sisters in U.S., 3,000 world. Nursing the sick poor in their homes and hospital; care of aged; domestic work in seminaries; home for working girls; office work; home missions; missions in Africa. Ages 17-30, high school education preferred. Aspirancy six weeks, postulate one year, novitiate two years. Black habit. Motherhouse: Wuerzburg, Germany. U.S. commissariat: Most Holy Redeemer Convent, 1616 Huntingdon Pike, Meadowbrook, Pennsylvania.

Oblates of the Most Holy Redeemer (O.SS.R.) Founded in Spain in 1864; recently established in U.S. Pontifical. 13 sisters in U.S., 1,000 world plus 500 Magdalens. Domestic work in seminaries, catechetics, social work at present. Community's main work is rehabilitating delinquent girls. Also located in Mexico. Eighth grade education. Aspirancy four years. Postulate six months, novitiate one and a half years, juniorate five years. Motherhouse: Spain. U.S. residence: St. Francis Xavier Mission House, Duxbury, Massachusetts.

Order of the Most Holy Redeemer, see Redemptoristine Nuns.

Most Holy Rosary, see Dominican Third Order.

Sisters of the Most Holy Sacrament (M.H.S.) Founded in France in 1851; established in U.S. in 1872; independent congregation in 1892. Pontifical, active and contemplative, simple vows. 202 sisters in U.S. Contemplation; teaching elementary and high school, boarding schools, teacher-training school; domestic work; catechetics; retreats; baking altar breads. No lay sisters. Ages 15-30. Eighth grade education. Aspirancy three years. Postulate six to eleven months, novitiate one year, juniorate five years. Black habit. Motherhouse: Convent of the Most Holy Sacrament, 409 West St. Mary Blvd., P.O. Box 2877, Lafayette, Louisiana.

Daughters of the Most Holy Saviour (F.SS.S.) Originally part of Daughters of the Divine Redeemer founded in Germany in 1849; independent congregation in 1914 in Slovakia; established in U.S. in 1951 by four German sisters. Pontifical, active, simple vows. 7 sisters in U.S., 80 world. Domestic work at present. Ages 18-30, some exceptions. Aspirancy six months, postulate six to twelve months, novitiate one year, juniorate three years. Black habit. Motherhouse in Bratislava, Slovakia, confiscated by Communist government and the sisters dispersed. U.S. novitiate: House of Nazareth Convent, Holy Redeemer College, 8555 Golf Links Rd., Box 5007, Oakland 5, California.

Sisters of the Most Holy Trinity (O.SS.T.) (Trinitarians) Founded in France in 1198 by St. John de Matha and St. Felix of Valois, founders of the Trinitarian Fathers; established in U.S. in 1920. Pontifical, active, simple vows. 68 sisters in U.S., 400 world. Teaching elementary school; domestic work; foreign missions in Italy and Madagascar. Also located in Mexico.

Ages 16-35, high school education. Postulate six to twelve months, novitiate two years, juniorate three years. White habit. Motherhouse: Rome, Italy. U.S. provincialate: Our Lady of Lourdes Shrine, 21320 Euclid Ave., Euclid 17, Ohio.

Most Holy Trinity, see Our Lady of the Most Holy Trinity, Society of.

Sisters of the Most Precious Blood (C.PP.S.) Founded in Switzerland in 1845; established in U.S. in 1870 from Germany. Pontifical, active, simple vows. 585 sisters. Teaching elementary and high school, academy, junior college; domestic work; promotion of liturgical movement; missions in Finland, Bolivia and Peru. Ages 16-30, two years high school education. Postulate eleven months, novitiate two years, juniorate five years. Black habit. Motherhouse: St. Mary's Institute, 204 North Main St., O'Fallon, Missouri.

Sisters Adorers of the Most Precious Blood (Ad.PP.S.) Founded in Italy in 1834 by Blessed Maria de Mattias; established in U.S. in 1870. Pontifical, active, simple vows. 1,038 sisters in U.S., 2,925 world. Ages 16-35, high school education. Aspirancy four years. Postulate six months, novitiate one year, juniorate five years. Preferable entrance dates February 1 and September 1. Black habit, red sash. Motherhouse: Rome, Italy.

Midwest provincialate: R.R. 1, Red Bud P.O., Ruma, Illinois. 455 sisters. Teaching elementary, high, and normal school; nursing; care of orphans and aged; home for working girls; domestic work; catechetics; mission in Puerto Rico.

Western provincialate: 1165 Southwest Blvd., Wichita 13, Kansas. 413 sisters. Teaching elementary and high school, academy, college; nursing; religious correspondence schools; care of aged; domestic work; home missions; missions in Brazil.

Eastern provincialate: St. Joseph Convent, Columbia, Pennsylvania. 170 sisters. Teaching elementary school and academy; care of aged; retreats; domestic work; home missions.

Most Precious Blood, see Charity of the Most Precious Blood, Daughters of the.

Most Pure Heart of Mary, see Franciscan Handmaids of the Most Pure Heart of Mary.

Missionary Sisters of the Most Sacred Heart of Jesus (M.S.C.) Founded in Germany in 1899; established in U.S. in 1908. Pontifical, active, simple vows. 368 sisters in U.S. Teaching elementary, high and normal school; hospitals, sanitariums, schools of nursing; care of orphans and aged; domestic work in seminaries and retreat house; missions in Peru, New Guinea, Africa and Australia. Ages 14-17 for aspirancy, 17-30 and high school education for novitiate. Aspirancy four years. Postulate ten months, novitiate one year, juniorate two years. Black habit, white for tropics. Generalate: Rome, Italy. U.S. provincialate: St. Michael's Convent, Hyde Park, Reading, Pennsylvania.

Servants of the Most Sacred Heart of Jesus (S.M.Ht.J.) Founded in Poland in 1894; established in U.S. in 1959. Pontifical, active. 6 sisters in U.S., 850 world. Domestic work at present. Community's purpose is the religious care of women workers, servants, and the poor. Ages 15-30, eighth grade education. Aspirancy two months, postulate six months, novitiate two years, juniorate two years. Motherhouse: Cracow, Poland. U.S. residence: 3840 Shannon Rd., Erie 1, Pennsylvania.

Missionary Sisters of the Mother of God (M.S.M.G.) Ukrainian-Byzantine Rite. Founded in Connecticut in 1944 by Archbishops Constantine Bohachevsky and Ambrose Senyshyn. Diocesan, active, simple vows. 22 sisters. Teaching elementary and high school; catechetics; domestic work; music, painting and embroidering in Byzantine style. Ages 16-35, high school or college education, or experience in office, medical, factory, domestic or farm work, social work or teaching. Those of Byzantine or Latin rites eligible. Black habit; also white habit with blue veil. Motherhouse: 813 N. Franklin St., Philadelphia 23, Pennsylvania.

Poor Servants of the Mother of God and the Poor (S.M.G.) Founded in England in 1869 by Mother Mary Magdalen Taylor, a convert who had worked with Florence Nightingale in Crimea; established in U.S. in 1947. Pontifical, active, simple vows. 18 sisters in U.S., 900 world. Nursing in hospital and convalescent home at present. Ages 16-26, good education. Postulate six months, novitiate two years. Training is in England and Ireland. No lay sisters. Black and blue habit, white for nursing. Generalate: Rome, Italy. Motherhouse: London, England. U.S. addresses: St. Mary's Hospital, Norton, Virginia; Maryfield Nursing Home, High Point, North Carolina.

Mother of God, see St. Francis of the Immaculate Virgin Mary, Mother of God, Sisters of the Third Order of; Immaculate Conception of the Mother of God, Missionary Sisters of the.

N

Poor Sisters of Nazareth (R.S.N.) Founded in England in 1851; established in U.S. in 1924. Pontifical, active, simple vows. 41 sisters in U.S., 1,600 world. Care of orphans, foundlings and aged. Ages 16-30. Aspirancy. Postulate six months, novitiate two years, juniorate five years. No lay sisters. Black habit. Motherhouse: London, England. U.S. novitiate: Nazareth House, 3333 Manning Ave., Los Angeles 64, California.

Religious of Nazareth (R de N) Founded in France in 1822; established in U.S. in 1952. Pontifical, active, simple vows. 8 sisters in U.S., 360 world. Teaching; nursing; domestic work; missions in the Holy Land. Ages 16-30, high school education. Aspirancy two years. Postulate six months, novitiate two years, juniorate varies. Black habit, recently redesigned. Motherhouse: Paris, France. U.S. residence: La Purisima Convent, 213 W. Olive Ave., Lompoc, California.

Nazareth, see Holy Family of Nazareth, Sisters of the.

Order of Notre Dame, see Company of Mary, Our Lady.

Sisters of Notre Dame (S.N.D.) Founded in Germany in 1850; established in U.S. in 1874 because of religious persecution. Pontifical, active, simple vows. 1,518 sisters in U.S., 3,827 world. Black habit, white for nursing and foreign missions. Motherhouse: Rome, Italy. U.S. provincialates:

Notre Dame Academy, 2851 Overland Ave., Los Angeles 64, California. 126 sisters. Teaching elementary school and academy; domestic work; nursing. Ages 16-30, high school education. Aspirancy three and a half years. Postulate six months, novitiate two years, juniorate five years.

St. Joseph Heights, 1601 Dixie Hwy., Covington, Kentucky. 328 sisters. Teaching elementary and high school, academy, schools of music; reading clinic; nursing; care of orphans; social work; administration and office work; domestic work; Negro mission. Ages 16-30, high school education or equivalent preferred. Aspirancy four years. Postulate six to twelve months, novitiate two years, juniorate five years.

Maryhill Convent, 5228 Everhard Rd., Canton 8, Ohio. 134 sisters. Teaching elementary and high school; convalescent home; catechetics; domestic work. Ages 16-30. Aspirancy four years. Postulate six months, novitiate two years, juniorate five years.

Notre Dame Educational Center, R.D. 6, Box 240, Chardon, Ohio. 566 sisters. Teaching elementary and high school, academies, college, schools of music and art, school for exceptional children; catechetics; domestic work; nursing; missions in India. Ages 16-30. Aspirancy three and a half years. Postulate six months, novitiate two years, juniorate five years. Five-week summer sessions for professional renewal and advancement.

Notre Dame Convent, 3837 Secor Rd., Toledo 6, Ohio. 364 sisters. Teaching elementary and high school, academy, schools of music, extension college, school for retarded children; catechetics; domestic work; administration and office work; nursing; missions in New Guinea. Ages 16-30. Aspirancy three and a half years. Postulate six to twelve months, novitiate two years, juniorate five years. Six-week summer sessions for professional renewal and advancement.

Sisters of the Congregation of Notre Dame of Montreal (C.N.D.) Founded in Montreal, Canada, in 1658 by Blessed Marguerite Bourgeoys; established in U.S. in 1860. Pontifical, active, simple vows. 4,000 sisters, 400 in U.S. Teaching elementary and high school, academies, domestic science, industrial and normal schools, business college, colleges; farming; home missions; missions in Japan and Central America. Ages 17½-30, high school education. Postulate six months, novitiate two years, juniorate two years, also six-week session for spiritual formation one year after profession. Temporary vow period six years. Black habit. Motherhouse: 3040 W. Sherbrooke St., Montreal, P.Q., Canada. Canadian provincialates: Notre Dame Convent, 38 Gloucester St., Ottawa 4, Ont., Canada; Joliette, P.Q., Canada. U.S. provincialate: Notre Dame Academy, 76 Howard Ave., Grymes Hill, Staten Island 1, New York. Novitiate in Bourbonnais, Illinois.

Sisters of Notre Dame de Namur (S.N.D.) Founded in France in 1803 by Blessed Julie Billiart; established in U.S. in 1840 at Cincinnati. Pontifical, active, simple vows. 2,939 sisters in U.S., 5,000 world. No lay sisters. Generalate: Rome, Italy. Motherhouse: Namur, Belgium. U.S. provincialates:

Bohlman Rd., Saratoga, California. 409 sisters. Teaching elementary and high school, college; missions in Hawaii. High school or college education. Postulate six months, novitiate two years, juniorate two years.

1561 No. Benson Rd., Fairfield, Connecticut. 290 sisters. Teaching elementary and high school; domestic work; missions in Brazil. High school or college education. Postulate nine months, novitiate two years, juniorate two years.

Ilchester, Maryland. 572 sisters. Teaching elementary and high school, academies, junior college, college, school for exceptional children, missions in Brazil. High school or college education. Postulate nine months, novitiate two years, juniorate two years.

Notre Dame Novitiate, Jeffrey Neck Rd., Ipswich, Massachusetts. 1,068 sisters. Teaching elementary and high school, academies, colleges; missions in Hawaii, Rome, Italy, Japan and Brazil. High school or college education. Postulate six months, novitiate two years, juniorate two and a half years.

Mount Notre Dame, 701 E. Columbia Ave., Reading, Cincinnati 15, Ohio. 600 sisters. Teaching elementary and high school, academies; catechetics; social work; home missions; missions in Rome, Italy. High school or college education. Postulate one year, novitiate two years, juniorate two and a half years.

Congregation of Notre Dame de Sion (N.D.S.) (Congregation of Our Lady of Zion) Founded in France in 1843 by two brothers converted from Judaism to pray and work for the conversion of Jews; established in U.S. in 1892. Pontifical, active (and contemplative branch), simple vows. Under the direction of the Fathers of Zion. 56 sisters in U.S., 2,000 world. Teaching elementary and high school; social work; catechetics; missions in Canada, England, South America, and Africa. Conducts Archconfraternity of Prayer for Peace and Good Will to Israel for the conversion of Jews. Little Office of the Blessed Virgin in choir. Three branches: teaching sisters; Ancillae who wear secular clothes and walk in the world; contemplatives. To age 30, high school education. Postulate six months, novitiate one and a half years, juniorate two years. Black habit. Motherhouse: Paris, France. U.S. provincialate: French Institute of Notre Dame de Sion, 3823 Locust St., Kansas City 9, Missouri.

School Sisters of Notre Dame (S.S.N.D.) Founded in France in 1598 by St. Peter Fourier and Blessed Alexia LeClerc; after suppression by Napoleon, reestablished in Germany in 1833 by Mother Teresa Gerhardinger; established in U.S. in 1847 by Mother Teresa Gerhardinger. Pontifical, active, simple vows. 6,404 sisters in U.S., 12,000 world. Black habit. Motherhouse: Rome, Italy. American provincialates:

Villa de Lourdes, 345 Belden Hill Rd., Wilton, Connecticut. 822 sisters. Teaching; domestic work; catechetics; missions in Puerto Rico. To age 27, high school education. Aspirancy four years. Postulate one year, novitiate one year, juniorate three years.

6401 No. Charles St., Baltimore 12, Maryland. 1,024 sisters. Teaching. To age 27, high school education. Aspirancy four years. Postulate ten months, novitiate one year.

Our Lady of Good Counsel Motherhouse, Good Counsel Hill, Mankato, Minnesota. 857 sisters. Teaching; domestic work; catechetics; nursing; missions in Guatemala. Ages 16-27, high school education for prospective teachers and nurses. Aspirancy four years. Postulate one year, juniorate six years.

320 E. Ripa Ave., St. Louis 25, Missouri. 1,229 sisters. Teaching; domestic work; catechetics and teaching in home missions and in foreign missions in Honduras, Japan, and Ryukyu Islands. To age 27, high school education. Aspirancy one to four years. Postulate one to one and a half years, novitiate one year, juniorate three years.

2110 Cooper Dr., Irving, Texas. 355 sisters. Teaching; domestic work; boys' home; institute for the deaf; catechetics; nursing. To age 27, high school education. Training at St. Louis provincialate until completion of Dallas motherhouse.

Notre Dame of the Lake, 700 West Highland Rd., 128 North, Mequon, Wisconsin. 2,117 sisters. Teaching elementary and high school, college, teaching blind and deaf, Indian mission school; nursing; domestic work; social work; publication— *The School Sister;* home missions; foreign missions in Guam and Brazil. To age 30. Aspirancy one to four years. Postulate one year, novitiate one year, juniorate three years.

Canadian provincialate: Notre Dame Convent, Waterdown, Ont., Canada. Also in Bolivia and England from Canadian provincialate.

School Sisters of Notre Dame. Founded in Czechoslovakia in 1853; established in U.S. in 1910. Pontifical, active, simple vows. 131 sisters in U.S., 1,100 world. Teaching elementary and high school, academy; domestic work; retreats; Indian mission. Ages 15-27, some exceptions. Aspirancy one to four years. Postulate six months, novitiate two years, juniorate three years. Motherhouse: Horazdovice, Bohemia, Czechoslovakia. U.S. provincialate: Notre Dame Convent, 3501 State St., Omaha 12, Nebraska.

Notre Dame, see also Our Lady, and School Sisters of Our Lady.

Nursing, see Mary, Nursing Sisters, Little Company of; Sick Poor, Nursing Sisters of the.

O

Olivetan, see Benedictine Sisters, Olivetan.

School Sisters of Our Lady (S.S.O.L.) Founded in Kalocsa, Hungary, in 1860, based on Notre Dame Order founded in France in 1598; established in Canada in 1960. Pontifical, active, simple vows. 12 sisters in Canada and U.S., 931 world. Teaching; religious art work; domestic work. Age 16, grade or high school education. Postulate six months, novitiate one year, juniorate six years. Black habit, recently redesigned. Motherhouse: Rome, Italy; formerly in Kalocsa, Hungary. Canadian provincialate: Gloria Art Studio, 546 Euclid Ave., Toronto 4, Ont., Canada. U.S. address: Holy Angels Convent, 348 Porter Ave., Buffalo, New York.

Our Lady, see Blessed Sacrament and of Our Lady, Religious of the; Mary, Our Lady, Company of; see also Notre Dame.

Missionary Sisters of Our Lady of Africa (W.S.) (White Sisters) Founded in Algeria in 1869 to assist the White Fathers in Africa and to work particularly among Mohammedan women; established in U.S. in 1929. Pontifical, active, simple vows. 63 sisters in U.S., 2,072 world. Missions in Africa: schools, hospitals, dispensaries, social work, catechetics, administration, training native sisters. In U.S. publish magazine, *Africa*. To age 35, high school education. Postulate nine months, novitiate one and a half years, juniorate one year. White habit. Motherhouse: Rome, Italy. U.S. provincialate: 319 Middlesex Ave.,

Metuchen, New Jersey. Novitiate: Mary Glenn, R.D. 2, Franklin, Pennsylvania. Canadian novitiates: Lévis, P.Q., Canada; Rosemère, Terrebonne Co., P.Q., Canada; St. Charles Garnier, P.Q., Canada.

Missionary Sisters of Our Lady of the Angels (M.N.D.A.) (Soeurs Missionnaires de Notre Dame des Anges) Third Order of St. Francis. Founded in Canada in 1919 by Mother Mary of the Sacred Heart (Florine Gervais); established in U.S. in 1949. Diocesan, active, simple vows. 250 sisters, 4 in U.S. Missions in Japan, Oceania, Africa, Peru: hospitals, clinics; teaching; care of orphans; catechetics; social work; training native sisters. Ages 18-30, elementary school education. White and black cotton habit. Motherhouse: Lennoxville, P.Q., Canada. U.S. address: St. Mary's Convent, 338 N. Main St., Union City, Naugatuck, Connecticut.

Religious of Our Lady of Charity of the Good Shepherd, see Good Shepherd Sisters.

Sisters of Our Lady of Charity of Refuge (O.L.C.R.) Founded in France in 1641 by St. John Eudes; established in U.S. in 1855. Pontifical, active and contemplative, minor papal enclosure, simple vows. Contemplation; care and training of disturbed and problem girls; direction of community of repentants, Sisters of Seven Dolors. Average entrance requirements and training: Ages 16-30, some exceptions, high school education preferred; postulate six months, novitiate two years, juniorate three years. White habit, black veil. Each monastery is independent. Write to Monastery of Our Lady of Charity of Refuge:

1125 Malvern Ave., Hot Springs, Arkansas. 20 sisters.

485 Best St., Buffalo 8, New York. 47 sisters.

1326 Winton Rd., N., Rochester 9, New York. 12 cloistered, 1 extern sister.

W. Main St., Carrolton, Ohio. 21 sisters.

Flaugherty Run Rd., Coraopolis, Pennsylvania. 37 sisters.

4635 E. Lake Rd., Erie, Pennsylvania. 15 sisters.

1625 Lincoln Ave., Pittsburgh 6, Pennsylvania. 5 cloistered, 1 extern sister.

4500 W. Davis St., Dallas, Texas. 24 sisters.

415 N. Glenwood Dr., El Paso, Texas. 20 cloistered, 8 Magdalens, 3 externs.

1900 Montana St., San Antonio 3, Texas. 36 sisters.

S. Reseca Rd., P.O. Box 737, San Benito, Texas. 4 sisters.

Edgington Lane, Edgewood, Wheeling, West Virginia. 29 sisters.

918 Porlier St., Green Bay, Wisconsin. 39 sisters, 45 Magdalens.

Sisters of Seven Dolors. Community of repentant women under the direction of Sisters of Our Lady of Charity of Refuge. Write to any monastery of that congregation for information.

Sisters of Our Lady of Christian Doctrine (R.C.D.) Founded in New York City in 1910 by Mother Marianne Guerney. Diocesan, active, simple vows. 67 sisters. Settlement houses; catechetics; discussion clubs; day nurseries; home visiting; summer camps; training catechists. Day hours of Divine Office. Postulate nine months, novitiate two years, juniorate five years. Motherhouse: Marydell Convent, Montebello Rd., Suffern, New York.

Sisters of Our Lady of the Cross (N.D.C.) (Soeurs de Notre Dame de la Croix) Founded in France in 1832; established in Forget, Canada, in 1905. Pontifical, active, simple vows. 80 sisters in Canada, 215 world. Teaching elementary and high school; care of aged; nursing; catechetics; home visiting; aiding retarded children. Age 14½, no educational requirement. Postulate six months, novitiate two years. Temporary vow period five years. Black habit. Motherhouse: Murinais, France. Canadian provincialate: 58 Eighteenth St. E., Prince Albert, Sask., Canada.

Our Lady of Evron, see Charity of Our Lady of Evron, Sisters of.

Congregation of Our Lady of Good Counsel. Founded in Canada in 1923 by Archbishop George Gauthier. Motherhouse: 5035 de la Roche, Montreal, P.Q., Canada.

Sisters of Our Lady of Good Counsel (N.D.B.C.) (Institut des Soeurs de Notre-Dame du Bon-Conseil) Founded in 1894 in Canada by Bishop Michael T. Labrecque and Françoise Simard. Pontifical, active, simple vows. 592 sisters, 4 in U.S. Teaching in rural areas, elementary, high and normal school; homemaking and Indian mission schools; domestic work; assisting African Sisters of Our Lady of Good Counsel, Mbarara, Uganda, Africa, an independent community founded by them. Age 17, eleventh grade. Postulate six months, novitiate one and a half years. Temporary vow period five years. Black habit.

Motherhouse: Chicoutimi, P.Q., Canada. U.S. address of Sisters of Our Lady of Good Counsel and African Sisters of Our Lady of Good Counsel: Mission House, 8 Lamartine St., Worcester, Massachusetts.

Our Lady of Good Counsel, see also Franciscan Sisters of Our Lady of Good Counsel.

Our Lady of Guadalupe, see Sacred Heart and Our Lady of Guadalupe, Missionaries of the.

Sisters of Our Lady of Help (N.D.A.) (Soeurs de Notre-Dame-Auxiliatrice) Founded in Mont-Laurier, Canada, in 1921 by Bishop F. X. Brunet. Diocesan, active and contemplative, simple vows. 180 sisters. Teaching elementary school and academy, Indian mission schools; domestic work in seminaries, rectories, etc.; missions to South America planned. Aspirancy. Postulate six months, novitiate two years. Temporary vow period three years or more. Motherhouse: Maison-Mère, C.P. 1000, Rouyn, Cté. Rouyn-Noranda, P.Q., Canada.

Our Lady of the Holy Angels, see Franciscan Sisters of Our Lady of the Holy Angels.

Missionary Sisters of Our Lady of the Holy Rosary (H.R.S.) Founded in Ireland in 1924; established in U.S. in 1954. Pontifical, active, simple vows. 14 sisters in U.S., 410 world. Missions in Africa. Teaching; nursing and allied work; social work; domestic work; publication—*Missionary Sisters.* High school education or equivalent. Postulate six months, novitiate two years, juniorate three years. Motherhouse: County Cavan, Ireland. U.S. regionalate: Holy Rosary Convent, 214 Ashwood Rd., Villanova, Pennsylvania.

Sisters of Our Lady of the Holy Rosary (R.S.R.) Founded in Rimouski, Canada, in 1874 by Bishop John Langevin and Mother Mary Elizabeth Turgeon; established in U.S. in 1899. Pontifical, active, simple vows. 881 sisters, 27 in U.S. Teaching elementary, high, domestic science and normal schools, Indian mission schools; catechetics; domestic work for lay sisters. To age 35, high school education. Grey and black habit. Motherhouse: Holy Rosary Convent, Rimouski, P.Q., Canada. U.S. address: St. Martin's Convent, Maine Ave., Millinocket, Maine.

Daughters of Our Lady of Mercy (D.M.) (Daughters of Mercy) Founded in Italy in 1837 by St. Josepha Rossello; established in U.S. in 1919. Pontifical, active, simple vows. 104 sisters in

U.S., 3,000 world. Teaching elementary and high school; day nursery; convalescent hospital; parish mission work; catechetics; domestic work. Ages 15-30, eighth grade education. Aspirancy two years, postulate eight months, novitiate two years, juniorate five years. Black habit. Motherhouse: Savona, Italy. U.S. provincialate: Villa Rossello, Catawba Ave., Newfield, New Jersey.

Missionary Sisters of Our Lady of Mercy (M.O.M.) (Mercedarians) Founded in Brazil in 1938; established in U.S. in 1955. Diocesan, active, simple vows. 9 sisters in U.S., 220 world. Teaching elementary school; domestic work at a seminary. Ages 15-30, high school education preferred. Postulate six months, novitiate two years, juniorate five years. Motherhouse: Brazil. U.S. novitiate: St. Raymond Nonnatus Convent, Lake St., Le Roy, New York.

Our Lady of Mercy, see Charity of Our Lady of Mercy, Sisters of.

Our Lady's Missionaries. Teaching. Motherhouse: 65 Clarendon Ave., Toronto 7, Ont., Canada. Novitiate: R.R.1, Richmond Hill, Ont., Canada.

Sisters of Our Lady of the Missions (R.N.D.M.) (Religieuses de Notre Dame des Missions) Founded in France in 1861; established in Canada in 1898. Pontifical, active, simple vows. 186 sisters in Canada, 1,200 world. Home and foreign missions: teaching elementary and high school, teaching music, drama and art, religious vacation schools; retreats for women; visiting the poor and sick; domestic and office work; dispensaries; care of orphans; publication—*Message*; foreign missions include Indochina, India, Pakistan and Burma. Ages 16-30, high school education preferred. Postulate six to twelve months, novitiate two years, juniorate two years. Temporary vow period six years. Black habit. Motherhouse: Hastings, Sussex, England. Canadian provincialate: St. Edward's Convent, 800 Yarwood, Winnipeg 3, Man., Canada. Novitiate: Sacred Heart College, Albert St. So., Regina, Sask., Canada.

Order of Our Lady of the Most Holy Saviour, see Bridgettine Sisters.

Society of Our Lady of the Most Holy Trinity. Founded in New Mexico in 1958 by Archbishop Edwin V. Byrne and Father James H. Flanagan. Diocesan, active and contemplative, simple vows. 8 sisters. Teaching; nursing in clinic. Aspirancy until completion of high school. Postulate nine months, novitiate one year, juniorate one year. Grey habit. Motherhouse: Immaculate Heart of Mary Convent, Holman, New Mexico.

Our Lady of Lourdes, see Franciscan Third Order.

Our Lady, Mother of Mercy, see Charity of Our Lady, Mother of Mercy, Sisters of.

Our Lady of Mount Carmel, see Carmelites.

Missionary Sisters of Our Lady of Perpetual Help (M.P.S.) 8 sisters in U.S. Mission work in parishes. U.S. address: Our Lady of Peace Convent, 601 Runnels St., San Antonio 8, Texas.

Sisters of Our Lady of Perpetual Help (N.D.P.S.) (Soeurs de Notre-Dame du Perpétuel Secours) Founded in Canada in 1892 by Father Joseph Brousseau and Mother St. Bernard. Pontifical, active, simple vows. 811 sisters. Teaching, domestic science school; care of foundlings and orphans; hospices; missions in Santo Domingo and Africa. Postulate six months, novitiate. Entrance dates February 10 and August 10. Black and white habit. Motherhouse: St. Damien de Bellechasse, P.Q., Canada.

Our Lady of Perpetual Help, see Franciscan Sisters of Our Lady of Perpetual Help.

Sisters of Our Lady of Providence (O.L.P.) Founded in Providence, Rhode Island, in 1955 by Most Rev. Russel J. McVinney as a modern community following recent directives of the Holy See. Diocesan, active, simple vows. 28 sisters. Catechetics; home visiting; social work; interracial centers; day nurseries; home for working girls and retired women. Work particularly among Negroes. Future plans include nursing, teaching, and care of delinquent girls. Ages 17-35, high school education preferred. No dowry or novitiate fees. Postulate six months, novitiate two years. Habit: grey jumper, white blouse, black veil. Motherhouse: Mother of Hope Novitiate, 2543 W. Main Rd., Portsmouth, Rhode Island.

Servants of Our Lady, Queen of the Clergy (S.R.C.) Founded in Canada in 1929 by Rev. Alexandre Bouillon and Mother Marie de St. Joseph Rimsuski; established in U.S. in 1936. Diocesan, active, simple vows. 203 sisters, 45 in U.S. Domestic work for priests. Ages 17-30, eighth grade. Postulate six months, novitiate two years. Motherhouse: The Cenacle, Lac-au-Saumon, P.Q., Canada.

Congregation of Our Lady of the Retreat in the Cenacle (R.C.)
Founded in France in 1826 by Blessed Thérèse Couderc and
Rev. Etienne Terme; established in U.S. in 1892 in New
York. Pontifical, active and contemplative, cloistered, simple
vows. 430 sisters in U.S., 1,300 world. Daily adoration; Divine
Office in choir; retreats; catechetics; missions in Madagascar.
To age 35, college education or equivalent for choir sisters,
high school for lay sisters. Postulate six months, novitiate two
years, juniorate five years. Motherhouse: Rome, Italy. U.S.
provincialates: Convent of Our Lady of the Cenacle, Mt.
Kisco, New York; Convent of Our Lady of the Cenacle, 3288
N. Lake Dr., Milwaukee, Wisconsin. Canadian addresses: 318
Lawrence Ave. E., Toronto 12, Ont., Canada; 3689 Selkirk
St., Vancouver, B.C., Canada.

Our Lady of the Rosary, see Dominican Congregation of Our Lady
of the Rosary.

Daughters of Our Lady of the Sacred Heart (F.D.N.S.C.)
Founded in France in 1882; established in U.S. in 1955. Pontif-
ical, active, simple vows. 20 sisters in U.S., 1,800 world.
Teaching elementary school; domestic work. Aspirancy one
year, postulate six months, novitiate two years. Training in
Ireland, England and Australia. Motherhouse: France. U.S.
address: St. Francis de Sales Convent, 424 Browning Rd.,
Bellmawr, New Jersey.

Sisters of Our Lady of the Sacred Heart (N.D.S.C.) (Religieuses
de Notre-Dame du Sacré-Coeur) Founded in Canada in 1854
at St. John, N.B., as Sisters of Charity of the Immaculate Conception from the New York branch of the Sisters of Charity
founded by Mother Seton; in 1924 the congregation was divided into two branches, English and French speaking, and
the latter took the above title. Pontifical, active, simple vows.
423 sisters. Teaching elementary school through college, including fine arts, music, etc.; nursing; care of aged and orphans. Ages 17-30, high school education; college preferred.
Postulate six to ten months, novitiate two years, juniorate
three to five years. Temporary vow period three years. Black
and white habit. Motherhouse: 125 King St., Moncton, N.B.,
Canada.

Our Lady of the Sacred Heart, see Dominican Third Order.

Sisters of Our Lady of La Salette (R.S.) Founded in France in

1930; established in U.S. in 1959. Diocesan, active, simple vows. 13 sisters in U.S., 4 Canada, 100 world. Care of shrine. Future plans include care of aged, work with youths, nursing, social work, and catechetics. Ages 15-35. Postulate six to twelve months, novitiate two years, juniorate three years. Black habit. Motherhouse: France. U.S. novitiate: La Salette Shrine, Attleboro, Massachusetts.

Oblates of Our Lady of the Snows (O.L.S.) (Eskimo Sisters) Founded in Alaska in 1954 by Ursuline Nuns. Diocesan, active, simple vows. 4 sisters. Teaching; nursing; social work; catechetics. Age 16 or high school education. Postulate six months, novitiate two years, juniorate six years. Motherhouse: St. Mary's Mission, St. Mary's, Alaska.

Sisters of Our Lady of Sorrows (O.L.S.) Founded in Italy in 1839; established in U.S. in 1947. Pontifical, active, simple vows. 31 sisters in U.S., 700 world. Teaching elementary school, teaching and care of retarded children; home and foreign missions. High school education. Motherhouse: Rimini, Italy. U.S. residence: Sacred Heart Mission House, Moreauville, Louisiana.

Our Lady of Sorrows, see Franciscan Missionary Sisters of Our Lady of Sorrows.

Our Lady of Victory Missionary Sisters (O.L.V.M.) Founded in Indiana in 1918 by Rev. J. J. Sigstein. Pontifical, active, simple vows. 392 sisters. Home missions: catechetics; religious instruction of exceptional children; home visiting; parish census; publication—*The Missionary Catechist*. Ages 18-30, high school education preferred. Postulate eleven months, novitiate two years. Blue habit. Motherhouse: Victory Noll, Box 109, Huntington, Indiana.

Congregation of Our Lady of Zion, see Congregation of Notre Dame de Sion.

Our Saviour, see Five Wounds of Our Saviour, Regular Canonesses of the.

P

Pallotine Missionary Sisters (C.M.P.) Founded in Italy in 1835 by St. Vincent Pallotti to help the Pallotine Fathers; established in U.S. in 1912. Diocesan, active, simple vows. 142 sisters in

U.S. Teaching elementary school, academy; hospitals, school of nursing; catechetics; social work; domestic work. Ages 18-30, some exceptions, high school education preferred. Postulate one year, novitiate two years. Black habit. Motherhouse: Limburg, Germany. U.S. motherhouse: St. Mary's Convent, 900 McCoy Rd., Huntington, West Virginia.

Pallotine Sisters, see Sisters of the Catholic Apostolate.

Parish Visitors, see Mary Immaculate, Parish Visitors of.

Passionist Nuns (C.P.) (Nuns of the Most Holy Cross and Passion of Our Lord Jesus Christ) Founded in Italy in 1770 by St. Paul of the Cross; established in U.S. in 1910 in Pennsylvania. Pontifical, contemplative, major papal enclosure, simple vows. Contemplation; retreats; making altar breads, vestments; art work. Choir nuns and lay sisters lead similar lives except that the lay sisters do not recite the Divine Office. Ages 18-25, high school education. Average training: postulate one year, novitiate one year, juniorate five years. Black habit, sandals. Each monastery is independent. Convent of the Sacred Passion, 751 Donaldson Highway, Erlanger, Kentucky (15 nuns); St. Joseph's Monastery, 1420 Benita Ave., Owensboro, Kentucky (14 nuns); Immaculate Conception Convent, P.O. Box 145, Clayton Rd., Ellisville, Missouri (8 nuns); St. Gabriel's Monastery, 1560 Monroe Ave., Dunmore 9, Pennsylvania (25 nuns); Our Lady of Sorrows Convent, 2715 Churchview Ave., Pittsburgh 27, Pennsylvania (24 nuns).

Passionist Sisters (C.P.) (Sisters of the Most Holy Cross and Passion of Our Lord Jesus Christ) Founded in England in 1851; established in U.S. in 1924. Pontifical, active, simple vows. 121 sisters in U.S., 1,250 world. Teaching elementary and junior high school; social work; retreats; catechetics; home missions; foreign missions in South America and Africa. Also located in Mexico. No lay sisters. Ages 15-30, some exceptions by dispensation, high school education. Postulate six months, novitiate two years. Black habit. Motherhouse: Bolton, England. U.S. provincialate: Assumption Convent, 530 Dexter St., Providence 7, Rhode Island.

Pious Society, Daughters of St. Paul (D.S.P.) (Missionary Sisters of the Catholic Press) Founded in Italy in 1915; established in U.S. in 1932. Pontifical, active and contemplative, simple vows. 93 sisters in U.S., 2,500 world. Writing, translating, editing and illustrating books; printing and bookbinding; producing religious films; radio and TV apostolate; Catholic book and film centers; teaching; catechetics; census and parish visiting; social work; publication—*The Family*; missions in Formosa, Korea, Africa, Peru, Philippines and Mexico. Ages 14-23, eighth grade education. Aspirancy one to four years. Postulate one year, novitiate two years, juniorate five years. Motherhouse: Rome, Italy. U.S. provincialate: Daughters of St. Paul Novitiate, 50 St. Paul's Ave., Jamaica Plain, Boston 30, Massachusetts.

Sisters of St. Paul de Chartres (S.P.D.C.) (Soeurs de St.-Paul-de-Chartres) Founded in Chartres, France, in 1694; established in Canada in 1930. Pontifical, active, simple vows. 214 sisters in Canada, 3,000 world. Nursing; teaching; all types of social work; foreign missions in Philippines, Korea, Japan, Africa, Vietnam, Siam. Also located in Marquette, Michigan. Ages 17-30, ninth grade education. Aspirancy one month, postulate six months, novitiate two years, juniorate two years. Black and white habit. Motherhouse: Chartres, France. Canadian provincialate: Notre-Dame-de-la-Paix Convent, St. Anne des Monts, Gaspé-Nord, P.Q., Canada.

Peekskill Sisters, see Missionary Sisters of the Third Order of St. Francis.

Sisters of Penance, see Congregation of the Sacred Heart, under Dominican Third Order.

Penance, see Penance and Charity, and Penance and Christian Charity under Franciscan Third Order.

Nuns of the Perpetual Adoration of the Blessed Sacrament (A.P.) Founded in Rome, Italy, in 1807; established in U.S. in 1925. Pontifical, contemplative, major papal enclosure, solemn vows. 81 nuns in U.S., 1,500 world. Contemplation; perpetual adoration; Divine Office; making altar breads; painting. Ages 18-30, high school education. Average training: postulate one year, novitiate two years, juniorate one year. Also located in Mexico. White habit. U.S. monasteries: Expiatory Shrine of Christ the King, 145 N. Cotton Ave., El Paso, Texas (21 choir nuns, 20 lay sisters, some knowledge of Spanish required); Monastery of Perpetual Adoration, 771 Ashbury St., San Francisco 17, California (23 choir nuns, 17 lay sisters).

Religious of the Perpetual Adoration of the Blessed Sacrament (Rel. Perp. Ador.) (Society of Perpetual Adoration) Founded in Belgium in 1857; established in U.S. in 1900. Pontifical, active and contemplative, minor papal enclosure, simple vows. 13 sisters in U.S. Contemplation; retreats; catechetics; providing vestments and sacred vessels to missions; directing Archassociation of Perpetual Adoration and Work for Poor Churches; other work on occasion. Choir and lay sisters. Ages 16-35, some exceptions, high school education. Postulate six months, novitiate two years. Black habit. Motherhouse: Watermael, Belgium. U.S. address: Convent of the Perpetual Adoration, 2907 Ellicott Terrace, N.W., Washington, D.C. Novitiate in Beallsville, Maryland.

Sisters of Perpetual Adoration of the Blessed Sacrament of St. Mary of Guadalupe (A.P.G.) (Adoratrices Perpetuas de Jesus Sacramentado de Santa Maria de Guadalupe) (Adoratrices) Founded in Mexico in 1879 by Mother Maria de las Mercedes; established in U.S. in 1925. Pontifical, active and contemplative, simple vows. 357 sisters, 14 in U.S. Contemplation for all; teaching elementary and high school, college; retreats; catechetics; making altar breads, vestments, banners, etc. Ages 15-30, grade school education. Postulate six months, novitiate two years. Motherhouse: Av. Lindavista 120, Mexico 14, D.F., Mexico. U.S. address: 2701 W. Travis St., San Antonio 7, Texas.

Perpetual Adoration, see also Benedictine Sisters of Perpetual Adoration; Dominican Nuns of the Second Order of Perpetual Adoration; Franciscan Third Order; Holy Ghost of Perpetual Adoration, Sister Servants of the; Sacred Hearts of Jesus and Mary and of Perpetual Adoration, Sisters of the.

Perpetual Help, see Our Lady of Perpetual Help; Franciscan Sisters of Our Lady of Perpetual Help.

Perpetual Rosary, see Dominican Sisters of the Perpetual Rosary.

Missionary Sisters of St. Peter Claver (S.S.P.C.) Founded in Austria in 1894; established in U.S. 1914. Pontifical, active, simple vows. 18 sisters in U.S., 5 in Canada. Support of missions in Africa: collecting and shipping funds and material; missionary correspondence; editing, illustrating, and printing books and magazines in African and other languages; making vestments and altar linens; office work, bookkeeping; domestic work; catechetics; publications include *Claver Almanac, Echo from Africa, African Youth* and Polish periodicals. Ages 15-35, high school education. Postulate six months, novitiate two years. Black habit. Motherhouse: Rome, Italy. U.S. provincialate: 3703 W. Pine Blvd., St. Louis 8, Missouri. Novitiate: St. Mary's Mission House, 123 W. Isabel St., St. Paul, Minnesota. Canadian address: 89 Wells Hill Ave., Toronto 4, Ont., Canada.

Sisters of St. Philip Neri Missionary Teachers (R.F.) Third Order of St. Francis. Founded in Spain in 1858; established in U.S. in 1956. Pontifical, active, simple vows. 25 sisters in U.S., 400 world. Teaching elementary school; care of Cuban refugee children in Florida; domestic work. Age 18, high school education. Aspirancy three years. Postulate six months, novitiate two years, juniorate three years. Training schools in Spain and South America. Motherhouse: Barcelona, Spain. U.S. provincialate: Immaculate Conception Convent, 148 Richards Way, Sparks, Nevada.

Pink Sisters, see Sister-Servants of the Holy Ghost of Perpetual Adoration.

Pious School Sisters (Sch.P.) Founded in 1829 in Spain as the female branch of the Pious School Fathers; established in U.S. in 1954. Pontifical, active, simple vows. 28 sisters in U.S., 1,370 world. Teaching; domestic work in seminaries. Ages 18-25, older by dispensation, high school education for prospective teachers, eighth grade for domestic workers. Postulate six months, novitiate two years, juniorate three years. Black habit. Motherhouse: Barcelona, Spain. U.S. address: Our Lady Queen of Angels Seminary, 15101 San Fernando Mission, P.O. Box 1071, San Fernando, California.

Little Sisters of the Poor (P.S.D.P.) Founded in France in 1839; established in U.S. in 1868. Pontifical, active, simple vows, vow of hospitality along with other three vows. 835 sisters in U.S., 5,500 world. Care of aged poor; centers for volunteer aides and oblates. Oblates, ages 17-50, single or widowed, make promises not vows. No lay sisters. Ages 16-40, high school education, college desirable. Aspirancy six months, postulate six months, novitiate two years, juniorate two to four years. Black habit and bonnet. Motherhouse: St. Pern, France. U.S. provincialates: 2358 N. Sheffield Ave., Chicago 14, Illinois (280 sisters); 819 Bushwick Ave., Brooklyn 21, New York (251 sisters, 24 sisters at 1035 des Seigneurs St., Montreal, P.Q., Canada); 4291 Richmond Rd., Cleveland 22, Ohio (280 sisters). Aspirancies in Detroit, Michigan, and Los Angeles, California; novitiate in Queens Village, New York.

Little Sisters of the Poor. Founded in Spain in 1873. Pontifical, active, simple vows. 12 sisters in U.S., 2,856 world. Care of aged. Also located in Mexico and Puerto Rico. Black habit. Motherhouse: Valencia, Spain. U.S. address: Sacred Heart Home for the Aged, 3290 N.W. Seventh St., Miami 35, Florida.

Missionary Catechists of the Poor (M.C.P.) (Misioneras Catequistas de los Pobres) Founded in Mexico in 1926 by Archbishop Juan Herrera y Piña; established in U.S. in 1960. Diocesan, active, simple vows. 190 sisters, 4 in U.S. Catechetics; training catechists; retreats for women and girls. Ages 15-30. Postulate six months, novitiate two years, juniorate two years. Black habit. Motherhouse: Villa de la Paz, Apartado 422, Monterrey, N.L., Mexico. U.S. address: 117 W. Fourth St., Lancaster, Texas.

Sisters of the Poor Child Jesus (P.C.J.) Founded in Germany in 1844 to teach poor children; established in U.S. in 1924. Pontifical, active, simple vows. 54 sisters in U.S., 2,000 world. Teaching elementary school and kindergartens, teaching art and music; domestic work; catechetics; missions in Colombia and Java. Age 16, eighth grade. Aspirancy three years. Postulate one year, novitiate two years, juniorate five years. Black and white habit. Motherhouse: Simpelveld, Holland. U.S. provincialate: Our Lady of Bethlehem Convent, 4567 Olentangy River Rd., Columbus, Ohio.

Poor Clare Missionary Sisters (O.S.C.M.) (Missionaries of St. Clare of the Blessed Sacrament) (Misioneras Clarisas del Santisimo Sacramento) Third Order of St. Francis. Founded in Cuernavaca, Mexico, in 1945 by Mother Maria Ines Arias and three other Poor Clare Nuns who received permission from the Holy See to found a missionary congregation, established in U.S. in 1954. Pontifical, active and contemplative, simple vows. 300 sisters, 25 in U.S. Hospitals, dispensaries, lazarets; care of orphans; teaching elementary and high

school, normal schools, universities; training lay missionaries;
fostering the Third Order of St. Francis; missions in Japan
and Central America; daily adoration; Divine Office in choir.
Ages 17-28, high school education. Postulate six months, novitiate two and a half years, juniorate three years. Dark grey
habit, black veil. Motherhouse: Cuernavaca, Morelos, Mexico.
U.S. novitiate: 6012 N. Walnut Grove, E. San Gabriel, California.

Poor Clares of Ireland. 17 sisters in U.S. Teaching grade. U.S.
address: St. Pius X School, 37 E. Emerson, Chula Vista, California.

Poor Clare Nuns (Order of St. Clare, Second Order of St. Francis) (O.S.C.) Founded at Assisi, Italy, in 1212 by St. Francis
of Assisi and St. Clare, and **Poor Clare Colettines** (Order of
Poor Clares of the Second Order of St. Francis of the Reform
of St. Colette) (P.C.C.) St. Colette (1406-1434) added new
constitutions to the Rule of St. Clare. Established in U.S. in
1875 from Italy; in 1878 Italian and German Poor Clares
formed the Franciscan Poor Clares, distinct from the Poor
Clare Colettines. They are, however, commonly considered as
one group, the Poor Clares. Each monastery is autonomous.
Some are subject to a Father General and Franciscan Provincial. The Proto-Monastery is in Assisi, Italy. World membership is 13,000. Pontifical, contemplative, major papal enclosure,
solemn vows. An austere life of prayer and mortification: year-
round fast and abstinence, straw mattresses, barefoot except
for outdoor work, rise at midnight to pray, Divine Office, strict
Franciscan poverty—property may not be owned even in common. Work includes making altar breads, vestments, laundering church linens, printing, arts and crafts. Requirements and
training vary. Average entrance ages 16-26, to 30 for externs, no
lay sisters, high school education preferred. Postulate six to
twelve months, novitiate one year, juniorate three years, on
average. Brown habit. Write to individual monastery. Alphabetized by state.

St. Joseph Monastery of the Poor Clares, 280 State Park Drive,
Aptos, California (P.C.C.) Perpetual adoration. 22 nuns, 2
externs.

Immaculate Heart Monastery of the Poor Clares, 28210 Elena
Ave., Los Altos, California (P.C.C.) 12 nuns.

Monastery of Poor Clares, 215 E. Los Olivos St., Santa Barbara, California (P.C.C.) 17 nuns.

Christ the King Monastery, Delray Beach, Florida (O.S.C.) 6 nuns.

Monastery of the Poor Clares, 5245 So. Laflin St., Chicago 9, Illinois (P.C.C.) 24 nuns, 6 externs. Especially dedicated to the Immaculate Heart of Mary for the Russian apostolate; will found a monastery of the Eastern Byzantine Rite. Candidates are being accepted to be trained for this purpose.

Corpus Christi Monastery, 2111 So. Main St., Rockford, Illinois (P.C.C.) 24 nuns, 3 externs.

Monastery of St. Clare, 509 So. Kentucky Ave., Evansville 14, Indiana (O.S.C.) 32 nuns, 4 externs.

Maria Regina Mater Monastery, 809 W. Sycamore St., Kokomo, Indiana (P.C.C.) 6 nuns, 1 extern.

St. Clare's Monastery of the Blessed Sacrament, 720 Henry Clay Ave., New Orleans 18, Louisiana (O.S.C.) 19 nuns, 5 externs, plus a group of Poor Clare refugees from Cuba. Publication—*Unity*, a magazine for all Poor Clares.

Monastery of St. Clare, 920 Centre St., Jamaica Plain 30, Massachusetts (O.S.C.) 41 nuns, 3 externs.

Monastery of St. Clare, 236 Westford St., West Andover (Lowell P.O.), Massachusetts (O.S.C.) 15 nuns, 2 externs.

St. Clare's Monastery of the Infant Jesus, 8650 Russell Ave., So., Minneapolis 20, Minnesota (O.S.C.) 15 nuns, 2 externs.

St. Clare's Monastery, 421 So. Fourth St., Sauk Rapids, Minnesota (O.S.C.) 15 nuns, 4 externs.

Monastery of St. Clare of the Immaculate Conception, 200 Marycrest Dr., Oakville, St. Louis 29, Missouri (O.S.C.) 7 nuns.

Monastery of St. Clare, 1310 No. Twenty-ninth St., Omaha 31, Nebraska (O.S.C.) 22 nuns.

Monastery of Poor Clares, Crosswicks St., Bordentown, New Jersey (O.S.C.) 29 nuns, 5 externs.

Monastery of Our Lady of Guadalupe, Nineteenth St. & Railroad Ave., Box 285-C, Rte. 1, Roswell, New Mexico (P.C.C.) 14 nuns, 2 externs.

Monastery of Poor Clares, 142 Hollywood Ave., New York 65, New York (O.S.C.) 37 nuns.

Monastery of the Blessed Sacrament, 3501 Rocky River Drive,

Cleveland 11, Ohio (P.C.C.) 25 nuns, 8 externs. Perpetual adoration.

Monastery of St. Clare, Girard and Corinthian Aves., Philadelphia 30, Pennsylvania (O.S.C.) 31 nuns, 1 extern.

Monastery of St. Clare, 1916 No. Pleasantburg Drive, P.O. Box 5134 B, Greenville, South Carolina (O.S.C.) 15 nuns, 2 externs.

Monastery of St. Clare, 1310 Dellwood Ave., Memphis 7, Tennessee (O.S.C.) 16 nuns, 4 externs.

Bethlehem Monastery, 1110 E. Warwick Rd., Newport News, Virginia (P.C.C.) 11 nuns, 2 externs. Perpetual adoration.

Monastery of St. Clare, 4419 No. Hawthorne St., Spokane 18, Washington (O.S.C.) 11 nuns.

Immaculate Conception Monastery, 7661 Burris St., Burnaby, B.C., Canada.

St. Clare Monastery, 2050 Haultain St., Victoria, B.C., Canada. 15 nuns.

Poor Clare Monastery, Bellerive, P.Q., Canada. 34 nuns, 10 externs.

Monastère des Clarisses, Lennoxville, P.Q., Canada. 11 nuns.

Monastère des Pauvres Clarisses Colettines, Rivière-du-Loup, P.Q., Canada (P.C.C.)

Monastère Sainte-Claire, Sorel, P.Q., Canada.

Poor, see also Dominican Poor School Sisters of Penance; Franciscan Sisters of the Poor; St. Francis Seraph of the Perpetual Adoration, Poor Sisters of, under Franciscan Third Order; Jesus Christ, Poor Handmaids of; Jesus Crucified and the Sorrowful Mother, Poor Sisters of; Morsel for the Poor, Sisters of the; Mother of God and the Poor, Poor Servants of; Nazareth, Poor Sisters of; Sacred Heart of Jesus and of the Poor, Servants of the.

Congregation of the Handmaids of the Precious Blood (H.P.B.) Founded in New Mexico in 1947 by Very Rev. Gerald M. Fitzgerald, S.P., and Mother M. Dolorosa. Diocesan, active and contemplative, simple vows. 31 sisters. Contemplation; Divine Office; daily adoration; nursing in clinics for needy priests and for the poor; domestic work in bishops' residences; care of altar linens. Community's purpose is the sanctification of priests. Ages 18-45, R.N. for nursing. Postulate six months, novitiate two years. Motherhouse: Villa Cor Jesu, Jemez Springs, New Mexico.

Missionary Sisters of the Precious Blood (C.P.S.) Founded in Mariannhill, South Africa, in 1885 to work among women and children there; associated with the Mariannhill Fathers; established in U.S. in 1925. Pontifical, active, simple vows. 44 sisters in U.S., 23 in Canada, 1,250 world. Teaching, nursing, social work, domestic work, and catechetics in home missions and foreign missions in Africa and New Guinea. Ages 17-30, eighth grade education. Postulate one year, novitiate one and a half years, juniorate four years. Black habit, white in foreign missions. Motherhouse: Aarle-Rixtel, Holland. U.S. provincialate: Precious Blood Convent, New Holland Ave., P.O. Box 43, Shillington, Pennsylvania. Canadian novitiate: St. Bernard's Convent, 685 Finch Ave. W., Willowdale, Ont., Canada.

Sisters of the Precious Blood (C.PP.S.) Founded in Switzerland in 1834 by Maria Anna Brunner, a widow; motherhouse established in U.S. in 1844 by the foundress and her son, Father Brunner. Pontifical, active with contemplative branch, simple vows. 801 active sisters, 3 contemplatives. Teaching elementary and high school; domestic work in seminaries, etc.; sanitarium; care of aged and orphans; retreats; missions in Chile. Contemplatives: making rosaries and rugs, weaving cloth, knitting machine crafts. Ages 18-30, high school education preferred. Pre-postulate six months, postulate six months, novitiate two years, juniorate five years. Training for contemplation includes regular Sister Formation program and one-year probation in cloister. Grey habit, black veil. Motherhouse: Convent of Our Lady of the Precious Blood, Regina Heights, 4830 Salem Ave., Dayton 16, Ohio.

Sisters Adorers of the Precious Blood (A.P.B.) (Soeurs Adoratrices du Précieux-Sang) Founded in St. Hyacinthe, Canada, in 1861 by Aurélia Caouette; established in U.S. in 1890 in Brooklyn; union of monasteries formed in 1945. Pontifical, contemplative, minor papal enclosure, simple vows. 900 sisters. Contemplation; retreats; foreign missions in Japan. Ages 18-35, choir nun applicants must have knowledge of Latin. Postulate six months, novitiate two years, juniorate at least two and a half years. White and red habit, black veil. Apply to motherhouses or individual monasteries. Motherhouse, French-speaking: Monastery of the Precious Blood, 2520 Rue Girouard, St.

Hyacinthe, P.Q., Canada (67 nuns). Motherhouse, English-speaking: Monastery of the Precious Blood, 667 Talbot St., London, Ont., Canada (27 choir nuns, 3 lay sisters, 4 externs).
Monasteries of the Precious Blood in Canada:
922 21st Ave., S.E., Calgary, Alta., Canada. 10 nuns.
11105—One hundredth Ave., Edmonton, Alta., Canada. 29.
St. Paul, Alta., Canada. 6.
Nelson, B.C., Canada.
3651 Hudson St., Vancouver, B.C., Canada.
190 Raymond Pl., St. Boniface, Man., Canada. 16.
3507 Assiniboine Dr., Charleswood 20, Man., Canada.
Alexandria, Ont., Canada. 14.
Rosedene Ave., Hamilton, Ont., Canada. 16.
P. O. Box 834, North Bay, Ont., Canada. 11.
774 Echo Dr., Ottawa, Ont., Canada. 29 choir, 10 lay, 7 extern.
202 Margaret St., Pembroke, Ont., Canada. 9.
716 Maryland Ave., Peterborough, Ontario, Canada. 10.
113 St. Joseph St., Toronto 5, Ont., Canada. 39.
Malpeque Rd., Charlottetown, P.E.I., Canada. 19.
Christ-Roi, P.O. Villemay, Levis, P.Q., Canada.
Joliette, P.Q., Canada. 31.
Notre Dame de Grace Ward, 563 Decarie Ave., Montreal, P.Q., Canada.
Nicolet, P.Q., Canada. 43.
Sherbrooke, P.Q., Canada. 41 choir, 8 extern.
Trois-Rivières, P.Q., Canada. 37.
Gravelbourg, Sask., Canada. 17.
403 River St. W., Prince Albert, Sask., Canada. 15.
2200 Twenty-fifth Ave., Regina, Sask., Canada.
Monasteries of the Precious Blood in the U.S.
1106 State St., Lafayette, Indiana. 8.
166 State St., Portland 3, Maine. 12.
700 Bridge St., Manchester, New Hampshire. 43.
Fifty-fourth St. and Ft. Hamilton Pkwy., Brooklyn 19, New York. 53.
R.F.D. 2, Bellevue, Marywood, Ohio. 11.
1208 S.E. Seventy-sixth Ave., Portland 15, Oregon. 27 choir, 5 externs.
Precious Blood, see also Most Precious Blood.

Sisters of the Presentation, see Dominican Sisters of Charity of the Presentation of the Blessed Virgin Mary.

Sisters of the Presentation of the Blessed Virgin Mary (P.B.V.M.) (Presentation Sisters) Founded in Cork, Ireland, in 1776; established in Canada in 1833; established in U.S. in 1854 at San Francisco. Black habit. Some are independent motherhouses, some have motherhouses in Ireland. Some are pontifical, some diocesan jurisdiction, active, simple vows. 6,500 sisters in world.

St. Augustine's School, 2630 Thirty-fourth Ave. N., Birmingham 7, Alabama. 4 Presentation Sisters of Mullingar.

St. Joseph's School, 1020 Thirty-second St., Birmingham 8, Alabama. 5 Presentation Sisters of Lismore.

Holy Angels Convent, 1300 E. Cedar, Globe, Arizona. 9 Presentation. Sisters of Crosshaven, Ireland. Teaching elementary school.

Presentation Convent, 281 Masonic Ave., San Francisco 18, California. Pontifical. 293 sisters. Teaching elementary and high school; catechetics; parish visiting; domestic work. To age 30, high school education. Postulate one year, novitiate two years, juniorate five years.

Sacred Heart Convent, 150 So. Davis Dr., Warner Robins, Georgia. 6 sisters. Teaching elementary school. Motherhouse and training in Cork City, Ireland.

Presentation Convent, Liberty Hill, Oregon, Illinois. 5 sisters. Teaching elementary school. Ages 18-30, high school education. Postulate six months, novitiate two years, juniorate three years.

Mount Loretto Convent, 1229 Mt. Loretto Ave., Dubuque, Iowa. Pontifical. 260 sisters. Teaching elementary and high school, college; catechetics; domestic work. Ages 16-30, high school education. Aspirancy six months, postulate six months, novitiate two years, juniorate five years.

Holy Family Convent, 366 South St., Fitchburg, Massachusetts. 200 sisters. Teaching elementary and high school, college; catechetics. High school education. Postulate one year, novitiate two years, juniorate five years.

Our Lady of the Presentation Convent, 189 Howard Ave., Grymes Hill, Staten Island 1, New York. 107 sisters. Teaching elementary school. High school education. Postulate six months, novitiate two years.

Mount St. Joseph, R.D. 2, Box 101, Newburgh, New York. Pontifical. 212 sisters. Teaching elementary and high school, college for sisters. At least 16, high school education. Postulate one year, novitiate two years, juniorate five years.

St. Colman's Convent, Watervliet, New York. Pontifical. 88 sisters. Teaching elementary school, teaching and care of retarded; day nursery; children's home; catechetics. Ages 16-30, high school education. Novitiate two years, juniorate three years.

Sacred Heart Convent, N. Broadway, Rte. 1, Box 40, Fargo, North Dakota. 190 sisters. Teaching elementary and high school; nursing; care of orphans; catechetics; domestic work; home missions. Ages 16-30, eighth grade. Aspirancy up to four years to age 16. Postulate six months, novitiate two years, juniorate three years.

Presentation Convent, Aberdeen, South Dakota. Pontifical. 338 sisters. Teaching elementary and high school, junior college; hospitals, schools of nursing; care of aged; domestic work. Ages 17-35, high school education. Postulate six months, novitiate two years, juniorate five years.

Presentation Convent, 8931 Kenney Rd., San Antonio, Texas. 17 sisters. Teaching elementary school. Ages 16-30, high school education. Postulate six to twelve months, novitiate two years.

Presentation Convent, Cathedral Square, P.O. Box 758, St. John's, Nfld., Canada. Pontifical. 383 sisters. Teaching; social work. Age 15. Postulate at least six months, novitiate two years, juniorate five years.

Sisters of the Presentation of Mary (P.M.) (Soeurs de la Présentation) Founded in France in 1796 by Venerable Mother Anne-Marie Rivier; established in Canada in 1858; established in U.S. in 1873. Pontifical, active, simple vows. 895 sisters in U.S., 3,100 world. Ages 16-27, high school education. Postulate six months, novitiate two years, juniorate three years. Black habit. Motherhouse: France. American provincialates: *St. Hyacinthe*, P.Q., Canada. Teaching elementary school, academy, normal schools, domestic science schools, classical college; retreats.

Sherbrooke, P.Q., Canada. Teaching.

1405 Fifth Ave. W., Prince Albert, Sask., Canada. Teaching elementary schools, academy; home for girls.

209 Lawrence St., Methuen, Massachusetts. 375 sisters. Teach-

ing elementary and high school; domestic work; catechetics. 465 Mammoth Rd., Manchester, New Hampshire. 520 sisters. Teaching elementary and high school, academies, college; domestic work; missions and novitiate in Davao City, Philippines.

Presentation, see Dominican Sisters of Charity of the Presentation of the Blessed Virgin Mary; St. Mary of the Presentation, Sisters of.

Daughters of Providence (F.d.l.P.) Founded in France in 1818 by Ven. Jean-Marie de Lamennais; established in Canada in 1897. Pontifical, active and contemplative, simple vows. 185 sisters in Canada, 415 world. Teaching in public and separate elementary and high schools; commercial and domestic science schools. Age 15. Postulate six to twelve months, novitiate two years, juniorate planned in near future. Temporary vow period five years. Black habit redesigned in 1952. Motherhouse: St. Brieuc, France. Canadian provincialates: 1300 Fifteenth St. W., Prince Albert, Sask., Canada; 845 Tiffin Rd., Cité Jacques-Cartier, Montreal, P.Q., Canada.

Oblate Sisters of Providence (O.S.P.) Founded in Baltimore in 1829 as a Negro community by Rev. James Joubert, S.S., and Mother Mary Lange. Diocesan, active, simple vows. 318 sisters. Teaching elementary and high school, academy, junior college; care of orphans; catechetics; retreats; office and domestic work. Ages 15-30, high school education. Candidacy five months, postulate six months, novitiate one year, juniorate two years. Entrance date is September 8. Black habit. Motherhouse: Our Lady of Mount Providence Convent, 701 Gun Rd., Baltimore 27, Maryland.

Sisters of Providence (S.P.) Founded in Kingston, Canada, in 1861; U.S. community established in 1873, independent in 1892. Diocesan, active, simple vows. 435 sisters. Hospitals, sanitorium, schools of nursing; teaching; day nurseries; children's home; care of aged; residence for working women; rest homes; shelter for unwed mothers; domestic work; catechetics; home missions. Ages 16-30, high school education, college or special training preferred. Postulate one year, novitiate two years, juniorate five years. Black habit. Providence Motherhouse of Our Lady of Victory, Brightside, Holyoke, Massachusetts.

Sisters of Providence, see Sisters of Charity of Providence.

Sisters of Providence and of the Immaculate Conception. Founded in Belgium in 1837. 7 sisters in U.S. Teaching elementary school. Motherhouse: Belgium. U.S. address: St. Mary's School, 2750 Ygnacio Valley Rd., Walnut Creek, California.

Sisters of Providence of St. Mary-of-the-Woods (S.P.) Founded in France in 1806; established in U.S. in 1840 in Indiana by Mother Theodore Guerin. Pontifical, active, simple vows. 1,496 sisters. Teaching elementary and high school, junior colleges, college; domestic and office work; nursing; day nursery; missions in Taiwan, Formosa and Peru. Ages 16-28, high school education. Aspirancy four years. Postulate eleven months, novitiate two years, juniorate two and a half years. Black habit. Motherhouse: Providence Convent, St. Mary-of-the-Woods, Indiana.

Sisters of Providence of St. Vincent de Paul (S.P.) Founded in Canada in 1861 by four Sisters of Charity of Providence from Montreal. English-speaking. Rule of St. Vincent de Paul. Pontifical, active, simple vows. 377 sisters. Nursing; teaching elementary and high school; care of orphans, aged, chronically ill, and unemployed servants; hostels for young women; making vestments and altar breads. Ages 17-30. Postulate at least six months, novitiate two years, juniorate three years. Black habit. Motherhouse: Heathfield, Box 427, Kingston, Ont., Canada.

Providence, see St. Ann of Providence, Sisters of; Charity of Providence, Sisters of; St. Mary of Providence, Daughters of; Our Lady of Providence, Sisters of; see also Divine Providence.

Providence of God, see St. Francis of the Providence of God, Sisters of.

Sisters of the Purity of Mary (S.P.V.M.) Founded in Mexico in 1903 by Mother Julia Navarrete and Rev. Alberto Mir, S.J.; established in U.S. in 1916. Diocesan, active, simple vows. 500 sisters, 21 in U.S. Teaching; catechetics; retreats; missions among Mexican Indians. Ages 15-30, high school education preferred. Postulate six months, novitiate two years, juniorate six years. Black habit. Motherhouse: Aguascalientes, Ags., Mexico. U.S. headquarters: 410 E. Richard Ave., Kingsville, Texas.

Q

Queen of the Clergy, see Antonian Sisters of Mary, Queen of the Clergy, Congregation of; Our Lady, Queen of the Clergy, Servants of.

Queen of the Holy Rosary, see under Dominican Third Order.

R

Recluse Missionaries, see Jesus and Mary, Recluse Missionaries of.

Redemptoristine Nuns (O.SS.R.) (Order of the Most Holy Redeemer) Founded in Italy in 1731 by Ven. Maria Celeste Crostarosa and St. Alphonsus di Liguori; established in St. Anne de Beaupré, Canada, in 1905; established in U.S. at Esopus, New York, in 1957. Pontifical, contemplative, cloistered, solemn vows. 850 nuns in world. Contemplation, Divine Office sung in Latin; sewing vestments for Redemptorist Fathers; making altar linens; painting; writing. Life is not as strict as in some contemplative orders: day is from 4:30 A.M. to 9:15 P.M.; the nuns sleep on straw mattresses but do not rise at night to pray, meat is allowed. Ages 18-30, high school education preferred, college and knowledge of Latin helpful. Postulate (educandate) one year, novitiate one year. Temporary vow period three or four years. Red, white and blue habit, sandals. Canadian monasteries: Redemptoristine Monastery, St. Anne de Beaupré, P.Q., Canada (French-speaking); Monastery of the Holy Redeemer, 43 Dundonald St., Barrie, Ont., Canada (English-speaking, 30 nuns). U.S. monasteries: Mother of Perpetual Help Monastery, Esopus, New York (8 nuns); Monastery of St. Alphonsus, Liguori, Missouri (8 nuns).

Refuge, see Our Lady of Charity of Refuge, Sisters of.

Regina Pacis, see Benedictine Sisters, Regina Pacis.

Servants of Relief for Incurable Cancer (Dominican Congregation of St. Rose of Lima) (O.P.) Third Order of St. Dominic. Founded in New York City in 1896 by Mother M. Alphonsa (Rose Hawthorne Lathrop, daughter of Nathaniel

Hawthorne). Diocesan, active, simple vows. 129 sisters. Nursing in homes for indigent incurable cancer patients regardless of race or religion in Hawthorne and New York City, New York; Philadelphia, Pennsylvania; Fall River, Massachusetts; Atlanta, Georgia; St. Paul, Minnesota; and Cleveland, Ohio. Ages 18-35, high school education, nursing experience helpful but not required. Postulate six months, novitiate one year. White habit, black veil. Motherhouse: Rosary Hill Home, Hawthorne, New York.

Daughters of Reparation of the Divine Heart (F.R.D.C.) (Filles Reparatrices du Divin Coeur) Founded in Canada in 1929 by Msgr. J. A. Bourassa. 135 sisters. Diocesan, active, simple vows. Care of foundlings; domestic work for priests; missions in Africa—nursing, catechetics. Ages 15-35. Postulate six months, novitiate two years, juniorate five years. Temporary vow period five years. Motherhouse: 14135 rue Cherrier, Montreal, Pointe-aux-Trembles, P.Q., Canada.

Sisters of Reparation of the Congregation of Mary (S.R.C.M.) Founded in U.S. in 1890 by Mother Mary Zita (Ellen O'Keefe). Diocesan, active, simple vows. 33 sisters. Social work; catechetics; home for friendless women. Dedicated to helping homeless, delinquent, and working girls, providing homes for them and helping them to find work. Ages 16-35. Novitiate one year. Black habit. Motherhouse: St. Zita's Villa, Saddle River Rd., Monsey, New York.

Reparation, see Sacred Heart of Jesus for Reparation, Handmaids of the.

Sisters of the Resurrection (C.R.) Founded in Italy in 1891; established in U.S. in 1900. Pontifical, active, simple vows. 434 sisters in U.S., 1,000 world. Ages 15-35, high school education. Older women and widows by special permission. Black habit. Motherhouse: Rome, Italy. U.S. provincialates:

Resurrection Convent, 7432 Talcott Ave., Chicago 31, Illinois. 221 sisters. Teaching elementary and high school; nursing; day nursery; home for working girls; retreats; catechetics. Postulate six months, novitiate one year, juniorate three to four years until college degree is obtained.

Mount St. Joseph, Castleton-on-Hudson, New York. 213 sisters. Teaching elementary and high school, junior college for sisters; children's home; rest homes for women and girls; retreats; catechetics; nursing. Aspirancy one to four years. Postulate six months, novitiate one year, juniorate five years.

Retreat in the Cenacle, see Our Lady of the Retreat in the Cenacle, Congregation of.

Sisters of St. Rita (O.S.A.) Third Order of St. Augustine. Founded in Germany in 1911 by Augustinian Fathers; established in U.S. *circa* 1950. 4 sisters in U.S., 300 world. Domestic work in monasteries, etc., at present. Ages 18-30. Black habit. Motherhouse: Wuerzberg, Germany. U.S. address: St. Monica Convent, 4332 Douglas Ave., Racine, Wisconsin. Canadian address: % Augustinian Retreat House, King, Ont., Canada.

Daughters of St. Rita of the Immaculate Heart (D.S.R.) Founded in Kentucky in 1951 by Mother Maria. Diocesan, active, simple vows. 12 sisters. Nursing home; domestic work. Ages 16-35, high school education. Postulate six to nine months, novitiate two years. Motherhouse: St. Rita's Convent, 288 S. Main St., Versailles, Kentucky.

Rosary, see Dominican Congregation of Our Lady of the Rosary; Dominican Sisters of the Rosary.

St. Rose of Lima, see Dominican Congregation of St. Rose of Lima; Servants of Relief for Incurable Cancer.

Rural Missionaries, see Dominican Rural Missionaries.

S

Sacramentine Nuns, see Religious of the Blessed Sacrament and of Our Lady.

Mission Helpers of the Sacred Heart (M.H.S.H.) Founded in Maryland in 1890 by Mother M. Demetrias. Pontifical, active, simple vows. 240 sisters. Home missions, missions in Puerto Rico and Venezuela: catechetics, training lay catechists; parish visiting and census taking, visiting public institutions; publication—*The Mission Helpers* and religious texts, visual aids, etc. Ages 16-30, high school education. Postulate nine months, novitiate two years, juniorate three years. Black habit, white in tropics. Motherhouse: Sacred Heart Convent, 1001 W. Joppa Rd., Baltimore 4, Maryland.

Missionary Zelatrices of the Sacred Heart (M.Z.S.H.) Founded in Italy in 1894; established in U.S. in 1902. Pontifical, active, simple vows. 294 sisters in U.S., 2,700 world. Teaching kindergartens, elementary and high school; care and teaching of mentally retarded; day nurseries; care of foundlings; catechetics; social work. Ages 15-30, high school education. Aspirancy four years. Postulate six months, novitiate two years, juniorate one year. Motherhouse: Rome, Italy. U.S. provincialate: Mount Sacred Heart, 265 Benham St., Hamden 14, Connecticut.

Society Devoted to the Sacred Heart (S.D.S.H.) Founded in Hungary and Czechoslovakia in 1941; established in U.S. in 1956. Diocesan, active, simple vows. 11 sisters in U.S. Conducts Catechetical College for sisters; training lay catechists; instructing converts; home and foreign missions. Community is training sisters as doctors, nurses, hospital technicians; teachers for exceptional children; writers, editors, designers and printers. Ages 17-30, high school education. Postulate six months, novitiate one year, juniorate three years. Habit: modern dress. U.S. motherhouse: 728 S. Hudson Ave., Los Angeles 5, California.

Sacred Heart, see under Dominican Third Order; Franciscan Sisters of the Sacred Heart; Grey Nuns of the Sacred Heart; St. Joseph of the Sacred Heart, Sisters of; see also Our Lady of the Sacred Heart under O listing and under Dominican Third Order.

Religious of the Apostolate of the Sacred Heart of Jesus (R.A.) (Religiosas del Apostolado del Sagrado Corazon de Jesus) Founded in Cuba in 1891; established in U.S. in 1960. Pontifical, active, simple vows. 30 sisters in U.S., 400 world. Teaching elementary school; social work among Spanish-speaking in Buffalo and Miami. Also located in Puerto Rico. Ages 15-30, high school education for prospective teachers, less for domestic workers, age 12 for aspirancy. Postulate six to twelve months, novitiate two years, juniorate six years. Black habit, white in Florida and Latin America. Motherhouse: Madrid, Spain. U.S. address: 288 Franklin St., Buffalo 2, New York.

Congregation of Consolers of the Sacred Heart of Jesus (C.S.H.J.) Founded in Czechoslovakia in 1916; recently established in U.S. Diocesan, active. 3 sisters in U.S. Nursing the sick poor in their homes; domestic work; home missions. Postulate six months, novitiate two years. Motherhouse: Czechoslovakia. U.S. address: 237 W. Magnolia St., San Antonio 12, Texas.

Daughters of the Sacred Heart of Jesus (S.C.I.F.) (Bethlemite Sisters) Founded in 1650 in Guatemala by Ven. Pedro de Betancourt; reestablished in 1840 in Colombia; recently established in U.S. Pontifical, active, simple vows. 7 sisters in U.S., 1,000 world. Care of aged and domestic work at present in U.S. Also located in Mexico. To age 30. Aspirancy one year, postulate one year, novitiate two years, juniorate three years. Motherhouse: Bogota, Colombia. U.S. address: St. Joseph's Hostel, 330 W. Pembroke St., Dallas 8, Texas.

Handmaids of the Sacred Heart of Jesus (A.C.J.) Founded in Spain in 1877 by Blessed Raphaela Porras and her sister Dolores; established in U.S. in 1926. Pontifical, active and contemplative, simple vows. 63 sisters in U.S., 2,700 world. Contemplation, daily adoration; teaching elementary school and academies; retreats; domestic work (lay sisters); missions in Japan. Ages 16-30 for prospective teachers, to 35 for lay sisters. Aspirancy. Postulate six to nine months, novitiate two years, juniorate three to four years. Black habit. Motherhouse: Rome, Italy. U.S. provincialate: Ancilla Domini Academy, 700 E. Church Lane, Germantown, Philadelphia 44, Pennsylvania.

Missionary Sisters of the Sacred Heart of Jesus (M.S.C.) (Cabrini Sisters) Founded in Italy in 1880 by St. Frances Xavier Cabrini, the first U.S. citizen to become a saint; established in U.S. by the foundress in 1889 at the suggestion of Pope Leo XIII to aid Italian immigrants. Pontifical, active, simple vows. 510 sisters in U.S., 4,500 in world. Teaching elementary and high school, colleges; hospitals, dispensaries, schools of nursing; care of orphans; day nurseries; catechetics; retreats; missions in Canada, Brazil, Argentina, Nicaragua, England, France, Switzerland, Spain and Australia. Missionaries are volunteers. Ages 16-25, high school education preferred. Postulate six months, novitiate one year. Black habit. Motherhouse: Rome, Italy. U.S. motherhouse: Columbus Hospital, 227 E. Nineteenth St., New York, New York.

Missionary Society of the Sacred Heart of Jesus (M.S.C.J.) Founded in Spain in 1942; established in U.S. in 1958. Pontifical, active and contemplative, simple vows. 15 sisters in U.S., 150 world. Teaching elementary school, catechetics, social work, publication—*Forward* in U.S.; teaching, care of orphans, nurses and doctors for hospitals and dispensaries, catechetics, and social work in missions in India, the Congo, and Peru; contemplation, Little Office of the Blessed Virgin. No lay sisters. Ages 15-35, high school education. Aspirancy. Postulate six months, novitiate two years, juniorate one year. Temporary vows annually for five years. Entrance dates: February 2 and June 21. Before leaving for foreign missions, the sister is allowed one week's visit at home. White cotton habit in Texas and warm climates, black wool in cooler climates, secular clothes when work requires it. Motherhouse: Madrid, Spain. U.S. novitiate: Queen of Missions Convent, Rte. 3, Box 75, San Angelo, Texas.

Oblate Sisters of the Sacred Heart of Jesus (O.S.H.J.) Founded in Rome, Italy, in 1894; established in U.S. in 1949. Pontifical, active and contemplative, simple vows. 22 sisters in U.S., 500 world. Life of reparation and prayer for the clergy. Perpetual adoration, Office of the Eucharistic Heart of Jesus; teaching elementary school, academy; retreats; catechetics. Ages 15-30, junior high school education. Postulate six months, novitiate two years. White habit. Motherhouse: Rome, Italy. U.S. provincialate: Villa Maria Teresa, 50 Warner Rd., Hubbard, Ohio.

Oblates of the Sacred Heart of Jesus (O.S.H.) Founded in France in 1843; established in U.S. in 1955. Pontifical, active, simple vows. 14 sisters in U.S., 1,000 world. Teaching; catechetics to Spanish-speaking. Also located in Mexico, Nicaragua, Guatemala and El Salvador. To age 25, eighth grade. Postulate six to twelve months, novitiate one year, juniorate one year. Training in U.S. and Central America. Motherhouse: Mont Lucon, France. U.S. address: Our Lady of Guadalupe Academy, 3233 Ellicott St., N.W., Washington 8, D.C.

Sisters of the Sacred Heart of Jesus. Founded in Sicily in 1889. 8 sisters in Canada. Teaching. Motherhouse: Ragusa, Italy. Canadian address: 254 Hellems Ave., Welland, Ont., Canada.

Society of the Sacred Heart of Jesus (R.S.C.J.) (Religious of the Sacred Heart) Founded in France in 1800 by St. Madeleine Sophie Barat; established in U.S. in 1818 at St. Charles, Missouri, by Blessed Rose Philippine Duchesne. Pontifical, active and contemplative, simple vows. 977 sisters in U.S., 7,000 world. Teaching; domestic work; retreats; catechetics; missions in Puerto Rico, Chile, Brazil, Colombia, Japan, Korea, Formosa, India and Africa—missionaries become members of the vicariate to which they are sent. Also located in Mexico. To age 30, high school education for choir sisters. Postulate six months, novitiate two years, juniorate five years, "second novitiate" of six months just before final profession. Lay sisters: postulate six months, novitiate two years. Black habit. Motherhouse: Rome, Italy. U.S. vicariates:

San Francisco College for Women, Lone Mountain, San Francisco 18, California. 179 sisters. Day nurseries, kindergartens, elementary and high school, college.

Convent of the Sacred Heart, 9101 Rockville Pike, Washington 14, D.C. 179 sisters. Teaching elementary and high school, college.

Convent of the Sacred Heart, 6250 Sheridan Rd., Chicago 40, Illinois. 173 sisters. Teaching elementary and high school, college.

Convent of the Sacred Heart, 334 No. Taylor Ave., St. Louis 8, Missouri. 155 sisters. Teaching elementary school, academies, college.

Convent of the Sacred Heart, Kenwood, Albany 2, New York. 291 sisters. Teaching academies, normal school, school of liturgical music, college; conducting teachers' guilds and clubs.

Missionary Catechists of the Sacred Heart of Jesus and the Immaculate Heart of Mary (M.C.) (Violetas) Founded in Mexico in 1929; established in U.S. in 1943. Diocesan, active, simple vows. 20 sisters in U.S. Catechetics. Motherhouse: Tlalpán, Mexico 22 D.F., Mexico. U.S. address: Our Lady of Sorrows Mission Center, 209 W. Murray St., Victoria, Texas.

Sisters of the Sacred Heart of Jesus of St. Jacut (S.S.C.J.) Founded in France in 1816; established in U.S. in 1903. Pontifical, active, simple vows. 101 sisters in U.S., 1,800 world. Teaching elementary school; domestic work; catechetics; nursing; missions in South America, Africa and England. To age 30. Aspirancy three years. Postulate six to nine months, novitiate two years. Black habit. Motherhouse: St. Jacut, Brittany, France. U.S. provincialate: Mt. Sacred Heart Convent, 606 Mt. Sacred Heart Rd., San Antonio 12, Texas. Canadian provincialate: Avenue des Oblats, Ottawa 1, Ont., Canada.

Servants of the Sacred Heart of Jesus and of the Poor
(S.S.H.J.P.) Founded in Mexico in 1885 by Rev. José de
Yermo y Parres; established in U.S. in 1907. Pontifical, active,
simple vows. 610 sisters, 70 in U.S. Teaching; nursing; social
work; care of orphans; day nurseries; catechetics; domestic
work; home missions; missions in Colombia, Honduras,
Guatemala, Cuba and Italy. Ages 15-30, eighth grade. Aspir-
ancy one to two years. Postulate six months, novitiate two
years, juniorate six years. Training in Mexico, U.S. and Rome.
Motherhouse: Apartado 92, 3 Poniente 1512, Puebla, Pue.
Mexico. U.S. address: Sacred Heart House of Studies, 3722 El
Paso St., San Antonio 7, Texas.

Handmaids of the Sacred Heart of Jesus for Reparation (A.R.)
Founded in Italy in 1918; established in U.S. in 1958. Pontifical, active and contemplative, simple vows. 4 sisters in U.S.,
330 world. Contemplation; teaching; social work; catechetics;
retreats; day nursery. Ages 15-26. Postulate six months, novitiate two years. Motherhouse: Italy. U.S. address: Sacred Heart
Convent, 725 N. Fourth St., Steubenville, Ohio.

Sacred Heart of Jesus, see Charity of the Sacred Heart of Jesus,
Daughters of; Dominican Third Order; also Most Sacred Heart
of Jesus.

Missionary Oblates of the Sacred Heart and Mary Immaculate
(M.O.) (Soeurs Missionnaires Oblates du Sacré-Coeur et de
Marie-Immaculée) Founded in Canada in 1904 by Archbishop
Louis Langevin. Pontifical, active. 283 sisters. Teaching in public and private schools, kindergarten, elementary and high
school, homemaking and vocation school; homes for working
girls; Indian mission; visiting and nursing the sick; catechetics;
religious correspondence courses for children; making altar
breads and vestments; bookbinding; arts and crafts; mission in
Brazil. Postulate six months, novitiate two years. Temporary
vow period five years. Entrance dates February 18 and August
18. Motherhouse: 601 Aulneau St., St. Boniface, Man.,
Canada.

Missionaries of the Sacred Heart and Our Lady of Guadalupe
(M.S.C.) Founded in Guadalajara, Mexico, in 1926; established in U.S. in 1956. 400 sisters. Teaching elementary and
high school; general and mental hospitals; catechetics and
social work among Mexican Indians; domestic work in semi-

naries, etc. In U.S. Little Office of the Blessed Virgin in Latin. Choir and lay sisters. To age 30. Aspirancy. Postulate six months. Novitiate two years. Temporary vow period six years. Entrance dates in January and June. White habit. Motherhouse: Ceylan 279, Colonia Cosmopolita, Mexico City, Mexico. U.S. address: 401 N.E. Madison, Peoria, Illinois.

Sacred Hearts, see Holy Union of the Sacred Hearts, Religious of the.

Little Sisters of the Workers of the Sacred Hearts of Jesus and Mary (P.O.S.S.C.C.) Founded in Italy in 1902; established in U.S. in 1948. Pontifical, active, simple vows. 21 sisters in U.S. Domestic work. Motherhouse: Rome, Italy. U.S. address: Sacred Hearts Convent, 117 Hope St., Stamford, Connecticut.

Sisters of the Sacred Hearts of Jesus and Mary (S.H.J.M.) Founded in England in 1903; established in U.S. in 1953. Pontifical, active, simple vows. 30 sisters in U.S., 500 world. Teaching elementary and high school; catechetics; social work; nursing. Ages 18-30, high school education. Postulate six months, novitiate two years, juniorate six years. Motherhouse: Essex, England. U.S. provincialate: Sacred Heart Convent, 88 Hecker Pass Rd., Watsonville, California.

Sisters of the Sacred Hearts of Jesus and Mary. Teaching. Motherhouse: Senneterre, P.Q., Canada.

Sisters of the Sacred Hearts of Jesus and Mary and of Perpetual Adoration (SS.CC.) Founded in France in 1797; established in U.S. in 1908. Pontifical, active and contemplative, minor papal enclosure, simple vows. 158 sisters in U.S., 1,500 world. Contemplation, vocal prayer, perpetual adoration. Postulate six months, novitiate one and a half years, juniorate four to five years. White habit. Choir, school, lay and oblate sisters.

U.S. provincialate: Regina Pacis, 1120 Fifth Ave., Honolulu, 16, Hawaii. 125 sisters. Teaching kindergarten, elementary school, academy; domestic work; retreats. Ages 16-50, high school education.

Regionalate: 330 Main St., Fairhaven, Massachusetts. 33 sisters. Teaching kindergarten, elementary and high school, academy. Ages 15-28, high school education for prospective teachers.

Canadian address: Pont Viau, P.Q., Canada.

Sacred Hearts of Jesus and Mary, see Franciscan Sisters, Daughters of the Sacred Hearts of Jesus and Mary.

Sisters of La Sagesse, see Daughters of Wisdom.

Religious of the Sacred Heart of Mary (R.S.H.M.) Founded in France in 1848; established in U.S. in 1877; established in Canada in 1943. Pontifical, active, simple vows. 848 sisters in U.S., 2,060 world. Teaching elementary school, academies, colleges; domestic work; missions in Cuernavaca, Mexico, South America and Africa. Ages 15-35, high school education. Postulate six months, novitiate one year, juniorate three years. Blue habit, black veil. Motherhouse: Beziers, France. Generalate: Rome, Italy. Eastern U.S. provincialate: Marymount, Tarrytown, New York (657 sisters). Western U.S. provincialate: Marymount, 6717 West Palos Verdes Drive So., Palos Verdes Estates, California (191 sisters).

Salesian Sisters of St. John Bosco (F.M.A.) (Daughters of Mary Help of Christians) Founded in Italy in 1872 by St. John Bosco and St. Mary Mazzarello; established in U.S. in 1908. Pontifical, active, simple vows. 267 sisters in U.S., 17,150 world. Teaching elementary and high school; day nurseries; care of orphans; catechetics; summer camps; domestic work; social work; foreign missions (volunteers only) in Canada—20 sisters, and Australia. Also located in Mexico and Philippines. To age 25, some exceptions, high school education preferred. Aspirancy one year, postulate six months, novitiate two years. Black habit. Motherhouse: Turin, Italy. U.S. provincialate: 41 Ward St., Paterson 1, New Jersey. Canadian novitiate: Pointe Verte, N.B., Canada.

Salvatorian Sisters, see Sisters of the Divine Saviour.

Sisters of the Company of the Savior (C.S.) Founded in Spain in 1952; established in U.S. in 1962. Diocesan, active, simple vows. 4 sisters in U.S., 73 world. Teaching elementary school; parish visiting. Age 15. Postulate six months, novitiate two years, juniorate five years. Black habit, white in warm mission countries. Motherhouse: Barcelona, Spain. U.S. address: St. Mary's Convent, 500 Pembroke St., Bridgeport, Connecticut.

Scalabrini Sisters, see Missionary Sisters of St. Charles Borromeo.

School, see Notre Dame, School Sisters of; Pious School Sisters.

School Sisters of St. Francis, see Franciscan Third Order.

Sisters of Service (S.O.S.) Founded in Canada in 1922 by Redemptorist Fathers A. T. Coughlan and George T. Daly to serve Catholics in rural and isolated areas; established in U.S. in 1939. Diocesan, active, simple vows. 121 sisters. Teaching, including Indian mission school; small rural hospitals, visiting the sick in their homes; parish social work; catechetics; homes for girls in large cities; home and employment bureau for domestic workers; meeting immigrants at ports. Ages 17-30, high school education. Postulate one year, novitiate two years. Grey dress and cap. Motherhouse: 2 Wellesley Place, Toronto 5, Ont., Canada. U.S. address: 608 Ninth St. S., Fargo, North Dakota (religious correspondence school for children in isolated areas, 4 sisters).

Servite Sisters, see Servants of Mary.

Mother Seton, see Charity, Mother Seton Sisters of.

Sisters of Seven Dolors, see following Sisters of Our Lady of Charity of Refuge.

Seven Dolors, see Holy Cross and of the Seven Dolors, Sisters of the.

Nursing Sisters of the Sick Poor, see Little Sisters of the Assumption; Sisters of the Infant Jesus.

Sick Poor, see Dominican Sisters of the Sick Poor.

Snows, see Our Lady of the Snows, Oblates of.

Sisters of Social Service. Founded in Hungary in 1923, Los Angeles foundation opened in 1926, independent community in 1953. Diocesan, active, simple vows. 139 sisters. Social work in diocesan agencies and parishes; home visiting; settlement houses; girls' camps; homes for working girls; day nurseries; nursing; catechetics; retreats; religious correspondence course; training lay volunteers; missions in Formosa and Mexico. Ages 18-30, high school education. Postulate six months, novitiate two years. Temporary vow period six years. Grey uniform; hat and veil for outdoors. Motherhouse: 1120 Westchester Place, Los Angeles 19, California. Canadian novitiate: Mount Cenacle, Fennell Ave. W., Hamilton, Ont., Canada.

Sisters of the Sorrowful Mother (S.S.M.) Third Order of St. Francis. Founded in Italy in 1883; established in U.S. in 1889. Pontifical, active, simple vows. 621 sisters in U.S., 949 world. Nursing and allied work, hospitals, sanatorium, schools of nursing; teaching elementary and high school; care of orphans, aged, convalescents; catechetics; missions in British West Indies. Ages 13-16 for aspirancy, 17-30 for postulate. Aspirancy two years. Postulate six months, novitiate two years. Grey habit, black veil. Motherhouse: Rome, Italy. U.S. commissariat and novitiate: Convent of the Sorrowful Mother, 6618 N. Teutonia Ave., Milwaukee 9, Wisconsin. Aspirancy and future provincialate: 2007 So. St. Louis, Tulsa 20, Oklahoma.

Sorrowful Mother, see Jesus Crucified and the Sorrowful Mother, Poor Sisters of.

Sorrows, see Franciscan Missionary Sisters of Our Lady of Sorrows; Our Lady of Sorrows, Sisters of.

T

St. Teresa, see Carmelite Sisters of the Third Order of St. Teresa.

Society of St. Teresa of Jesus (S.T.J.) (Teresian Sisters) Founded in Spain in 1876; established in U.S. in 1910. Pontifical, active, simple vows. 118 sisters in U.S., 3,000 world. Teaching elementary school, academies; care of orphans; domestic work; missions in Nicaragua. Also located in Mexico. Ages 15-30, high school education for prospective teachers. Postulate six to nine months, novitiate two years, juniorate five years. Brown habit, black veil. Motherhouse: Barcelona, Spain. North American provincialate: St. Teresa's Academy, 4018 S. Presa St., San Antonio 10, Texas.

St. Theresa, see Carmelite Tertiary Sisters of St. Theresa of Jesus, Discalced; Eucharistic Missionary Sisters of St. Theresa.

St. Therese, see Carmelite Sisters of St. Therese of the Infant Jesus.

St. Thomas Aquinas, see Dominican Third Order.

Sisters of St. Thomas of Villanova (S.T.de V.) Founded in France in 1661; established in U.S. in 1948. Pontifical, active, simple vows. 19 sisters in U.S., 800 world. Nursing; retreats; domestic work; missions in Africa. Ages 18-30, high school education. Aspirancy two years. Postulate six to eight months, novitiate two years, juniorate three years. Black habit, white for nursing and missions. Motherhouse: Neuilly-sur-Seine, France. U.S.

regionalate: Notre Dame Convalescent Home, West Rocks
Rd., Norwalk, Connecticut.

Trappistines, see Cistercian Nuns of the Strict Observance.

Trinitarians, see Sisters of the Most Holy Trinity.

U

Order of St. Ursula *(Ursulines) Founded in Italy in 1535 by St.
Angela Merici, first order of women dedicated to the education of girls. World membership in all branches is approximately 15,000. Ursuline nuns first arrived in Canada from
France in 1639, led by Ven. Marie of the Incarnation (Marie
Guyart). French Ursulines founded the first Catholic school
for girls in the U.S. in 1727 at New Orleans, Louisiana. Fourth
vow of the instruction of young girls.*

**Society of the Sisters of St. Ursula of the Blessed Virgin
(U.T.S.V.)** (Company of St. Ursula) Founded in France in
1606 by Venerable Anne de Xainctonge; established in U.S. in
1901. Pontifical, active, simple vows. 73 sisters in U.S., 200
world. Teaching elementary school, academies; catechetics;
missions in Africa. Ages 17-35, high school education. Aspirancy one month, postulate nine months, novitiate one and a
half years, juniorate four years. Black habit. Generalate: Tours,
France. U.S. motherhouse: Convent of St. Ursula, 26 Grove
St., Kingston, New York. Canadian motherhouse: Maxwell at
Oxford St., Sarnia, Ont., Canada.

Ursuline Nuns of the Canadian Union (O.S.U.) Founded in Canada from Tours, France, in 1639 by Venerable Marie of the
Incarnation (Marie Guyart). Canadian Union formed in
1953. Pontifical, active and contemplative, solemn vows. 1,000
members. Teaching elementary school, academies, college;
missions in Japan and South America. Lay sisters do manual
work and do not recite the Divine Office. High school education. Postulate six months, novitiate two years, juniorate three
years. Black habit. Generalate: 18 Donnacone St., P.O. Box
760, Quebec 4, P.Q., Canada. Provincialates: Loretteville,
P.Q., Canada; Rimouski, P.Q., Canada; Trois-Rivières, P.Q.,
Canada (established in 1697).

Ursuline Religious of the Chatham Union (O.S.U.) Founded in

Italy in 1535; established in London, Ont., Canada in 1860 by the Ursuline Congregation of Paris. Pontifical, active, simple vows. 442 sisters. Teaching elementary school, academy, school for retarded children, schools of music, college; social work; catechetics; mission in Peru. Ages 18-30, high school education for prospective teachers. Aspirancy one year, postulate one year, novitiate two years, juniorate five years. Motherhouse: The Pines, Chatham, Ont., Canada. U.S. address: Ursuline Convent of Our Lady of the Straits, St. Ignace, Michigan.

Ursulines of Jesus (U.J.) (Dames de Chavagnes) Founded in France in 1802; established in Canada in 1911. Pontifical, active, simple vows. 50 sisters in Canada, 1,400 world. Teaching; social work; catechetics; mission in Chile. Age 16, high school education. Postulate six months, novitiate two years, juniorate five years. Black and white habit. Motherhouse: Chavagnes-en-Paillers, France. Eastern provincialate, French novitiate: 1688 rue Cartier, La Fleche, P.Q., Canada. Western provincialate, English novitiate: 10647 Eighty-first Ave., Edmonton, Alta., Canada.

Ursuline Sisters of Mount Calvary (O.S.U.) Founded in Italy in 1535; established in Germany in 1838; established in U.S. in North Dakota in 1910. Pontifical, active. 71 sisters in U.S., 420 world. Teaching elementary and high school; nursing; catechetics. Age 17, two years high school education for postulate. Aspirancy. Postulate one year, novitiate two years, juniorate three years. Temporary vow period three years. Black habit. Motherhouse: Mount Calvary, Germany. U.S. regionalate: Holy Spirit Convent, 1026 N. Douglas Ave., Belleville, Illinois.

Ursuline Nuns of the Congregation of Paris (O.S.U.) Founded in Italy in 1535; Congregation of Paris formed in 1572. Black habit. Each motherhouse is independent.

Ursuline Motherhouse of Our Lady of Lourdes, E. Miami St., Paola, Kansas (1895). 116 sisters. Diocesan, active, simple vows. Teaching elementary and high school, academy; domestic work; care of deaf. Age 16, high school education. Postulate six months, novitiate two years, juniorate three years.

Ursuline Motherhouse of the Immaculate Conception, 3115 Lexington Rd., Louisville 6, Kentucky. 560 sisters. Teaching elementary and high school, academies, normal school, college; care of orphans. Ages 16-30, high school education. Postulate six to nine months, novitiate two years, juniorate five years.

Mt. St. Joseph Ursuline Motherhouse, Maple Mount, Kentucky. 502 sisters. Pontifical, active, simple vows. Teaching elementary and high school, academies, college. To age 30, high school education. Postulate six to twelve months, novitiate two years, juniorate two years.

St. Ursula Convent, 1339 E. McMillan St., Walnut Hills, Cincinnati 6, Ohio. (1910) 80 sisters. Pontifical, active, simple vows. Teaching elementary school, academy, choir school; catechetics. To age 30, high school education. Postulate six to eleven months, novitiate two years, juniorate five years.

Ursuline Motherhouse, 2600 Lander Rd., Cleveland 24, Ohio. (1850) 427 sisters. Pontifical, active, simple vows. Teaching elementary school, academies, college. To age 30, high school education. Postulate one year, novitiate two years, juniorate three years.

Ursuline Convent of the Immaculate Heart of Mary, Brown County, St. Martin, Ohio. (1845) 73 sisters. Pontifical, active, simple vows. Teaching elementary school, academies, Sunday schools, junior college; summer camp. To age 30, high school education. Postulate eleven months, novitiate two years, juniorate three years.

Ursuline Convent of the Sacred Heart, 2413 Collingwood Blvd., Toledo 10, Ohio. (1884) 249 sisters. Pontifical, active, simple vows. Teaching elementary school, junior military academy, high school, academies, college, school of music; summer camp. To age 30, high school education. Aspirancy four years. Postulate six to twelve months, novitiate two years, juniorate three years.

Ursuline Motherhouse, 3650 Logan Way, Youngstown 5, Ohio. (1874) 178 sisters. Pontifical, active, simple vows. Teaching elementary and high school. Ages 17-30, high school education. Postulate six to twelve months, novitiate two years, juniorate three years.

Ursuline Nuns of the Roman Union (O.S.U.) Founded in Italy in 1535; established in U.S. in 1727 at New Orleans; Roman Union formed in 1899. Pontifical, active and contemplative, semi-cloistered, solemn vows. 1,324 in U.S., 7,000 world.

Teaching; catechetics to blind and retarded children; training
lay catechists; home missions in Montana and Alaska; foreign
missions in Latin America, Africa, Far East and Greece. Also
located in Mexico. Divine Office in choir. Ages 18-30, high
school education, some college preferred. Postulate six months,
novitiate two years, juniorate five years, six-month tertianship
in Rome ten years after profession, second juniorate of two to
four months. Black habit, white in tropics. Generalate: Rome,
Italy. U.S. provincialates:

Western provincialate: 400 Angela Dr., Santa Rosa, California.
143 nuns. Teaching elementary and high school; Indian and
Eskimo mission schools.

Northeastern provincialate: 65 Lowder St., Dedham, Massachusetts. 197 nuns. Teaching elementary and high school.

Central provincialate: 399 S. Sappington Rd., Kirkwood 22,
Missouri. 611 nuns. Teaching kindergarten, elementary school,
academies, college.

Eastern provincialate: Two hundredth St. and Marion Ave.,
New York 58, New York. 373 nuns. Teaching elementary
school, academies, college.

Ursuline Nuns of Tildonk, Belgium (R.U.) Founded in Italy in
1535; established in Belgium in 1831; established in U.S. in
1924. Diocesan, active, simple vows. 97 sisters in U.S., 900
world. Teaching elementary school; catechetics; missions in
India and the Congo. To age 30, high school education. Postulate six to twelve months, novitiate two years, juniorate three
years. Generalate: Haecht, Belgium. U.S. provincialate: Ursuline Motherhouse, Blue Point, L.I., New York. Canadian
vicariate and novitiate: Bruxelles, Man., Canada.

V

Venerini Sisters (M.P.V.) Founded in Italy in 1685 by Blessed
Rosa Venerini; established in U.S. in 1909. Pontifical, active,
simple vows. 78 sisters in U.S., 800 world. Teaching elementary
and high school; day nurseries; catechetics; domestic work.
Ages 16-30, high school education. Aspirancy. Postulate six
months, novitiate two years. Black habit. Motherhouse: Rome,

Italy. U.S. provincialate: Venerini Academy, 23 Edward St., Worcester 5, Massachusetts.

Missionary Sisters of Verona (M.S.V.) Founded in Italy in 1875; established in U.S. in 1950. Pontifical, active, simple vows. 33 sisters in U.S., 2,000 world. Home and foreign missions—care of aged; maternity home; nurseries; social work; domestic work. Ages 17-27, high school education. Postulate six months, novitiate two years, juniorate two years. Mother-house: Italy. Black habit. U.S. provincialate: 1307 Lakeside Ave., Richmond 28, Virginia.

Victory, see Our Lady of Victory Missionary Sisters.

St. Vincent de Paul, see Sisters of Charity; Providence of St. Vincent de Paul, Sisters of.

Vincentian, see Charity, Vincentian Sisters of.

Violetas, see Missionary Catechists of the Sacred Heart of Jesus and the Immaculate Heart of Mary.

Virgin of Dolors, see Bethany, Consolers of the Virgin of Dolors, Sisters of.

Visitandines, see Visitation Nuns.

Visitation Nuns (V.H.M.) (Order of the Visitation of Holy Mary) (Visitandines) Founded in France in 1610 by St. Francis de Sales and St. Jane de Chantal; established in U.S. in 1799 in Washington, D.C.; confederated in 1952. Pontifical, contemplative, solemn vows. This order was founded to make the contemplative life possible for those unable to enter the more austere contemplative orders. Contemplation; perpetual adoration; Little Office of the Blessed Virgin in choir; teaching; manual labor; private religious instruction; fostering devotion to the Sacred Heart through the Guard of Honor of the Sacred Heart; making altar breads and linens and vestments; printing; painting. There is no age limit but there is a limit to the number of older candidates in each monastery. Widows are accepted. Eighth grade education. Average training: aspirancy one week, postulate six months, novitiate one year, juniorate three years. Black habit. General motherhouse: Annecy, France. Each monastery is independent and under the jurisdiction of the local Ordinary.

First federation of North America. Major pontifical enclosure. Write to Monastery of the Visitation:

2002 Bancroft Pkwy., Wilmington 6, Delaware. 29 nuns.

1820 Ponce de Leon Ave., N.E., Atlanta 7, Georgia. 12 nuns, 2 externs.

9001 Old Georgetown Rd., Bethesda 14, Maryland. 21 nuns.

Two hundred fifty-sixth St. and Arlington Ave., Riverdale-on-Hudson, New York 71, New York. 29 nuns, 4 externs.

1745 Parkside Blvd., Toledo 7, Ohio. 28 nuns, 4 externs.

5820 City Line Ave., Philadelphia 31, Pennsylvania. 23 nuns.

2209 E. Grace St., Richmond 23, Virginia. 32 nuns.

103, 1 Ere. rue, Comte Kamouraska, St. Anne-de-la-Pocatiere, P.Q., Canada.

114 Richmond Rd., Ottawa 3, Ont., Canada. 33 nuns.

Second federation of North America. Minor pontifical enclosure except Mobile, Alabama, which is major enclosure. Monastery of the Visitation:

2300 Spring Hill Ave., Mobile 17, Alabama. 34 nuns. (major enclosure).

1500 Thirty-fifth St., Georgetown, Washington 7, D.C. 51 nuns. Teaching academy and junior college.

2000 Sixteenth Ave., Rock Island, Illinois. 41 nuns. Teaching kindergarten, elementary school, academy.

Visitation Academy, Georgetown, Kentucky. 33 nuns, 3 externs. Teaching academy.

5712 Roland Ave., Baltimore 10, Maryland. 27 nuns. Teaching kindergarten and elementary school.

Mount de Sales, Catonsville 28, Maryland. 27 nuns. Teaching high school.

200 E. Second St., Frederick, Maryland. 26 nuns. Teaching kindergarten and elementary school.

720 Fairmount Ave., St. Paul 5, Minnesota. 41 nuns. Teaching elementary and high school.

3020 N. Ballas Rd., St. Louis 31, Missouri. 59 nuns. Teaching kindergarten, elementary and high school.

Elfindale, Springfield, Missouri. 20 nuns. Teaching kindergarten and elementary school.

Ridge Blvd. and Eighty-ninth St., Brooklyn 9, New York. 49 nuns. Teaching elementary school.

Rte. 5, Box 1370, Tacoma 22, Washington. 21 nuns. Retreats for laywomen.

1600 Murdock Ave., De Sales Heights, Parkersburg, West Virginia. 28 nuns. Teaching elementary and high school.
Wheeling, West Virginia. 46 nuns. Teaching academy.
Sisters of the Visitation of the Congregation of the Immaculate Heart of Mary (S.V.M.) Founded in Iowa in 1952 by Most Rev. Leo Binz. Diocesan, active, simple vows. 51 sisters. Teaching elementary school, academy; catechetics. To age 35, high school education. Postulate one year, novitiate two years, juniorate five years. Motherhouse: Visitation Convent, 900 Alta Vista St., Dubuque 3, Iowa.

W

White Sisters, see Daughters of the Holy Ghost; Missionary Sisters of our Lady of Africa.
Daughters of Wisdom (D.W.) (Montfort Sisters) (Sisters of La Sagesse) Founded in France in 1703 by St. Louis de Montfort; established in U.S. in 1904 after religious orders were expelled from France. Pontifical, active, simple vows. 405 sisters in U.S., 5,000 world. Teaching elementary and high school, academies, college, school for retarded children, teaching the blind, deaf and dumb; hospitals, nursing orthopedic and polio cases, school of nursing; care of orphans and aged; domestic work; missions in Africa and Latin America. Little Office of the Blessed Virgin in choir. Ages 16-30, high school education. Postulate six months, novitiate one year, juniorate one year. Grey habit. Generalate: Rome, Italy. Motherhouse: Vendee, France. U.S. provincialate: 101-19 One hundred-third St., Ozone Park 16, L.I., New York. Canadian provincialate: Convent of Notre Dame de Lourdes, 418 Montreal Rd., Ottawa, Ont., Canada. Teaching elementary school, academies; hospitals, sanatoriums.

X

Xaverian Missionary Sisters of Mary, see Missionary Sisters of Mary.

Xavier Mission Sisters, see Catholic Mission Sisters of St. Francis Xavier.

Z

Zelatrices, see Sacred Heart, Missionary Zelatrices of the.

Secular Institutes

Caritas Christi. Founded in Marseilles, France, in 1938; established in U.S. and Canada in 1954. Pontifical. 75 members in U.S., over 1,500 in world. By special dispensation, this institute has no community houses; members remain at home and at regular job, including during training. Prayer includes daily Mass, meditation, rosary, Compline in English, annual retreats. Members are teachers, secretaries, social workers, often as assistants in diocesan chanceries, Catholic Charity bureaus, etc., and all professions and occupations, manual and intellectual. They are encouraged to take part in diocesan and parish organizations. Ages 18-45, single or widowed, no special educational requirement, ill health not necessarily an impediment. Preparatory training at least six months, two years of doctrinal and spiritual formation. Vows, called "dedication" annually for five years following training, then perpetual. No habit. Membership is ordinarily kept secret except by permission, and anyone considering membership is asked not to discuss her intention except with her spiritual director or confessor. Write to: Very Rev. Patrick M. J. Clancy, O.P., 7200 Division St.,

River Forest, Illinois; Rev. Bennand Mailhiot, O.P., 2765
Chemain St. Catherine, Montreal 26, P.Q., Canada.

Institute of Daughters of the Immaculate Heart of Mary (Cordimarian Filiation) Founded by St. Anthony Claret in Barcelona, Spain, in 1850; established in U.S. in 1952. (Teaching sisters of Mary Immaculate, religious institute, also founded by St. Anthony Claret.) Pontifical. World membership over 2,000. Types of membership: consecrated, associated, or cooperators. Members ordinarily live in community. Prayer includes meditation, visit to the Blessed Sacrament, monthly day of recollection, etc. Members work individually in their professions, or in groups in catechetics, distributing Catholic literature, conducting social programs for youths, etc. Ages 15-40, under or over with dispensation, eighth grade education, single or widowed (married women may be cooperators), sickly and handicapped admitted if they can help themselves and earn a living. Three years' training while candidate continues at regular job or studies. Some take three vows, others one vow and promises; eventually perpetual vows and promises are taken. No habit. Membership kept secret. Write to: Director of Vocations, 4541 So. Ashland Ave., Chicago 9, Illinois.

Ancelles of Jesus-Maria (Handmaids of Jesus and Mary) Founded in St. Cloud, France, in 1947. Types of membership: Residents live together in homes called "Foyers"; semi-residents work outside while living in the Foyers; non-residents live in the world. Most members are non-residents. Prayer includes Mass, Office, and meditation. The institute does not have specific works for which it is responsible. Members work as family assistants, social workers, saleswomen, farm workers, nurses, governesses, professors, secretaries and all types of employment. Those who have insufficient health for a religious institute but who are not invalids, and those who have had to leave a religious institute may also apply. Vows of chastity and obedience, promise of poverty compatible with life in the world. No special habit. Members in Canada and U.S. Write to: Superior General, Ancelles de Jesus-Maria, Le Couarail, 46 bis rue Louis-Blériot, Buc (Seine and Oise), France.

Missionaries of the Kingship of Christ. Founded in Italy in 1919; established in U.S. in 1952, Canada 1958. Pontifical. 60 members in Canada, 3,400 world. Three branches, laywomen, laymen, and diocesan clergy. Members do not live in community. Two hours of prayer daily including Mass, meditation, Franciscan Office or Divine Office or Little Office of the Blessed Virgin, rosary or Franciscan Crown (seven decades, mysteries of the seven joys of Our Lady), etc. Work is done through the professions of individual members, such as medicine, domestic work, secretarial work, social work, etc., and organized Catholic Action; the institute has no group apostolate. Ages 21-35, single, Franciscan Tertianship. At least six months probation, two year novitiate while candidate continues regular job. Vow of chastity, promises of poverty, obedience, and the apostolate, renewed annually. No habit. Membership kept secret. Write to: Rev. Stephen Hartdegen, O.F.M., Holy Name College, Fourteenth and Shepherd Sts., N.E., Washington 17, D.C. Rev. P. Richer-M., O.F.M., St. Joseph Friary, 2010 Dorchester St. W., Montreal, P.Q., Canada.

Oblate Missionaries of Mary Immaculate (O.M.M.I.) Founded in Grand Falls, N.B., Canada, in 1952 by Father Louis-Marie Parent, O.M.I. Established in U.S. in 1956 in Lowell, Massachusetts. Pontifical. 1,086 members in Canada, 173 in U.S., 1,520 world. Two types of membership: Intern Oblates live in groups, may disclose their membership and are assigned to the official work of the institute. Extern Oblates remain at home, do not disclose their membership, and keep their regular jobs. Interns and Externs take the three vows, renewed annually. There are also lay missionaries who work in the home or foreign missions for three to five years and do not take vows; and auxiliaries, single or married, who do not take vows but promise, not under pain of sin, to follow the rule. Prayer includes Mass, visit to Blessed Sacrament, half hour meditation, rosary. Work includes teaching, nursing, social work, catechetics, office work, missions, care of aged, dispensaries— in Catholic and non-Catholic environments. The purpose is to re-Christianize families, professions, and society. Ages 18-35, single for Interns; 20-40, single for Externs; 20-30, single, for lay missionaries; no age requirements for auxiliaries; average health; high school education not necessary. Training given while candidate continues regular job or studies. Aspirancy six months, two years of probation. Lay missionaries have six months training; auxiliaries have one year of probation before taking promise. No habit. Located in many states and provinces in U.S. and Canada. Write to: Les Vieilles Forges, Comte St. Maurice, P.Q., Canada; 1258 Park Ave., Woonsocket, Rhode Island.

Opus Dei. Male branch founded in Madrid, Spain, in 1928; women's branch in 1930; established in America in 1949. Pontifical. Most of the members remain at home. The purpose is to spread the life of perfection among people of all walks of life, especially those of intellectual pursuits. Most members retain their jobs; in addition, the institute has residences for students, missions in Africa and Asia, and other works. All ages and education. Married persons may become associate members. Training includes two years of philosophy and four of theology while member continues at job. Private vows, which may be taken for life. No habit. Membership is not kept secret. Located in U.S., Canada, and Mexico. Write to: Very Rev. Ignatius Gramunt, 2132 Wyoming Ave. N.W., Washington 8, D.C.

Society of Our Lady of the Way. Founded in Vienna, Austria, in 1936; established in U.S. in 1956. Pontifical. 25 professed, 25 candidates in U.S., 500 world. Members do not live in community. Members retain occupations as waitresses, factory workers, office workers, accountants, bank officers, nurses, social workers, teachers, doctors, lawyers, etc. Ages 22-45, some exceptions, single or widowed, gainful employment. Initiation six to twelve months, probation two years. Spiritual training while member continues at regular job. Vows of chastity, poverty, and obedience; perpetual vows may be taken six years after first temporary vows, must be taken after ten years if member wishes to remain in institute. No habit. Discretion rather than secrecy. Write to: P.O. Box 17396, Los Angeles 4, California.

The Company of Saint Paul. Founded in Milan, Italy, in 1920; established in U.S. in 1958. Pontifical. 6 members in U.S., about 200 in world. Three sections: priests, laymen, laywomen. Members normally live in small groups (cenacles) but may if necessary live apart or with their families. Prayer includes daily Mass and adoration; recitation of parts of Divine Office in Latin or English is customary. Members work individually in such fields as social work, teaching, medicine, law, the arts, communication, business, etc., or in groups, counselling families, conducting a residence for working girls and students, helping unwed mothers and the aged, etc. Ages 18-30, two years of college education, college degree preferred. Three years training without interrupting education or work if possible. Vows of chastity, obedience and poverty, perpetual sixth year after first profession. No habit. Secrecy at discretion of individual member. Write to: 1601 Buchanan St. N.W., Washington 11, D.C.

Regnum Christi. Founded in Lucca, Italy, in 1935; established in U.S. in 1956. Diocesan. No community life. Prayer includes Mass, meditation, rosary, Office of Blessed Mother in Latin or English. Work includes catechetics, personal contacts, social work, spreading literature, parish organizations, giving spiritual aid to Italian immigrants. Ages 19-35, high school education or equivalent, single. Postulate six months, two years novitiate. Vow of chastity, promises of poverty, obedience, and apostolate, renewed annually, perpetual after ten years. No habit. Membership kept secret. Write to: Very Rev. Armando Pierini, P.S.S.C., P.O. Box 447, Chicago 90, Illinois.

Rural Parish Workers of Christ the King. Founded in 1942 in Cottleville, Missouri, by Alice Widmer and LaDonna Hermann. Diocesan. 4 members. Members live in community or at home. Prayer includes Mass, part of Divine Office in English, meditation. Life based on Rule of St. Benedict. Work includes catechetics, social work, work with youth, aged, and handicapped, cultural and civic activities; some members work to provide support for the group. Needed are nurses, doctors, teachers, stenographers, saleswomen, librarians, etc. Ages 17-35. There are also one-year volunteers, ages 18-30, high school education. Temporary private vows of poverty, chastity, and obedience for five to ten years and then perpetual. No habit. Annual home visit and vacation. Write to: Box 300, Rte. 1, Cadet, Missouri.

Schoenstatt Sisters of Mary of the Catholic Apostolate (S.A.C.) Founded at Schoenstatt, Germany, in 1926; established in U.S. in 1949. Pontifical. 65 members in U.S., 2,500 world. Intern members live in community and wear blue habit; extern members live at home. Work includes teaching, nursing, social work, domestic work, catechetics, formation of lay apostles, foreign missions in South America, South Africa, and Australia. Ages 17-27 for interns, externs may be older. Postulate six months, novitiate two years, two five-month tertianships. Promises. Write to: 3009 Cottage Grove Rd., Madison 4, Wisconsin; Rte. 1, Rockport, Texas.

Teresian Institute. Founded in Spain in 1911; established in U.S. in 1961. Pontifical. 16 members in U.S., over 2,000 world. Some members live in community. Prayer includes daily Mass, Office of the Blessed Mother, one hour of meditation. The main purpose is the Christian education of women and girls, and U.S. members teach in public and private schools. Age under 30, academic degree required for teaching, single. Six years spiritual and professional training given while candidate continues a job assigned by the institute. Promises of chastity, poverty, and obedience taken for life. No habit. Membership not necessarily kept secret. Write to: Miss Ann Mandiola, 312 Dartmouth St., Boston 16, Massachusetts.

Potential Secular Institutes: *The following are not yet officially recognized as secular institutes but are working toward that goal.*

Caritas. Founded about 1950 by Bertha Mugrauer in New Orleans, Louisiana. 8 members in New Orleans, Baton Rouge, and Abita Springs, Louisiana, and 1 in San Juanito, Chihuahua, Mexico. Members live in groups of two or three. Prayer includes daily Mass, Divine Office in English said individually, an hour to one and a half hours meditation. Purpose is to bring about a Christian society through a parish apostolate. Work includes home visiting, catechetics, encouraging active participation in the Mass, conducting adult education programs, taking part in civic groups for community improvements, training laywomen for parish work, conducting a religious day camp, training and supervising Caritas Missionary Volunteers, laywomen who work for a year in the Southern U.S., particularly among Negroes, and in Mexico; institute supported by a few of the members who are employed and by outside contributions. Ages 18-30, high school education, single or widowed. Most of the three-year training period is spent working in parishes in New Orleans, learning group techniques with children and adults, arts and crafts, music and the Liturgy. Vows of poverty, chastity and obedience annually for five to ten years, then may be taken for life. No habit. Membership is not kept secret. Write to: Miss Bertha Mugrauer, Talitha Cumi, Abita Springs, Louisiana.

The Dominican Secular Institute of St. Catherine of Siena. Founded in Paris, France, in 1947. Established in Canada in 1949, U.S. 1954. Diocesan. 21 members in Canada, 5 in U.S., 66 in world. Members do not live in community and the institute has no specific works; members work in offices, hospitals, schools, etc. Many devote themselves to charitable works; one member, for example, opened a hospitality house for the poor. Prayer includes Mass, parts of Divine Office or Little Office of the Blessed Virgin in Latin or vernacular, half hour of meditation, annual retreat. Ages 21-50, single or widowed, no dowry but candidate must be self-supporting. Candidate continues job while training. Postulate fourteen months, novitiate two years. Lifetime vows of poverty, chastity, and obedience after three temporary professions. No habit. Secrecy at discretion of each member. Write to: Miss Georgette Lefort, 500 Claremont Ave., Westmount (Montreal), P.Q., Canada; Rev. M. Guimond, 96 Empress Ave., Ottawa, Ont., Canada; Rev. Stanley J. Gaines, O.P., 1530 Jackson Ave., River Forest, Illinois.

Jesus-Caritas. Founded at Ars, France, in 1952, in the spirituality of Father de Foucauld, the "Apostle of the Desert"; established in Canada in 1956, in U.S. in 1958. Diocesan. 8 members in U.S. and Canada, 400 in world. See also Little Sisters of Jesus under religious institutes. There are also Little Brothers of Jesus and an independent lay fraternity, groups of men, women, and married couples. Members are not obliged to live in community but some may do so if they wish. Prayer includes daily Mass, meditation, parts of Divine Office in English, an hour of adoration, day or half day of solitude monthly, annual retreat. Members strive for a fraternal and universal love above all divisions of class, nationality, and race. Most members keep their professions, some work among the very poor in Africa and South America. Ages 21-40, high school education, unmarried or no longer bound by marriage ties. Spiritual training through correspondence, annual retreats, etc., while candidate continues regular job. After two and a half years, vows of poverty, chastity and obedience may be taken, renewable for six years, after which they may be taken for life. No habit. Membership may be revealed. U.S. and Canadian headquarters: Miss Anne-Marie de Commaille, 185 Claremont Ave., New York, New York 10027.

Madonna House Apostolate. Founded in 1930 in Toronto, Canada, by Baronness Catherine de Hueck, a refugee from Communist Russia; originally called Friendship House; first U.S. Friendship House established in Harlem, New York City, in 1938. Diocesan. Two branches: Domus Dominae for women, Domus Domini for laymen and priests. Total membership, men and women, 110 in Canada, U.S., and in missions in West Indies and Pakistan. Most members live in community. Prayer includes Mass, meditation, part of Divine Office in English, rosary, etc. Also day or two at a time spent praying and fasting in a place of solitude called "the desert." Social justice with emphasis on most neglected areas. Work with Negroes, Indians, Spanish-Americans, Mexicans, Gypsies; delinquents, prostitutes, prisoners, transients, alcoholics; labor union work, housing, credit unions, co-ops; catechetics, convert-making, Catholic Action movements, writing, library work; Cana camps in Stafford, Virginia, and Combermere, Ontario; summer school of lay apostolate, publication—*Restoration*. Ages 20-35, single or widowed, no educational requirements. Stages in training—working guests share in daily life at training center and observe the institute, must work at any task given them. If interested in the vocation, may become visiting volunteers who receive academic training. Staff worker applicants study the history, constitutions, etc., of the institute; after eight months make a retreat and then make one-year promise of chastity, poverty, and obedience; one more year spent at headquarters, then a year at a branch house, and another year at headquarters; then sent to home or foreign missions in teams or singly. No habit. Membership not kept secret unless instructed to do so by a bishop. Write to: Director General, Madonna House, Combermere, Ont., Canada.

Daughters of Our Lady of Fatima. Founded in Lansdowne, Pennsylvania, in 1949 by Rev. A. Paul Lambert. Diocesan. 7 consecrated members under vows, 50 associates, who do not take vows and may be married. Community life customary but not required. Prayer includes daily Mass, half hour of meditation, Divine Office in English, two annual retreats, etc. Work includes parish visiting and census, catechetics, and other work at request of pastors, such as teaching, social work, office work, nursing, or whatever the members are qualified to do. Ages 18-35, sometimes older, high school education, single or widowed. After six months of full time spiritual training, candidate receives professional training evenings or Saturdays while she works. Vows of poverty, chastity and obedience are now temporary but it is hoped that they may be taken for life in the future. No habit. No secrecy except at discretion of individual members. Write to: Fatima House, 25 N. Highland Ave., Lansdowne, Pennsylvania.

Regina House. Founded in Chicago, Illinois, in 1961 by Margaret A. Galvin. Diocesan. Community living not required. Dominican spirituality. Prayer includes daily Mass, Divine Office in English, half-hour meditation, rosary, annual retreat. Purpose is to penetrate the professions with Thomistic philosophy. Types of work include social work, psychology, psychiatry, guidance, nursing, teaching, etc. Age requirements are flexible, single, widowed, divorced, college education or professional training, moderately good health. Six months probation. Social vows of poverty, chastity and obedience. No habit. Membership preferably kept secret. Write to: Miss Margaret A. Galvin, 1033 Loyola Ave., Chicago 26, Illinois.

The following organizations are neither religious institutes nor secular institutes but offer a lifetime apostolate.

The Bishop's Helpers (formerly called La Paix). Founded in 1961 in Louisiana by Bishop Maurice Schexnayder. 4 members. Prayer includes daily Mass, half hour meditation, monthly half day of recollection, annual retreat. Members continue at their regular jobs, teaching, nursing, secretarial work, housekeeping, etc. Members do not live in community. Ages 20 or over, single or widowed, some professional ability or training. Candidates will be trained while continuing at regular job. Vow of chastity, promise of obedience, pledge of poverty, renewed annually, no perpetual vows. After five years, membership is permanent. No habit. Membership is not kept secret. Write to: Miss Barbara A. Plaisance, U.S.L. Box 532, Lafayette, Louisiana.

Daughters of St. Francis de Sales; Missionary Daughters of St. Francis de Sales; Salesian Missionaries of Mary Immaculate, Daughters of St. Francis de Sales. Founded in France in 1872 by Ven. Caroliné Carre de Molberg and a diocesan priest; established in U.S. in 1946. Pontifical. 100 members in U.S., 5,600 world. Under 55, married, single or widowed. Daughters of St. Francis de Sales: Live at home; prayer includes Mass, rosary, visit to Blessed Sacrament; individual apostolate, parish and diocesan work; act of consecration not binding under pain of sin; postulate three months, two years probation; training based on study and concentrated effort in practicing various virtues for a month at a time; no habit; membership usually kept secret. Missionary Daughters of St. Francis de Sales: make an act of total oblation through the society; home missionaries living in community; no habit. Salesian Missionaries of Mary Immaculate, Daughters of St. Francis de Sales: foreign missions; teaching, nursing, home visiting, etc.; annual vows of poverty, chastity and obedience; simple black habit and veil. Write to: Miss Delphine M. Madill, 4906 Argyle, St. Louis 8, Missouri.

International Catholic Auxiliaries. Founded in Belgium in 1937; established in U.S. in 1951, in Canada in 1952. Pontifical. 18 members in U.S., 16 Canada, 280 world. Members live in teams of three to six. Prayer includes daily Mass, half hour meditation and rosary. International teams provide technical and professional assistance in medical, educational and catechetical fields and cooperate with Catholic Action movements in missions in Africa, India, Vietnam, Formosa, Japan, Korea, Jordan, Syria and Lebanon. Centers for foreign students in U.S. and Canada. Ages 18-30, high school education, single. Three years spiritual, apostolic and practical formation, professional training if not already received. At end of training members take an oath to live in spirit of poverty, chastity and obedience for two five-year periods and then can take it for life. The temporary oath can be taken only if member intends to stay on for life. No habit. Membership not kept secret.

Write to: Crossroads Student Center, 5621 S. Blackstone, Chicago 37, Illinois; International Training Center, 1911 Av. Van Horne, Montreal 8, P.Q., Canada.

Martin de Porres Workers. Founded in Illinois in 1943 by Miss Mary Widman. 4 members with life dedication. Types of membership: life dedication; temporary promises; visiting residents; volunteers. Members do not necessarily live in community. Prayer includes daily Mass, half hour meditation, parts of Divine Office, rosary. Work is corporal and spiritual works of mercy in an informal way and as family to family. Ages 17-28, single or widowed. Spiritual training mostly while taking part in the apostolate. Promises of poverty, chastity and obedience may be taken for life as well as life dedication to the apostolate. No habit. Membership is not kept secret. Write to: Martin de Porres House, 3322 Washington Blvd., Chicago 24, Illinois.